The Palace Addiction

by

James Howland

Foreword

I survived the roller-coaster ride: as did we all.

I loved every twist and turn, up and down, and even the occasional plummet towards the floor. I spent long enough at Crystal Palace FC to realise that this was pretty much the norm. Somewhere along the line, somebody or something was always going to whip the rug from beneath your feet. But, what that does, is bring everybody involved closer together: the staff, the players and the fans. I was always highly aware that WE were in this together.

Never has this been more highly evident than in the CPFC 2009/10 season. James Howland's book, 'The Palace Addiction', reminds of this in such detail and with such passion. This is his story, but the book allows us to relive our memories and our own take on the times: it certainly did me, anyway.

The whole season was nearly wiped out when the players were 35,000ft in the air. That rare place where you are free of the trappings of modern technology (heaven forbid that we actually have to converse) and away from the spotlight of the media glare.

As Crystal Palace Football club stumbled into administration, the players were on a flight from London to Newcastle. I, on the other hand, was speeding through the countryside on a rattler. My aversion to flying having got the better of me; the one and only similarity that I can attribute to Dennis Bergkamp and myself. The powers that be deducted 10pts and I had to let that all sink in alone and free of my teammates. This time there was an 'I' in team. But, don't fret, I systematically set about everybody in the team so that they would have a landing gift as they all switched on their phones. I removed the 'I' from team. A promotion push turned into a relegation fight. Everything the club had been working towards had been pulled from underneath our feet: the pattern repeated. The rest of the season has gone down in history.

And, sometimes, out of adversity springs eternal hope.

Four fans in shining armour, with rather hefty cheque books under their arms, rode into Selhurst and saved the club. Life was breathed back into Crystal Palace Football Club: phoenix rose from the ashes. The last five years have been nothing short of a fairy tale. The baton is now held by Alan Pardew and his squad. The club is thriving and appears to know no bounds. Can Pardew take the club into Europe?

The fans can dare to dream… but this is the story before the new beginning.

League One beckoned and was a distinct possibility. Played out before your eyes, in this book, is James' story of life on the terraces.

I hope you get as much joy reliving that topsy-turvy season as I did.

Matt Lawrence

Contents

Chapter	Chapter Name	Page Number
	Before I Begin...	7
1	We All Follow the Palace	10
2	Little Problems	16
3	The Red and Blue of Barcelona	21
4	The Opening Day (...and the wedding...)	30
5	Devon	38
6	Controversial	40
7	Coach Travel	53
8	Crisis Club Come to Town	58
9	The World's Richest Team	63
10	The Day After the Days Before	73
11	A Happy Wife	76
12	Singing in the Rain	81
13	A Family Affair	86
14	Away to the League Leaders	89
15	Advice Going Forward and Filth Looking Back	96
16	Money Worries	99
17	The Welsh Adventure	101
18	Back on the Coach	109
19	Jesus is With Us	112
20	Old Friends	117
21	A Girl. At Football?	121
22	Football Friends	126
23	Turn Left at the First Tramp and Right at the Second	132
24	A Dark Cloud Arrives Over SE25	140
25	It Never Rains but it Pours	144
26	The Second Coming	149
27	Jordan's Master Plan	155
28	How the Hell did that Happen?	162
29	Thank You Mike	166
30	Excuse me Boyo	171
31	So what for 2010?	178
32	A Wasted Day	184
33	Palace. My Friend's Worst Nightmare	187
34	Football Rivalries	191
35	A Dark Day	198
36	My Only Palace	200

37	A Proud Moment	207
38	Once Upon a Time at Selhurst...	209
39	An Unhappy Wife	214
40	Crashing Back Down to Earth	223
41	Cup Fever	225
42	The FA Cup Hangover	233
43	Send them to Coventry	236
44	Be Loud, Be Proud, Be Palace	239
45	An Expensive Day	245
46	Warnock Leaves	253
47	The Return of a Legend	256
48	A Chance for Revenge	262
49	Running Out of Time	265
50	P Diddy's Red and Blue Army	272
51	Finally, a roof!	275
52	Career vs Football	281
53	Football Stress	287
54	Do or Die	295
55	Train Clientele	306
56	Palace Rise from the Dead	315
57	Jesus and Judus Return	319
58	A Great Day Out in Derby	323
59	Other Games	335
60	A Chance of Salvation	339
61	The Final Showdown	344
62	Doomsday: The Final Battle	358
63	...And so it Begins....	364

Before I Begin....

Well, I can't quite believe this. My very own book about my addiction – being a Palace supporter!

Without going any further, I'd like to thank you for taking an interest in my book. As with the majority of self-published material, I suspect that it isn't perfect. Due to budgeting restrictions (i.e. I don't have a spare five-hundred quid), it has not been professionally proof read. However, hopefully you'll be able to ignore the odd typo and forgive the occasional mistake so that you can still take some pleasure out of your reading experience. If there are any grammatical, factual or contextual errors that you take offense to or harm your enjoyment of the book in any way, please feel free to contact me and I can edit the manuscript for later additions.

Before you start, I would like to explain a few things. Firstly, although the events of this book take place between May 2009 and August 2010, the majority of writing was done between February and May 2014 – with plenty of editing and rewriting happening in the following 11 months! I kept a (very) brief factual diary of events at the time, which has helped me with the odd pub name, player performance or choice of beverage but the overriding majority of it was written from memory.

Secondly, everything written in this book is as true to life as possible. I didn't want to make things up or lie, even if it might have made for better reading at times. Although, writing the book four years after the events took place, coupled with the amount of alcohol consumed at the time, may have meant that some things are slightly exaggerated or possibly remembered differently by different people!

Finally, with the benefit of hindsight, even I can observe that at certain points, the honest and truthful nature of this book doesn't reflect well on myself or some of the decisions that I made at the time. However, I will point out that at the time of the events in this book, I was a youthful, naive and foolish student, still learning the ways of the world. And as youthful, naive and foolish students tend to do, I did drink a lot, which usually results in making youthful, naive and foolish decisions even more disastrous and embarrassing. However, I have come through this experience and learnt from it and as the youthful, naive and foolish twenty-five year old that I have become, I am no longer the borderline alcoholic displayed in this book. I am much more of a connoisseur of craft beer and have also have grown out of my love of Wetherspoons!

I also want to make a comment about the player contributions to this book. Around a month before publishing, I sent some speculative emails out to the current clubs of various players from the 2009/10 season. The response that I received was incredible and really supported my view that the squad from our year in administration were one of the most committed groups of players to ever pull on the red and blue. The team spirit was clearly outstanding and a key part of helping the club to survive the season and everything that was thrown at it. Clint Hill was going to send me a couple of lines about the season but he ended up finishing his e-mail by saying *'Sorry it's so long mate, once i started I couldn't stop.'* The passion for the club from all of them was as evident five years on as it was on the pitch in the club's darkest hour. I would like to say a genuine thank you to all of the players that responded to me to talk about the season.

And in one last little moment, before you can finally start hearing about the exciting adventures of a Football Addict in the romantic and picturesque towns of Doncaster, Plymouth and Coventry, I would like to take the opportunity to say a few words of thank you to the people who have assisted me with writing and editing this book.

Firstly, to my father. As well as leading me to football in the first place, he has encouraged and advised me throughout the writing of this book. Also, I would like to thank my friends, Pavel Mogilevski, Thomas Clarke and Ryan Clarke for their proof reading and advice on the project. I need to say a quick thank you to my friend Richard Sroka for his support on designing the front cover. I would also like to thank Stephen Goddard, author of the outstanding Rattles and Rosettes, Adam Keeble, author of Don't Put Baby In The Corner, and Michael Pudney, author of Just Visiting, for their advice and support on the project, despite none of them having met me in person.

Finally, I would like to say thank you to James Mitchell, a moderator on the BBS, Palace's online fan's bulletin board, for his time,advice and encouragement on the project, and Martin Steenson, a Palace fan with professional proof reading experience, for his time, effort and support, despite having not actually met me.

Behavioural addiction consists of a compulsion to repeatedly engage in an action until it causes negative consequences to the person's physical, mental, social, and/or financial well-being. Behaviour persisting in spite of these consequences can be taken as a sign of addiction.

The Palace Addiction

Chapter One – **We all follow the Palace**

Football doesn't always make sense. In fact, it rarely does. How can teams from the lower leagues on shoe string budgets beat top flight millionaires? How can world class players, like Steven Gerrard and Frank Lampard, fail so spectacularly to play well together? How can every fan in England support 'the unluckiest team in the world?' How can a new 'worst referee' be found every single week? How can the sport be immune to the biggest recession in decades and continue to grow in wealth as the population scrounges around for money? But most baffling of all, why on earth do football fans turn up, spending small fortunes, travelling all over the country to obscure towns and cities, despite being served up crap, week after week after week? Total and utter crap in many cases.

In fact, if you counted up all the minutes that a football fan spent talking about how crap their team was, you would probably find that they had enough time to do something fairly productive, such as curing cancer or saving the rainforest (or in some cases, saving their marriage). But why would anyone want to do something productive when they could be having a beer, ranting at referees and be despairing over just how useless their team is?

Despite the lack of logic, football is without doubt the most popular and in my humble opinion, best sport in the world. I'm not doubting the skill involved in other sports, nor the entertainment, but the emotion that you get in football is on a different level to anything else. You can experience anything from joy, pain, excitement, despair, anticipation, anger, surprise, fear, love, contempt, regret – and that's just in the pub beforehand. No wonder so many fans need a pint by half time to calm their nerves.

Admittedly, supporting Crystal Palace is more about the anger, pain and misery. The whole experience is cold, overpriced and full of disappointment – just like the pies served up in the ground. However, even mundane and average teams such as mine do have their moments. In the previous fifteen years, I have seen promotions, cup semi-finals, last day survivals, play offs, a win at Anfield and most importantly, a 5-0 thrashing of B*ighton. Although this has been evened out with two relegations, losing cup semi-finals, being thrashed in the play offs, getting drenched and slaughtered at Cambridge in the FA Cup, and losing at home to some small south coast side who wear Tesco bags. (that's Brighton for any non-Palace fans who don't share our irrational hatred).

However, like thousands of deranged men and woman, I follow my club up and down the country. Whether they are in Plymouth or Newcastle, Swansea or Norwich, come Saturday afternoon (or sometimes a cold Tuesday evening) I'll be there cheering on my team. Not that it does much good. We're still crap. But it fills a Saturday afternoon, lets me see my mates, releases my anger and gives me the chance for a good ol' piss up.

So why Crystal Palace? Why did I choose this particular method of self harming over all the others? I certainly wasn't from the area. I'd grown up in Ascot so Reading, Brentford or Aldershot would have been more logical addictions geographically. My Dad was born in Bromley and after being taken to Selhurst by his teacher (imagine the press hearing about a story such as this now), was hooked for life. He had then gone on to have three children and as a father, he had failed them. One Liverpool fan, one Manchester United fan and one Tottenham fan. And then came me.

At the tender age of seven, when my football addiction began, my three older brothers each grabbed a limb and pulled me as hard as they could towards their team. Eventually, I came up with a plan. Whoever wins the FA Cup, I'll support. Come cup final day, United beat Liverpool and that was it, I was a Manchester United supporter. For life right? You can't ever change your team.

A couple of weeks later, I walked up to my Dad while he was in the garden, mowing the lawn. "Daddy, who's that football team who you support?" I enquired.
"Crystal Palace, son," proudly professed my father.
"Well you've got four sons and none support that team so I am going to," I replied, as the perfect son. Since then, the United and Liverpool supporting brothers have been converted to Palace but the Spurs fan is still a lost soul. Although to this day, my Dad claims to have three and a half Crystal Palace supporters. About a year later, he took me to Wembley for my first ever live game to see us get promoted and it's been downhill ever since.

It was at Wembley that my Crystal Palace addiction started. I remember walking along Wembley Way with my father and brother, experiencing my first banter with an opposition fan as a Sheffield United supporter mocked my scarf. I remember freezing, not knowing how to react to this attack on my club. I remember sitting high in the gods at the world-famous ground as I learnt my first terrace chants of 'Ole, ole ole ole, Eagles, Eagles'. I remember the players looking tiny – far smaller than they had done on TV. I remember being told that I had to go to the toilet before the game as I wouldn't be allowed to go until half time otherwise. I remember celebrating as our striker, Bruce Dyer, looked like he had scored, only to realise that the ball had hit the wrong side of the side netting. And most of all, I remember the pure elation as David Hopkin scored the last minute winner for our club. It was the perfect day.

Many fans claim to fall in love with a club for materialistic reasons – their badge, their colours, their location, their song or even a player. But I can't say that it was our Eagle proudly perched above a ball on our badge. Nor was it the red and blue on the player's shirt or our song, Glad All Over, which I remember my Dad telling me at Wembley was played before every game at our home ground, Selhurst Park. It certainly wasn't a love of South London that made me fall for the club either. Although my Grandmother's decision to live in Bromley and raise her kids there undoubtedly played a logistical part as I can't imagine a Berkshire born kid would naturally fall for a second rate South London side. And as for falling in love with them for a player, it's one thing to love a club because of Bobby Moore or George Best, but it would be quite sad to lay the blame of my addiction at the feet of Marc Edworthy.

No, I leant to love all of those things by association with the club. It sounds cheesy but it was a feeling of togetherness and belonging that had drawn me to the club. Approaching the ground, I had felt close to my family – we were in this together. A feeling that returns on the rare occasions that we all attend games together nowadays. However inside the ground, I felt an entirely new feeling of togetherness. I'd only ever met one Palace fan outside of my family before – Jonathan, a boy who played for the same Saturday morning team as me. To be honest, I wasn't really sure that there were any more of us than that. I was laughed at by schoolmates for not supporting Manchester United or Chelsea. Suddenly, I found myself sat alongside tens of thousands of other Crystal Palace Supporters. I'd found where I belonged – nearly.

On that day, I knew where I belonged but I wasn't quite part of it yet. There was one thing missing. I didn't have a red and blue shirt. Everyone else did – although my brother pointed out that the guy behind us didn't have a shirt at all: just an eagle tattooed across the whole of his back. Despite the scorching hot May sunshine, I kept my Crystal Palace sweatshirt on all day and religiously wrapped my new 'Eagles at Wembley' scarf around my neck as I tried to fit in. I couldn't quite belong but I was going to do my best to try.

After that fateful day, the following years of my childhood saw me decline from a wide-eyed kid at Wembley, taking in the noise, colour and swearing that a first match brings, to an addicted and devoted supporter. I'm not really sure how the addiction happened. It started out as a harmless hobby. In the beginning, I would simply listen to the scores on the radio, when I had nothing else to do, and before I knew it, I was a teenager travelling up and down the country. I was going to every possible game, home and away. I was planning my life around football. Like any addiction, I don't know where or when I descended into dependence on football, but just like people hooked on drugs or alcohol, I seem unable to function without it.

My story begins as the 2008/09 season was coming to a close. Personally, I was 19 and coming to the end of my second year of university where I was training to be a Primary School Teacher. As for Palace, despite flirting with the play offs over Christmas, it had been a particularly depressing season. Mid table mediocrity. It's a strange thing, but in some ways I would rather have a relegation dog fight than sit in the middle of the table, filling my weekends with meaningless matches. You look up the table and long for the excitement and thrill of promotions and titles. Yet you also look down at the teams at the bottom. Yes, they would do anything to swap with you. But at least they get the passion that football fans crave for at the end of season big matches and full stadiums.

Crystal Palace, rarely for us, had none of that. Money problems had seen our better players slowly but surely desert us. The list was endless. Ben Watson,

Clinton Morrison, Tom Soares, Andy Johnson, Dougie Freedman, Scott Sinclair,Jobi McAnuff, Emerson Boyce and others had all gone. Mainly to the Premiership. The manager seemed fed up, the fans were fed up and the players were dusting off their flip flops, ready for their summer break. It had been months since we'd had a worthwhile game and the season had long since petered out.

Naturally, my first idea was to head to Doncaster for the final away game of the season. I woke up late, missed the coach and that was that. Well, it should have been. But me being me, I was determined to go. I called Robbie, who was in charge of coach travel at Palace, to make some alternative arrangements. I managed to get to my Mum's place in Egham from Twickenham (where I was at university) and frantically cycled to the A30 roundabout at Junction 13 of the M25 and met the coach.

I got on the coach and sat with my mates. Well, actually just behind them as that was the only space left on the packed coach, and off I went. I said hello to the person next to me. I didn't recognise him and he had bad BO. Brilliant. I used the age-old match day conversation opener. *"What do you reckon today then?"*
Well that was it. He was off. Terry (although he told me I could call him 'Tezza' if I wished) gave me an in-depth analysis of our season, each player, the manager and he seemed to have a full report on the referee too. After telling me every statistic of the season from our win percentage in the rain to how many goals we had scored from the left hand side of the penalty area, he finally professed that we had a 47.3% chance of winning. I suggested it might be closer to 47.6% but he wasn't having any of it.

He kept on wittering on about his love of Clint Hill and seemingly personal hatred of Julian Speroni – our goalkeeper and in my opinion, our best player. I bit my lip. Then he moved on to his expectations of us spending millions in the summer. I bit my lip harder – we were having financial difficulties and I expected more players to leave than join. Finally, he moved onto his dislike of some of our fans' songs and that some weren't 100% accurate. Apparently, not everyone in Preston lives on benefits as had been sung at one of the previous matches. My lip began to bleed.

After what seemed like a few months, we arrived at a service station and I crept away from him in a fashion not too dissimilar to how opposition strikers seem to manage to sneak away from Palace defenders at Selhurst Park i.e. without much difficulty. I then went to get a fry up with some of my friends. I had to analyse my life. A few of my close mates had stopped going to the away games. Palace were about as successful as a tortoise in a one hundred metre sprint, and about as exciting too. Yet I was still heading to South Yorkshire for what was likely to be a crap match, between two crap teams, with disinterested end-of-season crap support, in a crap town. At least Doncaster's new ground insured that it wouldn't be in a crap stadium too. The magic of live football...

Still, it wasn't all bad – I had a fry up, the highlight of any away trip (or home game in many cases too). If it wasn't for sausage, bacon, beans and a bit of fried veg, I don't think I would have the stomach for watching Palace (or the drinking that inevitably goes with it).

Anyway, back to analysing the worthwhile-ness of continuing with my unquestioning, blind support of Palace all over the country. I still had my season ticket and could do the decent away trips with my friends. Also, some of my closest friends were Brentford fans. Going with them allowed me to get the social side of an away trip, without the heart-ache and disappointment that Palace usually gave me. Then I looked around. One hundred or so Palace fans mulling around Watford Gap services. It was hardly Man United or Arsenal taking over Wembley Way or Milan City Centre with thousands of fans but it still gave me a sense of pride. We all had something in common. We were all here for the same reason. We were all as mad as each other. We all loved Palace. Even 'Tezza'.

When we got to the ground, a few of us headed around the corner to Lakeside Village, a small shopping centre by the stadium. It seemed to be designed as if it was in the middle of Disneyland rather than a grim town in the north of England. Unfortunately, it was also the only shopping 'village' this side of 1900 where it was difficult to find a bloody ATM. Maybe the rumours were true that they don't use cash 'oop north' and still trade farm animals as currency? Just as we were about to give up looking for cash and start hunting for poultry to trade, one of the coach regulars spotted one. Armed with crisp, freshly withdrawn notes, we headed to the Harvester Pub/Restaurant to indulge in some pre-match beer and banter.

After much heated discussion, none of us agreed on the team selection, formation or tactics, so we decided that we would leave that for our manager, Neil Warnock, to choose. Woe betide him if he gets it wrong. Any idiot/football fan knows what he should have done. We got into the ground, listened to the stewards as to where our seats were and then ignored the kind men in yellow and stood at the back. A group of about one hundred of us sang typically rude, irrelevant and sometimes not quite factually true songs (I hope Tezza didn't hear) about our manager, the opposing fans, Ron Noades (our former chairman), Ron Noades' mother, past players, current players and our un-dying love of all things red'n'blue and South London.

Bizarrely for Palace, we actually played really well. We passed it about, we created chances, we defended well and it was a joy to watch. Somehow, we managed to hit the woodwork three times without scoring. Feeling positive, I walked down to the front, ready to dash out for a 'cheeky' pint at half time. Just as I got there, Doncaster scored. Bastards. I waited for the few seconds after the re-start before charging to the beer kiosk and ordered 6 pints of lager (not all for me I hasten to add).

During the second half, I felt much more at home. Palace were crap. The songs dried up (at least Tezza would be pleased on the coach home). The team reverted to long, hopeful and ultimately fruitless passes, while the manager made terrible subs. I knew in the pub that I could do a better job. Doncaster went on to win 2-0. The season was ending in the same depressive manner that it had been played all year.

After the match, I received a phone call from my Dad. He rang me after every game to touch base and see how we'd played. He would usually follow the scores online and fill me in with the 'experts' view on the match, while I ignored that and gave him my own 'expert' opinion.

I returned to the coach thoroughly pissed off and beginning to sober up. Tezza got on soon after me. *"That ref was s***!"*.
"I don't think we can really blame him for the result," I replied calmly.
"We should have had two penalties in the first half!" he snorted back, while spitting out some crumbs from a pork pie he was munching on.
I considered his view, briefly, and then decided that rather than pointing out that the first claim was a clear dive that had left our other players laughing and the second appeal was when *our* player had handled in their box, I would agree. He then blurted out *"...and why were our bloody fans singing that they're a small team in Sheffield. Don't they know that Doncaster is 22.3 miles from Sheffield?"*
I pretended to be asleep. I had a long and uncomfortable journey home, being squashed against the window.

A few of us headed back to Thornton Heath for a couple more pints and discussed the "highlights" of the season. It was difficult. However, what was even more difficult was deciding how to spend Saturdays over the summer. No football? What on earth would we do? We could waste our weekends by drinking all day in London, but without a bit of s*** football to discuss in the middle of it, it just wouldn't be the same. It was during this discussion, and after a fair amount of alcohol, that I made an important pledge. A vow. I was going to do what I had always wanted to do, but had so far eluded me by the odd game. I, James Howland, was going to go to every Crystal Palace league and cup game, home and away, during the 2009/2010 season, and nothing or no-one was going to stop me.

Chapter 2 – **Little Problems**

Once the alcohol, and the inevitable hangover, had begun to wear off, I expected the idea to disappear. Yet strangely, it grew. The timing actually made a lot of sense. This was to be my final year of university. A point in life when you have more time to do silly challenges and waste your weekends. Mainly because most days feel like the weekend while at university anyway. Getting to Barnsley (to see the inevitable 1-0 defeat in the unlikely event that the match wasn't frozen off) on a Tuesday night in January was difficult at the best of times but it would surely be nigh on impossible if I had to work until at least three-thirty in the afternoon as a teacher. Then you have to consider the following day. I couldn't really expect the kids to do silent reading *all* day while I lay face down on my desk trying to catch up on some sleep. Besides that, I doubt even the most understanding head teacher would allow me to have regular half days to go up and down the country watching football. Very selfish if you ask me but that's just the way of the world. Although, the teacher strikes in 2011 were very carefully planned to be on the day of our League Cup Quarter Final at Old Trafford.

Of course, going to every game would have some difficulties. I suppose I would have to do *some* essays and attend *some* lectures at certain points of the year. I would also have to consider getting a part time job that was not only flexible with my university commitments, but more importantly, my football requirements. On top of this, I was still a student after all and wanted to enjoy my final year of the party lifestyle that I was used to. Or, if my parents happen to be reading, my educational lifestyle. Being able to go to football while teaching would be difficult, but going clubbing until four or five in the morning would categorically be out of the question. And certainly *would* result in silent reading for the children the next day.

Part of my desperation to do the challenge was very egotistic. I knew other people who'd done the same challenge and I wanted to be able to say that I had too. The feeling of time running out was one that I didn't like. I suppose it's odd that a nineteen year old would feel that he won't have another opportunity but I was weighing myself down with the approaching responsibility of teaching and the dawn of adulthood. Something that children spend their whole childhood wishing would come sooner, but the reality of adult responsibility to late teens and early twenties is terrifying.

Another motivation for the challenge was that ever since I was a child, I've had an almost autistic obsession over completing things. They were usually football collections such as Premier League Stickers or World Cup Coins but it was anything really. While at primary school, I'd fixated myself over completing the entire 'Wild West Lego' set before my best friend, Matthew, who was now one of my university flatmates. As well as that, Pokemon cards – I'd *had* to have the whole set (or 'catch 'em all' as the advert went). Even in my early teens, I'd fanatically gone around car-boot sales to buy every Only Fools and Horses and James Bond VHS. All of these obsessions had come and gone as I'd completed them. Unfortunately, I couldn't 'complete' Crystal Palace. I couldn't do it *all*. I mean sure, I'd bought every home and away shirt in the previous fifteen years, and bought every programme to every game that I'd ever been to, but when it came to matches, I could always do more.

There was always extra friendlies, youth or reserve games that I could attend and in each of the previous four years, I'd missed two or three competitive games. This annoyed me. *Really* annoyed me. Far more than it should have annoyed me. We'd only won two of the games that I'd missed but I didn't care. Win, lose or draw, I wanted to be there. I wanted to experience the banter of the crowd for each unique game, to cheer every goal and agonise over every misplaced pass. I'd missed those games and I could never get them back, unlike when someone had stolen my rare Charizard Pokemon card years earlier. There was no tracing my footsteps and finding a way back for football in the way that I had reclaimed my lost prized possession as a kid. I wanted to complete a Palace set – and not just owning every season review DVD/VHS since I was born and every home shirt since 1997. I wanted to go to every single league and cup game in the season.

That is why I felt I *had* to take my chance this time. I might not get another. I was angry at myself for not attending every game two years previously. I'd missed away games at Cardiff and Leicester by choice. Can you believe it? I'd actually made a conscious decision not to go. I hated every minute as I followed every kick on the radio, TV *and* internet. I'd missed John Bostock's first start, Victor Moses' debut and the end of a fifteen match unbeaten run to a last minute goal. I would never get the chance to experience the pride and pain of those events in the first person. They'd been and gone. I'd missed them. I hated that.

As the summer began, I left the idea in my head and started to try and enjoy the warm weather - watching whatever football I could in the pub, or Student Union when we needed to save money, with my friend Chris. He even persuaded me to go to Brentford's League Two title procession the following Saturday and I jumped at the chance to see some live football. After the traditional end of season pitch invasion (I say traditional but I've only seen three real pitch invasions at Palace games – the away section at Stockport, both sets of fans after West Brom beat us to gain promotion and Bristol City celebrating getting to a playoff final – which they lost), we headed to the pub for a night of heavy drinking, loud singing and even a bit of dancing. I woke up with a splitting head ache the next day for the final game of Palace's season. It was a dreadful 0-0 draw with Sheffield United. Surely a sign that sentencing myself to attend a further 48+ matches the following season was a bad idea.

Despite the result, the end of the football season is a depressing time for me. It feels like I've lost something from my life. Of course, I know that it is going to come back, and it actually gets easier as the summer goes on and I get into a football-less routine, but the initial shock of having no football to go to is horrifying. There is a sense of reflection and celebration akin to New Years Eve at the end of the season as fans discuss the year in the pub, and clubs hand out their end of season awards – Julian Speroni, our legendary keeper, won his second consecutive Fans' Player of the Year Award. A lot of people use the final match of the season as an excuse to get drunk too. However, my overriding emotion at the end of the 2008/9 season was sadness and loss. This feeling was enough to make me want to continue with the following season's challenge, despite the less than exciting football.

My first target was to get a job. I decided that if I wanted a part time job, where I didn't have to work during most days for lectures, every Saturday for football and the odd evening in the week, my best bet was a bar job. One of my friends was a manager at the Feltham Wetherspoons and I applied for a job there. Unfortunately, he had previously got another of our friends a job and based on his performance, the big boss declined my application. Following this rejection, I spent a few days wondering around pubs in Kingston, Twickenham and Teddington. This would usually sound like a brilliant few days. However, when I walk into a pub, I usually walk up the bar, order a pint of ale, drink it and then order another one. During these of days of wondering around pubs, I would walk up to the bar, ask if they were employing new staff, be told no and then walk out again. Sober.

After a couple of weeks of football-less Saturdays, I got a phone call from my Mum. I could tell that she was excited about something. Mainly because she was shouting *"James! James! Guess what?"* down the phone at me. I considered the options. Could my sister-in-law be pregnant again? Had my brother broken a world record? Had my other brother won the lottery?

"Erm... Tony Blair has announced he is gay?" was my flippant, thoughtless and needless reply. It seemed about as likely as any other option.

"What? No! Your cousin, Emily, is getting married!"

This was great news. My Mum is one of ten children and as a result, I have a lot of cousins. Out of my generation of the family, only my eldest brother had previously got married and this was to be a huge event. When you have about fifty uncles, aunties, cousins, cousins' kids and god knows who else to invite, before even considering friends, it must be tempting to save money and keep your special day restricted to immediate family only. Especially if you are a young couple and still working your way up the financial ladder. However, Emily and Mitch invited everyone; uncles, aunties, cousins. The whole clan.

For a brief moment, I shared my Mother's excitement. Weddings are fantastic celebrations and it's always hard not to be swept along in the emotion and romance of it all. I find it amazing that soap opera writers can look at these festivities and create a tale of misery and pain.

"She will be marrying Mitch on the 8th August and we're all invited!" she continued.

8th August? S***! That was the first day of the new season. Well so much for going to every game. The wedding was an unmissable family event. My mother would be heartbroken if I couldn't go, let alone if I *chose* not to go *for football*. Besides that, I didn't really want to miss it. Weddings are hardly every-week events like football. Even the summer's football drought couldn't cloud my judgement over that.

A couple of weeks passed and the final games of the season came to a close. The play offs came and went, the cup final came and went, the champions league final came and went and that was it. No more football. Not for at least a couple of months until pre-season started in July and then, eventually, in August, when the season began for real. And a whole week after the season kicked off, I would finally get a chance to go to a competitive match. To return to my spiritual home.

One of the highlights of a football supporter's summer is the day that the fixture lists are released. 17th June 2009 was the chosen day for the 2009/2010 season. The day before, Palace had been drawn at home to newly promoted Torquay in the first round of the League Cup. A highly unexciting proposition but at least it meant there was a date in the diary for a match. Something to look forward to through the long football drought.

Eventually the day was upon us. There was so much to anticipate. In some ways it was unfortunate that our three main rivals, Brighton, Millwall and Charlton, were all in the league below. While it is always nice to be above your enemies, those games are the ones that football fans crave and can really get excited about – despite our appalling recent record against Millwall. But there were plenty of other questions that would be answered. When would we play the newly relegated Newcastle United? There was talk amongst my friends of an overnight trip up there. Who would we play on the opening day? (even if I couldn't go) The last day? Boxing Day? When would we play Cardiff in their new stadium? Another of my ventures is to visit all 92 football league grounds. I had been to fifty-nine of them and hoped to add Peterborough and Middlesbrough as well as the previously mentioned two to my list this season.

Finally, sitting in my uni-room, with my laptop flipping between the BBS (the Palace online fans' forum), the official Palace website and the BBC website, I began to hear the news. The first information released was on the BBC website, the opening fixtures were there, early. A whole five minutes before the 10am release time. We had Plymouth at home. Not bad. Very winnable in fact. Right, who next? I frantically pressed F5 to refresh the page as if it was transfer deadline day. Finally, someone on the BBS, a usually reliable poster, said we had Newcastle home as our second home match. Oooh fantastic! Newcastle were a team in crisis and it would be good to catch them early in the season, when they were still adapting to life outside the Premiership. The next news that I received was that we were to travel to Sheffield Wednesday on the last game of the season. Boring. Or so I thought anyway. Still, it was exciting that the fixtures were here. Home to Ipswich on Boxing Day. Not bad.

Soon, the full fixture list was on the BBS, the BBC and the official Palace website. How did people live before the internet? I had all these sources of information at the click of a button. In the past, people had to gaze at teletext and wait for it to flick from page to page painfully slowly, most of which you couldn't care less about. Or even worse still, wait for the newspaper the next day. Imagine that! Waiting a whole 24 hours to hear when your team will play each fixture. I was excited. I was bouncing around the room like a puppy that has just been shown his new family. The new season was coming.

I then quickly scrolled down the page to see when Newcastle away was.... Wednesday 27th January 2010. ****! Well that ruined that. The game that I was looking forward to more than any other, the game that was furthest away from me, was a bloody midweek in January.

Undeterred, I ran around to my neighbour's house. Jak is an avid Brentford fan and had been doing something very similar to me while looking at their fixtures. We then compared schedules to see if there were any that we could travel to together. During the previous season, we had been un-coordinated and visited Bournemouth and Southampton on different trains, so we were determined not to miss out on any shared drunken adventures this season. However, except for one tedious looking link when we were at Blackpool and they were at Oldham, there was nothing. We were already looking at trains and planning our first away trips when I blurted out *"Sod the wedding, I doubt my Mum will speak to me ever again, but I'm going to every game next season!"* He agreed that it was the right thing to do. This was all the verification that I needed. So we headed to the pub to celebrate.

A few days later, whilst on a drunken escapade to Crocodile Creek at the Weymouth Sealife Centre(another story for another day), my friend Phill, the bar manager, received a phone call quite out of the blue. His big boss had been moved on due to personal misdemeanours and they were suddenly very short staffed. I had an interview.

Chapter 3 – **The Red and Blue of Barcelona**

Unfortunately, as time went by, Jak's 'wise' words began to seem less wise and the inevitable disappointed look in my mother's eyes became more prominent in my mind. I couldn't even blame alcohol for my over-confidence and socially-unexplainable decision this time. With a clearer head, I backed out of the decision to prioritise football over such a celebration. I couldn't miss a wedding so that I could watch Crystal Palace vs Plymouth Argyle, could I?

Pre-season was well underway and Palace had begun to sign players. Freddy Sears, a young, hungry and talented striker, had joined on loan for the season from West Ham. Darren Ambrose, a Charlton cast off, had signed after being released by our friends from the Valley. Stern John, a proven goal scorer, had arrived on a free transfer. Claude Davis, who had been decent on loan in the previous season, also signed on a free transfer. However, have no doubts about it, we were skint. Jamie Scowcroft, Shefki Kuqi, Rui Fonte, Anthony Stokes, Carl Fletcher, Leandre Griffit, John Oster and Paul Ifill had all departed. While no-one was devastated to see these players leave, the squad was looking very thin. There was also a transfer embargo put on the club due to money that was owed from signing Nicky Carle and Alan Lee in the previous season. Two players whom the club were now frantically trying to offload after they had failed to make an impact.

Desperate to see our new signings and feed my addiction, I made the short trip to Brentford for our first preseason friendly. Before the game, I was in The Griffin pub. Brentford's home ground, Griffin Park, has one main claim to fame. It is the only football ground in the country that has a pub on each corner of the stadium. During my first visit, my Brentford supporting mates had proudly taken me on 'the tour' of the drinking establishments and my favourite is the Griffin. It is a real football pub and it also serves a very good pint of London Pride. At the time, a personal favourite of mine.

None of my Brentford mates were at the match and I can only assume that their absence indicated how scared they were of the mighty Palace. However, a couple of my Palace mates, Dan and Colin, had made the short journey to West London.

My Palace friends are older than myself. About twenty years older to be precise. While I was often out clubbing until the early hours, they were at home with the responsibilities that are brought upon them by having families and jobs. Of course, that doesn't mean that they can't drink me under the table. Drinking with the 'Palace Vets', as I refer to them from time to time, has been my un-doing on a few occasions and would be throughout the season.

Dan had recently had his fortieth birthday and was starting to grey. He is tall – standing a well over six foot – and frequently visits the gym to keep himself in shape, although this gives him a slightly lanky appearance. Like Dan, Colin is also in his early forties, starting to grey and well over six foot. I look positively tiny in comparison when standing next to the pair of them, despite being 5"10 and a half. Yes, the half is important.

Colin wears glasses, which are usually complimented by a large grin, induced partly by alcohol and partly by his illogically positive attitude to Palace. An attitude not shared by Dan. He has a much more realistic view of the club. While he is fiercely defensive of Palace to 'outsiders', he misses the 'glory' days of supporting the club, i.e. when we weren't terrible, and is a lot quicker to point out the club's faults than his long-time friend.

As with every summer, Colin had made the same shocking fashion mistake that Dan was not willing to forgive him for. He wore sandals to football. He didn't quite complete the obsolete look by complimenting them with socks but the pub 'banter' was unforgiving nonetheless. Especially from Dan, who liked to try and keep in touch with fashion. Despite their different expectations of dress sense, they both took the, sometimes heated, abuse in good nature. Any lower league football fan needs a good sense of humour, especially once the match starts.

Dan had come to the game with his son, father and mother. He had promised his wife that he wouldn't get drunk as he was looking after their eight year old son, Max, so he only had a couple of *Coronas*. We did our best to corrupt his mind but he stayed loyal to his parental obligations. Like me, Dan had spent most of his child life growing up in Sunningdale, a small commuter village in Berkshire. However, unlike me, he is originally from South London and has spent most of his adult life living between the two.

Colin had also come to the game with his eight year old son, Adam. Unlike Dan, he hadn't promised his wife not to drink and was on the piss in his own style of pre-season training so he indulged in five or six pints of London Pride. Binge drinking parents. Broken Britain at its worst.

During the early nineties, the pair of them, along with some other friends who you will meet later, had travelled the country watching Palace but their catchment area for away games had gradually got smaller and smaller as they had got older and wiser. In the 1990/91 season, Dan had made a similar decision to me and had loyally attended every single match. However, there was one quite major difference when he did it. We were good. Very good! It was our most successful ever team; we finished third in the top division and had a string of England internationals playing for us at the time. With all due respect, watching Alan Lee and Shaun Derry just isn't the same as watching Ian Wright and Geoff Thomas. In Palace's terms, they were the 'glory days'. Days that I am gutted to have missed. I was only aged one at the time.

We all compared summers and discussed how we felt the season would go. It was pretty depressing stuff. They were surprised to hear that I still wanted to pitch up at every game during the coming season. Despite informing them at the final game of the previous campaign, they had wrongly assumed the fact that the beer was flowing had lead my mind astray.

While the pair of them questioned the sanity of my challenge, I defended my logic. When else would I get the chance to do it? I knew I would regret it if I didn't take on my task. No, it wasn't my task, it was my duty. My purpose. My... my... my... enjoyment. Ok, it wasn't quite a life changing experience, such as climbing Kilimanjaro or doing missionary work. However, it was something that I wanted to do, something that would be a challenge and something that was likely to piss off friends and family along the way as I inevitably missed birthdays, parties and maybe even a wedding.

Talking of weddings, I then explained the collision course that I was on with my Mum (and of course Emily). I still hadn't discussed the issue with her and the wedding was now only a few weeks away. It's not big and it's not clever, but when faced with a problem, I often find the best solution is to not think about it, head to the pub and hope it goes away. And it does, for a few hours, before returning the next morning, complete with a different sort of headache. I knew no one would understand why I felt that watching a meaningless early season game between Crystal Palace and Plymouth Argyle was so important to me but it was. What would be the point of going to every game, *except one*. Anyone could do that. It was hardly a show of dedication and barely even a challenge.

However, Colin and Dan were very supportive of my challenge. *"Of course you should choose Palace!"*
This was easy for them to say, they wouldn't be there to see the disappointment and embarrassment on my Mum's face when I told her. She was never impressed when I missed the Annual Family Christmas Party to attend an obscure Palace game, but this was another level. This wasn't a yearly event. This was the family event of the decade. *"It's only a cousin, it's not immediate family,"* chipped in Dan.
Done. If Jak, Colin *and* Dan all said that it was the right thing to do, it must be. The decision was proving to be much easier to make after a few drinks than it was while sober. We all had another pint (except Dan, who stayed loyal to his parenting obligations) to toast my venture and then headed to the game. It finished two all with Ambrose and Fonte scoring for us.

After the game, I went to meet my Felthamite friends in the Wetherspoons and continued drinking. I am glad that Phill was working behind the bar and none of my other potential employers because if you choose to believe certain eye-witnesses, I was loudly showing off my vast array of terrible accents and generally annoying people in the public house. I personally refuse to believe it.

The next morning I was minding my own business, reading the BBS while nursing a hangover, *(and had once again lost confidence in my previously definite decision to miss the wedding),* when two of my closest friends, Robin and Barlow, burst into my living room. Quite un-announced and quite rudely really.

Tom, usually referred to by his second name (Barlow), is someone who I have known since I started primary school. Amazingly, longer than I have known my love of all things red and blue. However I certainly have more love and affection for Palace than I do for Barlow. He had been on the end of most of our jokes through secondary school and this trend had continued into early adulthood. He never helped himself either. One insight into the mind of this man was his desire to join the police force, so he could drive a car fast. He followed up this scheme by going to uni; not because he needed to for his career, but for the 'university lifestyle'. Fair enough, spending your late teens and early twenties getting pissed and going on the pull in Bristol, Manchester or Leeds does sound like a productive and enjoyable way to spend three or four years. Naturally, he went to Broadstairs. A tiny village in Kent.

I have known Robin for less time than Barlow. We'd had the same friends through secondary school but we'd never had much time for each other. Mainly because he was such a grumpy git. Come to think of it, he still is. However, two things had brought us closer as friends. The first was attending a party together that neither of us wanted to go to. We met up early and found a watering hole that would serve us despite being underage and helped get into the party mood before making an appearance. When we finally arrived, two hours late, we discovered that it was more akin to a tenth birthday than a seventeenth. Beer was strictly off the menu. All that was missing was a clown and some jelly to go with the party games and cake. We returned to the pub.

The second event that sealed our companionship was our lads' holiday to Malia the previous summer. While we enjoyed many eventful evenings, mine and Robin's ultimate bonding moment was being team mates for a particularly tense game of drink-tion-ary. An adapted version of the family board game – Pictionary. It is no coincidence that I found early teenage friendship difficult with Robin. The fact that he wasn't a football fan seriously limited my ability to hold a conversation of any substance in my early secondary school days.

Unfortunately, Robin was not in a great place in July 2009. He had just lost his job, been evicted from his flat as he couldn't afford the rent and was now living at his parents' house; sleeping on the sofa.

After bursting in like Batman and Robin, leaving me about as enthusiastic for their enterance as I would be for Paul Peschisolido being subbed on against Palace with five minutes left, the pair of them continued to upset my fragile state even more by inexplicably loudly unleashing their own harebrained plan on me.

"*Come with us to France for a month*!" shrieked Robin, in a manner that thumped my already spinning head.

"*No not now guys, I've got a bloody hangover!*"

"*Not now you prick.*"

Barlow was showing his usual charm.

"*When? Where? How long for?*"

I loved the way that they seemed to think that summoning me to France without any details was likely to result in me saying *au revoir* to England and *bonjour* to frog's legs suppers.

"*We are taking my car and going!*"

"*We'll go to my Gran's house for a week!*" added Robin.

"...Then onto my Uncle's in the south..!" chipped in Barlow.
"...Then we'll drive to Barcelona and camp there!" explained Robin.
Barcelona? I hope they realised that isn't in France. They hadn't mentioned Spain.
At least, I don't think they had. They had blurted out the words so quickly
at me that they would have been hard to comprehend at the best of times.

However, the unpleasant physical effects following the heavy use of
alcohol that I was suffering from had made it even harder to keep up with the
Usain Bolt speed of conversation.
*"Then we'll go to Milan before heading to my sisters place in the Swiss Alps and
then back home!"* added Barlow.
This comment finished me off. *"Let's get a fry up and you can take me through
this slowly."*

For all of the faults of a hangover, they do have one saving grace. They
are the perfect excuse to head to the nearest cafe and indulge in some sausage
and bacon. After the third explanation, their message and vague route just about
resembled some form of sense in my mind. As loose and unplanned as the idea
was, it did sound like a fantastic opportunity. Neither of them had much money
so we knew that it would be on a shoe string budget but that suited me. As
students, we were well accustomed to being tight. *"So when do we go?"* I asked,
nearly convinced.
"5th August for a month!" enthused Robin, which was unlike him, because as I
said before, he is an incredibly grumpy individual.
Bugger! That's when it clicked. I had another decision to make. Marseille,
Barcelona and Milan or Bristol, Peterborough and Ipswich? There shouldn't really
be a decision to make. Unfortunately, as already discussed, a football addict's
mind doesn't always work the way that it should do.

Once again, when faced with a decision, I did the mature and adult
thing. I put it to the back of my mind, suggested that we got a crate of beer and
went back to Barlow's place. It worked for then.

After a few cans of cheap lager, the idea of a European tour got better
and better. Difficulties and practicalities became less and less important and a
ferry was booked; once we managed to type in the correct number plate of
Barlow's Ford Mondeo. Robin rang his Gran and asked her to get some beers in,
while Barlow rang his uncle and sister to let them know we were coming. It was
during the phone call to his sister that my eyes were opened to an ulterior motive
of the pair.

*"Hi.. How are you?... Yes we are coming... Yeah it's me, Robin and
James... Yes, James you know him... Yeah it's just someone else to help pay for
petrol."*
Bastard. I was honoured that despite being on two previous holidays with me, he
was willing to put up with me for a third trip abroad. But no. It wasn't for my
good looks, my charm, my intellectual conversation or even my general good
company as an extra drinking buddy. It was because of my bloody wallet. When I
questioned him after the phone call, he explained that he was trying to justify a

third person crashing on his sister's ski-lodge floor. It meant nothing to me. As far as I was concerned, that was it, our friendship was over. Fifteen years obviously meant nothing to him so they meant nothing to me either.

"Another beer James?"

"Cheers Barlow,"

He wasn't so bad after all.

I woke up the next day on Barlow's sofa with yet another hang over and a lot of questions about whether I should go or not. I would be lying if I said it was just the football that was holding me back. I also had my driving test coming up and couldn't afford to miss a month of lessons. Plus, I had a trip to Prague booked that I would have to pull out of. That city break had been carefully planned by me to fall during the first international break of the season in early September so that I wouldn't miss a game.

I also knew how skint my friends were and I wasn't exactly Roman Abramovich. I could see visions of us running out of petrol in a backwards French village that hadn't developed in 70 years, miles away from civilization and leaving us unable to fill up the car. However, the main drawback was the football. My dream. That is how sad the obsession had become. Other holidays, financial woes and learning to drive had all seemed insignificant compared to missing a few early season matches.

That day, I went home and told my Mum of the European plan. I was expecting her to be highly sceptical of such sketchy plans but she was surprisingly supportive. *"It's the chance of a lifetime. You're so lucky that you have friends with kind families that are willing to put you up."*

She was right too. The generosity, particularly of Robin's gran and Barlow's uncle, was astounding. They were willing to not only put up a relative for a week, who was rarely in touch, but also two of his friends who they had never met.

"So when do you go?"

"5th August"

"Oh no, you'll miss Emily's wedding!"

I hadn't even considered this. Despite drunkenly deciding to miss the wedding for football, I still hadn't made a final declaration of where my presence would be on that day. The Wedding was now extremely close and it would be exceptionally rude to drop out at this stage. However, the decision would be much more understood if I pulled out for a month-long holiday than a second rate football match.

"You must ring Emily and tell her!"

So I did. She was very understanding.

It was a mere ten days before we were due to depart to France. After putting the potential French, Spanish, Italian and Swiss adventure to the back of my mind for as long as I could, I had finally come to a decision. I was not going to go. It was a shame and it was not an easy dilemma to solve. However, I had made a pledge to go to every game and when James Howland makes a pledge, he keeps it. Sometimes.

I was dreading telling the guys that I was bailing. I hoped that they would still be able to afford to go without me (and my wallet). After delaying the moment for as long as possible, I summed them to the office, the Royal Foresters Pub in Ascot, and broke the news. I had a couple of pints of Dutch courage beforehand and then went for it.

"I'm really sorry guys, I'm not going to come to France with you, or Spain, or Italy, or Switzerland. I can't afford it. I have got other things happening and I can't justify buggering off for a month. I hope you can still go"

"We know."

"What? How? Aren't you pissed off?"

"We were. When you told us the other day while hammered at Phill's place, but we've changed our route since then."

"Oh"

Well that was easier than I expected.

Boosted by the easiness of telling the boys, I then broke the news to my mother.

"Why?" was her short and stunned response. I had to think quick. She wouldn't be impressed if I told her the real reason. So I used my second escape route. If you can't avoid thinking about it, lie.

"Oh I couldn't afford it and I need to get my driving out of the way for when I start to apply for jobs and they haven't planned it very well." I blagged.

"Very sensible James."

Phew. She bought it.

"At least you will be able to go to the wedding now."

S***! I hadn't thought of that. I was going to have to do something really drastic. I couldn't hide my thoughts. I couldn't lie. I couldn't even run away to the pub. I was going to have to tell the truth.

"I won't be going to the wedding Mum because Palace are playing at home that day."

She looked at me in disgust. And embarrassment. And some pity I think.

"Don't be silly James."

Over the next few days we argued. A lot. Eventually, I rang up Emily to explain and apologise. It was a horrible phone call to make. I felt like a spoilt brat at Christmas, cursing Santa, because he got a *Samsung Galaxy* rather than an *iPhone*. Emily was surprisingly sympathetic to my decision. Her father is a football fanatic and she was marrying a mad Evertonian so I guess she understood the dedication that came with being a football supporter to a degree. She suggested I came to the reception afterwards, even if I couldn't make the service. I was delighted with this compromise. Needless to say, my mother wasn't and neither were my brothers or other cousins. *"I hope you're not going to miss my wedding for football. That's if I invite you,"* was one chilling comment from my cousin, Jessie.

A few days later, I dusted off my suit, put on my best (well, only) tie and headed to my interview at Wetherspoons. I did consider bringing a brief case to boost my professional image even further but I decided that would be a little OTT. As a student, it was rare that I had the opportunity to wear a suit and it still had a little bit of an uneasy feeling about it. However, when you're not used to wearing a suit, it has almost magical powers. It made me keep my back straight and hold my head uphigh. I felt a great sense of pride and power flowing through my veins. Suddenly, I was invincible. People would look at me and not see a scruffy student but a fine young business man. They would think that I was coming back from a hard day in the city, making millions of pounds from buying and selling shares. I hopped off the train at Feltham station with an extra spring in my step and marched down the high street to the Moon on the Square Public House.

I casually went up to the bar and waited to be seen. I could feel all the enviable eyes staring at me and the magic suit. I was the smartest man in the establishment. A real high flyer. How could they possibly not employ me? I was in a deep self-satisfied thought when I heard a voice.

"You look like a right twat in that suit!" smirked Phillip from behind the bar. A group of regulars, standing close by, started laughing. All that power and pride rushed out of me as quickly as the suit had given it to me. Maybe it wasn't magic at all? Maybe it was on the dark side and had built me up to knock me down as if it was the British media. Maybe... but before I could think any further, which is usually a good thing, I was interrupted.

"Come over to this booth mate," called a bloke in a swish brown shirt and tie that was smarter than all the other workers behind the bar. He introduced himself as Vinnie, one of the middle managers at the pub. He offered me a cup of tea or coffee and then pulled out a clip board full of different papers. The interview began. It was a typically tedious interview for a part time pub job.

Why do you want to work for Wetherspoons?
For the money...
"I need a part time job and wanted to work for a well respected company that would look good on my CV."

What can you offer the company?
I can turn up for three shifts a week, pour some pints and clear some tables.
"I am a committed worker, my university schedule allows me to be flexible and I am keen to learn new skills."

What do you think your strengths are?
My ability to drink ten pints of Guinness and my loyalty to Crystal Palace Football Club.
"My determination, loyalty and commitment."

Where do you see yourself in one years' time?
Not working at f***ing Wetherspoons, that's for sure!
"I will hopefully have just successfully completed my degree and looking forward to starting my career in teaching."

Vinnie then concluded the interview after scribbling down my highly insightful answers and gave me an unconvincing handshake. Something that I think is inexcusable for any adult, especially one in a management position but so be it. He said that they'd be in touch and we then turned to go our separate ways. I was considering how it would be perceived if I left the interview and went straight to the bar when something suddenly popped into my head. I called after him *"Oh and one more thing, I can't work Saturdays or Tuesdays..."*
A day later I got a call telling me that I'd got the job.

Chapter 4 – **The Opening Day (...and the Wedding...)**

Saturday 8th August 2009 – Crystal Palace vs Plymouth Argyle, Selhurst Park

Crystal Palace: Julian Speroni, Nathaniel Clyne, Lee Hills, Shaun Derry, Patrick McCarthy, Neil Danns (Darren Ambrose, 60), Stern John (Alan Lee, 37), Victor Moses (Sean Scannell, 79), Freddie Sears, Matt Lawrence, Alassane N'Diaye
Subs Not Used: Nick Carle, Darryl Flahavan, Danny Butterfield, Johnny Ertl
Plymouth: Romain Larrieu, Jim Paterson, Carl Fletcher, Krisztian Timar, Jamie Mackie, Steven MacLean (Karl Duguid, 66), Rory Fallon, David McNamee, Gary Sawyer, Marcel Seip, Luke Summerfield (Alan Judge, 71)
Subs Not Used: Chris Clark, Craig Noone, Reda Johnson, Kyle Latheren, Ashley Barnes

There really is nothing like it. The feeling when you wake up in the morning of the opening day of the new football season. I'd had an early night the previous evening so I burst out of bed bright and early. It was hours until kick off but I was ready. I was excited. I skipped out of my room and downstairs, grinning all the way, shoulders up, head high. Football was back.

Then I stopped. Mum was getting ready for the wedding. Her new hat, her new dress, her best jewellery, her best make up, re-doing her newly-cut hair. My brother was getting ready for the wedding. His best suit, his smart shirt, his crisp tie, his classy cufflinks. She looked great. He looked great.
I had a red and blue football shirt on.

They both looked at me and simply shook their heads. I felt guilty. Of course I did. While my obsession with all things red'n'blue was well known, this was a seen as a new low for me. Even my football-obsessed uncles thought it was pathetic.

When it was time, I slipped off to Egham station and met my friend Dan on the train. I must have looked strange to say the least. There I was, in smart trousers and a football shirt, with my suit jacket over the top, carrying a smart, ironed shirt on a hanger and a tie stuffed into my back pocket. With hindsight, I probably should have just worn the shirt and left the Palace top behind but it didn't seem right at the time to head to SE25 without the colours of red'n'blue. Note to self: buy a Palace tie for such occasions.

We arrived at Palace around one o'clock and headed to the Wheeltappers, a Railway Man's Social Club by Selhurst Station. We had started drinking there about a year previously. From the outside, it looks like a scene out of Football Factory. It's in a dodgy alleyway, with a shut off, closed-looking entrance and a bloke on the door to collect a pound for entry. Inside, it looks slightly better, as long as you don't look at the broken ceiling or torn wallpaper.

However, it attracted our custom for three reasons. Firstly, it was cheap, very cheap, roughly £2 a pint cheap. Which in London, is, well, extremely cheap. No one ever minded buying a round in there. Secondly, it was often empty. We had previously drunk in the Clifton, which is right by the ground, but as soon as anyone returned with one round of drinks, the next person had to head off to get the next ones in; such was the build up of bodies at the bar. Instant service in the

Railway Club was a real selling point of the venue. Finally, despite its rough appearance, it was actually quite child friendly, which was perfect for Colin and Dan (and their kids I guess).

Dan and I once again met Colin and his son, Adam, in the pub. We were also joined by our friend and fellow season ticket holder, Kev, who went to school with Colin many years previously. While he isn't as tall as the other two, he still makes me feel small because of his large build. Unlike the other two, he has kept the grey hair at bay, something that the others put down to the fact that he has never married. Kev is a man of few words and often tends to sit 'on the fence' with his Palace views. Although, after a whisky or two, he has been known to be more controversial with his opinions, as well as repeat the same few, famous stories that he has – such as chatting up two girls on the Holmesdale terrace on one cold afternoon of terrible football to name but one. And when I say a whisky or two, I could just as easily be talking about bottles as glasses. Whatever the weather outside, Kev always wears the same thing – a large, thick, Umbro jumper. Come rain or shine, Kev is as loyal to the jumper as we are to Palace.

Jonathan was also with us, who is Colin's kind of nephew. The family link has never been fully explained to me and seems to change every time I ask about it. I'm not sure even they know to be perfectly honest. In looks, Jonathan appears to be a younger version of his (kind of) uncle. He is well over six foot, of a similar build and also wears glasses. However, his personality is less of the quick wit and humour possessed by his (kind of) uncle, and more random outbursts that demonstrate passion, if not intelligence. During games, Jonathan has a love of food like no other and religiously demolishes a couple of hot dogs in each match, sometimes three. Our group was completed by Dan's Dad, Peter, and his friend, Chris.

Palace fans, young and old, began to eccentrically discuss how the coming season would go and, I'm ashamed to say, any thoughts about the wedding couldn't have been further from my mind. Peter was negative, as usual, Colin was positive, as usual. Everyone was drinking, as usual. It was like we'd never been away. The reality was, the club were financially struggling and had a wafer thin squad but as the beers flowed, so did the excitement. The general feeling was that our new signings were decent and that we would once again be in mid-table. But to us, it didn't matter. All that mattered was that football was back.

Inexcusable opinions and excessive passion are what make football what it is. Without those things, it might still be a sport, it might still be entertainment, but it certainly wouldn't be one of the world's most talked about topics. I actually think what drives that passion on and gives football the edge over other sports is the tribal nature of it. You're in a pack and everyone cares about the same thing. You hunt as one. In other sports, both sets of supporters are mixed in together. In football, the two groups of supporters are kept separate, which creates a vocal, hostile atmosphere and no shortage of good humour between two similar groups of people.

Now don't get me wrong, I love going for a beer with opposition supporters before and after games, but during the match, it's war. Us vs Them. No barriers, give abuse, shout obscenities, cheer your team, laugh at the other's. The problem comes when people are unable to differentiate between football 'hate' and genuine 'hate' and it spoils over into violence. Something that has no place in the game.

It is easy to look at a football crowd and see a bunch of bloody-thirsty, aggressive blokes shouting and swearing. However, for the vast majority, it is simply a release of frustration and anger from real life in an environment that ultimately, doesn't matter. Work, family, university, school, money, illness; whatever stage of life you might be at, it all creates stress, worry and pain. To be able to release that in a football stadium has to be better than it coming out at colleagues, partners or children, right? However, that release of emotion can't happen unless you're genuinely passionate and desperate to win. Football has to feel as important as life and death, but that needs to be balanced by the little voice in the back of your head; reminding you of your sanity. Unfortunately, because of the history of violence at football, some people, understandably, will never see past that.

That passion and tribal nature also creates friendships. The way that a group of people, who would never usually socialise, get together and unite over something is very special. You only have to look at the demographic of our group to realise that. I couldn't imagine myself going for a drink with any of my companions in the pub that day without the Palace bond but the collective infatuation of one team can bring families together, even tenuous links such as Colin and Jonathan. Football can get three generations of a family to have a joint adventure every other Saturday. Where else could they go together for that *and* enjoy it?

It was the red and blue love that had made a 36 year old (Dan) and an 18 year old (myself) become good mates because we both happened to be exiled from South London to Berkshire. It was purely from travelling the country in the nineties with Palace that Colin and Dan, now such close friends, had met. Football gets a lot of bad press and sometimes deservedly so but the good that comes from football needs to be highlighted too.

Anyway, back in the pub, the eight of us decided that it was time to head to the ground. After emptying our bladders, we strolled out of the bunker that is the Selhurst Railway Club and into the alley, still carrying my shirt and tie. Early season games are supposed to be played out in the sun but this one wasn't. It was a fairly grey August day. Still, a reasonable, if unspectacular, well-spirited crowd was gathering and heading up the Holmesdale Road towards the ground. As we approached the stadium, with a sense of returning home after a summer holiday, I bought a programme. The excitement of seeing the new programme design, with a new player on the front in the brand new kit is magical. The wait was nearly over.

Then it was the chance to use my new Season Ticket for the first time.

Unlike previous seasons, Palace had actually managed to send out the season tickets before the opening game, which should be a bonus – although maybe it would be best to wait until after the game to make a judgement on that. However, using the new season ticket wasn't quite as exciting as buying the new programme. Based on previous experience, this was more of a nervous occurrence. Would it work?

We estimated that it had about a 50:50 chance. With a hesitant twitch, I handed over the plastic card to the teenager behind the counter. He scanned it, the turnstile clicked and I was in. Phew.

"Enjoy the game!" came the trained, almost robotic, comment from the entrance operator.

"I'll try," I replied with a sympathetic smile, in the cynical manner that football fans tend to, refusing to give any hint of optimism that the team might actually win or we might enjoy this whole over-priced experience.

I trudged up the two flights of stairs to the upper tier of the Holmesdale Road Stand where my season ticket was, taking in all the sounds that had been missing from my Saturdays over the previous couple of months.

"Selhurst Half-Time Super-Draw!"

"Daddy, can I have some chips?"

"Programmes! Get your match day programmes!"

"Wa'cha reckon today then?" "Gawd knows!"

There's nothing quite like ear-wigging conversations at football. No one ever agrees on anything other than that the referee is, inevitably, a wanker.

After re-emptying our bladders (once you've opened that seal...) we headed to our seats. In our familiar season ticket seats, we lined up in our usual formation: Jonathan and his outbursts (kept as far away as possible), Ron (Colin's Dad, who had joined us in the ground), Adam, Colin, Dan, me, Kev. It was fantastic to be back. The six of us were casually joking and enjoying the atmosphere in the minutes leading up to kickoff. Music was blaring out, anticipation was building and the reality of the new season was finally here. It had only been ninety-seven days since that un-eventful 0-0 draw with Sheffield United but it had seemed like forever.

Soon, the two teams came out to Glad All Over, Palace's song since the sixties. The first time that I'd heard the tune was before I'd even been to a game during a 'Worst Ever FA Cup Final Song' competition on the BBC's *Football Focus*. Without realising it was the Palace anthem, I'd declared *"This is rubbish!"* After hearing what I now considered to be a hymn at Wembley in my first ever live match, my parents had dug out an old vinyl record of the Dave Clark classic and I'd listened to it on loop until I learnt every word. Words that I now sing with such passion at the start of every home game. It was originally written as a love song but I can't imagine the band envisaged it being sung by thousands of blokes to declare their love for a football team every other Saturday. However, I think it is quite fitting that the club has adopted a love song. A man's love for his football team is just as strong as his love for his wife. Often stronger. Around the same time as the players took the field at Selhurst Park, Emily and Mitch had walked up the isle to Everton's own club song, 'Forever Everton'.

Palace were back in red and blue stripes after wearing a white sash kit for home games in the previous season, and Plymouth were in their traditional green. We quickly tried to work out who had been selected to represent us on the pitch as the players marched towards the halfway line for the customary handshakes.

Speroni was in goal, obviously – he had been for a few years by then. We had a solid-looking back line of Matt Lawrence, Paddy McCarthy, Nathaniel Clyne and Clint Hill. Pretty much as expected, good. In midfield, we had Shaun Derry (the club captain), good, Neil Danns, good, and Alessane N'Diaye, what?

He was an unknown, very young, French bloke who had signed in pre-season. Both times that I had seen him play, he had looked like a donkey playing up front. However, Neil Warnock had been quoted as comparing him to the former Arsenal captain, Patrick Vieira. Still, seeing him line up on the opening day of the season, in midfield, was a surprise. Inevitably, having seen him play, out of position, for about twenty minutes, we all gave our detailed opinions on whether or not it was right to start him.

One player we were all pleased to see starting was youngster, Victor Moses. He had become a teenage sensation at Palace when a national newspaper ran a report on him aged just 14 after he made his debut for England under 16s. By the age of sixteen, he had made his first team debut. Aged seventeen, he had scored his first goal in professional football. He had more natural talent than pretty much any other player that I had seen wear the Palace shirt, maybe with the exception of Italian International, Attilio Lombardo. However, despite all the positives, his Palace career had been fairly stop-start.

But his story is one of the most genuinely touching ones in football. He was born in Nigeria and at the tender age of eleven, his parents were murdered. He escaped the country and ended up in Croydon, where he was spotted by a Palace youth team scout. The club paid for him to attend Whitgift School and he developed his game at the club. Even if he didn't progress from being a talented Championship player, it was a magical story. But every Palace fan knew, he was far, far more able than that. Again, a case of the good in football and the way it had turned this orphan's life around was not focused on in the press. Millionaire footballers cheating on their super model wives or punching someone in a nightclub sells far more newspapers.

Alongside Moses, in a front three, were new signings; Stern John and Freddy Sears. None of us agreed with the manager on the starting line up. Football fans very rarely do – and often think they could do a better job. It's most fans' dream to be in charge of their team and be able to make those influential decisions. That's why the computer game, *Football Manager*, is so popular. It is essentially a game where you answer emails and watch matches, with little control over the outcome. Yet millions of copies are sold every year.

The game gives fans the chance to select the team, sign who they want and 'prove' that they could make a better fist of it than the bloke who has been charged with doing the job for real. The other advantage of *Football Manager* is that, as stressful as it can be, it doesn't seem to give the same early grey hair that the real job tends to trigger. However, despite the grey hair and judgemental supporters, the lucky 92 football league managers get to live out every fan's dream.

Eventually, the referee blew his whistle and the 2009/2010 Championship rollercoaster began. The crowd cleared their throats and began to sing some of the usual range of humorous, abusive and uplifting songs designed to motivate the team and mock the opposition. This was it.

Could this be our year? Promotion, the Premiership. No one was thinking of transfer embargos or financial worries here. As Simon Jordan, the club's rather outspoken chairman had said, promotion could change everything. And at the start of a season, no matter what your brain tells you, no matter what your mates tell you, no matter what the media tells you, no matter what the bookies tell you, you know that in the Championship, anything could happen. And that had to include winning the title with a record amount of points, right? A boy can dream.

Wrong, don't dream. Don't believe, that's when you get hurt supporting, as most people do, a crap team. Krisztián Tímár (Ever heard of him? No, me neither) put Plymouth 1-0 up after just five minutes. The small selection of West Country folk who had made the long trip to the capital city began to dance around in the away section to our right. ****. Palace were making my decision to miss the wedding even harder to justify.

Twenty minutes or so later, our new centre forward, Stern John, went off injured and was replaced by Alan Lee, a player we'd been desperately trying to shift throughout the summer after being the latest in a long-line of useless ex-Ipswich donkeys that we'd signed, double ****. Dan was already convinced that would be the last we saw of John – he was far from optimistic about our new, aging, centre forward.

Despite this, Palace actually had a few positives, Freddy Sears looked lively, Alessane N'Diaye had a vague resemblance to Patrick Vieira in how he played and Alan Lee looked slightly less useless than the previous season. However, at half-time, we were 1-0 down, at home, to poxy Plymouth Argyle. I expect there were a few tears being shed across South London at the wedding and that's exactly what I felt like doing during the disappointing opening half of the season.

Instead of breaking down and weeping, we formulated another plan – we went up to the Red'n'Blue bar and grabbed a beer. The general consensus was that it could have been worse. Looking back, I can't help but feel this was mere early season optimism, coupled with happiness to be out of the house and back at Selhurst Park on a Saturday afternoon. Rather than positivity based on any genuine belief. If the exact same half of football had been served up on a cold Tuesday night in February, I doubt we'd have been so generous in our analysis.

Anyway, after finishing our half time bevies, and once again emptying our bladders, we optimistically stepped back outside for the second half. Palace played with a lot more intent and the previously out-casted Alan Lee scored a firm header from a Victor Moses cross. The game petered out after that as both teams seemed content with a draw to get their points tally off the mark.

In the final few minutes of the match, I changed my shirt over, gave my Palace top and programme to Dan and walked out of the ground to a few strange looks as I was wearing a full suit. I rushed to Norwood Junction station and began my journey to Charlton of all places for the wedding. On the train, my Dad rang, as always. We discussed the positives and looked forward to the season ahead.

When I arrived at Charlton station, it was still busy from their opening game in League 1 after they had been relegated the previous season. Incidentally, they won 3-2 versus Wycombe Wanderers but as this was in the league below, who cares? I couldn't possibly write any more without saying 'Who the **** is laughing now?' Anyone who needs to, knows exactly what I mean. Anyway, while in the middle of a rival's territory, rather than burst into a lippy song and risk having my knee-caps rearranged, I jumped in a cab and arrived at the wedding just in time for the after dinner speeches.

Throughout what was a lovely, although incredibly drunken evening, I received many comments of disapproval at my decision but I stayed loyal to it; trying my best to justify the un-justifiable. I'd experienced just as much love and affection as I would have done at the wedding. Well, my mates and I had all jumped about and hugged each other after the Palace goal. Although, an early season goal wasn't exactly 'tears in your eyes' stuff like watching a young couple take their vows. Goals like that tend to come later in the season.

Just like the guests at the wedding had experienced the start of Emily and Mitch's marriage, I'd witnessed the start of something special too. The season. I didn't even have to listen to a priest's sermon in the middle, unless you count the PA man reading the half time scores. Personally, the more that I think about it, I find it hard to imagine people who *wouldn't* miss a wedding to see a one all draw between Crystal Palace and Plymouth Argyle.

However, I didn't convince anyone at the wedding that it was a rational or respectable decision. Still, I was on my way to completing the challenge. One down, (at least) forty-seven to go.

Throughout my career I've been fortunate enough to play with some really high calibre people. Looking back, I have to say that to be involved with Crystal Palace at that time fills me with great joy. Up to that point or after my time at Palace, I'd never been involved in a team that you could really call "a team". Each and every one of us really appreciated the role that we all filled and respected one another enormously. All aware that it was us as players that were to determine the future of a football club in adversity. For me to be Captain will forever fill me with pride.

Shaun Derry

Chapter Five –**Devon**

Tuesday 11th August 2009, Crystal Palace vs Torquay United, Selhurst Park

Crystal Palace: Julian Speroni, Clint Hill, Shaun Derry, Patrick McCarthy, Jose Fonte, Darren Ambrose, Neil Danns, Victor Moses (Sean Scannell, 73), Alan Lee (Kieran Djilali, 63), Danny Butterfield, Alassane N'Diaye
Subs Not Used: Nathaniel Clyne, Darryl Flahavan, Matt Lawrence, Johnny Ertl, Kieron Cadogan

Torquay United: Scott Bevan, Kevin Nicholson, Chris Robertson, Chris Todd, Tim Sill, Scott Rendell (Elliott Benyon, 70), Nicky Wroe, Tyrone Thompson (Michael Brough, 90), Wayne Carlisle, Danny Stevens (Mustapha Carayol, 70), Kieran Charnock
Subs Not Used: Mark Ellis, Martin Rice, Lee Hodges, Bon Joyce

The first date that any football league calendar receives is the first round of the League Cup. In this competition, Selhurst Park was to be visited by a side from Devon for the second time in four days. Torquay, a club newly promoted to the Football League. Their return after a two year absence pleased me for two reasons.

Mainly because I had previously been to their ground. Therefore, their football league return allowed me to tick off another ground out of the 92 with no effort required what so ever. I was also happy to welcome them back to the football league party because it's a pleasant enough place to visit and enjoy. I can put on my best pretentious attitude and enjoy scones on the harbour front, while discussing which way around the jam and cream go. In a Devon tea, it is cream on the scone then jam; in Cornwall, jam first followed by the cream. Not that I have spent a whole afternoon discussing this. That would be really sad. However, folk from Devon are definitely right. I hope I can say that without starting a civil war. The actual game was highly un-eventful. It felt a bit like the famous grammar book; Eats, Shoots and Leaves. I arrived just before kickoff, met Colin and family, watched us stroll to a 2-1 victory and returned home.

In many ways, it is games like this that sum up the addiction. I know I attended and I know who I attended the game with. I know that I had to sit in the Main Stand, rather than my usual seat in the Holmesdale Road as only one stand was opened due to the absence of some of the more rational thinking supporters. I know Darren Ambrose scored twice, including one penalty. Goals that I suspect were greeted with a grin, a smile and a satisfied round of applause, rather than the usual exuberance and euphoria of a Palace goal. I know I had a beer at half time in one of the lounges behind the unfamiliar stand, and it tasted better than my usual pint in the Red'n'Blue Bar. I know I didn't even consider not going – even if we had been drawn away from home I would have habitually attended. But how many of the four thousand fans who did show up remember much more than that? Even the fifty or so dedicated Torquay fans who made the 406 mile round trip on a Tuesday night must be struggling. Although I suspect they remember arriving home at 3am with work the next day.

I'll be honest enough to admit that I didn't know (well, remember) that Torquay had even scored until I checked some old reports. The game was dull and predictably forgettable, yet four thousand people religiously turned up after work and paid to watch the crap game that they knew they'd inevitably be treated to.

The following day, the draw for the next round pitted us at home to huge spenders, Manchester City. With Palace in a financial crisis and Man City's £150 million summer spending spree, the game was both exciting and terrifying in equal measures.

Chapter Six – **Controversial**

Saturday 15th August 2009, Bristol City vs Crystal Palace, Ashton Gate

Crystal Palace: Julian Speroni, Danny Butterfield (Matt Lawrence 90), Patrick McCarthy, Jose Fonte, Clint Hill, Alassane N'Diaye, Shaun Derry, Neil Danns, Freddy Sears, Alan Lee (Sean Scannell 90), Darren Ambrose (Victor Moses 90).
Subs Not Used: Darryl Flahavan, Nathaniel Clyne, Nicky Carle, Johnny Ertl.

Bristol City: Gerken, McCombe, Nyatanga, Orr, McAllister, Skuse, Hartley (Fontaine 90), Elliott, Sproule, Clarkson (Akinde 46), Maynard.
Subs Not Used: Basso, Johnson, Williams, Blackman, Brian Wilson.

Bristol C away. I have a few ideas what the 'C' might stand for but we'll stick with the title of this chapter for now. The two sides had played each other six times in 2008 and Bristol had seemed to have all of the luck. Last minute penalties, last minute goals, extra time winners, Palace missing penalties, dodgy refereeing decisions. Everything that could possibly go wrong against Bristol City, had gone wrong. Or so we thought. That was, until we met Rob Shoebridge. The day started well enough. I met Dan, Colin, Kev and our friend Steve on the train to Reading from Ascot with a crate of beer and a selection of hazelnut chocolate. More on that later. First, let me introduce you to Steve.

Steve is a real character. He looks like a nutter. He sounds like a nutter. He sometimes acts like a nutter. But he wouldn't hurt a fly. He is one of those people who you know is always going to provide a laugh. Colin often fondly talks about memories of Steve's cavalier attitude to trying to pull girls in clubs. I believe his outlook to pulling was similar to Thomas Edison's theory on failure. *"I have not failed. I've just found 10,000 ways that won't work."* Steve's infamous Stag Do further sums up his appearance and character. He had decided to be sensible and spend some time with his future father-in-law, not drinking, while his mates headed to the Wetherspoons in Leicester Square. Later that day, Steve turned up with his future father-in-law.
'Sorry mate, you're not coming in,' stated the bouncer on the door.
'What? It's my Stag Do!'
'Sorry mate, you've had enough. There's no way you're coming in!'
'What? You're joking, right? I haven't had a drop!'
'No chance mate. With those eyes, there's no way you're sober!'
Only Steve.

Another memorable story is when Steve managed to get a year-long ban from watching Palace. I'm sure there are plenty of people who think avoiding the depression of watching the team is a fantastic reward for someone. However, for some of us, that's pure torture. The incident happened at Highbury in the mid-nineties when the vast majority of the Palace fans were singing anti-Ian Wright songs after he had celebrated scoring a goal in front of us during a previous game, which had relegated us.

During one rendition, Steve decided to run down to the front of the stand and conduct the vocal away support. This made him an easy target for the disgruntled stewards and he was taken away. Dan once commented to me, reminiscing on the good old daysthat he missed so much, such as that John Solako inspired win at Highbury, that *"There was a big group of us who had sneaked into the Northbank* (the main home stand) *that day, singing about Ian Wright and no one questioned us, so god knows how Steve managed to get nicked from the away section!"*

Only Steve. He decided to represent himself in the trial. He lost.

I could probably write another book titled *'Steve. How? What? Why?'* But there is only so much of Steve anyone can take. If you happen to be reading this mate, then I'm sorry. I love you to bits you nutter but you really can have too much of a good thing. I suppose the worrying thing about Steve is that he was now a steward at Palace. In his words, *"because you get to watch 90% of the game and it's free!"*

Only Steve.

Anyway, we arrived at Reading station and sneaked out for a cheeky beer at The Three Guineas Pub, before catching our train to Bristol. We met our friend John in the pub. Another real character. John had recently given up his season ticket but was still a passionate Palace fan. He is best summed up as short, bald and controversial. If you ever want to know what John thinks, listen to what the majority of Palace fans think and he will probably (at least pretend to) believe the opposite. For example, he is the only Palace fan on the planet who rates Chris Day as a better keeper than Carlo Nash.

The group of us were all wearing our favourite 1996-1998 home shirts after Dan had declared the occasion was to be '90's shirt day'. This involved me wearing my oldest brother's top from the era as my one was for a seven year old with 'Lombardo 7' printed on the back. My brother is 6"3 and it's fair to say, the shirt drowned me.

As usual, the most exciting thing about the day was not the football. We had a plan for the train journey that didn't simply involve beer. On a train to Southampton towards the end of the previous season, 'The Sun' had insightfully informed us that the World Record for eating the most Ferrero Rochers in one minute was a mere seven. This seemed pitiful. This was a World Record that we could surely destroy.

James Boyd had become 'famous' for attempting, and failing, to beat this record on Britain's Got Talent. Since then, there had been a mini-craze across the country for attempting to become a World Record Holder at the said challenge. And that day, on that train journey, was to be our attempt to do just that.

The contenders were strong. We had all witnessed Jonathan destroy hot dogs and burgers during matches at such a speed that he surely owned a World Record or two already. Kev is large and therefore his mere physique made him a cert to do well. Finally, as Colin repeatedly informed us, he'd seen chicken wings go into Steve's mouth whole and return bare to the bone - less than a second later. Dan was quietly confident too. This was his competition. He'd supplied the chocolate mountain that lay before us and he wasn't going to let anyone beat him easily.

These are the rules of a Ferrero Rocher eating World Record Attempt:

- The Ferrero Rocher can only be unwrapped during the one minute time.
- Each separate Ferrero Rocher must be swallowed completely before eating commences on the next one. The challenger must eat the chocolates one after another; showing his/her mouth to be empty before starting to eat the next chocolate.
- It is at the attempters disposal to unwrap them all at once or as they are eating each one.
- No drinking is allowed.
- Only whole Ferrero Rochers completely eaten within the set one minute count towards the record total

As the outsider for the title, I went first. Nom. Chew, chew, chew, chew, chew. Until you try this challenge, you have no concept of how difficult it is. The bloody things won't break down. They're too big to swallow in one but the melted chocolate centre is too sticky to chew on. Anyway, on I went. Chew, chew, chew, chew, chew. Gulp! That's one. On to the next. Munch, munch, munch, munch, munch! Gulp! That was two. I eventually managed a reasonable four. It wasn't going to break any World Records (*Well, clearly, as I needed eight to do that*) but I was content with my attempt.

Dan went next and managed an even more credible five. Then came the surprise of the journey. An event so shocking that it will be forever remembered as '*The Moment that stunned First Great Western Trains and the West Country forevermore*'. An occurrence so unexpected that train staff are now required by law to stop their duties and quietly reflect on the surprise of that August, Saturday lunch time in 2009 as they pass this stretch of track. A moment so jaw-dropping that it puts the shock of Paddy McCarthy's 30 yard thunderbolt at Derby in the shade. Well, maybe not, but we were a bit taken aback. Jonathan, the fast food shoveller, the hungriest creature known to man-kind, the beast who laughs in the face of the portions on Man vs Food, the bookies red-hot favourite, managed a pathetic three. As loving friends, we would never let him forget this.

By now, we had started to gain a small audience. Colin and Kev gave reasonable efforts, much to the amusement of our fellow passengers, who were giving us a mixture of worried but encouraging looks. I think we were generally amusing the carriage but there was definitely a slight look of terror in some of their eyes.

Finally, John stepped up. Dan started the timer, One. Bang! Gone! Two! Bang! Gone! What? They were going down whole. He must have been practising! This was unbelievable! The whole carriage was on tenterhooks and took a huge deep breath in. Well, that's how I'd like to remember it. What actually happened is our group all shouted that he was cheating and needed to finish each one before moving onto the next, while a couple of annoyed passengers turned around to check out the fuss.

However, none of this seemed to affect John. Three! Bang! Gone! Four, Five, Six... He might actually do this. Seven... He was going to do it. Eight... He wasn't stopping. Nine... He'd smashed it. There was no doubting it, John was the new World Record Holder. If only we'd remembered to phone Guinness to get them to send one of their representatives on our train to verify the attempt then under the Ferrero Rocher section of the Guinness Book of Records, the name John Schembri would be immortalised forever. Probably. Unfortunately, it wasn't to be the last time that day than an official would be missing when he was needed to make an important observation.

When James Boyd 'performed' the challenge on Britain's Got Talent, Simon Cowell had been less than impressed. I can't help but feel that if he'd been on that train to Bristol and seen John in full flow, then the Queen might have been able to witness first hand this chocolate-eating extravaganza. Hell, she might even have had a go herself. Now that would have made good TV.

Full from chocolate and buzzing from beer, we arrived at Bristol Temple Meads Station.

"EAGLESSSSSSSSSS!" we all let out a customary cheer to announce our arrival. As I said before, it was this tribal nature that I loved. We were arriving in opposition territory and we were here to conquer.

I had been to three games away at Bristol in the previous couple of seasons and I also had a friend who attended university in the city, so I knew it well. I led the group out of the station, along the main road to a large roundabout, down a small road, straight over another roundabout and straight into the Wetherspoons pub. A short walk; no more than ten minutes. I was the hero, I'd found us a pub in no time. No wasted drinking time here. Smug mode on.

We all got a beer and began to partake in the usual pre-match banter. John was being usually controversial. Steve, who had decided to drink some West Country Loopy Juice that was probably brewed out the back in a bath tub, was beginning to look his slightly madder drunken state rather than his 'normal' mad *sober* state. Colin was being usually optimistic and Jonathan was chatting nonsense. As usual.

After indulging in a sufficient amount of pints, we came out of the pub and started the ten minute walk back to Temple Meads to jump into a cab.

"James, isn't that a back entrance to the station?" someone asked.

Bugger! Opposite the pub was another entrance to the station. Maybe I didn't know the area so well after all. Smug mode turned off.

Before jumping in a cab, we hid our remaining cans from the journey in a nearby bush so that we could return to them later. We didn't want to waste them or waste any money on more beer after the game. Apparently, women love a frugal man so I'm sure we would have been every girls' dream if they'd seen us burying our bag of booze in a bush.

The taxi ride was hilarious. Maybe not for the cab driver or anyone we passed but for us, it was. Jonathan, John and Steve were quite pissed by now and were shouting at anyone and everyone that we passed. The bellows from the back of the cab linked to anything and everything vaguely relevant.

"Wurzel, how's your combine harvester?" - Well, they're from the West Country so it's probably true that they own one.

"There's only one Dean Windass!" – After they had beaten us in the play off semi-final two seasons previously, he'd scored the winning goal against them in the final for Hull City.

"Gas Army!"- The nickname of their city rivals, Rovers.

"Did you cry at Wem-ber-lee?"– Back to the Windass moment.

"There's only one Nigel Martyn!"- A small celebration of the former England and Palace goalkeeper who we had signed from Bristol Rovers, nineteen years previously.

"Wolf whistle!"– Well, clearly no one shouted 'wolf-whistle' but fingers were put to lips and a screeching sound was made towards woman who happened to be passing by. It reminded me a bit of Calvin Harris' song, 'The Girls'

"I like them black girls, I like them white girls
I like them Asian girls, I like them mix-raced girls
I like them Spanish girls, I like them Italian girls
I like them French girls and I like Scandinavian girls

I like them tall girls, I like them short girls
I like them brown haired girls, I like them blonde haired girls
I like them big girls, I like them skinny girls
I like them carrying a little-bitty weight girls"

There really was no discrimination here. No girl was safe. John liked them all. In the chorus of the song, Calvin Harris claims 'I get all the girls' but I'm not sure any girls were going to be 'got' in Bristol that day.

Presumably out of fear of having an escaped party from a mental institute in the back of his cab, the driver informed us he was a Palace fan. It's amazing how wherever you go in the country, the cab drivers seem to support the away club that day. Whether it's out of fear of the reputation that goes before football fans or they simply want a tip, I don't know. However, almost without fail, they have a love of either your side or the other team from the city.

For example, on another day, this guy may well have claimed to be an avid Bristol Rovers fan and 'desperate' for us to win.

Eventually, we arrived at the ground around half an hour before kickoff. All of the pubs in the close proximity to the ground are 'Home Fans Only'. In the previous season, we had found a cricket club about a five minute walk from the stadium, which was more than happy to serve us but there was no time for that today. We headed past the gormless turnstile operators and into the small, un-covered concourse behind the stand.

In football grounds, it is illegal to drink within view of the pitch. This law was passed in 1985 and football is the only sport that it applies to. At cricket or rugby, fans sit in their seat and enjoy supping on a beer while taking the game in. I have a friend who watches both Reading Football Club and London Irish Rugby Club. Both sides share the same home ground; The Madejski Stadium. He sits in the same seat for both events. During a rugby Saturday, he sits in his seat with a beer in his hand but if he did the exact same thing in the exact same place a week later, he would be breaking the law.

Despite the irony, it's not actually a law that bothers me. Frankly, football fans are able to drink enough throughout the day without needing an extra ninety minutes. While the social side is vital to being able to enjoy football, if you can't get pleasure from the game without a beer, then you might as well give up and just go on the lash with your mates each Saturday. It would be a lot cheaper and involve a lot less travel. The whole purpose of this jolly up has to be centred on the football. Besides that, in order to make football a safe, family environment, the game has had to accept that there was a huge problem with violence in the past that needed to be, and has been, addressed. One of the controlling methods used was the ban on drinking in view of the pitch.

However, what was less understandable is that Bristol City refused to sell beer to away fans in their concourse despite having the facilities to do so and allowing the home fans to enjoy a beer in the ground. This meant that we had half an hour to sit on their tired, backless stalls, waiting for kick off. A half hour wait gave Jonathan enough time for two hot-dogs and a bottle of Fanta (this was a first half tradition of his). If only he'd managed a few more hazelnuts treats on the train, he wouldn't have had to spend so much in the ground. There again, knowing Jonathan, I expect he could have got through three boxes of Ferrero Rochers and still managed his hot dogs.

Eventually, after Jonathan had decided against a third hot dog, the game began. It was a fairly tame affair for most of the first half and the usual 'wit' went between the two fans.

"Did you cry at Wembley?" screamed the Palace fans, without a hint of irony that they had beaten us to get to Wembley in the first place.
"The wheels on your house go round and round!" replied the home faithful, obsessed with the idea that we came in a caravan. 'Tezza' would have been livid at the factual inaccuracies of people from the West Country calling Londoners 'pikeys'. Don't they know that the streets are paved with gold in our capital city?

However, the whole atmosphere and game changed on thirty minutes. Freddy Sears knocked the ball past the Bristol City keeper, Dean Gherkin; a player who had received so much 'banter' from the Palace fans in the past, not least because of his green goalkeeper jersey.

*"You're the s*** of McDonalds!"*

"Your Dad, was a cucumber!"

"Gherkin's in a pickle"

*"You taste s*** in a burger!"*

Anyway, as the ball went to the goal, Sears, along with four other Palace players, charged towards the corner flag in celebration. Goal! 1-0! Or was it? From our view, at the opposite end, we could see the ball bounce away. The players stopped celebrating. What was happening? My initial thought was that a City player must have hacked the ball away. However, the Palace player's reaction told me that it must have gone in before the defender had cleared the ball. I had seen us robbed in this way before. During an FA Cup match vs Leeds, we had scored a goal that was a good foot over the line, but the referee and linesman had somehow missed this vital fact; deeming the ball to have not crossed the goal line. Eventually, the game re-started with the Bristol keeper kicking the ball back to the middle of the pitch. Controversial.

Half time came and went with lots of disgruntled Palace fans as we tried to unpick the key incident of the half. The second half was again fairly uneventful, with Palace looking the slightly better team in my opinion, until the final moment. Our central defender, Jose Fonte, gave the ball away and Bristol scored in the last minute. Bastards. The home fans erupted and began the customary mocking of the away faithful.

As we trudged out of the jubilant stadium, thinking of what might have been, Steve and John were in full flow.

"That's what happens if you try and defend for ninety minutes," moaned John.

"Came for one point, got none," summed up Steve.

*"What a heap of s***, Warnock, sort it out!"* they both cursed.

Although, I managed to focus the pair of them on what was important to take away from the game. Filled with frustration and beer, I screamed towards the home dugout,

"Oi Johnson (the City Manager) *You're just a midget **** in a suit, you w*****!"* They both agreed with that.

Dan and I were slightly more positive in our post match reviews, Colin was moaning about the referee and Jonathan was at the burger bar, yet again. Kev was simply agreeing with everyone. He tends to do that. Life is easier that way and another reason that he's avoided turning grey as he hit 40. Having since read the BBC match report on the game, the neutrals were slightly more generous towards our performance than Steve and John, stating *'The Eagles had dominated the game, with Sears and Alan Lee always a threat.'* Football, the game of opinions.

As we argued on whether we'd deserved no points, one point or all three, while 'politely' telling any gobby home fan to '**** off' if they tried to take the piss, we soon realised that, having got a cab to the ground, we had no idea how to make it back to the station. We started to wonder down a side road which seemed to be the general direction of the bulk of the crowd.

"Is this the right way?" Colin checked with a policeman. The copper took a long look at us in our red and blue shirts. He frowned. He looked down the road at a sea of red, home supporters' shirts, shook his head and simply replied *"You don't wanna go down there, lads,"*in his thick, West Country accent.

He gave us some alternative directions and off we went. About twenty-five minutes worth of brisk walking later, we were somewhat unsure on where we were and how to get to the station. Wondering around a town that you don't know with a train that you have to catch isn't an ideal situation to be in. After a few minutes of searching, we found a cab to hail and had a somewhat more subdued taxi ride back to the station than the journey in the opposite direction. Thanks to Bristol's away section beer policy, it had been over two hours since we'd last had a drink.

As we'd got the cab, we had time to have one last beer in Wetherspoons and discuss the match. As soon as we sat down in the pub, a couple of Bristol supporters came over to us.

"Have you seen your goal?"

"No."

"Really? The one in the first half!"

"No."

"It's just as bad as the Reading-Watford ghost goal!"

This was a reference to a game in the previous season, where a shot from a Reading player was heading wide of the goal when a Watford player cleared it, seemingly stopping the ball going out for a goal kick. However, the referee and linesman seemed to not only believe that the ball had crossed the goal line, but also that it was between the posts and they incorrectly awarded a goal. It was the most baffling decision that I have ever seen in football.

"Did it go in then?" one of us asked, referring to the incident in our match.

"Yeah, it bounced out of the back of the goal!"

What the ****?! I don't like blaming the referee and it does amuse me how often football fans do (inevitably, he has acted like a 'wanker' if your team is on the wrong end of the result) but there really is no defending him here. If you haven't seen it, or need to review it to remind yourself just how shocking the decision was, you can view it here:

https://www.youtube.com/watch?v=nt7UXPy0vTo

Although this is a more light-hearted take on the events:

https://www.youtube.com/watch?v=XLgXdPfNdhs

The ball had hit the post holding down the net at the back of the goal and bounced out. Not understanding what had actually happened, Rob Shoebridge, the referee, deemed that it must have gone wide and hit the advertising boarding behind the goal so he gave a goalkick to Bristol instead of a goal to Palace. No wonder the team were fuming – Warnock had nearly exploded with anger. The Bristol fans thought it was hilarious. They were in full wind up mood now. However, it didn't stop at the goal, they started calling Palace cheats, Neil Warnock a cheat and Simon Jordan most names under the sun. To be fair, they were probably right about Jordan, our tango-faced chairman. They were laughing at our financial position and saying that we should be kicked out of the league as we still owed them money for Nicky Carle, who we had signed a year previously.

Banter is fine. We can usually take banter and to be fair to these guys, that's all it was. However, we were in no mood for it. We released John and Steve in full flow. The pair of them told the 'wurzels' exactly what they thought of Bristol City, Gary Johnson and the 'ghost goal'. This wasn't about being right or wrong, this was about standing up for our club in the same way that you would stand up for your family. Blind love. No one likes hearing the ones you love being attacked – that's why I dislike Charlton so much despite the lack of history in the rivalry. The two Bristolians didn't stand a chance and soon sulked off. We waved them off with a few shouts of *"There's only one Nigel Martyn!"*

In football, whenever there is an incident where a referee misses a goal, it opens up the debate about goal-line technology. Since that day, Premiership teams have installed technology to identify if the ball has crossed the line or not and instantly inform the referee. While it would have been useful on that miserable day in Bristol, I'm actually against goal-line technology. With it, we would have had a fairly un-memorable goal. Without it, we have one of the most talked about incidents in football and years worth of pub-moaning-material. Football, a game of opinions. Often ludicrous ones. You shouldn't try and take that away from the game.

I'm still bitter about that Freddy Sears goal and I'm still bitter about Tommy Black's goal against Leeds being missed by the officials in 2003. However, I'm still smug that the referee missed a foul on the Sunderland goalkeeper, allowing us to beat them and get to the Play Off Final in 2004. Just as I can still smirk at many incorrect refereeing decisions that have benefitted Palace over the years. The law of averages says that it must even out over the seasons.

I genuinely believe you make your own luck in football. As much as I dislike Manchester United, Sir Alex Ferguson seemed to get so many late goals, soft penalty decisions, dubious red cards etc. and there was a reason for that. He set his teams up to attack for ninety minutes. If you put the ball in the other team's penalty area enough, you're likely to get more favourable decisions in the crucial areas.

After finishing our drinks, we headed back to the station, via the booze bush.

"They've gone!" came the cry from Steve. Refusing to believe the claim, we all crowded around to check. Sure enough, the booze had gone.

"Werzel tramps!"

Only a group of football fans could moan about people pinching our booze from a bush while we were in the pub and call them tramps without the slightest hint of insincerity. But call them tramps we did. And much more too. I hope a fox had pissed on the beer.

Once we were over the devastation that losing beer causes, we found an off-licence to get some replacement bevies for the journey home. While the others bought some beer for the trip back, I received my routine post-match phone call from my Dad. He'd been listening on the radio and further filled me in on all of the controversy over the goal. Apparently, Warnock, true to character, had, rightly, gone ballistic in his post-match press conference.

When we got on the train, we found that the guard had not put out the ticket reservations. Still, we went to our seats that we had paid a reservation fee on and found people sitting in them. Usually, when you find somebody in your reserved seat, the conversation can go one of two ways. Either, they are typically English, apologise, and head off to queue up patiently for a cup of tea. Or, they might be typically English, a skin head wearing an England football shirt, look like something off the TV show 'Benidorm' and tell you to '**** off'.

In this case, we found a group of French men in our seats.
"Sorry guys, we've got the reservations here, these are our seats."
"Non."
Typically French. They were probably on strike from sitting in the correct seat. We began to protest but quickly realised that without the train's reservations on the seats, there was no way that they would be moving. Rather than cause an argument, we searched the busy train for another group of seats. A few carriages along, we sat down on a couple of double tables and opened a beer each. We began to talk about the game, and laugh about the meek way that the City fans had sleeked off with their tail between their legs after arriving so confident. There were quite a few people on the carriage but one man took exception to us.

We had noticed that it was the 'quiet' carriage and had therefore kept our voices to a low talking level. Quiet carriages are a brilliant idea. If you would rather not hear the usual train sounds that a public place brings, then you can pre-book to be in one and travel in peace. Therefore you don't have to listen to people on their mobiles or groups of drinking football fans, for example.

However, these were the only seats on the train and all rules were off. We certainly wouldn't have been in the 'quiet' carriage if the train company had done their job correctly and reserved the seats that we had booked. While we understood that it was unfortunate for this guy, we were confident that we were not being unreasonable. He obviously disagreed. What was frustrating, was that he didn't ask us to try and be quiet, he simply made comments to himself about how disgusting we were.

"Football fans, scum, always causing trouble, whatever they do," was his opening statement, just about loud enough to be in our earshot. He wasn't speaking to anyone; he was travelling alone. Well, this wound us up but we ignored him at first, staying in a 'classroom voice' as I would call it when teaching. However, the disdain kept coming from our disgruntled fellow passenger and

after a while, we did begin to play to his stereotype. Our voices raised as we started to discuss the respectable jobs, such as teaching or accounting that 'scum' could get these days. We also made a point of saying that the French bloke was in our seats and we hadn't chosen to be here. His tirade didn't stop there.

"Football fans should be banned from public transport!"

All in all, I was beginning think this chap wasn't over keen on 'The Beautiful Game'.

"There's never this trouble with Rugby fans."

Well, this comment really got to us. Dan and I had both regularly got the train to Palace from Sunningdale. This journey involved stopping at Twickenham station; the home of English Rugby. On a day when England were playing, the train would be packed. Even more so when the Welsh were in town as they had to change at Reading station. Dan has had plenty of problems with them not making any concessions for his young son, leaving him squashed and scared. Altogether, the train on a six nations day is quite frankly, horrendous.

My other experience of Rugby fans was attending university in Twickenham. The amount of times that I'd seen punch ups in the street after a day's drinking (without a break for the match) at the Rugby was ridiculous. There might not be the same 'tribal' nature in rugby as there is in football but there is still a load of blokes drinking too much, full of testosterone and that is always likely to end in a brawl.

So the notion, which we had all heard plenty of times before, that football fans are drunken hooligans and rugby fans are gentlemen of the middle class game, really hit a nerve. That was it. I took out my phone and played 'Glad All Over' on full volume. After the chorus, we proceeded to make a variety of 'shhh' sounds. Not big or clever, but generally speaking, we were pretty pissed off and this bloke was being obnoxious. At no point had he made any attempt to actually speak to us and ask us to be quieter or given us a chance to explain the situation.

Soon after, the guard came and realised that there was a building tension in the carriage. He politely checked our tickets and, after speaking to our Rugby-loving friend, led us up the train, past our seats and into the empty First Class section.

"I saw the look he gave you and knew I had to do something. He was being unreasonable so I thought I'd upgrade you guys!" explained the guard.

Controversial. But it gave us all the vindication we needed.

Around eight o'clock, after John and Colin had shared a bottle of wine in our new classy surroundings; we arrived back at Reading Station and went for a final pint at The Three Guineas Pub before heading off in our separate directions.

During the train journey back to Clapham Junction from Reading, the carriage filled up with extravagant hats, smart suits and summer dresses. There had been a race meeting at Ascot and the drunken crowd were beginning to make their way home. Anyway, as drunken people do, we began chatting to a group of guys, comparing our different days out. After a while, they mentioned that they had come from Brighton for the day.

Well that was it. The poor guys had to listen to our whole repertoire of anti-Brighton songs. And once we'd finished, we sang them again just in case there was any doubts as to our views on the south coast side. They learnt all about Alan Mullery's pilgrimage to Rome to meet the Pope and the head of the Catholic Church's less than positive response to his visitor, as well as hearing all about various victories over our bitter A23 rivals. To be fair to them, as non-football fans, they took it all in the good spirit that it was intended and laughed along with us.

All things considered, the football had been incredibly frustrating but it was a day that summed up the joys of an away day. Fun, jokes, beer, controversy, misery, anger, despair and friendship. It was a day that will live long in the memory for a number of reasons.

I now play with Jamie Mcallister, who played for City that day. He still laughs about it now! How bad it was and how they managed to get away with it was unbelievable...

I remember the ball sit up and Freddie Sears managing to finish it and we all peeled off celebrating and the whole of the City teams' heads dropped as they slowly walked back to kick off. Time seemed to slow as everyone looked at the ref and linesman, and they just looked lost!? Really?? How can they not see it was in?? Surely they saw it was 4ft over the line? The goals are deep at Bristol so surely it was at least that far over the line? It's wasn't even close...?

The City players then realised the ref was all over the place, and just played on that fact.They were even laughing as the game continued! I remember Neil going mad on the sidelines, but the game was still going on and we were still hammering the ref...the usual culprits... probably about 8 or 9 of us in fact..!!!!

The hatred between us and Bristol City was there before but after that it was heightened!!! Let alone for referees!!! There was just utter disbelief after the game, and seeing the replay on the coach on the way home confirmed the embarrassment!!!

Danny Butterfield

Chapter Seven – **Coach Travel**

Tuesday 18th August 2009, Ipswich Town vs Crystal Palace, Portman Road

Crystal Palace: Julian Speroni, Clint Hill, Patrick McCarthy, Jose Fonte, Danny Butterfield, Alassane N'Diaye, Shaun Derry, Neil Danns, Alan Lee, Freddy Sears, Darren Ambrose.
Subs Not Used: Darryl Flahavan, Nathaniel Clyne, Nicky Carle, Victor Moses, Sean Scannell, Lawrence, Ertl.

Ipswich: Richard Wright, Bruce, McAuley, Balkestein, Damian Delaney, Walters, Healy (Owen Garvan 52), Trotter, Martin (Quinn, 72), Priskin (Stead, 52), Wickham.
Subs Not Used: Supple, David Wright, Colback, Smith.

When I first started attending away games, aged sixteen, I used the official club coach. This had been to my mother's horror as she imagined a coach akin to Vinnie Jones' hooligan bus from the film *EuroTrip*. The reality was somewhat different. The Official Crystal Palace Supporters Coach was full of pensioners, who would later become my first away day friends. In the first couple of years on the Palace Away Trail, I had happily travelled up and down the country on a coach. I'd wake up around five am, travel to Selhurst Park for seven am and set off to a northern destination, partaking in football quizzes, cups of tea and eating a mountain of cheese rolls. At the end of five or six hours of travel, we'd arrive at the ground, have a couple of beers, watch the game and travel five or six hours home.

After a while of getting to know all the main characters on the coach, I'd arranged to be dropped off at Junction 13 of the M25, where I'd either climb a fence and walk home or be picked up by my mother. It's amazing to think that standing on a roundabout at a motorway junction just seemed so natural and normal back then. Two of my brothers picked me up once and they couldn't believe the situation and location that they were in. They went around the roundabout three times before they managed to stop and pick me up. Amateurs. My mum had the routine well rehearsed and would always managed to collect me first time.

During my days of coach travel, I made many friends who I still see at away games now. In particular, Garry, who is a middle aged man and worked in the city. Garry was aged 50 and happily married, without children. He was highly intelligent and had a fantastic sense of humour. He would always look out for me and was happy to go to the bar and buy my beer when I was underage. He had often talked about the season that he went to every game and was a big inspiration for me in my challenge. Unfortunately, Garry had recently stopped attending regular away games.

Before giving up the football bug, he would always sit next to Brian. An old man who was very set in his ways. Brian spoke a lot of sense and also had a good sense of humour. However, he was also stubborn and bitter. He once went eight months without speaking a word with his wife after an argument. They simply lived in the same house as separate beings.

On nearly every coach journey, Brian would discuss the same things; his hate of Julian Gray, how over-rated Dougie Freedman was, his hatred of Manchester United, his hatred of Liverpool, a bit more about Julian Gray, his hatred of David Beckham (as all this nonsense about him being any good only started after that 'lucky' goal from the halfway line at Selhurst Park versus Wimbledon), a bit more about Gray and Freedman, before finishing off with a twenty minute rant on Iain Dowie. Brian was fixed in his mindset and was never one to change his opinion. It must be said that I think he was someone who had been very logical and well-reasoned in the past but a mixture of old age and bitterness had made his views a bit skewed. A bit like Victor Meldrew in that sense.

However, he was dedicated to Palace and football. He had visited 91 of the 92 football league grounds, he always looked out for me as a youngster and I was very sad to hear of his passing away in 2011 after a long battle with heart problems.

Sitting opposite Garry and Brian, would be Mark and Alex; two of the nicest guys you could ever wish to meet. They are brothers and fanatically follow Palace through thick and thin. They really are both 'Mr Crystal Palaces'. Until their mother had been ill the previous year, they had gone about 15 years without missing a Palace game; home or away and they had an absolutely encyclopaedic knowledge of all things Palace. Also in our group of friends was Pauline, a thirty-year old tattoo enthusiast who loved Palace. The six of us had some fascinatingly geeky (and often repetitive) conversations about Palace as well as some highly competitive quizzes.

All of these were people who without football, I wouldn't socialise with but my life was enhanced by knowing and having as friends. Especially Garry, who I still occasionally go for beers with today despite him being thirty years my senior and him attending fewer games.

However, I'd moved on from this style of away day and intended on using the coach as little as possible during my mission. It was quicker and cheaper on the train. For example, a trip to Manchester by coach would involve leaving Selhurst Park at 8am for a 3pm kick off. I would have to leave my door in Twickenham at 6am to be in SE25 for 7:30. It would then be a five hour journey each way. By rail, I could get a train from Euston at 11am and be in Manchester for 1pm.

Also, train travel is, by nature, a lot more comfortable than coach travel. If your legs get stiff on a coach, there's not a lot that you can do whereas on a train, you can take a little stroll. On a coach packed full of football supporters, it is entirely possible to sit next to someone with bad BO/breath/any other personal hygiene issue or someone with an objectionable habit. Then, you're stuck with them. Again, on a train, you can easily take yourself away to another carriage and forget all about their existence, rather than be left to suffer for hours on end.

Unless of course, it happens to be on the tube in rush hour. Or even a commuters train into London but at least that's unlikely to last for hours on end –

despite Southwest Trains best attempts to delay as many services as they possibly can. My twitter feed is usually clogged full each morning with apologies from train companies.

And evidently, on a train, not only are you allowed a drink, but they almost encourage it. All of the long distance services in England sell overpriced cans of lager. It might not be decent beer and you are paying a high price as there is a lack of competition but after watching your team lose yet another lower league match, you often need a beer. And any beer will do. Although recently, even train companies are selling better beer with Virgin trains having their own craft beer. You certainly don't get that on a club coach.

With the cheap train tickets that rail companies offered for booking in advance, reduced further by using a young person's railcard, I rarely had to pay over £20 for a train ticket anywhere. I guess they were banking on the football supporting clientele purchasing their over-priced beer in large enough quantities to cover any deficits.

Sometimes, this meant that I had to get a train at a strange time, either arriving early or leaving a few hours after the match but I didn't mind this. It meant either more drinking time or a chance to get to know the city a bit. I've always been interested in geography and comparing different places. From a young age, I was fascinated by looking at maps and finding out where the different football towns in the country were. It seemed such a waste to arrive at a ground, go in, watch a game and leave without having a clue what the area is like. Except at Millwall. No one wants to know what South Bermondsey is really like.

A classic example of learning about a place is Derby. I had been to the ground twice by coach but I had never seen the city. When I finally discovered the city, I realised what a fantastic place it is to go drinking in – more on that later. By visiting the town, it gives the individual day a bit more character. When travelling by club coach, visiting Derby, Reading, Southampton, Coventry, Leicester or any other club with an out of town, identikit stadium, really is a very similar experience. However, now that I have been by train and seen a bit of the different towns, I can honestly say that I would much rather spend a day in Norwich than Coventry for example. Well, I would rather spend a day just about anywhere than Coventry.

One ground where that's not true is where I was heading for this midweek match; Ipswich. I have been to Ipswich by car, coach and train in the past. I liked returning there as it was generally a happy hunting ground for Palace, where we'd picked up some memorable victories. All three methods of travel involved the same routine. Arrive in Ipswich, head to The Station Hotel Pub opposite the station and by the River Orwell, drink until about 2:40 and then walk to the ground. I have seen Palace play away at Ipswich seven times and the closest that I have been to the town centre is being stuck in a traffic jam outside it with hoards of Saturday shoppers; while I was on my route to the stadium.

Despite my qualms with coach travel, for a midweek fixture, it was my best bet of making the match and being able to return home on the same evening. We set off from Selhurst at 2:30pm for the eight o'clock kick off and arrived around half past six. An incredible amount of time, including a long motorway service station break, to make it to a ground that is only 84 miles away from Selhurst Park. Official Coach Travel, sigh. Still, it was a good chance to catch up with some friends who I hadn't seen for a few months.

When we finally arrived, I went to the Station Hotel, had a couple of Suffork Ales and headed to the ground. It was a warm, August evening and perfect for watching football. Ipswich is one of the few championship grounds where the away fans are situated at the side of the pitch, which gives a better view. It must be an East Anglian thing because Norwich are the only other club who seem to do this. Well, other than Palace but I'm yet to experience being an away supporter there. Although, Palace fans are one of the only sets of supporters to be familiar with the idea of being 'away' at 'home'; having had both Charlton and Wimbledon as lodgers. However, I never attended one of those 'away' games at Selhurst Park.

After the controversy and fallout of the Bristol game, the small away following were eagerly awaiting the chance to get back into action. While the first half was highly uneventful, at least the referee didn't choose to ignore any of our goals this time.

Half time came and went and then, the match came to life. Four minutes into the second half, Darren Ambrose bundled home a cross from Alan Lee to put us 1-0 up. Both players were former Ipswich favourites, which made the goal even sweeter. A regular and cruel twist of football fate. As soon as the cheer for the goal went up, a bloke came running out of the concourse, still with a beer in his hand, to see what had happened. He realised we'd scored, punched the air and returned to the concourse to stop the stewards from confiscating his beer.

The game re-started and the bloke behind me rang his mate.
"'Alright Geez, we're one up. Ambrose. Yeah, just after ha...'"
"YEEEESSSSSSSSSSSSSSSSSSSSSSSSSSSSSS!"
Bang! Ambrose had done it again. The first may have barely trickled over the line as he scambled it home but his one was a thing of beauty. He'd curled the ball into the top corner from twenty-five yards. 2-0! For the first time in four days, we'd forgotten all about Mr Shoebridge and the Bristol debacle. Palace were back. Once again, the concourse-beer-drinker came charging out, not believing the second cheer. This time he punched the air, threw his remaining beer back to the concourse and charged up the staircase to give his mate a big bear hug. Pure elation.

Sure enough, as always with Palace, and presumably most other teams in the country, it wasn't meant to be easy. Alex Bruce, son of former Palace manager, Judas (apparently his birth certificate says 'Steve' but that sounds unlikely to me*[1]), scored to pull Ipswich back into the game. Then something very un-Palace like happened. Within minutes, we scored again. Neil Danns got the goal, assisted by Ambrose, who hadn't seemed a particularly exciting signing in the summer but was fast turning into a fans' favourite.

Late on, Freddy Sears nearly had the perfect moment to make up for the scandal of the previous Saturday. He rounded the Ipswich keeper but he took the ball too wide and couldn't get his elusive first goal for the club. Still, it was another lively performance and goals would surely start to flowsoon for the young loanee. At full time, the players came over to the Palace faithful to receive their well earned applause. It was a fantastic performance and a much deserved three points. 3-1 flattered Ipswich as it really could have been more.

The coach journey home was much quieter and less eventful than the train back from Bristol the previous Saturday, which was probably a good thing. Four games into my challenge and Palace had won twice, drawn once and been robbed once. I arrived back in London, extremely tired, around 1am. I then got a lift to my Granny's flat in Bromley and set a 7AM alarm for my 9AM start at the pub the next day. This was the first reminder to the fact that I wasn't making my life in the 'real-non-football-world' particularly easy on myself, thanks to my insistence of doing every single game.

*¹ In 2001, Palace were top of the league after 13 games and playing some brilliant football. Steve Bruce was the manager. He then walked out on the club to manage Birmingham City. Come the end of the season, Palace finished tenth while Birmingham, and Bruce, gained promotion. I, along with many other Palace fans, have never forgiven him.

Chapter Eight - **Crisis Club come to Town**

Saturday 22nd August 2009, Crystal Palace vs Newcastle United, Selhurst Park

Crystal Palace: Darryl Flahavan; Clint Hill; Shaun Derry; Paddy McCarthy; Jose Fonte; Darren Ambrose; Neil Danns (Victor Moses, 67); Freddie Sears (Sean Scannell, 67); Alan Lee; Danny Butterfield; Alassane N'Diaye
Subs Not Used: Nathaniel Clyne, Nick Carle, Matt Lawrence, Kieran Djilali, Johnny Ertl

Newcastle: Steve Harper, Fabricio Coloccini, Jose Enrique, Kevin Nolan, Danny Guthrie (Nile Ranger, 65), Danny Simpson, Ryan Taylor (Nicky Butt, 65), Alan Smith, Jonas Gutierrez (Geremi, 89), Shola Ameobi, Steven Taylor
Subs Not Used: Xisco, Kazenga LuaLua, Tim Krul, Tamas Kadar

Newcastle had dramatically dropped out of the Premiership on the final day of the previous season. The irony of the two 'Geordie Kings' (Kevin Keegan and Alan Shearer) both having spells as manager in the season that the North-East giants crashed out of the Premier League wasn't lost across football.

Five years previously, Newcastle had finished fifth in the top division, had crowds of well over fifty-thousand and were pushing to be in the Champions League with all its financial benefits. The famous club had slowly deteriorated as a side and slipped down the Premiership table, year on year. This could hardly be blamed on a lack of ambition either. Tens of millions of pounds were wasted on new, expensive international players, season after season, as the club tried to push back up the table. The club seemed more accident prone than Mr Bean as it shot itself in the foot, time after time.

'King Kev'(in Keegan) had returned to Newcastle late in the 2007/08 season; much to the delight of the Geordie faithful. Despite the fact that, by his own admission, he hadn't even watched a gamein two years, thousands of fans arrived at the St. James' Park to celebrate his home-coming. At Newcastle, this seems to be a re-occurring theme. Signings such as Michael Owen and Alan Shearer have prompted huge crowds to welcome them to the club on weekdays. Presumably all of these people just happened to have taken leave on that day as I'm not sure that the unemployed could afford extortionately priced football shirts and season tickets every year. Keegan's return was solid if unspectacular. However, early in the doomed 2008/09 season, the 'King of the Geordies' was to walk out of the club for the second time in his career, after the club signed and sold players behind his back.

Joe Kinnear was then appointed as his replacement, much to the anger of the fans, still reeling from Keegan being 'forced out of the club' by the 'Cockney Mafia' (Director of Football, Dennis Wise and Chairman, Mike Ashley). To be fair to the fans, appointing Kinnear was another strange decision. He hadn't managed for five years since he played a key part in Nottingham Forest's relegation to the third tier of English Football. Such was the immediate pressure on Kinnear, he went on an 'effin and blindin' rant at the media during his

introductory Press Conference. He was live on Sky Sports News and opened by calling one member of the local media a 'c***'. I wonder why football has such a bad reputation... The whole incredible interview can be heard here.
http://www.youtube.com/watch?v=i_NQqnc_ue0

Kinnear, who had previously had health issues while managing Wimbledon, was admitted to hospital with heart problems in February 2009. During his spell in charge, he managed just five wins in twenty-six matches and Newcastle were just above the relegation zone with twelve games remaining. With that form on the pitch and fifty thousand northerners baying for his blood in the stands, it is no wonder he had a heart attack. Anyway, the unfortunate events allowed the North-East supporters to be appeased by their owner once more. Enter 'King of the Geordies Mark II' – Alan Shearer. To be fair, after twice going for experienced managers and it not working out, Mike Ashley clearly wanted to try something different - inexperience. Shearer had never managed before (and hasn't since).

After the former England striker's 'heroic' return to save them, they lost six and drew three of his first nine games. He seemed to have got out of jail with a 3-1 win against fellow relegation strugglers, Middlesbrough, but Shearer managed to guide them to a couple more defeats; dropping them into the dreaded bottom three at the end of the season.

During their final game against Aston Villa, I had to leave a pub in Teddington rather promptly after jumping up in celebration at the side's fate being sealed. There wasn't a northern accent in the pub that day but there were plenty of Londoners in Black and White shirts. Were these the Cockney Mafia? I wasn't sure. Either way, my friends, Jak and Chris, decided it was best we left.

So how does this all affect Crystal Palace, myself and my challenge? Well, Newcastle had a huge wage bill after years of overspending on overrated players. After relegation, the club were put up for sale with minimal interest due to their enormous debts. Plenty of the players, who had got the club relegated, decided that they were too good to play in the league below and demanded a transfer. However, with their inflated wages, clubs weren't willing to splash out on them.

Although they were stuck with a lot of players (and wages) that they would have liked to have been rid of, Obafemi Martins, Sébastien Bassong, Habib Beye, David Edgar, Damien Duff, Michael Owen, Peter Lovenkrands and Mark Viduka all departed the club for much smaller fee's than they were originally signed for. There were even rumours in the press that Newcastle were still paying them a percentage of their wages, despite the players moving on to different clubs.

They hadn't signed a single player to replace the eight departures and with the club up for sale, no new manager was appointed to replace Shearer. Instead, they left assistant manager, Chris Hughton, in 'temporary charge'. Their pre-season had become a mockery after losing a friendly 6-1 at lowly Leyton Orient.

So in short, they had no manager, want-away players, a want-away owner and huge debts. Everything pointed to a club in crisis. There was plenty of talk in the media of them continuing their slide and having to battle at the wrong end of the table. When the fixtures came out and pitted us against them in August, early in the season, when they would still be finding their feet, it really gave us belief that they were there for the taking.

Eventually, the day came. It was a beautiful summer's afternoon with the heat searing down from the clear blue sky. Naturally, Kev still wore his thick, Umbro sweater as we headed into the dark pit that is Selhurst Railwayman's Social Club and began to sup beers, discuss the game ahead, and re-live the whole inevitable Saturday afternoon ritual. All of our regular group were there: Colin, Adam, Dan, Jonathan, Kev, Peter, Chris and myself. We were also joined by my oldest brother, Mark.

Despite being eight years my senior, Mark had started supporting Palace around the same time as me. He had begun life as a Liverpool fan. Being a loving father, my Dad didn't force him to support his side. In fact, he even took him all the way to Anfield to watch a match. All that way. In a car. With your Dad. As a fifteen year old. Four hours there. Four hours back.

Soon after his first long journey north, Mark decided to support a more local side. His father's side, Crystal Palace.

Dad...1
Son...0

Nowerdays, Mark rarely comes to Palace. He married his wife, Lise, in 2006 and they had had their first child, Zak, in 2008. Lise was now pregnant again. Understandably, he preferred to use his hard-earned money on the family, rather than spending a small fortune to watch Palace in what was usually a grim, cold and miserable second tier match. However, I had a promotion from the club for a free ticket and he jumped at the chance to see Palace against the biggest side in the league under the August sun.

Once again, the odd mix of people prompted passionate and enthusiastic discussion. I told them all about the Ipswich match, the bloke who missed the goals, and of my disdain towards coach travel. Don't worry, I'll save you from having to hear about the whole experience again.

Being football fans, we continued to moan about Mr Shoebridge and the Bristol disgrace. What would we talk about if the ref wasn't a w***er? We'd be lost. Football is definitely better for the odd howler by the referee. It was fair to say we talked a lot more about the anger that the referee had prompted in that match than the joy of the team's performance at Ipswich. Watch it again if you need to, just to remind yourself how bad a decision it really was.

The mood in the pub was wary but optimistic of the challenge ahead. Newcastle had drawn their opening match and won the two since then. Despite all the departures of key players, they still had an incredible forty-four players

listed on the back of the program that day. No wonder they were in debt and were expected to implode at any time. Hopefully starting today. Our start to the
season had been decent so we had every right to believe.

As kick off approached, we emptied our bladders before stepping out into the sunshine to stroll up the Holmesdale Road to the ground. While standing up against the urinal, Colin joked,

"Your brothers a bit posh, ain't he?"

To be fair, Mark is very well spoken. However, with family, you tend not to think of the ins and outs of how they speak. In his attitude to life, Mark would never be described as 'posh'. He works hard, he loves his family and is completely un-materialistic. However, in the context of drinking in a South London bunker, I guess he is.

"Yeah, we are from Royal Ascot in Berkshire, don't you know?" I replied, with my best attempt to imitate my brother's well-pronounced accent.

"So what went wrong with you then?"

Fair point, well made. I shrugged. I'm the youngest, I guess my parents must have given up by then.

As the teams were announced, the enormity of our task began to sink in. First, we had to deal with the unexpected news that club legend and goalkeeper, Julian Speroni, had picked up an injury. Speroni had been clattered in the first half of the game at Ipswich. Although he had received treatment, he had continued and played the rest of the game so it was mystifying that he was to be excluded from the team sheet for this match.

Looking at the so-called 'crisis club's' side was frankly terrifying. They had two former England Internationals, two current Argentine Internationals, a six and a half million pound full back and a ten million pound centre half playing. If that's a crisis, I want one at Palace.

The match attracted a large crowd, six thousand more than had attended the opening match against Plymouth just two weeks previously. While this created a good atmosphere, it did frustrate us as the bar was too packed at half time to get a drink – supporting a crap team does have some benefits. Palace were up for this game and while football fans often over-estimate the effect of having a loud and passionate crowd behind the team, it does definitely give everyone a boost. The Selhurst faithful believed.

However, the actual result was a bit numbing. Within two minutes, the home crowd had been silenced. Kevin Nolan, a regular Premiership goal scorer, who had often been touted as a potential England player, put Newcastle 1-0 up.

*"Speroni would have saved it!"*came my all-knowing cry. When a player is absent from a team, whether it is due to injury or because of not being rated by a manager, they instantly become an invincible super hero. With no way of disproving their logic, supporters of the said player can claim that they would have performed a million times better than the player who was chosen to do the

job by the manager. It is the 'what if?' logic that keeps football fans returning week after week.

Twenty minutes or so later, the game was effectively over as Newcastle scored a stunning second. The crowd were down, the players were down and as quick as any belief had been built, it was gone. The rest of the game was fairly uneventful and finished as a comfortable 2-0 away win for the crisis club. Crisis, what crisis?

Who knows, maybe if Speroni hadn't been injured that day, he'd have saved that opening goal, Newcastle would have grown frustrated, had a massive internal punch up on the pitch, had half the team sent off, Palace would have won, Newcastle's good start to the season would have been squashed and the press would have been able to print the headlines that they'd penned in anticipation. Newcastle fans everywhere should make a toast to Speroni's mysterious injury before each Premier League game they play because without it, who knows where they would be now. What if...

Anyway, back in the real world, the game had proved to be somewhat of a reality check. We had been miles behind Newcastle all over the pitch. Palace had now won once, drawn once and lost twice. When you've won and are delighted with the team, any records are obviously going to include every possible winning match so that they can emphasise your greatness. However, when moaning about your side, it's very easy to conveniently leave out a League Cup win against Torquay.

"Lies, damnedlies and statistics"

Our record of won 2 (including a very impressive away win at Ipswich), drawn 1, lost 1 (where we had been robbed) had changed in space of one game to won 1 (against a useless Ipswich side) drawn 1 and lost 2. Neither was technically a lie depending on how you bent the facts. Maybe football fans and politicians aren't so different after all?

After the game, Colin, Adam, Jonathan, Kev and I went for a 'sobering' drink in the Red'n'Blue Bar above the Holmesdale Road stand. We had been so effortlessly outclassed by Newcastle that the prospect of The World's Richest Football Club arriving in South London five days later, was to put it simply, daunting.

Chapter Nine – **The World's Richest Team**

Thursday 27th August 2009, Crystal Palace vs Manchester City, Selhurst Park

Crystal Palace: Julian Speroni, Nathaniel Clyne, Clint Hill, Shaun Derry, Paddy McCarthy, Jose Fonte, Darren Ambrose (Ryan Smith, 72), Neil Danns, Victor Moses (Nick Carle, 80), Freddie Sears (Sean Scannell, 72), Alassane N'Diaye
Subs Not Used: Darryl Flahavan, Matt Lawrence, Alan Lee, Danny Butterfield,

Man City: Shay Given, Micah Richards, Wayne Bridge, Stephen Ireland, Shaun Wright-Phillips, Robinho (Craig Bellamy, 72), Gareth Barry, Joleon Lescott, Emmanuel Adebayor, Kolo Toure, Carlos Tevez (Nigel De Jong, 90)
Subs Not Used: Nedum Onuoha, Pablo Zabaleta, Stuart Taylor, Martin Petrov, Vladimir Weiss

May 1999, Manchester City became the second ever club who had won a European trophy to be relegated to the third tier of football in their home country. The first was FC Magdeburg of Germany. The following season, 'Citeh' managed to get promoted by the skin of their teeth. They soon forgot all about those dark days of the club's lowest point as they gained a second successive promotion in 2001 to return to the Premier League. Once there, they found it a bit more difficult and 'yoyo'd' between the top two divisions before settling in the top flight.

In 2007, they were purchased by a dodgy Thai bloke called Thaksin Shinawatra. During his time in charge of the club, the former president of his homeland had all his assets frozen due to various charges of corruption. I wish the Premier League had a 'Fit and Proper Persons Test' to make sure that only the right sort of person is allowed to run a football club. Oh wait, they do...

After a year of uncertainty under the corrupt owner, City were bought by Abu Dhabi United Group and within hours the club had smashed the British Transfer record. If Newcastle were seen as a club in crisis, Manchester City were anything but that. The spending had continued for over a year now and they meant business. They had spent £127 million the previous season, which had been followed up by a further £118 million in the summer so they rolled up at Selhurst Park hoping that they might snatch a draw. After all, this was about £245 million more than we had spent in the same period.

Strangely, this story doesn't begin in the Railway Club. That comes later. Much later. About a day and a half later to be exact. This story begins in a field... What? ...in late August... Any guesses? ...in Reading... Got it? ...with a load of pissed/drugged up teenagers... Surely you've got it now? ...there's some music... Yup, the Reading Festival.

The Manchester City game had been moved by Sky TV to a Thursday night. A bloody Thursday. Since when was Thursday night a night for football? Tuesday, yup, Wednesday, ok, Monday or Friday, annoying but do-able. But Thursday? Even the most fanatical fans need a day off!

From Wednesday 26th until Monday 31st August, I was going to the Reading Festival with my mates. I'd already decided that I was going to have to 'nip off' to Peterborough on the Saturday to get my Palace fix. Incidentally, that game had been moved to the Saturday evening by our friends of football inconvenience at Sky. A real bugbear of mine is Sky changing kick off times. Of course, the reality is, Sky put so much money into the ~~business~~ sport that when they say jump, the ~~businesses~~ clubs have to say *"How high?"*

And rightly so. If you dance with the devil, expect to get burnt. Of course, the influx of money that such high profile worldwide TV coverage brings has given a lot of benefits to the football world. The image of the game has been cleaned up. A world brand like the Premier League simply cannot have a reputation of hooliganism and thugs. The coverage to keep up to date with your team is now phenomenal and there are hundreds of live games every year, from every division in England.

However, matches get changed, sometimes with little notice, players get highly inflated wages and fans get priced out of going to games. All the while, the sport is filled with parasites, who are all after their slice of the great big fat cake.

I once paid decent money to book a train up to Leicester for a midweek match. I'd organised to stay with my friend who was at uni there and all my plans were set. That was until just thirteen days before the game when Sky TV decided to switch the match from a Tuesday to a Monday. I simply couldn't afford to pay the last minute train fares (having splashed out once already) and had to miss the match. To make matters worse, we lost 1-0 to a last minute goal. We'd have definitely won on the Tuesday. Probably.

Anyway, back to the dirty fields of the Reading Festival Campsite. In all our enthusiastic youthful wisdom, we had decided that it would be a brilliant idea to get 'Early Bird' passes to the festival. This meant that rather than turning up on the Friday, when the music began, we got to arrive on the Wednesday and sleep under the stars for a couple of extra nights. Well, get pissed on cheap booze and then crash in a cold, poorly assembled tent for the night.

I'd anticipated the City cup game to be on the Tuesday night so I could have gone to it before the festival but the TV coverage meant that I'd have to leave the festival and trek to London on my second night under the stars. Annoying. However, the Thursday night coverage of this game, meant that the Peterborough game was pushed back to the Monday so at least I didn't miss any of the music days for either match. Maybe Sky aren't so bad after all!
This was the plan:
Wednesday – Arrive at the campsite and put up our tent.
Thursday - Enjoy a day in the sun before heading to Palace in the evening.
Friday – Let the music begin and enjoy a day of drinking before heading back to the campsite to sit around the fire.
Saturday - Continue to soak up the British Summer festival experience. Sun, Drink, Music and Fun.
Sunday - Take in a few more bands and beers before settling down for our last night under the stars.
Monday – Heading home for the SSS combination (s***, shower shave) before going to Peterborough. My new best friends at Sky had made it a 5:00PM kick off

so I might even have time for a quick snooze before setting off. Simples.
Incidentally, here is the 2009 reading line up.

Reading 2009		
Friday 20th August	**Saturday 21st August**	**Sunday 21st August**
Kings of Leon	Arctic Monkeys	Radiohead
Kaiser Chiefs	The Prodigy	Bloc Party
Placebo	Maximo Park	Yeah Yeah Yeahs
Fall Out Boy	Ian Brown	Vampire Weekend
Deftones	The Courteeners	Brandnew
Funeral for a Friend	Enter Shikari	
	Eagles of Death Metal	
NME/Radio 1 Stage		
Jamie T		Lost Prophets
Friendly FIres	Glasvegas	AFI – Gallows
Florence and the Machine	White Lies – The Maccabees	The Gaslight Anthem

...and here is what actually happened for those few days.

Wednesday– Arrive in Reading and find one of our mates didn't have an early bird pass. Pay for an over-priced ticket from a tout. Queue up. Drink some homemade Skittles Vodka in the queue. Not big. Not clever. It tastes like a 5% alco-pop. It is actually straight vodka with skittles in it. Fail to put my tent up properly. Drop my phone down a toilet. Start chatting up some girls. Fail to succeed in chatting up some girls - mainly down to my obscene drunkenness. Find myself entirely lost in a field, which is apparently not 'my' field. Realise I'm very cold and my clothes are ripped. Finally find my half assembled tent at 5:30AM. Sleep for a couple of hours.

Thursday – Wake up. Hung over. Start drinking (again). Head to Reading. Buy a new £10 phone. Head to Palace. Drink some more. Watch Palace. Drink more. Go back to Reading. Crash in a cold tent.

Friday – Wake up. Hung over. Aching. Head to Reading. Buy a KFC. Find out that it wasn't Adebayor who'd scored for City the night before, but Tevez. Use the town's toilets. Start drinking (again). See some music. Continue drinking. See some more music. Go back to the cold campsite. Sit around a fire drinking more. Crash out in a cold, unassembled, leaking tent.

Saturday – Wake up to a rumour that Rolf Harris had died. Hung over. Hurting. Find my tent covered in some kind of gunge. Find out that the Harris rumour isn't true. Head to Reading. Buy a KFC. Use the town's (now quite destroyed) toilets. Start (painfully) forcing some cans of crap cider or lager down my throat again. Watch some bands. Watch two of my best friends have a 'poo' fight. Drink some more. Watch some more bands. Drink a bit more. Go back to the cold, miserable campsite. Sit around a fire, drinking more. Crash out in a cold, unassembled, leaking, frankly disgusting tent.

Sunday – Wake up. Hung over. Aching. Fairly broken. Head to Reading. Can't afford KFC. Get a free bacon sandwich from a local Church. Wished I'd known about the free bacon sandwiches before. Use the toilets (now too hung-over to even notice what they look like but it's unlikely to be good) Head to the festival. Can't force down drinks. Watch some bands. Try a beer. Don't finish a beer. Listen to some music. Die a bit inside. Sod this, I'm leaving now. Leave, beaten. **Monday** – Wake up. Just. Thank god I'm in my own bed. Head to Peterborough.

All in the name of fun right? Who's going next year?

I hope that anyone who has been to a festival in their youth can relate to some parts of my Reading adventure and look back with a weary, embarrassed smile but don't get me wrong, I'm not telling you about this to boast of my behaviour or with any pride in it. I certainly wouldn't let events unfold like that now. It was only my naivety of youth and addiction to Palace that made me refuse to make a choice between going early to the festival and going to the game. I would be unlikely to try both these days – and certainly not without a quick trip home to have a shower and change of clothes. I would also be able to recognise the ability to enjoy the music (and indeed football) without quite so much excessive drinking. I'm merely telling you about my time in the fields to state my inappropriate starting point for the game to try and explain some of the events of the evening.

Anyway, rewind to before my tent looked like a festival toilet. It's Thursday Morning and my head is pounding. It was only to be expected. I crawled out of my tent, which was inexcusably hot in the morning as tents tend to be. Ouch. Sunlight. My. Head. Hurt. I'd barely slept. I needed water. I looked around the campsite. There was a lot of empty cans on the floor. I vaguely remember upsetting friends of friends the night before by throwing their full cans of beer onto the fire to watch them explode. Not a great introduction.

I then looked for my phone. Bugger. Ah yes. Toilet-gate. Not clever. I then looked at my tent. It was still there. Just. I vaguely remember trying to hammer in some pegs. I'd failed. I looked at my booze stash. Most of it had gone. Bugger. I didn't have a huge budget; about thirty quid for five days. I then looked at my clothes. Dirty and ripped. Hmmm. My friend Phill was the first to see me. He just looked at me, shook his head, muttered the word 'twat' and walked off. All in all, I don't think Skittles Vodka had been a complete success.

I then started talking to a girl who was in our campsite. The idea of our camp was to get as many people as possible so that we could all look out for each other's stuff. I was with a group of school friends, Phill and his friends and Phill's friend's friends. Anyway, I didn't know this girl but I started chatting to her. I saw that she was reading about Brentford in the paper. It only turned out that she knew my mates, Chris and Jak. In fact, she was an ex-girlfriend of Jak's. I couldn't believe it. However, she seemed less surprised.

"Oh my God, you discovered that four times last night. Just shut up!"
I'd obviously made a good impression the night before...

Later on that day, I set off to the match. Smelling, dirty and drunk. The best way to get a good seat on any train – even on the most packed of trains I'd have backed myself to get a set of six seats to myself. When I arrived at Reading station, I wasn't allowed in. I'd brought four cans with me for the journey as I was meeting Dan half way. Apparently, during the festival, the police weren't letting anyone into the station with booze. This did seem rather strange to me. Thousands of people were getting really pissed and stoned in a field nearby so no-one can take any alcohol *out* of Reading. I'm still not entirely sure on their reasoning.

It's almost like they were attempting a world-record for having the most amount of booze ever recorded in a Berkshire town. Idiots, surely they knew that there is only one world-record worth talking about. John's Ferero Rocher munching masterpiece.

Anyway, thanks to the Police's prevention of beer entering the train station, I stood next to the officer who was applying the rules as strictly as a steward in the away end at Elland Road and downed two of my cans before throwing two away. Even with (maybe especially with) the benefit of hindsight, this ban didn't seem to be very productive to me. I was allowed to stand outside the station downing beers alone, but I was not allowed to take them onto an hour and a half train journey to share with my friend.

I met Dan on the train at Sunningdale and explained the madness of Reading station. When I first got to know him, I was just seventeen and I have learnt a lot of my football drinking habits from him. However, after my early afternoon beers, even he looked at me in a slightly concerned manner. I think he realised I'd been drinking. However, I wasn't too drunk for a sober companion at this stage. Maybe a little bit too smelly, but not too drunk.

I did offer to run out at Clapham Junction to purchase the cans that we, particularly I, clearly needed. Luckily, he politely declined. I say luckily because I hadn't bought a ticket for the entire journey. I'd made the completely rational decision that they were over-charging (and I was skint) so I would only get one as far as Clapham Junction. I felt completely justified. Dan wasn't so sure. Anyway, my desperation for a crap can of lager had made me willing to go through the barriers without a thought towards how I was going to get back in again afterwards.

The drunken antics of the night before continued to cause problems. On the way to the game, I remembered that I was supposed to be taking some American tourists to the match. When I had finished sixth form three years earlier, one of my best mates, Lewis, had moved to New York. Twice I had been out to visit him and met some of his new American friends. One of them was currently on 'vacation' in England (and naturally, was heading on to Amsterdam) with a group of pals.

Lewis had promised his mate that I would take him to a football game. I'm not sure that going to Barnsley vs Crystal Palace would have appealed to the 'fanatic' Manchester United, AC Milan *and* Real Madrid supporter. However, seeing Manchester City, Robinho and more importantly, Crystal Palace, certainly did. Unfortunately, having lost my phone, I had no way of contacting my Yank guests to tell them how to get to the ground, where I could meet them for a drink or even tell them where Crystal Palace actually is. Bloody skittles vodka – depriving Palace of a US supporters club.

Eventually, we arrived at the Railway Club. There was a fairly large group of us in the pub and as it was in the school holidays, Colin was able to bring Adam to a midweek game. Jonathan and Kev were there of course. Also, 'mad-eyed' Steve's brother, Dave, joined us with his fiancé and Colin's friend Ricky was there too. We discussed the team, City's financial revolution and whether we wanted them to play their first team or reserves.

Our team didn't really matter to be honest. Most of our players were hard-working, decidedly average footballers; put together by a club in a financial crisis. Of course we wanted Moses to play, but past that, we really weren't too fussed.

Colin, mainly for his son, wanted City to play their big guns. No matter what any football fan tells you, it is great to see some of the world's best players play live (even against your own side!). And if your team actually manages to get a result against them, it's a story you can re-live forever. I was more in the camp of wanting Palace to win at any cost and frankly, our best chance was if City decided we were small fish to fry and played their reserves.

The other pre-match debate was whether we would enjoy being taken over by a foreign investor, Manchester City style. Of course, every football fan is desperate for their club to be successful but at what cost?

Success brings its own problems. Further inflated ticket prices for example. It's not a cheap hobby to watch your club slog it out in the second tier but some of the top clubs are able to charge double what I was paying. Of course, a bit of success makes you more attractive to Sky TV, who as I've already discussed, can make your club bend over and squeal like a pig if they wish. Who's ever heard of playing on a Thursday nights for God's sake? There's also the feeling of your club becoming a toy to a multi-millionaire, who could walk away at any moment. So many clubs have been promised riches and been left with their club hanging by a thread.

Every fan dreams of building a team full of local lads, giving their all for the club. However, the days of clubs winning a European Cup with eleven players born within ten miles of the stadium (as Celtic did in the sixties) are long gone. The reality now is: If you want success, you have to pay for it. Literally and metaphorically.

Anyway, the beers flowed as well as the conversation did and by this stage, my sleep and food deprived body was beginning to struggle. Colin suddenly turned to Dave's fiancé and mentioned that I was training at Saint Mary's University. She was about to begin studying there and naturally, wanted to talk about the uni and get some advice. So there I was, wearing ripped clothes, stinking of a cow field, pissed as a fart, discussing the benefits of doing a teaching degree and the pro's and con's of the course. I have no idea what advice I gave but I assume it was insightful and productive. I'm told that she still asks after me with an extremely worried look on her face.

As we went to leave the pub, we saw the City team on the TV.

Shay Given - £8m

Micah Richards – Youth Player

Wayne Bridge - £12m

JoleonLescott - £22m

KoloToure - £16m

Steven Ireland – minimal fee

Shaun Wright-Phillips - £9m

Gareth Barry - £12m

Robinho - £32.5m

Emmanuel Adebayor - £25m

Carlos Tevez - £25.5m

Total: ONE HUNDRED AND SIXTY TWO MILLION POUNDS.

At the time, it was the most expensive starting eleven ever played. In case that wasn't enough to make it past a Palace side, assembled mainly of youth players, freebies and loans, they also had Craig Bellamy (£14m), Nigel de Jong (£17m) and Pablo Zabaleta (£7m) on the bench. Eighteen million pound centre forward, Jo, and £17.5 million pound Roque Santa Cruz didn't even have to sit on their arse picking up splinters at Selhurst Park that evening to earn their fortune. It's fair to say, City took the cup seriously. However, the magic of football is, you never know.

From that point on, the evening only went downhill. As we left the pub, I still had over half a pint left. I was in no state to down it so obviously I did the sensible thing and left it, right? No, no I did not. I hid the pint glass out of view of any staff working in the pub and took it out with me to drink on the short, five minute walk to the ground. As we turned onto the Holmesdale Road, which was full of police and stewards, my mates told me to put down the beer. I gave the remainder of my Guinness a twirl, downed it and chucked the glass into a bush in some poor fellow's garden. Classy.

With us in our usual seats, and me finally without a beer, Palace actually started the game quite well (from what I remember). One of the reasons that I'm so obsessed and passionate about my club is the unexplainable pride in them. Not just on the pitch either. When a football fan is asked who they support, they never hesitate or mumble. They reply from their heart, with their head held high. We are proud of our team; our identity.

Of course, there are moments in games when we're proud of the individual players representing us – every time Moses beat a player with skill, every time Matt Lawrence threw himself in for a tackle or Speroni made a save. Sometimes we're proud of the team as a collective unit. It is always a special moment when the players look up at thousands of away fans singing *'We're Proud of You, We're Proud of You, We're Proud of You, We're Proud!'*
In certain games I'm sure they've taken inspiration to go and win the match from

that but fans aren't only proud of their team when they're winning.

At the end of matches we've lost and spent most of the game glumly sitting in silence, fans will often pipe up and defiantly sing of their love for the team in the final few minutes to show the players and away crowd that the result doesn't matter, we're still devoted to our team. Indeed, at the end of the nothing season in 2008/09, I stayed behind with thousands of others after the final whistle to applaud the players and sing of our pride – even though there had been little to be proud of on the field. Whatever happens on the pitch, we're still a proud member of the Crystal Palace club.

It's not just at matches either. I love answering the question of 'Who do you support?' – even if it is often met with a confused and baffled face from an inquiring glory hunting supporter. I'm proud to support a team that most would turn their nose up at. I'm proud to support a team that no one else in my school or work place or university lectures supported. However, it has made me very defensive. It's made me want to stand up for my team and be verbally aggressive towards people who put them down, but don't mean to argue or confront others. I simply want to I want to tell the world that I love Crystal Palace Football Club and I'm proud to represent them.

It's a pride of the team – coupled with alcohol – that makes me scream Palace songs as I walk home at three in the morning from a night out. People who don't know me can confuse it with aggressive or confrontational behaviour but they're wrong – I'm just intoxicated and in love with *my* football team. Winning, losing or drawing doesn't matter to fans. Singing and supporting is more about being a part of something collective; something special and being proud of that. However, against The World's Most Expensive Ever XI that night, I had every right to be proud of my team for their performance on the pitch and it was me, not the players, who was letting us down.

In my incredibly drunken state, I began to get quite excited. This is where the problems began. Victor Moses had started and was causing the expensively assembled City defence all sorts of trouble, Freddy Sears, still searching for that elusive goal thanks to Rob bloody Shoebridge, went close three times (I had to check that with reports after the game such is my clouded memory of the actual match) and our defence was holding firm against the most expensive forward line in world football.

Naturally, I was regularly jumping up as Palace created chances and, being drunk, stayed up slightly longer than was really necessary. The people behind weren't happy. Of course, after paying decent money to see a game you don't want to have a blocked view but in a thrilling cup tie, you also have to accept that people will be jumping up and down from their seat.

What really annoyed me was that we were in our usual season ticket seats, where we had sat for years and we never had people behind us. I was used to standing, jumping and cheering when I wanted, as I wanted, without having to consider the folk behind me. However, playing a top side, we suddenly had a large crowd and after Moses had once again managed to beat his man and have a shot well-saved by City's keeper, Shay Given, I once again jumped up. Once again they moaned, but this time, I snapped.

"We sit here every f***ing match and we never have anyone behind us. Man City rock up and suddenly everyone wants to be here. All we're doing is enjoying the game and you lot are f***ing moaning."

Unfortunately, although my actions were fuelled by an arrogant sense of standing up for my right to support the team, they were simply the words of an aggressive and confrontational drunk. My poor fellow supporters looked bemused. While I don't think I'd done a lot wrong in terms of getting into the game by jumping and standing as it was only for the key incidents, my reaction to them was entirely unnecessary and unattractively alcohol fuelled. Like me, they simply wanted to enjoy sharing their pride of the team and my actions were stopping them from doing that. They may well have been season ticket holders who had moved seat for this cup game. Either way; they understandably didn't appreciate my foul-mouthed rant. Luckily, they didn't rise to it.

When half time arrived, Dan and I darted up to the Red'n'Blue Bar. It was even busier than usual as everyone was after a quick drink to toast the highly impressive first half performance. We had been un-necessarily polite about the first half of the Plymouth game when we were in the same bar a few weeks earlier but we were now rightly full of praise for our team. I managed to get to the packed bar quickly and catch the gormless bar tender's eye.

"Five bottles of Heineken, please mate." I asked before turning to speak to Dan, and suddenly there was a hand on my throat. A middle aged bloke, who was about my height but much larger built, had grabbed me.

"I was f***ing next, you little twat!"

Unlike when Phill had used the same word earlier in the day, I didn't feel this was justified.

He felt he was next at the bar and that I had pushed in. I have little doubt that he had been at the bar before me. However, I'd had my back to him and hadn't even registered his existence, let alone consciously pushed in front of him. Getting a quick beer during the short half time interval is a unique experience and the Great British tradition of organised queuing tends to go out of the window. However, there is a general understanding of politeness to make sure that people who arrived at the bar before you, get served before you. Most people have been on both sides of injustices when it comes to order of service at the bar. However, during a fifteen minute break at a football match, it really is a smash and grab situation; more like feeding time at the zoo than fully grown adults trying to get a beer.

Anyway, although I could completely understand his frustration, it was a total over-reaction. There had been no deliberate provocation this time, unlike what I had aimed at the people who I'd abused in the seats, who'd managed to laugh my stupidity off. Now I am not, and never have been, any use in a confrontation. I froze. Just as I had done as a seven year old on Wembley Way when confronted by a (much more harmless) Sheffield United fan at my first match. I am not an aggressive person and I don't like violence. Luckily, Dan pushed the idiot away and, realising that Dan was well over six foot tall, the angry man left in a huff. The bar tender returned with our beers, open mouthed at the bizarre situation, checked I was ok, took my money and moved onto the next punter.

"Who's next?"

"ME!" replied about five blokes, each waving a note under his nose. Based on my experience, I assume that started a riot.

The second half began and despite my drunken state, I could just about justify my actions for most of the night so far. Not all, but most. The people behind had been over-reacting to my standing in the first half and the moron at the bar was totally at fault for the needless scuffle. However, my attitude and behaviour was about to make a further nose dive. City dominated the second half. Shaun Wright-Phillips scored early on and Carlos Tevez added a second midway through the half (although by the time I was back in Reading, I was convinced it was Emmanuel Adebayor). Palace weren't in the game at all. The previously rocking atmosphere fell flat.

In the disappointment, I decided that standing up as much as possible was a good idea. My lonesome attempts at singing 'Stand Up if You Love Palace', with the single intention of annoying the people behind me, fell on deaf ears and embarrassed faces. Even my friends looked on red cheeked, asking me to sit down.

My embarrassment grew a few days later when I found out that not only had my American visitors managed to make it to the game without me, I realised from their pictures on *Facebook* that they had sat a few seats behind me. Fortunately, they hadn't recognised me at the game as the drunken idiot. Well, if they did, they were far too embarrassed to come and say hello.

On the journey home, I continued to embarrass Dan, chatting nonsense to people on the train. It's fair to say, when he'd first taken me under his wing at Palace, he didn't envisage having to babysit a naughty teenager in the way that he needed to that night. He was all for drinking at football but being around me that evening wasn't enjoyable for anyone. I finally arrived back at the campsite well after midnight. It's a wonder that I made it back at all really. The festival is a good twenty minute walk away from Reading station and there's dozens of identical fields of campers as I'd found out the night before.

I'm sure you will have gathered that I'm a big drinker at football. However, this was the only time in my life so far that I really felt I'd over-done it. It hadn't helped that I'd drank so much the night before, had barely slept and had a minimal amount to eat. However, these were all my choices and my mistakes. I'd embarrassed myself, embarrassed my friends, ruined the match for other Palace fans and offended people. As far as the challenge was concerned, I'd nowbeen to six matches but the reality was, I knew very little about what had happened in this one.

Chapter Ten – **The Day after the Days Before**

Monday 31st August 2009, Peterborough United vs Crystal Palace, London Road.

Crystal Palace: Julian Speroni, Clint Hill, Shaun Derry, Patrick McCarthy, Jose Fonte, Darren Ambrose (Ryan Smith, 69), Neil Danns, Freddy Sears (Matt Lawrence, 75), Alan Lee, Danny Butterfield, Alassane N'Diaye (Victor Moses, 69)
Subs Not Used: Nathaniel Clyne, Nicky Carle, Darryl Flahavan, Sean Scannell

Peterborough United: Lewis, Martin, Williams (Lee, 85), Morgan, Zakuani, Frecklington, McLean, Boyd, Mackail-Smith, Diagouraga (Coutts, 66), Batt (Rowe, 69)
Subs Not Used: Keates, McKeown, Pearce, Green.

As I said before, I'd given up on the festival a night early. The enormous amount of alcohol consumed over the five days was too much for my body to take and I couldn't face another night of sleeping in a cold, damaged tent. I was also desperate for a shower and a proper wash. The next morning, I was relieved to wake in my own bed but I still felt horrendous. Tired, hung-over and showing the early signs of catching a cold. I rolled over, burying my head into my pillow and sent an embarrassing apology to Dan for my actions at the Manchester City game.

The game was on a Bank Holiday, when the trains never run properly, and being in August, I hadn't moved into my university flat yet, so I was based at my Mum's house in Egham. This meant that I needed to travel into London, get the tube across the city and then a train up to Peterborough. So although it wasn't a long trip distance wise, it was going to take ages to get there.

As well as the bank holiday trains, I had another problem – money. I had only just started working at Wetherspoons and I had massively overspent at the festival. I simply didn't have a penny. I had to do something that I hate doing – I borrowed money off my mother. Just enough to buy a programme and a sandwich to get me through the day. I didn't feel the need for a beer.

I got a lift to Staines station and set off. When I arrived in Peterborough, I used my printed map to find the ground, only stopping at Subway to grab a sandwich. The discounted 'Sub of the Day' was all I could afford. I had to argue with the 'Sandwich Artist' behind the till as he said that he couldn't serve me tap water. It wasn't an argument that I'd usually pursue but financially, it's all I could afford.

I then headed to the ground; arriving a full hour and a half before kickoff. Normally, this would give me a chance to head into the pub, which was packed full of Palace fans, next to the away end. But I was in no mood to have a beer. The idea of drinking was a horrendous thought. Besides, I didn't have £3 to spare on a pint. Which was probably for the best after the Manchester City game.

Being a Bank Holiday weekend and a new ground for many Palace fans, including myself, there was a large away following. It was also a rare chance to stand at a game. Since the Hillsborough disaster, terraces have been viewed as unsafe and banned in the top two tiers of English football. I had jumped at the chance to be on my feet for the game.

However, when I arrived, my body was aching and the thought of standing was not an attractive one. I got a program, which incidentally was outstanding, before I queued up at their small ticket office to try and change my standing ticket for a seated one.

"Hi mate, I've bought a standing ticket but I want to sit. Is there any chance that I could swap it for a seat?"

"Yeah sure, it will be £2 to change it," he replied.

Bugger. Realising that two quid was too much spend on something is a particularly low moment in your life.

"Look mate, I haven't got any cash with me and I injured myself playing football last week. I really can't stand. Any chance you could do me a favour?" I lied. I didn't think the true story that I'd been jumping about like a lunatic in a mosh pit for three days while pissed up so my shins were hurting a bit would buy me any sympathy.

"No, sorry,"

Damn. I gave my best disappointed face and turned away with a fake limp, in a desperate and pathetic attempt to gain some pity.

"Oh go on then, as a one-off!"

Well, I didn't mind it being a one-off, not one bit. In fact, I really couldn't envisage the need to change my standing ticket at Peterborough to a seated one again in the future and even if I did, I expect that it would be long after this chap had left his job. I also suspected it was unlikely that he would leave an identification poster of me to warn his replacement about allowing me any leniency of the rules for a second time.

With a grateful grin and a respectful nod, I handed over my ticket to the kind member of staff.

"Errrrm... this is already a seated ticket Sir"

To say that I felt like a pratt is quite an understatement. I tried (and failed) to regain some dignity by blaming the Palace ticket office before I hobbled (as quickly as you can fake hobble) off to the away entrance of the stand.

After the embarrassing encounter with the ticket office, I made my way into the ground. As I do with all stadiums that I visit for the first time, I took a selection of photographs before I sat down in my front row seat to read my programme. Being in the front row meant that I would have a terrible view of the game. It also meant that I would inevitably be on TV every time the ball came near our corner. Looking and feeling as rough as I did, I hoped that I wouldn't be spotted by too many people.

The sun was beating down but as I'd been feeling so delicate in the morning and anxious for my sniffles not to develop into a full blown cold, I'd brought my big winter coat with me - which looked ridiculous. I saw some of the coach regulars and had a bit of a catch up, trying to hide the fact that I knew next to nothing about the previous match. I also met the youngest Palace fan that I'd ever known. A fanatical pair of new parents had brought their three day old son along to the game for his first Palace match. If that's not a case that Child Protection needs to look at, I don't know what is. I'm not worried about the kid being around swearing and shouting and boozed up fans, it's just surely cruel to introduce one so young to a lifetime of misery.

Peterborough had drawn one and lost three of their opening games since gaining promotion the previous season, so the mood amongst the Palace faithful was confident. Eventually, the game started. Within five minutes, Palace had a corner and my cheap, recently purchased phone buzzed in my pocket.

Colin – *'Just seen you on TV. You look in an even worse state than the other night.'*

Great. It buzzed again.

Colin - *'And why the f*** are you wearing that big coat?'*

Fair comment.

Just like the Manchester City game, I remember very little of the match. Not because of alcohol this time but because it was a highly forgettable game. Peterborough took the lead just after half time and Palace equalised soon after. Alan Lee scored our goal. It was hardly a screamer. It hit him on the back of the leg and he knew very little about it as it trickled over the line. Still, as the saying goes, they all count. Palace captain, Paddy McCarthy, was sent off late on for two yellow cards as the game petered out for a draw.

Dad rang me after the game, slightly later than usual, and I wearily pulled my new, cheap phone out of my pocket.

"Hi Dad, how's it going?"

"Hi James, what was the score?"

What was the score? What was the score? I couldn't believe it. It had been nearly an hour since the game ended and he hadn't bothered to look up the score. I was shocked and disgusted. I couldn't understand how he could cope that long without knowing the score. It was worse than that. He hadn't followed the game at all and knew nothing about it. I filled him in.

The journey home was a tired one and I struggled to stay awake. I had a couple of weeks to relax with no football (and no tents!) due to the international break. During the break, and after pay day, I had carefully planned a trip to Prague with my friends Chris, Phill and Steve (the ex-Wetherspoons one, not the Palace supporting one) so I had that to look forward to. After booking it in the summer, Steve quizzed me *"I thought you were doing every Palace game next season?"*

"Why do you think I've insisted on booking it for that weekend?!" I replied, smugly.

Overall, it had been a satisfying (if a little weary) trip. Palace had got a reasonable result; I'd visited another new ground out of the ninety two and was another game into my challenge. I was certainly relieved that I hadn't had to stand through the game on my aching legs and I was definitely ready for a long sleep and an even longer alcohol detox.

Chapter Eleven – **A Happy Wife**

Saturday 12th September 2009, Crystal Palace vs Scunthorpe United, Selhurst Park.

Crystal Palace: Julian Speroni, Danny Butterfield, Jose Fonte, Matt Lawrence, Clint Hill, Neil Danns, Shaun Derry, Darren Ambrose (Freddy Sears 64), Victor Moses (Ryan Smith 64), Alan Lee (Sean Scannell 46), Alassane N'Diaye.
Subs Not Used: Darryl Flahavan, Nathaniel Clyne, Johnny Ertl, Nicky Carle.

Scunthorpe: Murphy, Spence, Jones, Mirfin, Williams, Wright, Sam Togwell, O'Connor (Sparrow 82), Hayes, Woolford (Thompson 76), Forte (Hooper 86).
Subs Not Used: Slocombe, Byrne, Canavan, McCann.

Since the Peterborough game, I'd had a great time in Prague. I'd tried to feed my addiction in Eastern Europe as we planned to watch Czech Republic play San Marino. Unfortunately, the game had been moved to the other side of the country and we had to watch the game in a disinterested pub. The home side won 7-0 with four goals scored by Milan Baros, a player I detested after he had dived not once, not twice but thrice, while playing for Liverpool against Palace in a game at Anfield in 2004. Not that football fans hold a grudge. We got our revenge though. He was kicked off the pitch by our angered defenders as Palace beat them in the return match and he missed their Champions League Semi-final as a result. What goes around, comes around.

The unlikely highlight of our city break was Prague Zoo. I'm not particularly an animal lover but my friend Steve is. The incredible range of animals that they had and the impressive habitats that they had created, in a stunning location, made it a brilliant day. The cheap booze was very good too and ensured that the alcohol detox had been short lived.

Anyway, on to the game. There are very few things that I know about Scunthorpe as a team or a place but here is a selection:

1) Legendary England Cricketer, Ian Botham, made one appearance for Scunthorpe United FC.
2) Kevin Keegan started his playing career there.
3) Palace manager, Neil Warnock, played for them.
4) Their ground, Glanford Park, was the first of the modern style new-built grounds in England.
5) The town can't seem to decide whether it is in Lincolnshire, Humberside or North Yorkshire.
6) Dan's wife, Carol, is very proud to come from Scunthorpe.

None of them are as impressive as the St. Vitus Gothic Cathedral that stands in the *Pražský hrad (Prague Castle)*, overlooking the Czech capital, but I don't think anyone else needs to know anything else about Scunthorpe as a town or club to be honest. Carol had done well. Many folk from Scunthorpe rarely make it further than their yearly family holiday to Cleethorpes but she's been living in the South for years now with her non-funny speaking husband.

Dan had been to Wembley with his wife twice in the previous season for the Football League trophy, where Scunthorpe lost 3-2 to Luton, and League One Play Off Final, where they beat Millwall by the same scoreline. Who'd have believed that Scunthorpe United would play at Wembley stadium twice in a matter of months? Dan had enjoyed seeing Millwall lose on their big day out every bit as much as his wife had enjoyed Scunthorpe winning. She'd enjoyed the win, and booze, so much that she'd responded to a group of mouthy Millwall fans by flashing in their direction as her tube pulled out of Wembley Central station.

In the aftermath of their promotion, Carol and I had both been confident enough (well, either confident enough or too caught up in our own trash talking) to bet each other £10 on who would emerge victorious in the match between our two sides and come match day, I was confident. Since that playoff victory, Scunthorpe had won just once and lost their other five league matches. This included losing both their away games 4-0 so despite only having two more points than them ourselves, all of us were sure of getting the comfortable victory that we needed to get our season back on track. The mood in the Railway Man's Club was positive and light-hearted as we all enjoyed winding up Carol ahead of our easy victory.

Although, Dan didn't really join in. He was far too experienced with Palace for that. The years of abject average-ness had taken all confidence and trash talking ahead of playing smaller teams away from him. He'd seen the banana skin script too many times before. He once reminisced to me about 1990-91, the season that he'd gone to every game.

"That season was amazing James. Everywhere we went, we expected to win. And we backed it up!"

He certainly didn't feel like that anymore – even at home to Scunthorpe. Although, maybe it was purely out of fear of his northern wife that he avoided joining in with our jibes.

Adam was particularly buoyant as the game, and inevitable victory, had fallen on the day of his 8th birthday. Hopefully Palace would deliver him the perfect present. Maybe we could match Cardiff and Sheffield Wednesday's combined efforts against Scunthorpe and give him eight goals for his eighth birthday. Even I thought that was a tad on the hopeful side but it didn't stop me suggesting it to Carol.

Whether it was because of our teasing or if it was more down to Scunthorpe's poor early season form, I don't know but at the last minute, the usually over-confident Carol backed out of our bet. This only added to our strong pre-match belief. Being Palace fans, we should have known better.

Soon, quarter to three came; we emptied our bladders and headed to Selhurst. Dan took Carol to the away end before joining us in our season ticket seats. At the two Wembley matches, Carol had made friends with some

Scunthorpe fans and was planning to meet them in the away end for this fixture, although she didn't have their numbers so nothing definite had been planned. From our position, high above the Scunthorpe fans in the Arthur Wait stand, Dan was pleased to see that Carol had found her friends so that she wasn't alone. It can't have been too hard; there were only a couple of hundred or so northerners in the away end that holds nearly three thousand.

Palace started dreadfully. Within four minutes, Danny Butterfield, our full back, had slipped up and we went 1-0 down. The rest of the half didn't improve much and by the time we went up to the Red'n'Blue bar during the interval, we were more than ready for a beer. We all expected Dan to receive a text from Carol to laugh at our 'performance'. However, she obviously had more class (or concern) than we had shown in the pub pre-match. Still, we knew that Scunthorpe were favourites for relegation and Palace were more than capable of turning the game around.

The second half continued in the same vein as the first. Palace were useless. Misplacing passes, losing tackles and failing to offer any kind of goal scoring threat. Scunthorpe got a second. Then a third. They were floating through the heart of our defence as easily and gently as the River Vltava flows through the heart of Prague. 3-0 down at home to the smallest club in the division. Pathetic.

Colin grabbed Adam by the hand and left. Mr Positive very rarely leaves a game early and I'd certainly never previously seen him leave a whole twenty minutes before the end. But he simply could not be so cruel as to make his son watch any longer. Poor Adam, on his birthday. I turned to Kev.
"Pub?"

I had never left a game early before but I had never seen such a pathetic performance before. Kev wanted to stay. God knows why. Poor Dan had to stay. He'd usually be the first to leave but he knew he was meeting his wife outside the away end at full time. He sat there, head in hands; without a sign of his usual daft grin or beaten sense of humour – he couldn't believe how far we'd fallen into mediocrity over the previous fifteen years.
"Watching this is just pointless!" he declared with an exaggerated shake of his head.

Within two minutes, Scunthorpe hit a fourth. ****! Kev got up to leave but this time, it was I who decided to stay. If we were going to lose 4-0 (or maybe more) at home to bloody Scunthorpe than I wanted to be able to say that I stayed until the end. Loyal.

At least it couldn't get any worse. Could it? Palace began to come into the game. Well, as much as a team that is 4-0 down, at home, to bloody Scunthorpe, can get 'into' the game anyway. Seemingly out of pity, Scunthorpe gave us a penalty. With the game long lost, the players decided to let Freddy Sears take it rather than our usual penalty taker, Darren Ambrose, so that he could get his first goal for the club. Unfortunately, his tame penalty was saved. His whole loan move was turning into a complete disaster.

After the game, Neil Warnock, as usual, said it exactly as he and most Palace fans saw it.

"I hope the lads go home tonight as embarrassed as me. We can't play like that. I can't think of a bigger embarrassment in my career.

All you can do is apologise to the fans who I thought were terrific. I would crucify the manager if I was one of them after that.

I don't think Scunthorpe have scored a good goal. I'm not knocking them, we absolutely put it on a plate for them. They must think they won the pools."

With our tail well and truly between our legs, we headed back to the Social Club while Dan went to meet Carol. She entered the pub with a huge, well-justified grin on her face. To her credit, she didn't say much to wind us up after our previous arrogance. She didn't need to. Although I must admit, I doubt I would have been as restrained. Kev, Carol, Dan and I 'enjoyed' a few drinks before we left Kev and headed to The Falcon at Clapham Junction, where we met my friend Chris – the Brentford fan.

When we arrived, he told us about the controversial Emmanuel Adebayor running the entire length of the pitch to celebrate in front of the fans of his former club, Arsenal, which had nearly prompted a riot as City won 4-2. However, we weren't interested in other results. Dan and I didn't like football that evening. But Carol did. Carol liked football a lot. She reminisced to Chris about the game.

"I just felt so sorry for them."

Smug bitch!

"They were just so rubbish," she continued. Although this was a fair comment, you could tell she really enjoyed saying that. We'd all had a few more beers and by this point in the evening, she was beginning to show her delight at getting one over her husband. And me, especially after my pre-match arrogance.

"and then when they got the penalty, I was pleased that they were going to get one. But no, it was just soooo pitiful."

The drinks continued to flow and the jibes got less disguised. As for my quest, it wasn't proving to be a challenge. Well, watching the football was but that's only to be expected with Palace. However, other than the football, it was simply me having fun – having a social life. By the time Dan and Carol left us in the pub, she'd taken to quietly singing *"4-0, 4-0, 4-0, 4-0".*

Ok, having to sit through her taunting wasn't fun but most of it was – the boozing, the friendship, the moaning. Even without her tunes, I don't think anyone was in any doubt over the score but she felt the need to make sure.

"4-0, 4-0, 4-0, 4-0".

She was unrelenting by now.

In terms of performances, it surely couldn't get any worse. Or any better in terms of being able to justify negativity as football fans love to do - it was certainly the most humiliating result that I had known Palace have. The day was only partially saved by having a good evening drinking with friends. Win or lose, we're on the booze. A motto recited by many football fans to justify their expensive hobby. The depressing experience certainly epitomised my belief that the social side of football is more important than the match. As a teenager, I would have returned home straight after the game, in a bad mood, and spent the evening moaning on the Palace internet forum. As it was, I spent the evening laughing and joking in a pub.

While the result and the performance still hurt, I know which of the two post match experiences is healthier for you. Well, maybe not healthier for your liver but in terms of using the football to release emotion without letting it spill out into real life, heading to the pub with friends, having a drink and laughing about it, has to be better than being bitter at home on your tod. Once again, it was certainly a day on the Crystal Palace rollercoaster that will live long in the memory. And probably even more so in Dan's house.

Chapter Twelve – **Singing in the Rain**

Tuesday 15ᵗʰ September 2009, Queens Park Rangers vs Crystal Palace, Loftus Road.

We arrived in Shepherds Bush around six o'clock and the rain was lashing down on the busy London streets; shoppers were trying to protect their new purchases made at the recently-opened Westfields, commuters were rushing back home in their perfectly fitted suits and people everywhere were protecting themselves from the rain in whatever way they could: umbrellas, hoods, coats or simply hiding under any kind of shelter they found. Not football fans though. Football fans are too tough for that. A mixture of red and blue stripes and blue and white hoops strode out into the heavy downpour – eyes fixed on the pub, minds on the game.

Shop's shutters were slammed down as the frantic and miserable London rush hour mood was further damped by the weather. It was a very different scene to the images that I'd imagined as a child from their name appearing on Grandstand's *Final Score*. I'd assumed they played at a picturesque'Queens Park', similar to the gardens at Hampton Court Palace. But no. They didn't. They played here. There were no bright green, freshly cut lawns and certainly no daffodils, snowdrops or bluebells; just grey pavements, heavy traffic and miserable, overworked Londoners 'living' their life at 100mph. The place is a disappointment. Just like the team - they'd spent millions over the previous three years, but had never looked like getting promoted.

As we walked across Shepherd's Bush Green (although it was more brown than green as the weather had cut up the grass), we passed an incredibly trampy looking Palace fan who was under an estate agent cover, cowering from the heavy rain. He was on the third of the six cans of 9% Carlsberg Special Brew that were lying beside him. If ever we needed a reminder that we were a Croydon club, that was it. Maybe, just like our opposition for the day, 'Crystal Palace' didn't live up to our great name and the Palace that had once stood proudly at the top of the hill.

Dan, Colin, Kev, Jonathan and I headed past Croydon's finest to the Walkabout on the Green. We were drenched by the time we arrived. There was a large Palace following in the pub and all the usual songs were being belted out. While we stripped off layers and hung them on the backs of wooden stalls in the pub to dry, Dan took the whip to the bar and bought us a round of drinks. Still reeling from the previous weekend's game, we began to sink beers. With each beer we drank, the horrible memory of the Scunthorpe game began to fade and confidence for the evening began to grow.

In the pub, the songs were generally about our love of the club, and hate of Brighton. Although, occasionally, an idividual player would be deemed worthy of a chant. Most players have their own song which is sang after a moment of brilliance on the pitch (or occasionally after a moment of stupidity and the inevitable red card that follows) but only the most lauded are 'honoured' with their name being sung in the pub pre-match. One man who'd earnt the right to have his name echo around the Shepherds Bush Walkabout that night was our goalkeeper and hero, Julian Speroni.

He defines the word legend. Yes, his displays alone warrant the tag. He's single handedly won us points on so many occasions by making world class save after world class save – he's even got the odd assist from a long kick up the field. However, he's more than that. Far more.

His Palace career couldn't have started much worse. He was only three games in, fresh from Dundee with some dodgy long hair, which was soon to morph into an even dodgier ponytail, when he made the now infamous mistake against Everton, where he tried to take the ball around Kevin Campbell, losing the ball, the match and his position in the team for three long years. Like the club itself, Speroni didn't do things the easy way. Starting with a huge cock up and having to come back from the abyss is about as Palace-like as you can get. For one mistake, he had to watch from the sides as Gabor Kiraly, Scott Flinders and Iain Turner were all selected ahead of him. Not once did we hear of the slightest grumble in the South London Press about needing to move on, despite the fact that he has proven beyond doubt to be far more able than any of the men who kept him out of the side.

Despite his loyalty, when Warnock arrived, there were rumours within days that he wanted to replace our recently-reinstated number one. Rumours that the new manager refused to play down. The result, Speroni became simply too good to be dropped. Winning the Fans' Player of the Year award and keeping his crown for the following season. And the one after that.

I met him once in his period of exile from the team. He was in the club shop, posing for photos and signing autographs for kids. He seemed relaxed and content – almost as if he viewed making a youngsters day with a quick pose just as important a part of the job as keeping a clean sheet for the first team. My Dad and I spoke to him and told him that with Kiraly out on loan, we wanted him to start. He was gracious, thankful and seemed genuinely touched. He clearly wanted to play but respected the decision to leave him out. He knew it was up to him to earn his position back and when he got the chance, boy did he do that!

If we're being honest, football fans tend to turn a blind eye to incidents off the pitch as long as the player performs on it. I dare say that if Speroni was seen fighting in the street or caught cheating on his wife or partaking in any other such unforgiveable behaviour that seems to follow professional footballers around like a bad smell, the majority of us would ignore it and still worship him for his performances on the pitch. If Wayne Rooney had come off the streets of South London and into the Palace academy, would so many of our fans condemn his behaviour? I highly doubt it. Just as many Mancunians won't have a bad word said against him and Evertonians didn't until he dared to move on.

However, off the pitch, Speroni is as gracious as he is on it. He conducts himself with decency and honour, and regularly takes the time to meet and greet fans outside the stadium. Adam once arrived in the pub absolutely beeming after his Dad had taken him to the player's car park to meet his idol – and his hero didn't disappoint. He's the definition of a good sportsman, commited but fair. He's as quick to console as he is to celebrate in victory. He's a family man and a church goer – reportedly fitting into the community effortlessly, despite the obvious difference of being a highly paid, famous footballer, a local legend and Isuspect, a hero to many of the parish too.

So yes, of course Jules is a legend for making the odd save that leaves the Selhurst faithful as stunned as the thwarted opposing centre forward, but he also has a come-back story, a dodgy haircut, a humble nature, a subtly determined spirit and a loyalty beyond question in his locker. A true gentleman, a truly great player and a truly great man.

'*Manos de Dios*' or '*Hands of God*' has been used to describe our hero but I think the phrase could be expanded to:

Manos de Dios
Hombre de honor
Espíritu de guerrero

Hands of God
Man of honour
Spirit of a Warrior

Soon after seven o'clock, Dan received a call from John, our controversial friend who'd come to Bristol with us to see Rob Shoebridge forget his glasses. He told us that the game had been cancelled due to a waterlogged pitch. It was still smashing it down outside but we hadn't even considered the possibility of the game being postponed. Having to cancel a game so early in the season, before the pitch had faced the rigour of much of the season's play, would appear tin-pot. A bit like Loftus Road – QPR's cramped stadium.

We shared our newly acquired information with the other Palace fans in the pub. Sky Sports News was on the screens and hadn't mentioned anything about the cancellation but we were adamant. John had told us. The longer this went on, we became centre of attention to more and more people so we frantically tried every avenue and gain confirmation that the game had indeed been called off. Suddenly, because of John's call, we were the 'in the know' guys in the pub.

However, without anyone other than John (seemingly including all of the major broadcasting centres) knowing what was going on, people began to get sceptical. It would be typical of him to go on the windup and leave us looking silly. Fellow Palace fans were accusing us of bullshitting as the frustration changed to uncertainty and eventually anger. Finally, with the outbreak of civil war threatening as arguments got heated, Sky Sports caught up with John and confirmed that the game was off. Relieved and vindicated, we waited for the apologies to roll in.

What to do next? Well, carry on drinking. Clearly. Despite our newly found, alcohol-fuelled confidence, the Scunthorpe game was still very much in our minds and we were quite happy to not have to sit through another performance like that. Realising that he now had time and would miss his usual selection of stadium food and multiple hot dogs, Jonathan decided to indulge in a Walkabout burger.

Burgers always have a tempting picture which inevitably, the actual burger never lives up to. And sure enough, there was an alluring photo of a large bun, filled with a huge slab of beef, freshly washed lettuce and tomato, and finally topped off with large onion rings. Jonathan was sold.

What arrived would soon gain legendary status. True to the picture, there was a large bun. There was indeed a generous layer of lettuce on the bottom and the world's most enormous tomato filled most of the surface of the bun. One gigantic onion ring lay on top of the tomato. And on top of that, was a tiny burger. Like, a *really tiny* burger - it can't have been more than one and a half inches wide. Inside the six inch bun, it looked pitiful. Nearly as pitiful as some of our performances under Peter Taylor.

Colin, Dan, Kev and I roared with laughter. Jonathan stared in disbelief. Once we'd composed ourselves and Jonathan had double checked the picture one last time to ensure that the burger wasn't supposed to be a quarter of the size of the bun, he decided to take it back.

"And what's wrong with it sir?" asked a puzzled bar tender.

"Just look at it!" snorted an astonished Jonathan. The young bloke behind the bar looked blankly at him. *"The size!?"* Jonathan questioned, as no response was forthcoming from across the bar.

"They're meant to be like that," explained the bar tender, as if he was Arsene Wenger in a press conference claiming to have missed the latest offence by one of his entirely innocent players. Like Wenger's claims, the bar tender's had to be a lie.

"I've worked here for three years and no one has ever complained before." That *surely* had to be a lie. He looked like he was only just eighteen apart from anything else. Anyway, he went and got his boss.

"What's wrong with it?" asked a confused manager. We really couldn't keep a straight face. Those of us who hadn't bought a burger thought it was hilarious. A few of our fellow Palace fans, who'd now accepted that the game had *definitely* been cancelled, joined in with the laughter. What was wrong with the burger really didn't need explaining. Still, there's nothing quite like good customer care and selling a high quality product. Something *Walkabout* had clearly forgotten to include in their induction training.

Managers defending their goods, claiming to be totally ignorant to the products faults, really do come across like a Premiership manager. Despite everyone knowing that Ashley Young or Will Buckley or whichever other overrated cheat has dived, their boss will never admit to it. To be fair to

Walkabout, they might have got away with the tiny burger if it hadn't been put in such a ridiculously oversized bun (and it wasn't for us meddling kids).

Finally, they agreed to change his burger. It returned about five minutes later with a second tiny burger in it (and probably a large dollop of slither).

As the evening continued, frustration and anger grew in the pub again (aimed at QPR's ground staff this time rather than the size of the establishment's burgers) because Chelsea were able to play a Champions League match just three and a half miles away at Stanford Bridge. The game was on the multiple TV's around the pub, taunting us. We decided to stay in the pub until nine. Then we would head back to The Falcon at Clapham Junction before the trains were crammed full with Chelsea fans. Partly to make sure we had a comfortable journey but mainly because we all hate Chelsea and their fans so they were best avoided at all costs.

I arrived back in Egham around eleven o'clock and having been drinking all evening, without my usual ninety minute, legally-enforced detox, I was completely pissed. As I tried to get off the train, I gave Dan a long farewell, drunkenly discussing arrangements for the next game. Suddenly, the doors closed. Trapping me. Half on, and half off the train. After a short struggle, I broke free, stumbling onto the platform as I fell forward.

I looked around, trying to maintain my cool, hoping nobody had noticed. A bit like Del Boy from Only Fools and Horses did after falling through the bar. Just like Del Boy, people probably did look and I definitely felt like a right plonker. I put my head down and left as quick as I could. Without uttering a word, my response was similar to Del's famous line.
"Drink up Trig, we're leaving!"

After door-gate, I staggered home and fell asleep on the sofa, watching the goals from the evening's games that had avoided the weather. Despite the football being called off, maybe even because the football had been called off based on the previous performance, it had been a brilliant evening drinking with my mates. Certainly a huge improvement on the Scunthorpe match.

Chapter Thirteen – **A Family Affair**

Saturday 19th September 2009, Crystal Palace vs Derby County, Selhurst Park

Palace: Julian Speroni, Clint Hill, Shaun Derry, Paddy McCarthy, Jose Fonte, Darren Ambrose, Neil Danns, Sean Scannell (Nick Carle, 88), Alan Lee, Danny Butterfield, Johnny Ertl
Subs Not Used: Victor Moses, Darryl Flahavn, Lee Hills, Kieron Cadogan, Ryan Smith, Alassane N'Diaye

Derby: Stephen Bywater, Paul Connolly, Miles Addison (Kris Commons, 81), Dean Leacock (Shaun Barker, 78), Lee Croft, Robbie Savage, Rob Hulse, Gary Teale, Dean Moxey, Jake Livermore (Stephen Pearson, 67), James Vaughan
Subs Not Used: James McEveley, Saul Deeney, Paul Dickov, Lee Hendrie

The day after the QPR non-match, I moved back into my flat in Twickenham with my university housemates. Darrell, Matt, Dave and Adam. Four Chelsea fans. Despite my previously mentioned 'hatred' of Chelsea and their fans, I loved the banter that came with the flat. While it was often 4 v 1, I was never slow to take them on as it had always been harmless, well spirited and good humoured in the way that football should be. After spending a summer at my mum's house, it was great to have my independence back.

The Derby match was to be a special one as it was the first of the season that my Dad had attended. It was his Bromley up-bringing that was my connection to South London and ultimately, Crystal Palace Football Club. There is something quite magical about different generations of the same family going to football together. Up and down the country, fathers and sons bond over having the same fanatical love of their team.

I look forward to the day when we can take my nephew, Zak, to a match so that three generations of Howlands can cheer on the red'n'blue together as one. Something Colin and Dan both love doing as the middle generation with their fathers and sons.

At every stage in life, football can unite father and son. As a young child, boys look up to the father and aspire to be like them. Replicating their choice of football team gives them something to share, a mutual love. In most families, Dads are the breadwinners and not around in the week due to work, so the chance to have some father/son time on a Saturday is golden. I loved the early games that my Dad took me to, often with my brothers, as we all shared the love of our club together.

As a teenager, children often find talking to their parents difficult. And vice versa. Supporting the same team and having somewhere to go for a day out together without the moody teen complaining or being embarrassed to be spotted with his Dad, can make the usually awkward relationship easy. Discussing most things with a teenager is difficult as they think parents have no understanding of anything in their life, and adults have no idea what to talk to them about. However, anyone can discuss how pathetic Palace's defending has been or argue over whether to play three or four defenders in a match.

My parents split up when I was eleven and the first thing my father did was purchase 'Half Year Season Tickets' for the pair of us. It certainly guaranteed him my presence for every other weekend. There would be no avoiding weekends with Dad in order to go to a party or whatever other teenage social event popped up as there was no way that I was going to miss Palace.

When people enter the frantic life of early adulthood and university, children often forget to make time for their parents. Having your parents come and visit you could mean having to turn down a night out. A horrendous thought and let's face it, when you're not pissed at uni, you're usually hung-over.

The idea of dealing with your parents trying to discuss how your degree is going or asking you about your fragile finances, while your head is pounding is not an enjoyable one. Indeed, any parent questions are seen as intrusion or treating you as a child. Students are able live on their own and pay their own rent (using a loan) at the same time as being competent in using a microwave, a toaster *and* a sandwich-maker to create a wide variety of dishes. They are clearly young, independent adults and parents should treat them as such. In fact, other than when you're asking for a loan from the Bank of Mum and Dad, going to a football match is the easiest conversation with your parents while at uni.

I love going to football with my Dad. When he originally gave up his season ticket, his intention was to go to about one game a month but the reality was that he was coming less and less. He had a new wife, a busy job, a house to look after, four sons and a grandchild to see, a new extended family on his wife's side and a garden that he loved to work on. The truth was that he had plenty of things that he would rather do than watch Crystal Palace. I simply couldn't understand it. In fact, I hated it. I was desperate for him to come more. He'd only been to two games in the previous season – neither at the Mecca of football, Selhurst Park.

After university has finished, there is a brief period where the football isn't required for the relationship. Attending and discussing matches is simply done out of habit and for the odd bit of enjoyment (if you can call watching Palace 'enjoyment'). Both father and son are happy with their life, could easily chat over a meal and not feel the need to fill any voids in conversation with football chat. However, having a moan about a crap referee or re-watching a goal on the internet is a good way of blocking any women in their life out of the bonding session.

Eventually, over time, parents head into retirement and children begin to pick up a decent wage so the roles reverse. The son's life is full of new experiences while the dad is winding down. Not knowing what to talk about or where to go with their parent, who is slowly morphing into Victor Meldrew, the child decides to take the Dad out to the football. At least that way he can rant and rave irrationally without being humiliatingly out of place, embarrassing the whole family in public.

The final stage also works well for babysitting. Colin would happily leave his son with his Dad so that we could dash up to the Red'n'Blue bar at half time. Grandson would be happy to be with Grandad, Grandad would be happy with Grandson, and Colin would be happy with a beer.

Whatever age the pair of you are, watching football requires no effort, no awkward conversation and offers a shared interest. Football, for the easy family relationship.

On the Saturday morning of the Derby game, my Dad came and met me at my new flat and we went for a fry up in Teddington, which is always a good way to start a day. Another perfect father/son bonding experience. Who doesn't enjoy bacon and sausage? After breakfast, we headed off early to the ground to pick up a ticket for my Dad and then on to the Railway club for a pre-match drink. Meat, beer and football. Forever keeping men happy.

In the pub, Dan, unable to stop himself laughing, told me that my train door exploits had kept most of the carriage in hysterics for the rest of his journey. My father looked at me and shook his head. I don't see what he was embarrassed about. I couldn't have done any more to improve an otherwise mundane train journey for my fellow passengers. James Howland, free entertainment provided.

The actual match was highly uninspiring. Palace weren't great but we needed a win after the previous Saturday's disgrace. We won 1-0 thanks to a Darren Ambrose goal. The main thing that we all noticed about the goal was how calm Ambrose was when shooting. He had so much time in the penalty area but he just waited and waited until the goalkeeper committed himself. Only then did he finally slot the ball into the bottom corner.

After the game, I felt we had been incredibly lucky to get a result but my Dad believed we'd edged it and deserved our win. As always, a game of opinions. Despite the distinctly average performance, the mood in the pub post match was ecstatic. To be honest, anything was better than losing 4-0 at home to bloody Scunthorpe.

Chapter Fourteen - **Away to the League Leaders**

Saturday 26th September 2009, West Bromwich Albion vs Crystal Palace, The Hawthorns.

Crystal Palace: Julian Speroni, Danny Butterfield, Jose Fonte, Patrick McCarthy, Clint Hill, Darren Ambrose (Alan Lee 61), Alassane N'Diaye, Neil Danns, Shaun Derry, Victor Moses, Sean Scannell (Nicky Carle 72).
Subs Not Used: Darryl Flahavan, Lee Hills, Johnny Ertl, Claude Davis, Kieron Cadogan.

West Brom: Carson, Zuiverloon (Reid 60), Olsson, Martis, Mattock, Jara, Mulumbu, Dorrans, Koren (Wood 78), Moore (Cox 60), Bednar.
Subs Not Used: Kiely, Barnett, Teixeira, Meite.

Despite the victory over Derby, I still had very little cause for optimism ahead of our trip to the Midlands. West Brom sat top of the league with twenty points from their eight games. We had a mere eight. To make the trip even more daunting, Albion had thrashed third placed Middlesbrough 5-0 the previous week, away from home. Newcastle, West Brom and Middlesbrough had been relegated together the year before, were favourites for promotion and were currently meeting expectations, sitting in the top three places of the league. Simply put, it was a case of damage limitation.

I set off early to Birmingham on my own. I had booked a train that meant I was arriving at Birmingham New Street around eleven thirty AM to get the cheapest travel possible. I had looked into meeting up with one of my cousins who lived in the city but none of them were available to go for lunch.

I took my laptop with me and used the lonely train journey as a chance to catch up with some university work. The new semester had started and I had been set no fewer than eight assignments. While most of them weren't due to be handed in until March, my schedule was hectic with going to the football, working at the pub and trying to still have a social life at the same time.

One benefit of working and having heavy restrictions on when I was offering my services to Wetherspoons, was that I had to work on Friday nights. This might sound mad. However, at university, student nights tend to be midweek when venues need to offer deals to get people in. Who better to market to than lay-about bums with nothing better to do and a desire to drink? Cheaply.

I found that I was going out in the week with uni-friends and then at the weekend, my friends who had Monday to Friday jobs would give me a call and I'd be off out again. This wasn't appreciated by either my wallet or my liver. Working on a Friday not only gave me some extra cash but it also saved me a lot by avoiding the expensive Friday nights out. Sticking to the cheaper student nights was definitely the way forward.

Anyway, having worked the night before, I'd avoided the usual Saturday morning hang-over so I was able to spend some much needed time on research for my assignments. I'd downloaded a few chapters on the theory behind positive behaviour management in the classroom and began making notes.

After I arrived at Birmingham New Street, I wandered towards Snow Hill station, where I needed to catch a train to The Hawthorns. I went slowly, peering into pub windows to see if I could spot any other Palace fans that I could join for a drink. Although I wasn't travelling to the game with anyone in particular, I knew plenty of people going to the match who I would happily share a beer and some football chat with. I hoped they felt the same about me.

I didn't spot anyone. It was far too early to head to the ground. Even the coach wouldn't have arrived with the regulars who I knew would be drinking in the stadium. Suddenly, something caught my eye. A Fullers pub sign. In Birmingham. I was surprised to see the Chiswick brewery have a pub up there so I strolled towards it. In Twickenham, we were just down the road from the brewery and most of the pubs were Fullers, but it was a pleasant surprise to find one up there.

It was called The Old Joint Stock and looked like a grand building from the outside. It had large steps leading up to a huge, wooden double-door. When I entered, I discovered a fantastic Victorian pub. It was a magnificent room dominated by an imposing, glass-domed ceiling, underneath which, was an island bar.

Despite its impressive interior and exterior, the pub was fairly empty inside. I went to the bar and got myself a pint. As you'd expect in such a brilliant location, the ale was kept incredibly well despite being over a hundred miles from the brewery. It was also much cheaper than you would find beer in Chiswick.

I had my pint and debated whether I wanted another one or if it was worth heading to the ground to meet the coach regulars. It was still a bit early but I could get a beer in the stadium. However, I'd noticed something. There was a group of Bolton fans in the pub.

Bolton Wanderers, the side who have spent longer than any other club in England in the top division without winning it. Surely a miserable experience. However, the ones across the bar from me looked like they were having a good time over a few beers and seemed harmless enough so I got another pint and went to say hello. To my surprise, they were having a far from miserable experience.

There is an amazing understanding between fellow football fans. Most of us are like-minded and see meeting people as one of the many benefits of travelling to away games all over the country. Straight away we bonded. They'd travelled down to the midlands as Bolton were playing away at Birmingham City. Most clubs have things in common. Whether it be players, historic games or mutual likes and dislikes. Most teams are happy to share our dislike of Millwall for example.

In this case, the link they made was former Palace and Bolton Assistant Manager, Neil McDonald. They saw him as a real club hero. Palace fans nicknamed him Ronald McDonald. The poor guy probably did a similar job at both clubs. However, at Bolton, he was part of their most successful management team of recent years whereas at Palace, he replaced the popular Kit Symonds in a disappointing season for the club. Football, a game of biased opinions.

Another common theme of chatting to non-Palace fans is their belief that Selhurst Park is the hardest ground in the country to find. This is simply not true. By rail, there are three, yes THREE, stations within a five minute walk. I don't believe that any other club in the country can claim that. By car, you simply go around the M25 until the A23 exit and take the A-road most of the way to the ground, which is clearly signposted. I was soon to find out the reason for the misconception.

The short version is that northerners are idiots.

The (only slightly) longer version is that away fans arrive at London from the north, try and travel through Central London and inevitably get both caught in traffic and lost. They then blame Selhurst Park. Blasphemy.

Anyway, despite their moronic views of the accessibility of travelling to South London, they were top guys. Like me, they loved having a beer, cheering on their team and then heading back to the pub to moan about the degree of incompetence of their side and the referee. As I said previously, only fellow fanatical ~~mugs~~ football fans can understand that mentality. The stories that we shared might have been about different teams in different divisions but ultimately, they were fairly similar.

Cheer, drink, hope, drink, begin to believe, drink, have your dreams crushed, drink, moan, drink.

It's only the rare moment of jubilation that catches us by complete surprise, such as winning at Anfield or getting promoted against all odds, that keeps us returning week after week. Blind belief. And supporting a mundane club like Crystal Palace or Bolton Wanderers makes those moments even rarer and therefore even more cherished. It's those moments of unsuspecting joy that ensure when Saturday, three o'clock comes, every football fan, at every ground, believes their team will win. No rationale can persuade them otherwise. That is why we got on. Well, that coupled with the fact that they seemed like really decent guys and we all had a beer in our hand.

They also had some Australian friends with them, who were on holiday from Down Under. I wondered if the Aussies call England 'Up Over' but I didn't ask. There were more important things to discuss – football. The Socceroos supported Newcastle United but I was shocked at how much they seemed to know about Palace and the rest of English football. They lived in Newcastle (*in New South-Wales not the North-East*), hence supporting the English namesake as well as their home-town team. Despite being born and living on the opposite side of the world, they were absolutely fanatical about all English football after they'd spent a few years living over here when they were younger and had caught the football bug. They certainly hadn't let it go.

Needless to say, I stayed for another beer with them. And another. And one more for good luck. (Palace would need it!) Around twenty past two, I said my goodbyes. They told me about another good ale pub they'd be taking their custom to post match and I agreed that I'd nip in before getting my train home. I rushed to the station and made the short trip to The Hawthorns. In the ground, I met up with Brian from the coach and even had time for a quick bottle of Carlsberg before the game.

The match started well. We'd all had high hopes for Victor Moses at the start of the season but his campaign had been up and down so far. In fact, other than the Man City game, it had probably been more down than up. Maybe it was because he was returning to the ground where he'd scored his first professional goal or maybe it was that he appeared to have been given more space on the pitch but whatever the reason, he was certainly up for this game. He tore their usually solid defence apart.

He wasn't on his own either. The whole team played well. Very well. By the time I supped on a half time beer, my three o'clock optimism seemed justified for a change. It was 0-0 and Palace had been the better side. I just hoped that we wouldn't live to regret missing our chances.

The second half continued with Palace playing well. Alessane N'diaye put us ahead with his first ever professional goal. The Hawthorns seemed to be turning into a happy hunting ground for Palace's goal-less youngsters - N'diaye was following in the footsteps of Lewis Grabban and Moses in breaking their professional ducks at the ground. Our French-born midfielder bundled his way past a defender on the edge of the area and slotted the ball beyond the goalkeeper from close range. There was a hint of handball but nobody in the away end cared. And by a 'hint', I mean that he definitely controlled the ball with his arm. Maybe luck was starting to even itself out after the Shoebridge debacle.

Once they'd fallen behind, West Brom finally began to take the game to us, forcing Julian Speroni and his defence into their top form to keep them out. But keep them out they did. The small following in the away end erupted when the referee blew his whistle for full time. It wasn't quite winning at Anfield or Old Trafford but this was some result. This was one of those rare moments of jubilation and boy, did we intend on enjoying it. Since losing 4-0 at home to lowly Scunthorpe, we'd won both of our matches, including away at the league leaders. All aboard the Crystal Palace FC rollercoaster.

Maybe the 'lucky' extra beer in the pub had worked after all.

After I'd finished jumping about in the away section, I headed back towards the small, local station and queued up for a train. Understandably, the home fans had made a quick exit. They hadn't felt the need to applaud their side off the pitch, whereas the Palace fans had stayed behind to cheer their heroes off. This meant the few hundred away fans were at the back of a long queue and had a long wait ahead. We filled the time by singing about our victory and informing the locals of our views on Brighton and Hove Albion. My only brief break in song was to take my usual post-match call from my father and let him in on the party.

When I got back to Birmingham, still ecstatic, I went to meet the Bolton fans in the pub that they had said they'd be in. They were in a similar mood to me. In previous seasons, under Sam Allardyce (and Ronald McDonald), Bolton had finished in the top eight of English football for four consecutive seasons. An amazing achievement for a club of their size and finances. This culminated in playing in the UEFA Cup and getting a result away at German giants, Bayern Munich. A trip that my new companions reminisced about with a huge amount of understandable pride and passion.

However, like most clubs who over-achieved, they wanted more. Allardyce was ludicrously sacked so they could 'move onto the next level'. For another more humorous example of clubs believing they should achieve more, look up Charlton Athletic sacking Alan Curbishly.

Anyway, it wasn't quite on par with the highs from the Allardyce era but they had won 2-1 away at Birmingham City with a last minute goal. There really isn't a better feeling than stealing a win with the last kick of the game, away from home. I felt it was justice being served as Kevin Phillips had scored a last minute winner against Palace on my previous visit to St. Andrews – home of Birmingham City. One of the Bolton lads described the whole emotion of their game to me in great detail.

Bolton had scored early on and led for most of the match. With six minutes left, heartbreak as Birmingham had equalised. A draw would have been a decent, if disappointing, result for the Lancashire side after leading for so long. However, right at the end, Bolton got a free kick. It hit the post and rebounded for their Korean substitute, Chung-Yong Lee, to score. It's not the most thrilling story in the world by itself – in fact, I doubt you care – but the passion and excitement of the storyteller had me hooked. Before that day, I'd had no interest in Bolton Wanderers but I knew exactly how he was feeling, I knew the joy that goal had brought him and I completely shared it.

We were all in party mood. They'd won in the last minute. We'd won at the league leaders. We'd only met that day but everyone wanted to buy everyone a drink. I didn't have enough time before my train to accept too many so I accepted one and bought one back for the same guy. As I went to leave, I swapped numbers with one of them. He put his name as Lee Chung-Yong on my phone so I entered mine as Fan Zhiyi, the former Palace and China captain. It somehow seemed right to know each other as our favourite Asian footballers.

I continued to text him about football for a couple of years after that. I never saw them again and never did learn their real names. Well I did but I'd soon forgotten them. I've always been useless at remembering names. Except in the classroom luckily. Learning thirty names on the first morning of teaching a new class is easy; yet remembering one or two names in a pub seems to be a task akin to climbing Everest for me. One of life's mysteries. Well, it's not really, it's down to alcohol. But still, it's quite a contrast in ability for doing the same task in a different setting.

On the way up, I'd been happy to sit alone and do some work. I wasn't intending on doing either on the way home. Although, the mood that I was in would have resulted in extremely positive behaviour management. Still, I was on a high from the football and I wanted to celebrate. That meant three things: beer, singing and companionship. You might think that it's obvious that you'd need companionship for the singing. However, anyone who's ever received a voice mail from me at three in the morning after a Palace victory will verify, I'm more than happy singing at the top of my voice as a soloist.

As I wasn't quite drunk enough to break out into song alone, I walked along the train until I found a group of Palace fans who I recognised. I only knew one by name but the rest were familiar faces. The one I 'knew' was called Chris and wrote for the Croydon Advertiser. He is a lovely guy and goes to lots of away games with his wife. A truly dedicated Mr and Mrs Crystal Palace couple.

Along with Chris and the other Palace fans, we drank, sang and celebrated all the way back to London. I knew very little about these guys. Even their names. Once again, they probably told me their names but god knows what they are. If only they were in a classroom, I'm sure I'd know. However, that didn't matter. We all had a bond. A connection. We were all Palace, we were all pissed and we were all exceedingly happy that night. We arrived back at Euston and our rendition of Glad All Over echoed around the station and into the tube.

I got the Northern Line to meet Brentford supporting Chris in The Hole in the Wall pub by Waterloo Station. Chris had been to football that day too but his experience had been somewhat different. All his mates had sulked off home after Brentford had lost 2-0 away at lowly Yeovil, who hadn't won in their eight previous games. However, he was just as booze filled as I was and wanted to continue drinking to hide the pain of the defeat. The two of us sank pints as we discussed our travels. Well, I enthused about mine and he moaned about his.

After a few pints, we jumped on a train back to Strawberry Hill to head home. By the stage that we were at Vauxhall, Chris had decided that Brentford were getting relegated and I had decided that Palace were going to win the league. We probably both agreed that referees were wankers. A common ground for any football fan.

Just as the train pulled out of Vauxhall, my face sank.
"What's wrong mate?" enquired a puzzled Chris. He hadn't seen me without a stupid grin on my face all evening.
"My bag! It's in the pub!" I replied, horrified at my stupidity. In my bag, was my laptop. On my laptop, was my university work. Although it was early in the term, I'd made a decent start on it. Besides, I really couldn't afford a new laptop and you simply can't pass a degree without a computer these days.

Also, my laptop had my spreadsheet of every football match that I'd ever been to on it. Yes, I know that's incredibly geeky but I had built it up over many years and was in no mood to lose it. In fact, I'd been particularly excited to update it with our fantastic result that evening. Yes, I know that's exceptionally sad but please don't stop reading because of it.

Anyway, when we got to Clapham Junction, we jumped off the train, got the next one back to Waterloo and dashed back to The Hole in the Wall. I rushed over to the table where we had been sitting, grabbed my bag, checked the laptop was still inside and breathed a huge sigh of relief. I'd been incredibly lucky. I bought Chris a pint to thank him for coming with me and then we attempted to return home. Successfully this time.

It had been a fantastic day. By far the best of the season so far in terms of football but the whole day had been good. Days like that make being a football addict, and completing the challenge, worthwhile. I'd supposedly travelled alone but I'd been in company all day. Meeting the Bolton fans had been a highlight. Like me, they were fanatical about their team. Although my team wore red'n'blue and were from London and theirs wore white and were from 'oop north, everything else about our love was the same. We could completely identify with each other.

Being a football supporter is a bond. Throughout life I've seen it as an easy conversation starter with millions of people across the globe loving the game. It really is an international language. Sometimes that leads onto a close friendship that lasts years. Sometimes it simply gives you a good conversation or memorable day as it did on that trip to Birmingham. Sometimes it even starts an argument. What it always does, is provide passion and debate. As long as people are intelligent and respectful to each other, having a passion for something has to be a good thing. People without a passion for something, whatever that passion might be, are boring.

I remember early in the season when we turned up the music to "The Proclaimers – 500 Miles" and "Ive got a feeling" by The Black Eyed Peas. Everybody gave everything on our own dance floor – The Crystal Palace changing room.

It started when our fitness coach did some break dancing and the whole squad joined in. Ever since that game, it was our own little pre-match ritual. It was such a blow for me that I sometimes felt really knackered from it – even before the warm up! Managers in charge must have thought that this bunch of players were absolutely crazy.

Johnny Ertl

Chapter Fifteen – **Advice Going Forward and Filth Looking Back**

Tuesday 29th September 2009, Crystal Palace vs Sheffield Wednesday, Selhurst Park

Crystal Palace: Julian Speroni, Clint Hill, Shaun Derry, Paddy McCarthy, Jose Fonte, Darren Ambrose (Nick Carle, 72), Neil Danns, Victor Moses (Ryan Smith, 76), Alan Lee, Danny Butterfield, Alassane N'Diaye (Sean Scannell, 55)
Subs Not Used: Nathaniel Clyne, Darryl Flahavan, Lee Hills, Johannes Ertl

Sheffield Wednesday: Lee Grant, Tommy Spurr, Lewis Buxton, Darren Purse, Etienne Esajas, Darren Potter, Richard Wood, James O'Connor, Leon Clarke (Marcus Tudgay, 62), Luke Varney (Akpo Sodje, 62), Michael Gray
Subs Not Used: Tommy Miller, Mark Beevers, Frank Simek, Richard O'Donnell, Jermaine Johnson

After two consecutive victories, Palace were flying. Not even Rob Shoebridge could stop us now...

I headed to the Railway Club for about five thirty. The pre-match drinking was to serve two purposes. Firstly, to help me endure the football and, secondly, as pre-drinks for a night out – The Fresher's Ball. However, thanks to the challenge, I wouldn't be having pre-drinks with my peers, young lads and lasses, but I would be in a dingy bar with two, greying, middle-aged men.

The Fresher's ball is one of the first big nights of the uni calendar and I was looking forward to an evening with my housemates. Even if they were Chelsea fans. The start of the year at university is brilliant as it is not only a chance to catch up with friends who you haven't seen over the summer but also a chance to meet the new freshers. In the Railway Club, I was wearing a chequered shirt and jeans rather than my usual football attire as I was ready for the clubbing post match.

When my Dad heard of my plans, he enquired if I was taking a lady to the ball. I imagine he was envisaging a grand event in a large, clean, wooden-floored magnificent hall, well-lit by crystal chandeliers, decorated with sweet-smelling flowers and an orchestra playing classics in the corner. I imagine he envisaged couples turning up – Men in Black or White tie, arriving with a lady on their arm in an elegant cocktail dress, and treating them as such. He couldn't have been further from the truth.

The Oceana Nightclub's 'ballroom' was dark, with its only lighting coming from the various flashing lights and lasers flying around the room. Groups of drunken teenagers turned up with whoever they happened to have found as their new university hall mates; girls wearing next to nothing, blokes in jeans and a t-shirt. Colin was horrified when he saw my shoes, a pair of red converses. He muttered that there was no way that you would get into a club 'in his day' wearing them.

Despite our twenty years age difference, it was a rare moment where I felt young and he looked old in my eyes. 'In my day'... who says that? I guess his forty year old hair had turned grey and therefore moaning about 'young'uns' would inevitably follow. Wearing 'smart shoes' to somewhere that's only going to ruin them is a stupid idea anyway – summed up well by an *Inbetweeners* scene where Simon has to swap his brand new *Nike* trainers with a tramp, in booze covered, dirty black shoes, to get into a club.

There would certainly be no flowers in Oceana. The only decoration in our 'ballroom' was a tired and tacky, overbearing disco ball hanging above the sticky, dirty dance floor, where people jumped around, often hugging their new found friends. A few people pair up with whoever they can get close to and rather than actually dancing at the 'ball', they give a public showing of waggling tongues and wandering hands. The music is thumping, as the bass clearly makes more impact, meaning and vibrations than words or a tune ever could, and instead of supping on sophisticated cocktails, people down shots of tequila, Jack Daniels and cokes, or even worse, VK Alco-pops, at the bar

It wasn't my scene, but I did it. Everyone did. It's just what you do at university. You get drunk and you get on with it. The people that you're with determine how good the night out is – not the location. I'm not saying that I'd have preferred the evening that my Dad imagined either. I'd have been just as hopelessly out of place there too.

There was one setting that I wasn't out of place – Selhurst Railway Club. Colin and Ricky, a Palace fan and one of Colin's friends from way-back, joined me there. For various reasons, Dan, Kev and Jonathan couldn't make the game and being a school night, Colin had left Adam at home. I'd met Ricky at the Sheffield United match on the final day of the previous season but I didn't know him very well. Like Colin, he had a primary school aged child. The week before, he'd had parents evening and had been furious to find out that his kid had been hiding under the desk at school.

"I said the to the teacher, I'll sign whatever you need me to sign to say that you can do whatever you need to do to grab him by the collar and get him out!" he declared. *"I said to him* (his son)*, what are you doing? You idiot!"* he continued. Despite his borderline corporal-punishment views, it was interesting to discuss the issue with him.

I was only twenty and within a year, I intended to have my own teaching job – a mystifying prospect based on the evidence of my behavior in this book so far. The one part of the profession that scared me was dealing with angry parents, who were much older than me and might not respect me thanks to my young age. Ricky turned to me and gave me some advice that I have kept in my mind ever since.

"If there's a problem, just let the parent know. I don't want to get to parents evening and find out about something that's been going on for months."
It was simple advice but made complete sense. I nodded, thanked him and went to the bar to get another three pints of Guinness.

From there on the conversation only went downhill as the beers went down our throats. Soon it was time to release our bladders and head to the match. It wasn't only Dan, Kev and Jonathan who'd stayed away. Colin's Dad wasn't at the match either. To be fair, there seemed to be about three other people in our entire block. It was a tiny attendance – just twelve thousand or so. Crowds had been slowly dropping for years. I think they knew something.

The match was a dreadful 0-0 draw. I would love to give you a full and detailed description of the game, analysing why we didn't get the goals we desired and admiring the defensive positional play of the Palace defenders but to be frank, there is nothing to tell. I was bored at the time and you'd be bored reading about it. Like so many games, the events around it meant more to me than the actual football.

The football was only lowered by our conversation. Between the three of us, with nothing on the pitch to distract us, we managed to shock and entertain in equal measures the few people who were in our vicinity. Discussions went between alleyways, women and kebab shops. I don't think anyone needs to know any more than that.

After the pitiful game, I rushed off to Twickenham to meet my friends who were half way through a pub crawl, before we got a taxi to Kingston to head to Oceana Nightclub. In spite of the football, it had been a good evening. Having said that, in this case, my insistence on going to every match had been annoying. I wasn't happy with the challenge. As much as clubbing wasn't my scene, seeing friends was, and joining a night out half way through is never as good as being there from the start. There again, if missing a wedding wasn't a reason to give up, then this certainly wasn't. I was now eleven games into my challenge and Palace were settling into the predicted mid table position.

Chapter Sixteen - **Money Worries**

Saturday 3rd October 2009, Crystal Palace vs Blackpool, Selhurst Park.

Crystal Palace: Julian Speroni, Nathaniel Clyne, Clint Hill, Shaun Derry, Paddy McCarthy, Darren Ambrose (Lee Hills, 86), Neil Danns, Sean Scannell (Nick Carle, 58), Alan Lee (Alassane N'Diaye, 66), Danny Butterfield, Johannes Ertl
Subs Not Used: Darryl Flahavan, Kieran Djilali, Kieron Cadogan, Ryan Smith

Blackpool: Paul Rachubka, Stephen Crainey, Keith Southern, Neil Eardley (Hameur Bouazza, 86), Brett Ormerod (Billy Clarke, 73), David Vaughan, Alex Baptiste, Jason Euell, Jay Emmanuel-Thomas (Ben Burgess, 45), Rob Edwards, Charlie Adam
Subs Not Used: Joe Martin, Alhassan Bangura, Matthew Gilks, Marcel Seip

One benefit of being back in Twickenham was the butchers opposite my flat. They did incredibly tasty baguettes with their high quality meat, and the staff were always friendly and knew how to sort out hungry students. Amazingly, they remembered and embraced my friend Jak and I (as 'Palace' and 'Brentford') whenever we returned, even years after leaving the area. I'm more than happy to give them some free advertising. Check out their website.
http://www.agmiller.co.uk/
During the week, Rock Investments, the company that owned Selhurst Park, had gone into administration, which added yet more uncertainty to our financial position. There were even some rumours that we would be evicted from Selhurst Park; home to the club since 1924. When I was at Clapham Junction, finishing my baguette on my way to the ground, I received a text from my mate Jak.
'Fit girl in a palace shirt on page 67 of The Sun'.
I looked at my watch, looked at the electronic train times above the platform and saw that I had two minutes. I ran down into the subway, rushed to the small paper shop, frantically exchanged a pound coin for a paper, sprinted back through the crowds to platform 15 and jumped on the train as the doors shut. Mission-not-so-impossible.
I opened the paper to enjoy my reward. Unfortunately, there wasn't a fit girl in a palace shirt. There wasn't even a girl. There was a palace shirt though. It was an action picture of our full back, Nathanial Clyne. I read the caption.
"The promising youngster is likely to be one of the first players to leave the Eagles to help to balance the books"
I read the article. It was saying that the club was thirty million pounds in debt. What had Simon Jordan done? What had Jak done? The bastard.
I arrived at the Railway Club around one thirty and all of the regulars were back. Ricky joined us again and this time he had his son with him, who incidentally was not under the table. If he had been, I would have been sure to inform Ricky straight away. We told the others that they'd missed absolutely nothing in the week, which they were annoyingly smug about.

However, that wasn't what everyone was talking about. Page 67 of *The Sun* was what everyone was talking about. It couldn't be true. It simply couldn't. We'd sold so many players for large fees and signed players on the cheap. It was only four years since we'd been in the Premiership and taken the riches that come with it. And in two of those years, we'd been receiving 'parachute payments' to support the club post relegation. After much debate, we decided that like most things in *The Sun*, it had to be made up. We couldn't be that far up s*** creek!

Blackpool arrived at Selhurst Park full of confidence after a good start to the season and were sitting in sixth place. The match was a strange one. It was heaped with controversy and goals but Palace didn't actually play that well. Alan Lee had put us 1-0 up early on and Neil Danns had made it 2-0 before half time. We went to the Red'n'Blue bar at the break, pleased with the score line and slightly unsure how we found ourselves in such a comfortable position.

The away side came back strong after half time. Alex Baptiste scored a header to get Blackpool back into the game and soon after, seemed to have scored a second to get them back on level terms. Typical bloody Palace to throw away the lead from such a good position. However, luckily, the referee judged Baptiste to have pushed his marker as he went for the header and harshly disallowed the strike. Within a couple of minutes, Darren Ambrose ran through on goal and lobbed their keeper to restore our two goal lead. Replays later showed that Ambrose had been offside. Maybe referees aren't so bad after all? Well, except Rob Shoebridge, he's still a wanker.

Alassane N'Diaye, who was fast turning into the shock performer of the season, scored a fourth goal to give us a flattering 4-1 win. After the game, we went back to the Red'n'Blue bar for a quick drink before I continued to celebrate the win with Kev, his Umbro jumper and Jonathan in the Railway Club by downing yet more beer. A few pints later, we'd forgotten all about the average performance but we certainly remembered the 4-1 score-line. That's what will be in the history books.

What we also knew by this point was that we had won three games out of four and suddenly found ourselves looking up the table rather than down. We were just two points off the play offs with a game in hand. Quite an impressive turn-around since the Scunthorpe debacle.

Chapter Seventeen – **The Welsh Adventure**

Saturday 17ᵗʰ October 2009, Cardiff City vs Crystal Palace, The Cardiff City Stadium.

Crystal Palace: Julian Speroni, Clint Hill, Patrick McCarthy, Jose Fonte, Danny Butterfield, Shaun Derry, Darren Ambrose (Sean Scannell, 46), Neil Danns, Victor Moses (Freddy Sears, 16), Alassane N'Diaye, Alan Lee (Stern John, 77)
Subs Not Used: Darryl Flahavan, Nathaniel Clyne, Lee Hills, Johnny Ertl
Cardiff: Marshall, Mark Kennedy, Mark Hudson, Gerrard, Matthews, Rae, Whittingham, Burke (Feeney, 88), Joe Ledley, Chopra, Bothroyd (McCormack, 61)
Subs Not Used: Enckelman, McNaughton, Gyepes, Quinn, Taiwo

The previous weekend had been another international break and again, I'd put it to good use. I'd spent the weekend in the fantastic city of Edinburgh with Brentford Chris. Originally, Jak was supposed to join us and we were going to come back via Hartlepool to see Brentford play.

However, as always, things didn't go to plan. The game was moved to the Friday night and Jak had an exam, which meant no football and no Jak, but that didn't stop Chris and I having a brilliant first trip to the Scottish capital. It was to be the first of many jolly ups to Edinburgh that I would go on after I fell in love with the city; good pubs, deep history and a friendly atmosphere – all overlooked by Edinburgh Castle, the stunning fortress that is beautifully lit up at night at the top of Castle Rock. What's not to like? It's certainly an improvement on the concrete jungle, filled with groups of aggressive skinheads and tarty women that is Glasgow Town Centre. I must say that I prefer Hibs to either Celtic or Rangers too – although Dumbarton will always be my main Scottish team as my Grandad came from the area. Although I never met him, family loyalties stay strong in football.

He might not have been as picturesque as the castle or as gentle as the rolling hills around the city but one of the benefits of having an experienced manager like Neil Warnock in charge was that we always knew that he could get a reaction from the players. After the Bristol debacle, we'd gone to Ipswich and won. After the Scunthorpe game, we'd got ten points out of a possible twelve. He built an 'us against the world' siege mentality – a bit like William Wallace – and he had supporters and players alike in believing in everything he said. If nothing else, he was a great motivator.

Next up was Cardiff City, which was another daunting task. They had narrowly missed out on the play offs in the previous season and were expected to challenge for promotion again. The Welsh side had started the season well and currently sat in third place behind Newcastle and West Brom, who had returned to the top spot since losing to us. However, we were on our own mini-run of good results and headed to Wales in a positive mood. The beauty of the Championship is that anyone can beat anyone – there's no turning up at games already beaten as most of the Premier League teams do every year at Old Trafford, Stamford

Bridge and other such grounds.

I had been to their previous ground, Ninian Park, three times but this was my first visit to the newly opened Cardiff City Stadium. The old stadium had not been a happy hunting ground as I'd witnessed two defeats and a 0-0 draw. I'd seen the new ground during the previous year while it was in its late stages of completion as the old and new stadiums are right next to each other.

For the previous season's match, I'd spent a whole weekend in the Welsh capital with my brother, William, who was at university in the city; even taking in an International Rugby match. Other than the chance to return to the scene of our Play-off win against West Ham, the main positive that we'd found to 'egg chasing' was that you could take your beer out to the seats and drink while you watch the sport. During the match, my brother had turned to me and whispered, (very, *very* quietly as there were a lot of very, *very* big Welsh men about who seemed to love the game and wouldn't appreciate two drunk English guys slagging it off) *"There doesn't seem to be a lot of skill involved. Just a load of strong blokes pushing each other!"*
Just in case any of the over-sized Rugby fanatics happen to be reading and do take offence, I don't think I could possibly comment any further on my brother's observation.

Unfortunately, (for me, not him!) William was in America on a placement year abroad so I couldn't spend the weekend with him this time. I'd argued that Cardiff was abroad but apparently that is different. I took my passport just in case...

As with the West Brom game, I travelled to the match alone and used the opportunity to catch up on some university work. In my bag, I'd packed some sandwiches and bottles of lager to save money. I'd been in Tesco a week before and found myself a bargain. Due to the outer box of a pack of small, French lagers breaking, I'd got twenty little bottles for just £3.50. My own French bargain – a bit like Alassane N'Diaye was proving to be for Palace. They say women love a frugal man so if there's any reading, what with this *and* the bush-beers in Bristol, I *must* be the one for you. The deal was perfect, combining two of a student's favourite things; cheapness and alcohol. I was loving being back at university, although I must admit, I was not feeling as close to my flatmates as I had in the previous year.

Anyway, I took five small bottles. They were only 200ml each so it was the equivalent of just under two pints. Lost in my studies, I didn't actually open them until I had entered enemy lines and crossed the Welsh boarder. I drank a couple as I wrote some notes on the benefits of a primary school teacher reading aloud to the class each day. Most of the research said that it was vital for children's reading and writing development. However, I didn't find anything saying that this shouldn't involve Crystal Palace Football Programmes so I assumed that would be fine for my daily classroom reading.

Soon enough, I arrived in Cardiff, ate my sandwich and put the three un-touched bottles to the bottom of my bag. Close to the station is a Wetherspoons

Pub, which based on previous seasons, I expected to find some other Palace fans in. The Cardiff Central Wetherspoons (also known as 'The Prince of Wales') is an old, converted theatre, which made for another fantastic drinking venue. A lot of pubs refused to sell to Wetherspoons as they were undercutting prices so 'spoons found themselves buying dis-used properties as a cheaper way of opening new pubs.

I went in, got myself a pint of ale and sure enough, I found some Palace fans who I vaguely knew. The hot-topic of conversation was Mark Hudson. The former Palace captain, now of Cardiff, had split opinions when he was our player, and continued to do so a full fifteen months after leaving the club. I was one of the supporters who had rated him during his four and a half year stay with us, but he did get a lot of abuse from the stands.

After finally winning over most fans with some strong performances, he left on a free transfer when his contract ended. To Charlton. Not a popular decision. Personally, I was a more disappointed that he had left than the fact he went to 'the clowns' and I didn't hold a grudge. I was however in the minority. Either way, justice came for Mark Hudson as he captained Charlton to relegation in his one and only season at the club before moving to Cardiff the following summer.

Partly thanks to the bitterness of the people who I was with, partly because it was a new stadium and partly because I knew that there would be people who I wanted to see in the ground, I left after just one pint. I knew the way to the ground as I'd effectively done it before when I'd visited Ninian Park.

The stadium itself was nothing spectacular. In fact, it was almost identical to Reading, Derby or any other 'new-build' stadium. A round bowl, all the same colour seats, all four stands the same, everything the same. No character. No life.

It's such a shame to see a ground like Ninian Park go. Admittedly, for financial reasons, clubs do need to have new stadia. Non-match day events are vital for their cash flow and who is going to pay good money to host an event in a crap looking location? Match day corporate hospitality is important too. Wining and dining clients at football is very popular with businesses and they do not want to hire a cramped box in a falling down stadium – much like the facilities at Selhurst Park at the time.

As a one off, a group of friends and I hired a discounted box above the Whitehorse Lane End, where we found a tiny space and a fuzzy old TV. I highly doubt it was a setting that would inspire anyone to invest any money in anything. The Palace boxes were one of many areas of the club that had suffered from years of neglect, which was costing the club money.

So put simply, the much criticised 'prawn sandwich brigade' may be a joke to the working class man on the terrace, but they help to fund a new centre forward a lot more than your average supporter.

Despite the need to move for the good of the club, Ninian Park was a great little ground. It had been the scene of my first ever father-free away trip and had a small terrace behind the goal with a low roof. The atmosphere was electric and it was a bloody intimidating place to go. The home crowd really got on top of away players and fans alike. It certainly had more soul than any new ground and Cardiff would have to work hard to keep the atmosphere that they were known for.

As I approached the turnstile of the familiar looking stadium, a steward asked to check my bag. He had a little rummage through, saw my laptop, checked out my remaining sandwiches and then pulled out my bottle of orange squash. I'd brought the squash for the journey down but not finished it.

"Sorry boyo. You can't take this in," he declared.

"What?" I said with a look of disbelief, expecting him to burst out laughing. Sadly, the laughter didn't come. I'm not sure he knew what laughter was. He looked like a Welsh Rugby fan who'd just been told that there's no skill involved in his beloved sport. Nope, squash-gate was no laughing matter for the large, bald Steward 261.

"It's not alcohol," I explained "You can sniff it if you like."

"You are not permitted to take any bottles into the ground due to health and safety reasons," he explained. There was probably a 'boyo' in there somewhere to go with his thick, Welsh accent but I was still in too much shock to take it all in.

"But it's plastic!" I protested to no avail.

Using all the common sense that he had, he made me a final offer, "You can down it now or simply leave it here."

So, in a child-friendly version of my Reading festival train station exploits, I downed half a litre of orange squash. It's lucky he didn't find the three glass bottles of lager that were at the bottom of my bag. They might have really been a health and safety issue.

Sure enough, inside the ground, there was a familiar looking concourse, serving Pukka Pies and bottles of Carlsberg. This really could be any ground in the country. Except Reading. Reading have Waitrose to do their catering. They are based in Royal Berkshire don't you know?

I ordered a pint and found Brian with a few of the other coach regulars. As usual, Brian told me how much he hated Julian Gray, Iain Dowie and Dougie Freedman. Especially Freedman. Today, Mark Hudson had joined his not-so-exclusive list of scumbags too. It was ironic that all four had played a key part in our last victory in Cardiff, some five years previously.

After what seemed like an age of Brian's moaning, we finished our beers, emptied our bladders and went out to watch the game. I'd agreed to sit with him after he'd offered to purchase the match tickets if I gave him the money. I was happy to do this at the time because as I explained on the way to Ipswich, despite his moaning, I had a lot of respect for the pensioner.

He'd been very ill and missed a lot of the previous season so I felt sorry for him too. I was also impressed that, after his health scare, he'd made a huge effort to cut down on cigarettes and alcohol to improve his well-being. However, during the match, he was too much to take. Moan, moan, moan, moan, moan. It was un-relenting.

Although not even Brian could complain when, for the second match in a row, Palace got off to the perfect start. Darren Ambrose put a deep cross into the penalty area, Alan Lee headed the ball back across goal and a Cardiff defender put it into his own net. Mark Hudson. I'd been in the minority before the match by standing up for him but we all loved him now. Maybe he still had a bit of red'n'blue left in his heart or maybe he simply was a useless defender as many Palace fans had believed him to be. Either way, he'd accidently put us 1-0 up.

It didn't last long. Cardiff equalised four minutes later. They controlled the rest of the half and not for the first time, Julian Speroni had to be on top form in goal to keep the home side out. The second half was a better performance from Palace in terms of holding Cardiff at bay but it made for a dreadful spectacle as it petered out into a 1-1 draw. BBC summed it up by stating *"The second half was lacklustre and niggly, with neither side deserving to take all three points."* Games like this really do make you appreciate the good times even more.

As the teams left the pitch there was a scuffle between the two sets of players. For the first time, the home crowd let out an intimidating roar. A noise which was the norm at their previous home across the road, but had been noticeably missing from their new stadium. Shaun Derry, our club captain, seemed to be in the middle of it, which wasn't exactly a rare occurrence, but from our biased view in the away end, he appeared to be the confronted rather than the confronter. The players were dragged apart in the centre circle but the situation flared up again as they entered the tunnel.

In his press conference, Cardiff manager, Dave Jones, accused Shaun Derry of making a racist remark to their striker, Michael Chopra. The allegation was later withdrawn and an apology was sent. Derry was well respected in the game by players and fans alike. The false allegations left a bad taste in the mouth. Jones had already angered the Palace faithful with comments about our players, particularly Claude Davis, in the previous season after the match at Selhurst Park. These two incidents were to be the start of an on-going 'mini rivalry' between the two clubs.

I had about an hour and a half until my train so I went back to the Wetherspoons for a quick pint and some cheap food. Made even cheaper by my 20% staff discount. The manager who served me was amazed to see a London payslip in Wales. He clearly hadn't done the appropriate research for his job as a manager of a pub by Cardiff station on a match day or he'd have realised that there was a thousand or so Londoners in the city for the game.

After finishing my food, I stopped off at an off-licence to pick up four cans of Guinness before heading to the station. On the platform, I found a couple of Palace fans who I knew. John (not my bald, angry friend John, a different one) and yet another different Chris. Both of them are lovely chaps, heading towards retirement and full of Palace knowledge.

Chris goes to every game, home and away, and John is his close friend, who goes to a lot of the matches. John also is a keen member of the '92 Club' and each season he makes it his priority to get to any new grounds so that he can re-join the club. The game in Cardiff had taken him back up to 91. As well as visiting every league ground in England and watching Palace play all over the country, he gets to the vast majority of England games all over the world.

As much as I always enjoy both of their company, they are far bigger tea drinkers than beer drinkers. In fact, I don't think I've ever seen either of them with an alcoholic beverage. This was fine but I was very conscious that I was drinking and they weren't. I took a look at a group of Palace youngsters who were enjoying a beer but decided that I would rather stay with Chris and John.

My friendship with them makes very little sense. They are at a different stage of life to me and won't thank me for pointing out that they were closer to triple my age than double it. As well as the age difference, they have different morals to me and expectations of an away day. They have different political views and an entirely different taste in music. I can't imagine them dancing about freely to the Arctic Monkeys or Jamie T at three in the morning. And they certainly don't have the same fashion sense as myself; both wore tweed jackets and smart trousers to games. We are different in almost every way. However, despite our differences, I could enjoy a two and a half hour train journey with them. Why? Because they were Palace, and that was enough. That was the bond we shared.

I discussed the game with them and they both agreed that it was a good result. Although John, who isn't happy unless he's got a worry of some sort, thought that we needed to be more attacking and relied too much on the goalkeeper. I sighed. We were away at one of the league's top teams and what is the point in having such a brilliant shot stopper if we don't rely on him in some of the tougher matches?

Anyway, we set off back to London and I set about drinking my beers. Just after leaving Newport station, the train came to a stop. The young Palace fans, who I'd decided against drinking with, suddenly charged through our carriage. Within a minute, they'd all charged back the other way and one of them had blood flying out of his hand.

The morons had smashed the glass to get the emergency hammer out before smashing a window on the train. What can only be described as the actions of a 'twat'. Couldn't they read? *'Break glass in case of emergency'.* Clearly, this had raised alarm.

The group of idiots, realising how stupid they'd been, then proceeded to run up and down the train - begging people to act as a witness to say that they couldn't have done it. I don't think they were clever enough to understand the *'CCTV in operation'* signs around the train. Maybe they'd needed a teacher engaging them at school by reading Crystal Palace books to them as a child to support their reading skills? Surely this counted as supportive research to my theory? Deep in thought, I took a large swig of my beer. I hoped this wouldn't detract from the credibility of my groundbreaking breakthrough in the theory of primary school reading.

John confronted one of them in his own self-caused panic.

"Sort your hand out. You're running up and down here throwing blood about. I don't want your blood. You might have HIV."

While John was technically right, saying this to someone who's in the state of mind to smash a train window for no particular reason, might not have been the best idea. The youngster turned and looked at John, eyed him up, stepped towards him and began to speak.

"Mate! You saw us. We were sat here weren't we? It can't have been us. You'll tell the guard won't you?" he begged. His plea was pathetic. He was so panicked that anyone could have said anything and he wouldn't have cared. He simply needed an alibi and was so focused on that, nothing else mattered. John shook his head, came and sat back down and worried that he'd get AIDS off a desperate kid. I can't help but feel that sentence makes him sound like a paedophile so I hope the rest of the explanation clears up that he certainly isn't.

We stayed there for over an hour. John worrying, Chris drinking tea andme getting pissed. Looking back, this might not have been the most appropriate action but at least it wasn't me causing offense for once. The guard had called for the police but they weren't forthcoming. We had left the last Welsh stop, Newport, but we hadn't crossed the bridge back into England yet. Neither of the English or Welsh police forces wanted to take responsibility for the yobs.

Unfortunately, the delay meant that my seemingly large beer supply disappeared and proved inadequate for the journey. Thanks to the kids, the beer-serving buffet carriage had been shut. Why they couldn't simply refuse to serve them and keep it open for the rest of their law-abiding customers, I don't know. However, luck was on my side. Somehow, thanks to Steward 261's incompetence, I still had three small bottles of French lager.

Naturally, John began to worry about me having glass out around the 'thugs' and that the Police would be after me too. I reassured him that I wouldn't share my booze (or even the empty glass weapons) with the kids who'd mucked up our journey and that seemed to calm him down.

Eventually, the train slowly rolled towards Bristol Temple Meads, where the police met us to pick up the kids. I expect there were some unhappy mothers driving one hundred miles west that evening. The whole experience was incredibly frustrating. Not only had it held me up but it also gave any non-football fans on the train an excuse to spread the word about backward football hooligans causing havoc. I can only imagine what the Moaning Michael who'd seen us upgraded on the way back from Bristol would say.

I got off the train at Reading and got the slow train back to Twickenham, which gave me a chance to reflect on the day.

It hadn't been as satisfying as the West Brom game in terms of either the football or the social side. In fact, like the football, the social side could have been described as *'lacklustre and niggly'* at times. Yes, football had still been a bond. I'd had people to talk to and subjects to talk about all day but for various reasons, the bond hadn't been quite as strong as it was at the West Brom game. Sat on my own, on the ever-so-slow train, I briefly considered if I was still enjoying my challenge. Of course, giving up wouldn't mean not going anymore, but it would allow me to be more selective on where I went and who I went with.

In the interest of balance, I began to reflect on the good bits of the day: the result which meant we were now five matches unbeaten, being able to tick off a new stadium which helped my other challenge of visiting the 92, and seeing some fellow Palace addicts, which meant I would never run out of things to say. After the brief moment of weakness, I decided the show (well, challenge) must go on.

Chapter Eighteen - **Back on the Coach**

Tuesday 20th October 2009, Leicester City vs Crystal Palace, The Walkers Stadium.

Crystal Palace: Julian Speroni, Patrick McCarthy, Clint Hill, Jose Fonte, Alassane N'Diaye (Claude Davis, 79), Shaun Derry, Neil Danns, Freddy Sears, Nicky Carle (Stern John, 71), Alan Lee (Darren Ambrose, 71), Danny Butterfield.
Subs Not Used: Darryl Flahavan, Sean Scannell, Nathaniel Clyne, Johnny Ertl.

Leicester City: Weale, Neilson, McGivern, Brown, Oakley, Howard (Waghorn, 65), King, Dyer (Gallagher, 45), Fryatt (Campbell, 79), Wellens, Hobbs.
Subs Not Used: Morrison, Logan, N'Guessan, Kermorgant

Due to it being a night game with no trains back to London and my friend Tom, who had previously been at Leicester uni, transferring course to Farnham, I was back on the official club coach. Despite this, I arrived at Selhurst Park for the ridiculously early leaving time in a positive mood. I'd been to Leicester four times before and never seen us win there but Palace were currently unbeaten in five and flying up the table. We had nothing to fear.

I stepped onto the coach, handed Robbie, the coach steward, my ticket and before I could sit down, I heard a familiar voice.
"Julian Gray can't even get into the bloody Barnsley team now. Five games it took. Five poxy games it took them to realise that he's a useless turd."
In one sentence, all the positivity within me had been sucked out. It's 112 miles from Croydon to Leicester and even slower on a coach.
"Hi Brian," I sighed. He'd saved me a seat next to him and I didn't feel I could turn it down. Garry, who would usually work as a 'voice of reason' buffer between Brian and the rest of the coach, had long given up on the away trips thanks to meeting a new woman.

This was something that Colin and Dan had taken a huge amount of time warning me about. At the slightest mention of girlfriends, Dan would get on his high horse, point his finger at me to support his all-knowing lesson in life and revel in his own brilliance, while Colin laughed and agreed in the background. They insisted that they made no football compromises to their wives when they first got together so now they were married with kids, going to all the home games and few away trips made it appear that they had cut down for their beloved. Geniuses.

Anyway, the entire coach journey was spent trying to disengage my brain from Brian's ranting while at the same time, maximising its use to solve Mark and Alex's quizzes. Thankfully, the expedition was a lot shorter than my first coach trip to Leicester.

On that horrific day, the traffic had been so horrendous that it took us six hours to get there. The driver had broken the law and carried on driving (well, crawling on the busy roads) past his limit of the amount of hours he was legally allowed to drive for or we would have missed the kick off. It was one of the few occasions that I had been grateful for the early leaving time. Well, as grateful as I could be after spending six long hours travelling to Leicester on a Friday night, not getting a beer and then watching us lose 2-0. Before finally spending three hours travelling home. Supposedly, for enjoyment?

Luckily, on this occasion, we arrived at the ground in plenty of time. Brian continued to tell me about Julian Gray's failure at Barnsley and also kept enquiring if I knew what the unemployed (and unemployable in his opinion) Iain Dowie was up to. I didn't. I did however, have a beer. Thankfully, we were soon joined by some away-day regulars, who had made their own way to the ground, or I think part of me might have died that night, listening to Brian's rambles. My ears had RMI (Repetitive Moaning Injury).

In the hour and a half before kick off, I managed to drink five pints of over-priced Green King IPA. You would always expect beer to be more expensive in an event venue but the difference in price was staggering. If I hadn't been on the coach, I would probably have been drinking in the town centre Wetherspoons. At the time, 'spoons had IPA at 99p a pint. I was paying £4.25. It didn't taste any better. In fact, it tasted a lot more bitter. Maybe if I drank too much, I'd turn into Brian.

Eventually, the game came. Once again, I'd foolishly agreed to sit with Brian. Mind you, the away following was so small that everyone was sitting within about ten seats of each other anyway. The game started and sure enough, Brian decided that the referee was a wanker. I don't know if he'd mentioned it before but he also took the opportunity during the match to say how much he disliked Julian Gray.

Half time came and I needed another beer. The game was 0-0 and Palace were sitting back, trying to play for a draw. Between the turgid football, cramped coach and Brian's moaning, it's fair to say I wasn't having the best time in the world. The contrast between this trip to the Midlands and the West Brom one, only a few weeks previously, was depressing.

Midway through the second half, Nicky Carle gave away a needless penalty. There had been no danger as the Leicester player had his back to goal and was as far away from Speroni's net as he could be while still in the box. Leicester striker, Matty Fryatt, took the penalty which was expertly saved by Julian Speroni. The away end erupted in relief but the joy was short-lived as Paul Gallagher, who always seemed to score against us, whoever he played for, netted the rebound.

Unknown to us at the time, he had entered the penalty area before the kick was taken meaning that the goal shouldn't have stood. Maybe Brian was right, the referee was a wanker. Not quite up to Rob Shoebridge's level of incompetence and wanker-ness but he had still made a mistake that cost us all the same. What wasn't the referee's fault was that after the goal, we never looked like getting back into the game. Gallagher, predictably, scored a second late on and we lost 2-0.

My dreadful record at Leicester had continued. In fact, the crap form in the city wasn't restricted to games that I had attended. Since they'd moved to

The Walkers Stadium in 2002, Palace had never won there in five, now six, attempts.

The coach journey home was more peaceful as Brian, and many others, slept all the way. Presumably dreaming that one day, Palace would actually win a match in Leicester. Although I was disappointed that the peace wasn't broken by a phone call from my Dad to inquire about the game. Eventually, I rang him. He didn't answer as it was late and when I spoke to him the next day, he told me that he'd forgotten that we were playing. I spent the trip back to London chatting quietly to Mark and Alex. They were always good company and keen to talk about any football matter from non-league to the Premier League to the Spanish League. True football fans.

It was lucky that I had them to talk to as I couldn't go to sleep myself. The plan that I had was to get off the coach at Junction 13 of the M25, clamber over a fence, walk through a private fishing area, climb through another fence, go down a dark path, walk along the pavement next to the slip road off the motorway, sneak through a business estate and back into Egham. From there, the twenty-minute walk to my Mum's house became a lot easier. Simple. Quite how I persuaded people that I'm sane enough to teach children, I don't know.

Anyway, in order to make sure I could remind the driver to briefly pull off the motorway, sleep was not an option. A driver had once missed my drop off on the way back from Wolverhampton and I'd been incredibly lucky that he'd turned the coach around to go back and drop me off. I imagine there were some thoroughly pissed off customers that night.

I was simply going for the football – a long trip for a dour game. Relying on the football being enough to make the journey worthwhile is a risky tactic. There is limited socialising and limited variety in coach travel. It wasn't that I didn't like the company that I was in. I didn't even really mind Brian. He was harmless and well-meaning enough. I just felt very trapped. I knew there was more to away travel than this. I intended to enjoy my challenge and not simply just 'do it'. I was spending far too much time and money on it for that. Although I didn't question the challenge when I got home, I knew this was exactly the type of game that I would soon stop going to. However, unlike my Dad, I would still be glued to whatever coverage I could find.

Chapter Nineteen – **Jesus is with Us**

Saturday 24ᵗʰ October 2009, Crystal Palace vs Nottingham Forest, Selhurst Park.

Crystal Palace: Julian Speroni, Clint Hill, Shaun Derry, Patrick McCarthy, Jose Fonte, Darren Ambrose (Lee Hills, 90), Neil Danns, Freddie Sears (Victor Moses, 35), Alan Lee (Stern John, 63), Danny Butterfield, Johnny Ertl
Subs Not Used: Nathaniel Clyne, Darryl Flahavan, Claude Davis, Alassane N'Diaye

Nottingham Forest: Lee Camp, Wes Morgan, Kevin Wilson, Paul Anderson (Gareth McCleary, 45), Paul McGugan (Luke Chambers, 68), Dele Adebola, Nathan Tyson, Chris Cohen, Chris Gunter, David McGoldrick, Paul McKenna
Subs Not Used: James Perch, Joe Gardner, Paul Smith, Radoslaw Majewski, Joel Lynch

The season was now a quarter of the way through. Overall, Palace had started the campaign well and my challenge was on track. The Leicester result had been disappointing but far from devastating. However, Forest's season was going even better than our own. As it should have been after spending big in the summer. They sat six points ahead of us in the table and arrived at Selhurst Park on the back of five successive victories.

The Midlands team (yes, yet another one!) had spent six million pounds – more than anyone else in the division - on eight summer signings, as well as bringing in three high-profile loan players on big wages and were one of the bookies favourites for promotion. It wasn't quite as much as Manchester City's £200 odd million but in comparison to us, it might as well have been. It demonstrated that even in the lower leagues there is a hugely uneven playing field – a gap that seems to be ever widening in football with every new mega-world-wide TV deal that is signed by the Premier League, and every overseas owner that invests in a club as his latest asset/toy.

It was typical of me to pick the year with the most northern division possible to attend every game. While it was lovely to look down a division, laughing at little old Millwall and Charlton, it would have been nice to have some London company other than QPR. The 2009/10 Championship was stacked full of teams from the Midlands: West Brom, Leicester, Derby, Coventry and Nottingham Forest. It was unfortunate that these were to be some of the shorter journeys during the season.

Around one thirty, I met the usual guys in the usual place and drank the usual beer. Pre-match, fans are generally either full of optimism so they trash talk their sides chances up or, feeling nervous, joke about the predictable and miserable outcome of the game. Our expectations were certainly on the nervous side in the pub.

For this match we were joined by my friend 'Tom the Twin'. An unimaginative nickname based on the fact that he had an identical twin brother. He was someone who I knew from my secondary school days and had only been to Palace once before, a 1-0 defeat to Portsmouth on Boxing Day 2004. His main memory for the day was how grumpy I had become once my beloved team were losing.

People always find it surprising that I only really had one close friend at school who loved watching live football. Being a group of lads, some of them would follow the general football results a bit and most of them would join in with a kick about. However, none of them really had the bug for supporting a team like I did.

I guess that shows that I can, very occasionally, talk about topics other than football. Although I do have to admit, the other person showing little or no interest in hearing about Crystal Palace doesn't usually stop me from rambling on. I mean, if only they knew about the charm of my Saturday afternoons in South London, I'm sure they'd be converts. I see it as my passage in life to show them the light. I'm pretty sure they'll thank me one day.

Anyway, Tom had decided to give live football and Crystal Palace another go. Which is more than can be said about his twin brother, Ryan. Not even watching us beat Liverpool 2-1 in the League Cup on his only visit to Selhurst Park had managed to persuade Ryan to return. I took Tom's more open-minded approach as a sign that he had taken the intelligence from the womb that they'd shared.

He may have got the intelligence but he wasn't the most confident of people. Some people will burst into a room of strangers and make everyone take notice. Some prefer to sit quietly and take in their surroundings without causing a fuss. Tom was certainly more of the latter.

It's surprising that he was shy as a mop-haired teen because in his early twenties, he took life by the scruff of the neck and tried living all around the world. Something that takes a huge amount of self-confidence and requires a willingness to throw yourself out there to engage with everyone you meet. I find it even more ironic that after a year of university in Leicester, he'd become homesick and transferred to a course that he could do from home. He'd happily live on the other side of the world to his family, but being in Leicester was just too much to take. Make of that, and Leicester, what you will.

To be fair to Tom, it must have been hard for him to join in with the conversation. I guess listening to me enthuse about something he had minimal knowledge about was difficult to keep up with. Therefore, throwing him into a position where he had to keep up with five of us talking passionately about the club, supposed debts and stories of people who he didn't know, was rather difficult for him. That's before you take into account all the 'in jokes' that any group of friends inevitably has.

Despite all this, Tom listened keenly. Occasionally, I, or Dan, who he used to babysit for, would turn to him and try to translate the Palace talk into an understandable dialect. For example, he was in no doubts about our opinions on Rob Shoebridge. After hearing the tale of woe from Bristol, even Tom agreed that the referee sounded like a wanker. However, he did what a lot of people do when they don't know the people they're with and can't keep up with the conversation. He drank.

Boy did he drink. We were in the pub for just over an hour and we'd had three pints each. Tom hadn't wanted to get into a round, which was fair enough, but he'd managed to sink five pints on his own. By the time that we emptied our bladders and made the short, damp walk to the ground, he was well on his way to being pissed. Usually, he wasn't even a particularly big drinker.

By the time that the players walked out to Glad All Over, we were all in a confident mood. I'm not sure why I'm telling you this as you might have noticed that it seems to be the same at pretty much every game. It is. Come three o'clock, no matter what the odds are or who the opponents are or what all logical evidence suggests, every fan believes that their team might win – even if they'd been sure of a defeat only a few hours earlier. And if you ever stop getting that 'winners' feeling, it's time to assess what you are doing with your weekend.

After the game began, I did wonder if Tom had known something we didn't when getting boozed up. It was a pretty dire match. Five minutes before the interval, we sent Tom, as the non-palace supporter, to the Red'n'Blue Bar with our cash to get the beers in. As he left, Palace got a free kick.

It was right on the edge of the area and the ground went silent, anticipating the shot. It's amazing how expectant a football crowd is for a free kick when you consider, David Beckham aside, how rarely a goal is actually scored. In my twelve years of going to Palace, I could only remember witnessing one or two successful direct free kicks. One in particular from Lombardo against Oxford United. It would surely take a divine intervention for us to score.

Adam and Colin turned to each other.

"How much for a goal Dad?" asked the optimistic son. I couldn't believe his cheek. Not only was he on a goal bonus from his father for his Saturday morning team, he now wanted a goal bonus for Palace strikes.

However, I knew where Adam's hopeful outlook on Selhurst life came from. His father never gave up on Palace. Clutching at straws didn't cover it, he'd clutch at thin air. His Dad was also very superstitious. He would often want us to sit in a specific 'winning' order at matches or tell us he was wearing a 'lucky' item of clothing. Thankfully, he'd not had 'lucky underwear' yet as he had a horrible habit of putting his lucky charms right in your face.

"Three quid!" replied Colin. The generosity came from a mixture of being a loving Dad, believing that tempting fate would rip him off, and being ever-optimistic on all things Palace.

"We're Winners!" he used to claim to his son, while making a 'w' with his fingers, every time Palace lost a game. Darren Ambrose stood over the free-kick. We'd seen him score one at Brentford in pre-season but that was more down to a huge deflection and the goalkeeper's incompetence than anything else.

The ref blew his whistle. Ambrose ran up. Bang. He curled it right into the top corner, bouncing off the underside of the crossbar and into the goal. 1-0 Palace. Poor Tom had missed it. I grabbed Adam and threw him in the air. Colin put his hand into his pocket with a huge grin on his face. Only bettered by the even bigger grin on his son's face. I didn't think there was a better feeling than seeing Palace score but on that day, Adam might just have found it. Seeing Palace score AND getting paid for the privilege.

As we were about to leave our seats for half time to collect our beers from Tom, there was a mass brawl between most of the players and management. I say a 'brawl' as that is how these things are reported in the press but it was much more like handbags (as these things usually are). Twenty two players pushing, shouting and probably pulling each other's overpriced haircuts.

The scuffle had started between Palace full back, Clint Hill, and Forest full back, Chris Gunter. I think it's just as well for Gunter that so many other players did dive in. Dan used to lovingly describe Clint Hill as a 'man's man' but he could quite easily be described as a 'scouse maniac'. Gunter wouldn't have stood a chance. Once it had all calmed down, the ref booked both players and the game re-started.

Suddenly, out of the PA system, came a voice. No, it wasn't Mr Parker being asked to leave the stadium. Nor was it an announcement to let some poor bloke know that his car had been clamped. It wasn't even to tell someone that his wife had given birth (an unbelievable public broadcast during a match against Manchester City in 2001 for which the crowd gave the man a round of applause and his wife, presumably, gave him a divorce). Nope it was none of them. *"...and Billy Davies* (The Forest Manager at the time) *is really throwing his toys out of the pram on the touchline..."*

Somehow, the radio had been played through the speakers to be heard by the entire crowd as well as the players. Davies soon moved on from his pram days and had a toddler style tantrum about the mistake.

After the commotion, the referee blew his whistle for half time, the home crowd let out a satisfied roar and we headed up to the bar to collect our drinks. Poor Tom, after missing both of the half's key events, was waiting patiently for us with our beers. He'd bought four bottles of Heineken for us as instructed and he'd also bought a pint for himself, which was already half gone.

I had to feel sorry for Tom. Once again, with all of the action coming in the final minutes of the half after we had sent him off on a beer run, he had nothing to add to conversation about the game. Within five minutes, he'd finished his pint and nipped off to buy a second one. Piss head.

We finished our bottles and headed back to our seats, leaving Tom to finish his second pint. We'd barely sat back down when Forest equalised. My hopeless friend had managed to miss another goal. Colin turned to me about ten minutes into the second half.

"Where's your mate?"

I shrugged *"Drinking?"* I wasn't sure if Tom was simply enjoying the boozing so much that he was keen to get every drop that he possibly could or, if he was *not* enjoying the football so much that he was drinking to get himself through it. Either way, he was certainly drinking. A lot.

Eventually, Tom, slightly swaying, made his way up the steps to join us in the stand.

"Jesus has returned," someone shouted, referring to his long, tangled hair. From

the way he was walking, he did look like he'd turned a lot of water into a lot of wine but he certainly hadn't shared it with the rest of the party. Well, that was it, from now on he would be known as 'Jesus'. Maybe it had taken a divine intervention for Palace to score a free kick after all.

Other than the Jesus puns, which deteriorated at the same rate as the football, the rest of the game was highly uneventful. This was particularly disappointing for the Son of God as he had managed to miss both goals. Originally, we had thought he was upstairs at the bar when the goals went in, but by now it was assumed that he'd been upstairs with his father, looking down on the action.

In his post match press conference, Davies was a sulking teenager. Unhappy that his team had failed to break down a resilient Palace side, he blamed anyone and anything except his expensively assembled side. At this rate of rushing through life, he'd be a pensioner within the week. He certainly moaned enough and would seem at home angrily waving a walking stick in disgust.

After the game, Kev, Jonathan, Jesus and I headed back to the Railway Club where we continued to discuss the game. Jesus was still lost in the conversation and still drinking. As the evening went on, we moved on to more general football talk and also discussed the big black cloud of finances that loomed over the club. A few beers later, Kev turned to me, *"Is Jesus ok?"*

We all looked over; he was leaning forward on top of the table with his eyes barely open.

"I think it's time to get going," I said so we, well I, drank up and left with him. Tom wasn't much of a conversationalist on the way back; he certainly wasn't up for any preaching. Some people get louder when they're pissed, whereas others simply go quiet and want to sleep. Jesus was ready for bed. Luckily for him, I was going back to Ascot to meet some friends, including his twin brother, so I was able to keep him awake. Without me, I expect he'd have woken up in Reading (the final stop on the line).

Thirteen league games done, thirty three left to go. The challenge was coming along nicely and Palace were continuing to get some decent results.

Chapter Twenty – <u>**Old Friends**</u>

Saturday 31st October 2009, Preston North End vs Crystal Palace, Deepdale.

Crystal Palace: Julian Speroni, Danny Butterfield, Jose Fonte, Claude Davis, Nathaniel Clyne (Lee Hills 73), Shaun Derry, Johnny Ertl, Neil Danns, Darren Ambrose, Alan Lee (Stern John 73), Victor Moses (Ryan Smith 56).
Subs Not Used: Nicky Carle, Sean Scannell, Kieron Cadogan, Alassane N'Diaye.

Preston: Lonergan, Jones, Collins, Chilvers, Nolan, Parry (Sedgwick, 66), Carter (Shumulikoski, 59), Chaplow, Wallace, Mellor, Brown (Parkin, 60)
Subs Not Used: Henderson, Hart, Mawene, Elliott.

For the second season in a row, going to Preston, one of the most depressing places in the Championship, sparked something magical. Fourteen months previously, I'd missed the coach to Preston. I'd stayed up late drinking as I waited for news after hearing that my sister-in-law had gone into labour. Around midnight, I received the brilliant news that my nephew, Zak, had been born. Stupidly, I continued drinking until about three in the morning and overslept.

Anyway, I woke up on the morning of this match to the brilliant news that my niece had been born. She didn't yet have a name but there was a new member of the Howland clan. Hopefully, another Palace fan. I also hoped that she would give us more luck than Zak had. We'd lost 2-0 on the day that he was born.

At the start of the season, the club had given out some free 'bring a friend' coach vouchers. As I wasn't allowed to bring my barely-hours old niece while the hospital kept her in for observation, Brian and I had done a deal where we would use them for each other so that we both got one free travel to an away game. I'd got my free coach for this game and I would get him free travel to Sheffield United in December. It was far from ideal but I couldn't afford to turn down a freebie. Besides, not even Brian could dampen my mood after the news I'd received that morning.

Motivating myself to go to Preston was one of the harder jobs of the early part of my challenge. Especially on the coach. When I started to cut down on away games the following season, Preston would be one of the first for me to give the cold shoulder to. It is a typically grim northern town and a thoroughly depressing place to visit. In fact, on the 12th October 2009, a survey of 10,000 people, carried out by respected market researchers YouGov, claimed Preston had the worst cultural offering in the country. Preston is also home to the street in the UK with the highest crime-rate (Glovers Court). I assume it got its name as a warning that you require of a pair of boxing gloves to keep you safe. Although, maybe 'Stab-vest Court' might have been more apt.

This was my fifth visit to Preston, including once making two trips in four days – neither of which we won - and it hadn't endeared itself to me on any of the previous four visits. The one saving grace of the place was that it was the host of the very impressive National Museum of Football. Something that has since been relocated to a more deserving home. Only an addict would keep returning to such an unappealing place as a sick kind of self-harming. Before we had even set off, I vowed that this would be my final visit to the town - to avoid me having to buy even more Christening presents as much as any other reason.

At the end of the long trek north, we finally arrived in Preston. I'd received an update that Julian Gray had now been released from Barnsley and Dougie Freedman couldn't get a game at Southend. Freedman was a club legend, having scored over one hundred goals for the club, including some vital ones. He had stayed at the club well past his best but the majority of fans still worshipped him, ignoring his shortcomings. While I could see that people were letting sentiment cloud their views on the striker's ability at the end of his spell at the club, it really didn't bother me. Unlike Brian. Brian had grown bitter about it and held poor Dougie personally responsible.

Having been three times before to the museum, I decided not to make one final visit. While the museum was inspiring in a geeky sort of way, beer was calling my name after being cooped up for so long. We went into the concourse and from there, saw that the final side of their ground regeneration had been completed. They now had four impressive stands and a smart looking stadium. Selhurst Park had dropped even further down the list of decent Championship grounds.

Inside the stadium, I met up with Garry. He was attending the game with Mary, his new partner, who lived in Lancaster, so it was only a short trip for them; allowing my mate to see Palace away from home for the first time that season.

Garry had been approaching twenty years of marriage when I first met him and he attended every Palace game. Since then, he had separated from his wife, met someone new and no longer had the Palace away bug. In fact, the change in his attitude was striking. When he was newly separated, the first thing that he sorted was ensuring that he had enough finances to still follow Palace around the country. Eighteen months on and he wasn't fussed about watching the team.

On reflection, I can't help but feel attending the football was filling a void in his life towards the end of his marriage. It can't be the sign of a happy marriage that the bloke is absent every Saturday. Preferring a trip to Preston to being with your wife simply isn't healthy. I definitely think that the football addiction gave Garry the escape from reality that he needed during that part of his life.

Since meeting someone new, he no longer felt the need to travel up and down the country on a weekly basis for football. Instead, he spent weekends with his new partner. A football team is a man's first love and it would be careless to lose that. You can find other loves in life but you should never forget your first love. Mary now filled Garry's heart and he didn't need the club's love as much as he once did. However, the old flame was still burning in the background of his life.

Especially as I hadn't seen him for months, it was brilliant to have a good catch up with Garry. He still had the same intelligent, quick-witted sense of humour and level-headed attitude to life that I respected and liked. We had a few pints of expensive bitter in the ground, while he told me about how happy he was with life and I told him about the games that he'd missed.

During the game, it was good to have a well-reasoned buffer between Brian and I. Watching the game with Garry, as well as Brian, gave the conversation a lot more balance. It was filled with as many bad quick-witted puns as it was with negative and repetitive moans. There is more to life than Julian Gray and watching the game as a three reminded me why I had enjoyed going to football with these guys so much in the past.

It was a stark contrast to my home life at the time where relationships with my flatmates had turned sour. For some reason, we weren't getting on as well. There were no major incidents or conflicts but the others, particularly Darrell and Matt had stopped talking to me or making any effort with me. This was particularly hurtful from Matt, who I had known since I was at primary school. I'd obviously done something to upset them but neither of them had the guts to challenge me on whatever I'd done. I'm certainly not claiming to be completely innocent in the fall out. I tried to raise the issue and resolve whatever it was with them on a number of occasions, but my efforts were rebuffed and any issues were denied. It pains me to say but the change in their attitude started when I stopped playing *FIFA* and *Football Manager* to focus on my studies, work, nightlife and football. Computer games that their lives seemed to revolve around.

The four of them also become close friends with another Chelsea supporter and it was fairly evident to me that they wished that he was living with them. It was unfortunate that myself and him had little in common and never really got on. He was far too brash and arrogant for me. However, the four of them seemed to love him. Their attitude seemed to be that he was one of 'them' as a Chelsea fan and I wasn't.

For them, supporting a football club was about their club and no other. An attitude matched by their refusal to accept any blame on their club for any defeat. It was *always* the referee's fault. Any kind of praise for the opposition was definitely out of the question. They certainly didn't want me talking about Chelsea or having an opinion on anything to do with their club. Matt was a season ticket holder with his Dad and sister. On the regular occasions when his sister didn't go, he would offer the ticket to his flatmates. On one occasion, none of the Chelsea fans could go but I was free. He didn't want me at the match as a non-Chelsea fan and the ticket went to waste.

What had previously been a fun environment, filled with football banter and friendship, was fast turning into a miserable and lonely place of living. Without the solid foundation of friendship, there was no fun in 'banter'. It became arguing. When I once suggested that a referee had been right to send off a Chelsea player, I was told to '**** off' and that I was an idiot. That was the end of the 'conversation'. Rather than act like spoilt brats and swearing at me, I was desperate for them to make a 'Shoebridge joke' in retaliation. However, like most of the time, I was met with being ignored - rather than engaged in any form of dialogue.

Anyway, it made me appreciate the escape from my flat and the Palace supporting company even more. Like with John and Chris, I didn't have a huge amount in common with Garry and Brian, although I shared some of Garry's love of rock music, but they were Palace. That was enough. That was a bond. Palace had started the game ok but it had got scrappier and scrappier. Ten minutes before half time, Preston took the lead. It was lucky that the company was good as the football was still crap. Brian, Garry, Mary, who was now an adopted Palace fan, and I slumped back into our chairs.

However, within two minutes, Palace were back on level terms. The ball had been lumped forward towards Alan Lee, who nodded it down for Darren Ambrose to finish superbly from outside the area. It's fair to say that the Ambrose signing hadn't particularly excited me at the time but it had been proved a Warnock masterstroke. That was the midfielder's eighth goal of the season from midfield. And it was a beauty.

The rest of the match was highly uneventful as both teams seemed satisfied with a point. Palace had welcomed my niece into the world with a better result than they had mustered up for Zak eighteen months previously, but it was hardly befitting of the beautiful little girl. 1-1 at Preston North End.

The coach journey home was long and slow. Another reminder of what was wrong with coach travel. At least I did manage to sleep for some of the way back. After five gruelling hours, I got off the coach at Junction 13 and met my mother, who drove me to Egham station where I could get a train back to Twickenham.

I certainly intended the upcoming Sheffield United game, which I had a free ticket for, to be my final one on the coach. Palace had got a decent result, it had been good to see Garry and I was still on a high after hearing my brother's news in the morning. However, overall it had been a very long day. I definitely stood by my vow never to return to Preston North End. Incidentally, my sister-in-law is yet to have any more children. Coincidence? I think not.

Chapter Twenty-one – **A girl. At football?**

Tuesday 3rd November 2009, Queens Park Rangers vs Crystal Palace, Loftus Road.

Crystal Palace: Julian Speroni, Clint Hill, Shaun Derry, Jose Fonte, Darren Ambrose, Neil Danns (Lee Hills, 85), Stern John (Alan Lee, 67), Danny Butterfield, Johnny Ertl, Claude Davis, Alassane N'Diaye (Freddy Sears, 45).
Subs Not Used: Nathaniel Clyne, Nicky Carle, Victor Moses, Sean Scannell.

QPR: Cerny, Fitz Hall, Mikele Leigertwood, Wayne Routledge, Buzsaky, Gorkss, Ben Watson, Faurlin, Simpson, Gary Borrowdale, Taarabt.
Subs Not Used: Heaton, Peter Ramage, Vine, Agyemang, Alberti, Ephraim, Ainsworth.

The week had been a fairly traumatic one for our family. Mark's baby girl had been kept in hospital but mercifully, mother and baby were now stable. I'd been to see her the previous day and had been the first in our family to find out the tiny girl's name. Nemie.

For the second time that season, we headed to Shepherds Bush. Armed with the knowledge that under no circumstances should we purchase a Walkabout burger. Mainly because if they remembered us, the chef would almost certainly spit in it. This time Dan, Colin, Kev, Jonathan and I were joined by a couple of others.

Rewind a few weeks and I was texting a girl. Not a species known for their knowledge or love of football. It was Phill's sister, Natalie.
Natalie – Football is silly
Me – No it's not.
Natalie – Yes it is.
Me – How do you know?
Natalie – I've had to watch it on TV.
Me – That's not real football. I meant actually going to the games.
Natalie – It's still silly.
Me – How do you know? You've never been.
Natalie – That's a fair point.
Me – You should give it a try.
Natalie – Yeah I suppose.

So there we had it. I had one chance to convert her. As I said before, it was my passage in life to enlighten the ignorant to the path of CPFC. Her parents regularly drank in the pub where I worked and gave me strict and detailed instructions about looking after her at the game. I had been warned. Although her Dad couldn't get it into his head that I supported Palace not QPR.

Her Dad, Jim, is an Arsenal fan and her mother, Sharron, is a Chelsea supporter. Both of them had an outdated view of football from when they used to go on the terraces. Her Mum is as tough as anything and used to go to games herself but even she had a deep rooted belief that football was no place for her little girl, who was 18 by now.

"You will look out for her won't you?" she'd checked, while I was clearing glasses from her table at the pub one afternoon.

I frowned, pushed my lower lip to one side in concern and crouched down next to her.

"Well actually, I'm a bit worried. A few of the old boys are coming back for this game and talking about a meet up..."

...but I couldn't keep a straight face any longer. Both of her parents were far from gullible but they'd fallen for it hook, line and sinker. The looks on their faces were priceless. They gave me a slap on the arm and ordered me back to work.

I'd decided that she was more likely to enjoy an away game with the better atmosphere and extra drinking time than a home game at a half-empty Selhurst Park. Realising that taking her to Barnsley or Preston was likely to not only put her off football but also make her hate me, I thought the QPR game would be perfect. It was local and the away end would be a sell-out. I bought two more tickets for the match, enabling me to sit with her.

This had meant I had a spare ticket, which I'd sold to 'Mad-Eyed Steve', who'd been with us in Bristol. I definitely could have used a photo of Steve to continue the trouble making wind up that I'd fed Natalie's parents. One picture of him and there's no way that she'd have been allowed to come. Or wanted to.

As we did on the first wet attempt, we all met up at Clapham Junction to get the train to the Bush. Once there, as we had done before, we headed to the Walkabout, an Aussie bar, and began to see off pints. The re-arrangement had certainly suited us. On the original date, we were still licking our wounds from the Scunthorpe match but since then, we'd only lost once in seven games. We were much more confident about getting a result this time, although QPR were in fine form too and sat in the playoff positions.

Due to a lack of decent ale, I was drinking Guinness. Unfortunately, on match days, lots of pubs serve beer out of plastic 'glasses'. Walkabout was one of those pubs. A plastic cup is never great for beer but with Guinness, it really affects the taste. Dan and I had a long and detailed discussion about this abuse of the Irish drink. Eventually, we decided it was unlikely that a group of leprechauns would suddenly declare war on Australia in the name of blasphemy against Guinness. Unlikely, but just about possible. Kangaroos, should stay on amber alert and Nicky Carle should always keep one eye on Paddy McCarthy.

Half way through the night, Steve had one of his many crazy ideas.

"I'm thinking of getting some food," he muttered innocently while picking up a menu to muse through.

"NO! Don't do it!" we all shouted with concern. He looked quite scared, unaware of what the problem was so we explained burger-gate from the original fixture. He put down the menu. Unfortunately, this wasn't to be his final crazy idea of the evening.

Natalie fitted in surprisingly well with the pre-match banter. She was definitely being won over by the football experience. It wasn't a completely new experience for her as she often went out with her brother's mates so was used to being the only girl with a group of lad-ish guys. She was also used to the boisterous nature of gigs. Indeed, it was at Reading festival that I had become close friends with her. Her first ever gig was in the mosh pit; watching the heavy metal band Slipknot so she was well prepared. Finally helping her feel part of the gang, she had a pint in her hand for most of the night which always helps.

Although on his round, Jonathan, ever the gentleman, decided to get Natalie a WKD alcopop. He'd assumed, being a woman, that she'd rather have that than a pint. He obviously hadn't watched her drinking lager all evening prior to that point – either that or, without his usual burger, he was as lost as a spinach-less Pop-eye.

Soon before we left, Steve came back from one of the many toilet breaks that we'd all needed that night and had some groundbreaking news. He got all of our attention by shouting in each of our faces, far louder than necessary, and pointed across the pub. We looked on as a burger came out from the kitchen. It looked juicy and tender but more importantly, it filled the bun.

Maybe our complaints had reached the Walkabout headquarters and they'd taken on our advice. Acting Food Standards Consultant was to be one of the many important roles that we would take on during the season. Either that or they'd simply run out of burgers on our previous visit and bought some crap ones from the Iceland opposite to use as replacements.

As we were getting our things ready to leave, still gutted that he'd been denied the chance to have a decent burger, Steve had another of his crazy ideas. He returned from the bar with a tray of shots of Bundaberg Rum. I'd discovered at a young age that shots and I don't get on. They make me sick. Instantly. The smell of it made my stomach churn and brought back memories of many ill-advised nights out.

I looked at the rum in my hand, then at the three-quarters of a pint of plastic affected Guinness that I had left in my other hand. Finally, I glanced towards the gents to judge how far away I was – just in case of an emergency. I wasn't going to risk it. While the others necked their rum in one, I poured the spirit into my plastic pint glass and downed the rest of my beer.
I wasn't sick but I don't think it helped me that night.

Feeling very jolly, we left the pub and headed to the ground. Inside, we went our separate ways. I sat with Natalie and the others were a couple of blocks along from us. The first half was fairly dull and I spent most of it explaining what was happening to my female friend and football virgin. Midway through the half, QPR got a soft penalty and led 1-0 at the break.

At half time, after which, Natalie and I moved to sit with the others, Warnock brought on Freddy Sears, who *still* hadn't scored for us. Following the Bristol debacle, we'd given him a generous amount of support but we'd long since given up on him. Warnock had claimed that he was still battling to come to terms with the non-goal.
"If he's that weak mentally, he ain't going to make it!" professed Dan in his

assured and experienced manner, and I've got to say, I agreed with him.

Having said that, it was probably Sears' best performance for us. He was excellent that night and won us a penalty which was scored by, you guessed it, Darren Ambrose. I spent a large amount of the second half trying to get Natalie to pose for a picture in a Palace scarf. She had been won over by the football experience but I think she was less convinced about Crystal Palace. For the third match in a row, it ended one all with Darren Ambrose scoring our goal.

Not for the first time against QPR, Speroni was unbelievable between the posts. After the game, Warnock insisted *"Julian Speroni is the best keeper in this division by a mile and I don't see anyone better in the Premier League."* Nobody who was there that night, whether they were QPR, Palace or Natalie, could disagree with our manager.

After the match, we headed back to Clapham Junction to go for one last drink at the Falcon. Natalie and I had lost the others in the crowd leaving the stadium so we made our own way back. The train back was packed full of Palace fans and Natalie learnt some new songs, not all of them polite. Just as many fathers do to their kids at football, I asked her not to repeat them to her parents. I didnt want to get into trouble.

As we walked down the steps off the platform at Clapham Junction, the drunken chanting from behind us suddenly changed from abuse about Brighton. *"There's only one James Howland, one James How-land!"* A true, and in many people's opinion, gracious fact. Well, probably not true – a quick google search suggests that there's quite a few of us. However, there was only one James Howland walking down the steps from Platform 1 at Clapham Junction and that *was* me. Of which, there really is only one, thankfully.

The elderly chap next to me on the staircase asked *"Who are they singing about?"* with a puzzled look on his wrinkled face. *"Errrm, that would be me I think,"* I replied, slightly embarrassed. He seemed quite content with my answer, as if it was a common occurrence at London stations for a group of lads to be singing about the bloke next to you. Satisfied, he continued with his onward journey.

In the Falcon, I negotiated the purchase of Colin's programme. I hadn't seen any being sold on the way to the ground and wanted one for my collection. Another sad hobby of mine that clutters up a sizeable amount of room in my mother's house. The transaction was simple. Supply and demand. We both had what the other one wanted. I wanted a programme and Colin wanted cash to buy a pasty. Everyone was happy.

Well I was, until I got onto the train with Dan and Natalie and realised that I'd left the damn thing in the pub. Idiocy doesn't do it justice. No wonder I never had any bloody money. Once on the train, I was in full wind up mood. We were in high spirits (rum to be precise), Natalie had enjoyed the game and we'd all had a lot to drink. I spent the majority of the journey winding her up about coming from Feltham and the low-lifes that lived in the area.

Now, when I've had an excessive amount of alcohol, the world outside my bubble of who I'm with, tends to not exist. Dan had given me plenty of anxious, warning looks on the train which had gone completely over my head. He'd seen people looking over at me in disgust and could see where the situation was potentially heading. Luckily, I was already safely off the train at Twickenham when the 'low-lifes' got off at Feltham. I guess if they really were as low as I was telling Natalie they were, the evening could have ended very differently.

After leaving Dan and Natalie on the train (I managed to get off without being trapped in the door this time), I decided to go into the Twickenham Weatherspoons to make the most of the Ale festival. I'd been cycling past (which was clearly a brilliant idea after an evening of drinking) and remembered that a couple of friends had said they would be in there. I locked up my bike outside the pub and went in to join them. I ordered myself a pint of a Yorkshire Light Ale and I really enjoyed it.

The second pint I had was called 'The Iron Lady' and the beer's picture was of Margaret Thatcher herself. I remember chatting to my friends about her and whether she was good for the country. Like most drunk people in the country, who are propping up a Wetherspoons bar, we were far too ill-informed to have a reasonable argument either way really. However, like most drunk people in the country, who are propping up a Wetherspoons bar, we had a long and passionate debate anyway.

What we could agree on, was that it was unlikely to be selling well in the Liverpool 'spoons. Or anywhere that had ever had a coal mine. Still, at least the Iron Lady wasn't in a plastic 'glass'. That might have affected the taste she left behind.

The match had reaffirmed what I loved about football. In truth, the game had been unremarkable but the socialising was top notch. Football had once again brought together people who would never usually mix and a good time had been had by all. Even Natalie. My work was done.

Talking of Natalie, I'd kept my promise to her Dad. I mean, yes, I'd got her drunk with a load of blokes. And ok, I had let her witness a huge amount of aggression and bad language at the match (not all from me). And technically, yes, I had nearly started a brawl on the train home before leaving her alone on it with a guy more than twice her age.

But *other* than that, I'd completely looked after her. She was fine, wasn't she? I did send her a text the next day, just to make sure.

Chapter Twenty-two – **Football Friends**

Saturday 7th November 2009, Crystal Palace vs Middlesbrough, Selhurst Park.

Crystal Palace: Julian Speroni, Clint Hill, Shaun Derry, Jose Fonte, Darren Ambrose, Neil Danns (Nick Carle, 81), Freddie Sears (Alassane N'Diaye, 90), Alan Lee, Danny Butterfield, Johnny Ertl, Claude Davis
Subs Not Used: Nathaniel Clyne, Stern John, Victor Moses, Sean Scannell, Kieran Djilali,

Middlesbrough: Brad Jones, Justin Hoyte (Julio Arca), 69), Leroy Lita (Johnathan Franks, 78), Sean St. Ledger, Gary O'Neil, Adam Johnson, Marcus Bent, Jonathan Grounds, Rhys Williams, David Wheater, Isaiah Osbourne.
Subs Not Used: Mark Yeates, Marvin Emnes, Danny Coyne, Joe Bennett, Tony McMahon

After a fantastic baguette from the butchers opposite my house, I headed to the Railway Club for one thirty to meet the others. The three consecutive draws had left Palace in thirteenth place; seven points above the drop zone, five away from the play offs. The football was as average and mediocre as you could imagine. Palace, as most fans believe of their team, don't generally do mid-table but we'd been there the year before and were heading there again.

Of course, there were some success stories; Ambrose had been a revelation, N'Diaye had been a surprise performer in midfield, and Speroni was outstanding as always but overall, mid-table was what we had expected and mid-table was what we were getting. Warnock teams don't tend to under achieve.

However, there had been plenty of disappointments too and we couldn't blame them all on Rob Shoebridge. Neither Alan Lee nor Stern John, who I'd had such high hopes for at the start of the season, looked like scoring any goals. Never ideal for a centre forward. Freddy Sears had been another pre-season flop and was yet to score (well, yet to score when the referee was looking). The hopeless Calvin Andrew was our final option up front. The less said about him the better. Palace seemed to specialise in non-scoring strikers.

Goalless Stern John had become a hate figure in many fans eyes as he appeared lazy. His casual style was shown up even more by the incredible work rate of the rest of the team. Warnock had them running through brick walls for the club. He'd filled the squad with players like Matt Lawrence, Clint Hill, Shaun Derry, Paddy McCarthy, Jonny Ertl and Claude Davis, who were all tough characters. None of them were the most gifted players but boy, would they put their body on the line and fight for the cause. I doubt there has ever been a more committed Palace side. Fans can forgive players for a lack of ability, which is just as well because Palace have had plenty of limited players over the years, but what fans won't forgive is a perceived lack of effort.

Newly relegated Middlesbrough had started the season well and were only outside of the play off positions on goal difference. They had some quality players, especially Adam Johnson who had torn us apart while playing for Watford the season before. They'd also signed former Palace striker, Marcus

Bent, in the week leading up to the game. As any football fan will testify, it's an unwritten rule that former players will *always* score against you. Bastards.

Although we had only lost one game in the previous nine, we weren't in a particularly positive mood in the pub. Which is strange looking back. I guess we preferred to focus on the fact that we hadn't won in five. Football fans tend to feel a lot more comfortable when they're in their default mode of miserable. Great expectations bring great disappointment. The first harsh lesson learnt while supporting a mediocre football team such as Palace. I wonder if the three-day old baby from the Peterborough game has learnt that yet.

Of course, it might have been that I simply hadn't drunk enough to build up any pre-match bravado and wipe that lesson from my brain. At quarter to three we drank up, emptied our bladders and headed to the ground. 'Boro started well and missed a few early chances. Marcus Bent was the main offender. Maybe there is a reason that the former players' rule has never been written down and formalised after all? Throughout the first half, Adam Johnson destroyed our full back, Danny Butterfield, beating him time and time again.

The Palace right back was a real fan's favourite. When he'd first arrived at the club in 2002, Danny had been outstanding and instantly nailed down a first team place. He was a reliable defender, a great crosser and even popped up with the odd goal. Over his six years at the club, he'd lost his form and inevitably his place. First to Emmerson Boyce and now to Nathaniel Clyne.

However, Butterfield offered a lot more to Palace than simply being a player. Teammates would regularly pick him out as one of the jokers in the squad who was vital in keeping up morale within the camp. More importantly than that, he seemed to genuinely love playing for Palace and care about the club. A combination that will win over any set of fans. Unfortunately, none of that helped him out on that afternoon. Johnson was simply too good for him. Eventually, 'Butts' stopped him. Well, kicked him. He got a yellow card for his troubles.

In the second half, Palace began to come into the match. Butterfield upped his game and got to grips with Middlesbrough's star winger, Shaun Derry and Jonny Ertl began to win the midfield battle and Palace started to offer a bit more of a threat going forward.

Just after the hour mark, we took the lead against the run of play. No prizes for guessing who scored it. Ambrose. Like the Derby game, it was a calm finish, where he took his time to slot it past the goalkeeper from close range. It is staggering to think that Charlton had released him on a free transfer the previous summer. He now had ten goals in twenty games. Including our only goal in each of our last four consecutive matches. An impressive return for any player, let alone a midfielder.

With Speroni once again putting on a brilliant performance under late pressure from 'Boro, Palace held out for the rest of the match. The 1-0 win was greeted by a huge eruption of joy and relief from all four sides of the ground. Well, except the small Middlesbrough following in one corner. It would be a long, long trip back to the North East for them.

Filled with pride, Dan, Jonathan, Kev and I bounced out of the stadium, down the Holmesdale Road and back to the Railway Club. Palace were definitely now on a run of 'one loss in ten' rather than 'one win in six'. The joy of statistics is that they can tell you whatever you want them to and at that moment, it suited us for them to say 'Palace are amazing.'

We had lost our default factory settings and our mood was far from miserable for the evening. The miserable and pessimistic frame of mind would stay clear of us until at least the next morning when we woke up with dry throats and pounding heads. Made even worse for me as Phill had put me on a twelve hour shift, starting at 9AM the next day. Git. Still, the evening after a win isn't a time for worries like that. The evening after a win is an evening for celebration. And beer.

Once we had a beer in our hand, we began to crowd around my programme to look at the table and work out what the permutations of the day's results were. As we were stuck in mid-table, any win would have us calculating how many points off the play offs we were, but any defeats would see us totting up how far clear of the dreaded drop zone we were. It was the early days of Smart Phones and none of us had one to get an up-to-date table.

Smart phones have been revolutionary in every walk of life. It's simply incomprehensible to imagine living without one nowadays. Football fans used to take wirelesses to matches to try and keep up to date with other scores from around the country. This led to an enormous amount of wires getting crossed as people desperately tried to listen to a dodgy signal in a loud crowd. I don't know how the wires got crossed as I thought that was the point of the small radios. Wireless. I guess people were simply making up rumours to confuse others for a laugh.

In the pub, after much debate, we decided that we were either four or five points off the play offs and either eight or nine or seven points clear of relegation. It depended on who'd heard the scores correctly in the ground. Oh, if only we'd known of the instant information at our finger tips that we'd have had access to with a smart phone. Never mind smart, they should be called Genius Phones.

The four of us drank happily for a couple of hours. Eventually, Dan decided it was time to return home to see his wife. Scunthorpe had lost 4-1 that day and it would not have been a good idea to risk crossing her. We finished our drinks and left Kev to get his bus home. Jonathan, Dan and I got the train to Clapham Junction, where we would head our separate ways. As we stepped off the train at the UK's busiest station, I turned to Dan, *"One more?"*
He looked at his watch, smiled and texted his wife.

We went to the Falcon and were pleasantly surprised to discover that they had a beer festival on. Beer festivals are a unique experience. As you would expect, they are packed with beer, stale smells and men with beards. I loved them. At the time, I regularly attended them with mates to sample different breweries' concoctions. Often, you wouldn't be able to find the majority of beers available at the festival in your average pub. Almost without fail, Robin, Barlow and I were the youngest there. We could only have been more out of place if we were women.

There are three types of people who attend beer festivals. The first is the lovely old man, with a beard, who has been allowed out by his loving wife to sample two or three halves. The second is the beer geek. They usually don a beard and have a clip board and pen to mark the beers. They can sample different brews for hours and never get drunk. The third is a piss head. Although not compulsory, they often have a beard and are there to simply get lashed up. The piss head is often disappointed that they can't find Fosters so they look for the 9% stout (*loopy-juice*) so that they can get hammered on it in the shortest time possible.

I would usually put myself down as a 'trainee geek'. I couldn't drink as much as them, but I had been known to take a pencil along to take notes on the different pints. Well, half pints. I would always drink in halves at festivals so that I could try a wider range. Unfortunately, turning up after a Palace victory meant that I was more in the third category that evening. The Piss Head.

I led the others to the side bar that was selling the festival beers. Enthusiastically, I put down a deposit on a 'festival glass' and asked for a beer with a ridiculous sounding name that I had never heard of before. Dan and Jonathan looked at each other, considered the complications of getting a rare ale and decided that they couldn't be arsed with all the fuss.
"Two pints of Fosters please," they asked at the regular bar.

I joined them with my ale and Jonathan gave us both a strange look. He slowly rose his large frame from the stool that he was perched on, squinting and pushing his glasses back up his nose towards his eyes, leaving his nearly full pint at the bar, and said *"Don't tell anyone I came here."*
He then made a hurried exit. Dan and I looked at each other and burst out laughing. It was bizarre – even stranger than Palace's Argentine signings under Mark Goldberg.

So many questions. So few answers. A bit like the Palace Argies, where had he gone? He wasn't married. He had no responsibility to anyone. Why couldn't we tell anyone? He lived with his parents but he was 27. Surely he hadn't been given a curfew. Was he banned from the Battersea area? Was he actually a secret spy and had been spotted by someone from the Russian mafia? Why the rush? It was unlike any Palace fan to leave a pint. 'Win or lose, we're on the booze' was the motto. In the end, we decided that there was no rhyme or reason to it. He was simply odd.

After I returned my pint glass to retrieve my deposit, we headed home. We were still laughing about Jonathan and overjoyed with the result when we were on the platform. I'd known Dan for a couple of years at this point but I still wasn't sure that we were friends or if we simply went to football together. We were twenty years apart in age. Something that his son found hilarious.

Without football, we wouldn't have known each other. Let alone be friends. There would simply have been no reason for us to meet. However, we spent a lot of Saturdays together drinking. I looked at him on the platform and realised that it wasn't simply a case of both being Palace and that being enough, it was more than that. I realised that he was a genuine friend. The common ground of supporting Palace had brought us together and over time, we'd gone from football mates to true friends. Once again, football had enriched my life.

A life that needed enriching as the idea of going home wasn't a good one. Darrell was entirely refusing to talk to me – he seemed to be going through a bit of a crisis. He was skipping lectures and having secretive relationships with some of our friends. However, despite not uttering a word to his flatmate in months, he still cowardly refused to discuss the reasons or any issues that he had with me. I was confused and hurt. The others weren't much better. While Matt kept things civil, it was clear that he had some sort of problem with me too. I'd never been close to Adam so we maintained the easy, light-hearted companionship that we'd always shared, which suited us both. Dave was the only one who gave me any kind of friendship. On the whole, the flat was a lonely place. Luckily, I had enough of a life outside it that I was barely there.

From Clapham Junction, keen not to head home, I went to meet Chris and Jak, two of my closest friends who I had also got to know and bonded with through football. We often said between the three of us that it's unlikely we would have taken such an instant interest in each other if we'd been typical armchair, Manchester United-type fans. We all understood the lower leagues and what going to football was really about. The pair of them were supposed to have been to an FA Cup game in Gateshead that day with Brentford.

Typically, the lovely people in charge of the TV companies had given no consideration to the fans attending the match. The real fans. Knowing that the game might be moved, Chris and Jak waited for confirmation of the date before buying train tickets. The game had indeed been moved to the Sunday. Not a problem. They booked up. At a later date it was then moved back to the Saturday. They couldn't afford to shell out for the second time and missed out on the game. A stadium and a town that they're unlikely to get another opportunity to visit with football.

At their house, we played *PES* on the *Playstation*, got a Chinese takeaway and I drank some Asda Smart Price cider. I'd gone from real ale to real crap. My hosts looked at me in embarrassment. The financial drain of going to football had hit me hard. There weren't many people who I could meet up with after a day of drinking at the football but I knew Chris and Jak wouldn't mind. They were true football fans of a crap team too and completely understood the experience. As well as the state that it could leave you in.

Although, I don't think they've ever ended up drinking Smart Price Cider – that was more a reflection on my wallet than the football that I'd watched. Having said that, with Palace's fragile finances, maybe the club would have to make some cut-backs on the alcohol provided for match-day hospitality packages.

The next morning, my alarm would wake me up far earlier than I was ready to leave my slumber. Sure enough, I had a dry throat and a pounding head. Luckily, I had some Paracetamol too as I had a long shift ahead of me. Phill always did have a crap sense of humour – although the torturous shift was made easier by watching non-league Northwich Victoria knock Charlton out of the FA Cup. Who the **** is laughing now?

Other than painkillers, I also had a couple of other things to get me through the long day ahead. Firstly, I was still on a high from the game. A good result can keep me smiling for days. Usually until the next game brings me crashing back down anyway. Secondly, I'd left the game content that football had brought me an even better result than beating Middlesbrough. Friends. It takes a certain type of person to support a crap football team. I was confident that watching Palace would lead me to more like-minded individuals and inevitably, more friends.

Chapter Twenty-three – **Turn left at the First Tramp then Right at the Second.**

Saturday 21st November 2009, Coventry City vs Crystal Palace, The Ricoh Arena.

Crystal Palace: Julian Speroni, Clint Hill, Shaun Derry, Jose Fonte, Darren Ambrose, Neil Danns (Alassane N'Diaye, 90), Freddy Sears (Stern John, 70), Alan Lee (Calvin Andrew, 70), Danny Buttefield, Johnny Ertl, Claude Davis.
Subs Not Used: Nathaniel Clyne, Patrick McCarthy, Nicky Carle, Victor Moses.

Coventry City: Westwood, Wright, Bell, Best, Clinton Morrison (Madine, 90), van Aanholt, Gunnarsson, Cork, McIndoe, Barnett, Wood.
Subs Not Used: Konstantopoulos, McPake, Eastwood, Cranie, Cain, Grandison.

I'd spent the days leading up to the Coventry game in Plymouth with Rob, who is one of my best friends from secondary school and was at university in the navy town. I'd gone down with Robin, who was now back from his European adventure, and his girlfriend, Lindsey. We'd spent most of the time in a pub or a club, and a good time had been had by all.

One of the highlights of the trip was visiting Plymouth Gin Factory. I was delighted to discover that their Sloe Gin is nearly as delicious as my father's. Drinking gin is supposed to make you depressed but I'd argue that watching Palace lose is a far more toxic mood killer. In fact, drinking excessive amounts of gin after a defeat has been known to numb the pain and raise my mood. Crystal Palace Football Club, turning beliefs upside down.

In Plymouth, the Friday-night drinking had continued until four in the morning on Saturday and I needed to catch a 7:30 train from Plymouth to Reading, where I would change trains and head to Coventry. A frankly horrendous experience. The start of the journey should have been charming as the train weaves in and out of the cliffs of the Devon coastline. It is my favourite stretch of rail in the country but unfortunately, I spent it with my head on the table and my eyes shut, while desperately trying not to vomit.

I certainly had to question the challenge. This was not an enjoyable way to spend a weekend. Something had to give. Either I had to make sacrifices about what I did around the games or I had to sacrifice the dream of doing every match. I really wasn't keen on either choice. What was the point of going to football if it was at the expense of socialising with close friends? Wasn't that the whole point of football? I was out looking for new friends which meant I wasn't around on Saturdays to see the bloody good ones that I already had. In the past, I'd missed a shocking amount of friends' birthdays and ventures out because I'd been away following Palace. Trying to do both on that weekend had made for a very uncomfortable experience.

It wasn't until I got to Reading, a whole three hours away, that I began to feel like something resembling a human being again. At the station, I got some breakfast. Bacon can solve most of the world's problems. I did consider getting a 'hair of the dog' but the mere idea of it made my stomach swirl. Drinking to save yourself from a hangover is very effective but it can't be a good idea, right? To be honest, I think it would be the start of a slope towards the dangerous world of alcoholism.

I classed myself as a binge drinker with a bad habit. However, I also had confidence in myself that I could stop when I needed to. While at university, I intended to enjoy drinking copious amounts of booze on a regular basis in the name of fun. I knew full well that this care-free stage of my life would not last forever and I had no intention of drinking in such volumes once I started teaching the following year.

After some bacon, sausage and beans *(no eggs, I don't like eggs. I've tried but we can't get along. It's about the only food that I don't eat but I think they're disgusting. A bit like Shefki Kuqi, I can see the appeal and what they offer but I just don't like them)*, I boarded my train to Coventry. It really did feel like I was being sent there as a punishment.

On the crowded train, a young lady sat next to me. We introduced ourselves to each other in the awkward way that people do when they are set to be squashed together on a long journey. It's not that you have any interest in them or they have any interest in you but it just seems the polite thing to do. She studied at Reading University but grew up in Coventry so she was going to visit her parents for the weekend. I assume she needed some washing done or had run out of food.

It turned out that she was a fashion student. I told her that I was on my way to the football. Her face sank. I don't think that she had a particularly high opinion of football fans and certainly wasn't relishing being sat next to one for the next couple of hours. I was impressed that despite her obvious disapproval of my absurd journey, she continued to engage me in conversation. I certainly got a more positive reaction from her when I started to discuss teaching.

We also shared an interest in Reading nights out. As I'd grown up in Berkshire, I knew her university town really well. Between us, we listed every pub, bar and club in Reading town centre before discussing why we didn't like each one. Although she did admit that it was better than being in Coventry. Most people are very defensive and proud over their home town, but I have never heard anyone, anywhere, stand up for Coventry.

As we approached Didcot, she said something that totally flabbergasted me.
"I design and make nearly all of my own clothes."
I'd noticed the she was wearing a pretty quirky jumper on top of an equally outlandish dress but I'd simply put that down to her being a fashion student. Fashion was (and still is) a mystery to me. A night out in Shoreditch will usually result in me looking around at groups of trendy people and trying to decide if they are fashionable or actually in fancy dress. I'm never sure.

Anyway, I wasn't sure if she was winding me up. I had no idea how possible her claim was and it did seem like a big task to make your own clothes. I'm not sure that I'd have had the time to do it while at university and I certainly didn't have the know-how. I did wonder where it stopped. Were her undergarments home made too? I didn't ask. It seemed a little forward. I was simply the football thug who she'd happened to end up next to on the train.

She showed me some of the stitching that she'd done and the odd subtle mistake. I guess my puzzled, tired and hungover face told her that while I was listening keenly, I still wasn't sure whether I believed her or not. She then ended any doubt.

She took out her highly impressive portfolio of designs from her bag. I had a flick through. I didn't have a clue whether what I was looking at was fashionable or not but it looked flippin' good to me. Especially, when she showed me the original design of the jumper that she was currently wearing. As I took in her designs, she explained the statement that each outfit was supposed to make. I dared not ask what statement I was making in dirty jeans and a football shirt. Scruffy Yob, I suspect.

She told me that she dreamed of designing and making her own label. Practising by making her own clothes would leave her in the best position possible to make that dream a reality. While the practise was helpful, the main reason that she did it was simply out of love for design and fashion. I guess that making your own clothes should put an end to every woman's worst nightmare; turning up to a party where someone else is wearing the exact same dress as you.

By the time we went through Banbury, she was asking me about the football and my predictions for the match. I'd converted another. Once we'd established where Crystal Palace actually was, she wanted to know, 'Why Crystal Palace when you come from Berkshire?'

I told her that it was the family heirloom and it was simply my duty to look after and cherish the love of Crystal Palace Football Club before passing it on to my children and them to my children's children. Which, roughly translated from bullshit to English, reads 'My Dad happened to be from Bromley and I, being a loving son, copied him and now I'm addicted to following the club.' Oddly, she seemed to identify more with the first explanation than the truth.

Yet again, travelling to football had got me talking to somebody who I had very little in common with and would be unlikely to meet in normal circumstances. However, this time, it wasn't even the Palace bond that we shared. Our interests were as different as they could possibly be. David Beckham and David Ginola were just about the only vague links that I could think of between football and fashion. But what was the same, was our passion for something. We'd both taken time to hear about the other's obsession.

It really doesn't matter what your passion is but what is important, is to have one. Mine was football. Hers was fashion. We were both able to learn from each other. She'd expected a football fan to be a yob. I'd expected a fashion expert to be a snob. Hopefully, her stereotype had been challenged as much as mine had. We'd both seen that sparkle in each other's eyes and engaged in that.

I think we had anyway. She might just have wanted someone, well anyone, to talk to about something, well anything. Even if that meant football. Either way, my alcohol-abused body felt a lot better after chatting to her. It had been a much healthier and more productive method of curing my hangover than getting a new pint and starting again.

I was joined on the train at Leamington Spa by my friend David. When he got on, my new fashion friend did offer her seat to him but he declined after I gave him a look. Frankly, she was a lot better looking than he is. David was studying chemistry at Warwick University. The flip side of travelling around the country was that although I didn't see friends from home as much as I would have liked to, I did get to see others who were based elsewhere. David is my oldest friend. I've known him since I was born but our friendship hasn't always been as natural as it is now.

He is someone who it is important that I stay in touch with because we do get on well and he is incredibly kind-hearted. He is probably the most reliable and fair person I know. As a sulky teenager, these aren't always traits that are valued as much as they should be. Therefore I often neglected him in favour of others. However, by the time that I'd left school, I'd realised what a good friend he was to me and we're still very close now.

I'll be completely honest. Without the football excuse, I doubt I would have been to Warwick to visit David during our three university years. However, football was an excuse. I could easily have just gone to the games and not seen him but whenever Palace were in the area, I would invite him along. Sometimes I would go up a night early to stay with him.

He is a typical Liverpool 'supporter'. He's never been to Anfield and is unlikely to ever go. However, he does have real soft spots for his Dad's team, Bournemouth, and for Crystal Palace after knowing me for so long. Whenever he had the chance, he would jump at it to come and cheer on the Palace with me.

I had a really good catch up with David. He told me about spending fifty hours a week in a lab. I told him about my teaching lectures. Prancing about with primary school equipment sounded a lot less taxing and a lot more fun than his degree did if I'm being honest.

I also filled him in on Palace's season so far and my challenge. He hadn't been since seeing us lose 1-0 at Birmingham City to a last minute Kevin Phillips goal the year before. Other than that, he'd been something of a good luck charm, witnessing a 2-0 win at Forest and a remarkable 3-0 at Wolves. One of our many, usually non-scoring centre forwards, Jamie Scowcroft, had scored a thirty yard volley in the latter.

Since being in the pub after the Middlesbrough game, I'd had a chance to study the table. I now had no doubts as to our definite position in the league so I was able to let him know. We were in thirteenth place. Five points away from the play offs and eight clear of relegation.

We finally arrived in Coventry over five hours after I'd left Plymouth with a somersaulting stomach and a hurting head. It takes just 59 minutes to go from Euston to Coventry. I can't help but feel I could have planned the trip a bit better.

My train journey had been as different from the coach travel as possible. I'd certainly never met a fashion designer on an official club coach. Also, neither she nor David had moaned about anything. Especially not Julian Gray. Maybe she would have done if she'd seen him get sent off in Sunderland. Although I doubted the likelihood of her ever witnessing either Sunderland or Julian Gray, or getting angry about it even if she did.

I'd also been glad that there were toilets on the train because it was touch and go in Devon as to whether I would need to run to them or not.

Like Preston, Coventry is a dire place that I had vowed to never return to. It had been bombed in the war and the resulting re-build was grey, pragmatic and depressing. It reminded me of a big Bracknell and anyone who's ever been to Bracknell will realise that is certainly not a compliment. Dull buildings, lots of roundabouts, lifeless streets and very little in the way of a soul. On this November afternoon, the weather was dreary, like the buildings. I can't help but feel that they'd have been better off leaving it in its flattened post war state. If only my new found designer friend had been born in the 1950s. I'm sure she could have planned a much more attractive looking home town for herself.

I wouldn't mind Coventry's ugliness if it could keep itself to itself. However, on the beautiful banks of the River Cam in Cambridge there are many outstanding buildings. Unfortunately, there is one that sticks out like a saw thumb. The Erasmus Building. A concrete, grey monstrosity. A thorn amongst the roses. Unsurprisingly, it was designed in the post-war 1950s by the same architect who had designed Coventry Cathedral. Due to there being very little architecture from this era as money was so tight, it is now a Grade Two listed building and can't be knocked down. It's a small bit of Coventry that ruins the picturesque banks of the river flowing through the pretty town.

Coventry is also the only place in the country where I have ever been given directions based on the tramps. Amazingly, the directions were spot on and I'd been able to find the pub (and the tramps) to meet my mates with relative ease. And no, my mates weren't the tramps. The phrase 'send them to Coventry' is well and truly justified.

One person who had been 'sent to Coventry' was Palace legend, Clinton Morrison. If Palace were my first love, then Clinton was my second. Aged 7, I'd been right behind the goal at the Holmesdale Road end as he scored the winning strike on his professional football debut against Sheffield Wednesday in the final game of the doomed 1997/98 season. As I'd grown up, so had my hero. He scored over one hundred goals for us over two spells. I loved Warnock and he was definitely the best man for the job but he hadn't rated our Clinton. Despite finishing as our top scorer in his final two seasons for the club, Warnock let him go. No one had scored goals consistently for Palace since then.

I, and Morrison, were still bitter about this as he was just four goals behind Ian Wright's post-war goal scoring record for the club. A record that I have one hundred percent confidence he would have broken if he'd been able to stay for another year. In my mind, it was not sentiment that made me want him to stay, it was the fact that I genuinely believed he had a lot to offer the club. Releasing my hero was the one decision of Warnock's that I couldn't agree with.

We walked past the boarded up pubs (as well as the tramps that didn't seem to have moved since my previous visit) and I recalled the stories of the soulless town centre to David. In four visits, no one had been able to recommend me a decent pub. He wasn't surprised and was less than complimentary about the town's nightlife, which he had experienced during his time in the Midlands. He explained how no-one from the university chose to live there, opting for the nearby Leamington Spa instead.

When we did enter the town centre, we came across a new low. Outside a charity shop, there was a whole family cuddled up on a battered and torn sofa, watching the TV screen in the window of the second hand shop next door. Both parents were nursing a can of Stella, while the kids were sharing a bottle of coke. Broken Britain at its worst. I felt sorry for the British Heart Foundation. Surely this shop couldn't be raising any money for a great cause with such clientele outside.

As we wondered through the town, we both commented that we saw more Manchester United shirts than Coventry City ones. We briefly considered getting a pint in the Wetherspoons but David still didn't have a match ticket and I was still feeling a bit fragile so we passed on the chance. We had plenty of time before kick off so rather than jump in a cab, we headed to the local bus station. There, we found more morbid souls who had nothing positive to say about the town that they inhabited or its football team.

Eventually, the bus to take us to the ground arrived at the badly sign-posted station. Despite growing up in a village with no buses and only one train every half an hour, it's amazing how quickly you get used to London transport. The arrogance of living in London makes the irregular services elsewhere incredibly frustrating.

The stadium is just as soulless as the town. I'd been to Highfield Road, their previous ground, for the final game of their penultimate season in their traditional home. It was a classic stadium, tightly surrounded by rows of terraced houses and as it wasn't quite big enough for the club, it was packed full with a vocal crowd every week. The stands were on top of the pitch, home fans loved going there and it felt like a vital part of the community.

The Ricoh Arena, their home since 2005, was just like any other new stadium. Round, soulless and in the middle of nowhere. While the stadium is right out of the city, it shouldn't have taken nearly an hour to get there. The painfully slow bus seemed to cover every grim and lifeless back street in town as light drizzle started to run down it's scratched and graffiticovered windows. It picked up the grand total of about six people before we finally arrived at the half empty ground at 2:45.

The Ricoh was anything but embraced by the community. It was more like a motorway service station than a local heritage. It is no wonder that children were choosing to follow one of the glory teams on television rather than attending matches at their local club with their Dad. Who would want to watch football there?

The ground was as drab as the town centre and so is Coventry's football. They haven't finished in the top six of any division since 1970. In each of my previous visits, the home crowd had seemed withdrawn and beaten before a ball had even been kicked. Palace had been to the Ricoh four times and won 4-1, 4-2, 2-0 and 2-0. The Coventry crowd's apathetic feelings towards their newish home, weary town and average football made it one of the least intimidating grounds to visit. I had no doubts that played a large part in our outstanding record there. It was a town, and team, in depression.

We had a mad rush to buy David a ticket and get into the ground before kickoff. Inside, there was no time for a pint so for the second time in the season, I'd be watching Palace sober. A terrifying thought. As we left the concourse, I bumped into Brian. Once again, he'd got us seats together. Within seconds, he'd started moaning about the usual subjects. I couldn't face it. I knew Brian and I knew that he meant well but it wasn't fair to make David sit through the game listening to the old man's dreary drones. I grabbed David and we slipped off, pretending that we'd lost him in the crowds.

The game was played on an awful pitch, in terrible conditions, between two poor teams, with a referee who felt the need to blow up for everything. It had absolutely no flow to it. The atmosphere was as damp as the weather. Midway through the terrible first half, Palace scored. True to the match, it was as scrappy a goal as you will see. The ball bounced about in the penalty area and fell kindly to Freddy Sears. As he had done all season, he mucked it up, skewing his weak shot wide.

Thankfully, it fell kindly to Darren Ambrose to tap it in. Goal number eleven for the season and the fifth game in a row that he'd scored. The Palace fans at the far end of the ground went nuts after checking the linesman hadn't raised his flag. An action that was copied by the goal scorer, which suggested that it had been a close call. The regular chant of 'We always win at the Ricoh!' echoed around the half-empty, damp ground.

Soon after, Palace had a decent penalty shout when Ambrose was bundled over. The Palace players, fans and manager rose as one to claim our prize but the referee waved our appeals away. As always, the referee had proved to be a wanker, who hated all things Crystal Palace. I checked my program to see if it was Mr Shoebridge. Unfortunately, I couldn't blame him this time. Not entirely anyway. He'd probably had a pre-match word with this official.

Half time came and went (still without a beer) before Leon Best equalised just two minutes after the re-start. I sat in silence; hungover, fed up and wishing that I was anywhere else in the world but in a ground that could hardly muster a cheer for a home team's goal. A ground where Palace were now looking flat and unlikely to pick up a win in the heavy rain. Where had my challenge taken me? Not to a place that I wanted to go. That's for sure.

Late on, Clinton Morrison was fouled near the touchline. Believing he'd dived, Warnock shouted over towards my former hero. Once up, Clinton hobbled over to Warnock to explain exactly what he thought of him. He was waving his arms about dramatically and shouting in our manager's face. Love him or hate him, Clinton always wore his heart on his sleeve. This huge overreaction reiterated to me how gutted Morrison was to have left Palace. He certainly blamed Warnock.

Freddy Sears and Alan Lee were replaced with Calvin Andrew and Stern John. None of them looked like scoring. It was lucky that Ambrose was coming up with the goods because our four strikers had two goals between them all season. Well, three, but Rob Shoebridge hadn't been looking for one of them. Calling them useless was being very kind. Morrison had managed five goals for Coventry already that season.

Palace huffed and puffed but couldn't find a winner. While it wasn't an awful result, it had been dreadful to watch. There had been very little quality and it had not been helped by the awful conditions that it had been played in.

The journey home was long. Not as long as my journey there but still long. Stupidly, I'd booked a return ticket to Reading. This meant that I had a longer distance on my original train returning south and yet again, I'd have to get the ever-so-slow train back to Twickenham from Reading, stopping at every small village in Berkshire. A train line that I'd been grateful for as I grew up in one of those villages but I was far from grateful for that evening – it was painful. Who needs to get off at Early? Or Winnersh Triangle? Or Virginia Water? Or Sunningdale? Ok, maybe Sunningdale can stay on the line as it is *my* hometown and had served me well in the past for Palace games, but as far as I was concerned, the rest could go.

As well as lengthening my journey, my travel choices meant that no Palace fans would be on my train home. After David got off at Leamington, I was alone. Further denting my depressive mood (maybe the gin had affected me after all?), my train to Reading was delayed so I sat on it; tired, bored and sober.

I thought about the challenge. Was it worth it? I'd had a brilliant time in Plymouth. I certainly wouldn't have changed going there. However, despite some positives, I couldn't say I'd really enjoyed the day out in Coventry. I'd felt crap from my hangover throughout, I'd travelled 450 odd miles to a crap town and the game had been, well, crap – like the weather. I love David and I love Palace but were they really worth all that effort? I wasn't sure.

Having booked three days off work to go to Plymouth, Phill had me coming back down to earth with a bump. I had another twelve hour shift the next day. Despite how I felt, it was just as well really. Three days of drinking and some incredibly overpriced train tickets had left a gaping hole in my wallet.

Chapter Twenty-four - **A Dark Cloud Arrives Over SE25**

Saturday 28th November 2009, Crystal Palace vs Watford, Selhurst Park.

Crystal Palace: Julian Speroni, Clint Hill, Shaun Derry, Jose Fonte, Darren Ambrose (Alassane N'Diaye, 90), Neil Danns, Victor Moses (Ryan Smith, 84), Alan Lee (Calvin Andrew, 76), Danny Butterfield, Johnny Ertl, Claude Davis
Subs Not Used: Nathaniel Clyne, Nick Carle, Freddie Sears, James Comley

Watford: Scott Loach, Adrian Mariappa, Henri Lansbury, Danny Graham, Heidar Helguson (Liam Henderson, 84), Lloyd Doyley, Jon Harley (Nathan Ellington, 61), Tom Cleverley, Craig Cathcart, John Eustace, Lee Hodson
Subs Not Used: Scott Severin, Richard Lee, Dale Bennett, Matt Sadler, Michael Bryan

I woke up early to do some university work before heading to the game. Needing to borrow a book, I'd gone into Darrell's room and was shocked to find that it had been emptied out. He'd briefly mentioned going to his girlfriend's house a few days earlier and I hadn't seen him since. Our relationship had become so strained that it wasn't unusual for me to go days without seeing or speaking to him. However, to find out that your flatmate has moved out without telling you was quite a shock. I later discovered that he'd dropped out of university too. When we'd first moved into the flat, I'd been closest to Darrell but for reasons unknown to me, he'd stopped talking to me since the summer. It is fair to say that I felt hurt, if a little relieved, that he'd gone. It sealed the end of our friendship but the reality was, living with him had been uncomfortable for months.

After completing some work, I headed to Selhurst. For once, I had a change in my Saturday routine. Rather than joining my usual group in the Railway Club, I met some other friends in The Thomas Farley, Thornton Heath. It wasn't even so that I wouldn't be tempted to let slip to the rest of the group about Jonathan's dark Falcon secret from the previous home match. Like Steve Bruce departing for Birmingham, we never did find out why he'd left in such a rush. No, the reason for deserting my usual companions was that by coincidence, a couple of my other friends were both coming to Selhurst for the first time that season.

Garry was attending his first home game of the campaign so he had arranged to meet Brian and I there for a drink. Traditionally, the three of us arrived at the three different stations so we didn't meet up at home games, but we picked Thornton Heath for a beer because that would be easiest for Brian, who found too much walking difficult.

I arrived in the pub early, just before 1 o'clock because I was going to meet another friend afterwards. The three of us drank Green King IPA and had a catch up. I told Garry that he'd pretty much witnessed the entire season in one match when he'd gone to Preston. 1-1, Ambrose scored. That really could define a lot of the games thus far.

Although he didn't say anything, I knew Brian wasn't happy with me. He felt very betrayed that I'd let him get me a ticket next to him and then not used it. My pretence that I'd lost him in the crowd hadn't fooled anyone. I explained to

Garry, who understood my reason – that I didn't want to put David through the endless in-match moaning.

I was happy to listen to Brian on a coach or before games but it was really ruining matches for me to have to put up with him while the action was going on. Apparently Brian had told Garry in no uncertain terms what he thought of me not sitting with him after he'd gone out of the way to get me a ticket. With hindsight, I should have been braver and simply told the old man that I didn't want to sit with him rather than always going along with his plans so I didn't upset him. Either way, Brian was never the same with me again.

After a couple of pints, I moved to the downstairs pool hall and met my friend Jim. He is about fifteen years my senior and I'd met him at a pre-season friendly in Stevenage a few years previously. We'd got talking as the only Palace fans who'd arrived an hour and a half before kickoff and I couldn't believe it when I found out that he'd travelled from Sunninghill. The next village along from my birthplace. We got on really well and have stayed friends ever since.

When I first met him, Jim was divorced. He'd mentioned his children so I'd asked him what age they were and how many he had.
"I've got three girls. They're eight," he'd replied.
It had taken me a few seconds to process what he'd said.

He had the triplets to stay every other weekend so he went to Palace in the intervening weekends. He'd driven me to quite a few away games and it had worked well for both of us. He got some company and I got free travel. However, he was another man who had found love away from Selhurst Park so attended games much less frequently. His new wife was now pregnant and he once again had more responsibilities than cheering on the Palace.

He was with his mate Del. I'd met him a few times and he was a nice enough guy. He went to games with his two daughters, who were sat at the side of the pool table, patiently sipping a glass of coke, waiting for their Dad to be ready to take them to the match. Whenever I saw them in the pub, they seemed bored. However, they had a love of Palace which allowed them to put up with their Dad's pre-match routine as they got to see the game afterwards.

We had a couple of pints before heading to the ground where I met up with my usual crew. Watford had started the season well and sat four points ahead of us; only outside the play offs on goal difference. Just like Middlesbrough, who we'd dispatched of a fortnight earlier.

The game started perfectly. Inside two minutes, Victor Moses, returning to the side, beat his man and fired across the goalkeeper to put us 1-0 up. Warnock had been reluctant to start the youngster who had been under constant speculation about a move to the Premiership. Many reports claimed that we were relying on his sale to keep the club afloat. However, playing ahead of the goalless Sears, the eighteen year old rewarded his manager with a goal.

We were still in shock that someone other than Ambrose had scored when it happened again. Danny Butterfield put in a deep cross that was headed in at the back post by Alan Lee. Finally, after twelve games since the same man had scored away at Peterborough, one of our strikers had put the ball in the damn net. Hallelujah! Palace didn't really know how to react to going 2-0 up after just six minutes. The rest of the half was fairly flat and by half time, the crowd were getting a little bit edgy.

Just before the break, Lee undid all of his good work. The clumsy striker gave away a needless penalty. The psychological difference of going into the interval at 2-1 rather than 2-0 is enormous. Expertly, Speroni saved the penalty. Once again he showed why he is a club legend. Surely it had to be our day now.

The mood in the Red'n'Blue bar at half time was a little uneasy. When we're losing, we're pretty relaxed. We know how to deal with that. However, to be winning so comfortably brings a different issue. Expectation. Anything but a straight forward win would now be disappointing, especially after the let off of the penalty.

We downed our beers and agreed that we needed (at least) one more goal to be sure of the result. I had seen Palace throw away plenty of two goal leads but I'd only seen us f*** up a three goal margin once. That criminal game was against poxy Stockport in 2000 and has haunted me ever since.

The second half started almost as well as the first. What we hadn't taken into account at half time was that we hadn't had the part of the game yet where Darren Ambrose scored. It really was a case of 'when' not 'if', considering the form that he was in. Moses received the ball in our own half and ran forward with power and intent. Sensing the danger, Watford players dived in, trying to take him out and take a tactical booking for the team.

Fortunately for us, he was far too strong, quick and skilful for that. When he was on form, he was unplayable. The young winger took the ball all the way to their penalty area, before passing it to Ambrose, who was just outside the box. Our top scorer appeared to have missed the chance to shoot but off balance, and on the turn, he curled the ball perfectly into the top corner. 3-0. It was game over and there was elation in the stands.

Palace comfortably saw out the win which left us just two points off the playoff positions. The game had marked Warnock's one hundredth in charge of the club and what a way to commemorate the occasion. After the game, I headed to the Railway Club with Jonathan and Kev. We celebrated into the evening with pint after pint of Guinness. However, the players' celebrations were somewhat cut short. Simon Jordan informed them and the rest of the staff after the game that he wouldn't be able to pay them their wages for up to ten days.

It is easy to judge players as overpaid and not living in the real world. However, just like everybody else, they have mortgages to pay and families to feed. To put in such a brilliant performance before receiving news like that, must have been devastating. It is also important to remember the non-playing staff, who would be on much more realistic wages. Most of the players should have been savvy enough to put some money aside but financially, other employees and some of the younger players might not have been able to do that.

Warnock was the one to tell the press. As always, he spoke with authority and confidence, using his sense of humour to defuse any tension. He hadn't been paid either but that wasn't going to affect him. He was the ultimate professional.

The next day, I watched the FA Cup draw after my shift at the pub. I wanted us to get either a home draw, which would be easy for me to attend, or an away game to a club who I hadn't visited before. What we got, was neither. Sheffield Wednesday away. It was the most depressing draw possible. A long distance trip to a ground that I'd already been to three times before and would visit again on the final day of the season.

I looked up train tickets and the cheapest that I could get with the short notice was £65. I sighed. It looked like I would once again be back on the coach.

The financial situation became apparent about six weeks prior to us going into administration. A lot of the boys used to visit the treatment room before training for strappings for their ankles and I remember one morning Danny Butterfield coming out aghast. Nigel Cox, the head Physio, had informed all the boys requiring strappings for training that they needed to buy their own and that the club could only afford matchday strappings. We as players knew then that things weren't right.

Shaun Derry

Chapter Twenty-five – **It Never Rains but it Pours**

Saturday 5th December 2009, Crystal Palace vs Doncaster Rovers, Selhurst Park.

Crystal Palace: Julian Speroni, Clint Hill, Shaun Derry (Nick Carle, 80) , Jose Fonte, Darren Ambrose Neil Danns (Freddie Sears, 67), Victor Moses, Alan Lee (Calvin Andrew, 67), Danny Butterfield, Johnny Ertl, Claude Davis
Subs Not Used: Nathaniel Clyne, Sean Scannell, Ryan Smith, Alassane N'Diaye

Doncaster Rovers: Neil Sullivan, James O'Connor, Gareth Roberts, Billy Sharp, James Chambers, James Hayter, John Oster (Mark Wilson, 80), Martin Woods (Sam Hird, 86), Jason Shackell, Dean Sheils, James Coppinger (John Spicer, 84)
Subs Not Used: Lewis Guy, Ben Smith, Byron Webster, Simon Gillette

It had been a week and the players still hadn't been paid. There had been rumours in the previous month about late payments but nothing official from the club. Obviously, we'd known about the money troubles; there'd been the two transfer embargoes for failing to pay other clubs, as well as the rumours in *The Sun*. However, we'd done what any responsible people would do and buried our heads in the sand. Blindly believing that things couldn't possibly be that bad. They were.

Jordan was claiming that the failure to pay the players was nothing to worry about and simply a 'minor cash flow problem'. His arrogance was as shocking as my ignorance had been. As well as having a transfer embargo on the club and being unable to pay its employees, there were rumours of HMRC issuing the club with a winding up petition over unpaid bills. It was clearly far from a 'minor cash flow problem'.

Since his match winning performance against Watford, Warnock had taken every opportunity to big up Victor Moses. He told the press that the Premier League side who landed him would be very lucky indeed. Our experienced manager claimed Moses was the most gifted player that he'd ever worked with and he could go right to the very top. Every interview that he did, he talked about him leaving. Although it would be devastating for his team to lose such a talent, he knew the importance of selling him for the club. The press valued Moses at £5million, which could potentially save Crystal Palace Football Club from financial meltdown.

Looking back now, with a slightly more cynical viewpoint, I can't help but wonder if Warnock was simply fed up of the late pay packets. Moses' sale would raise the money needed to pay him and the rest of the squad for a few months. Since the players hadn't been paid, the papers had been packed full with rumours about which players would leave in January alongside Moses. It wasn't even questioned that he would be departing.

The press were reporting that the players had to be paid by 14th December (two weeks after the money was originally due) or they would be allowed to walk away from the club for free. There were rumours of the players having a meeting and agreeing not to exercise their right to do that but it was hardly reassuring. To make matters worse, there was also background rumours about the club owing money to a hedge fund.

All in all, our discussions in the pub were a bit more realistic than before. These were no longer simply rumours in *The Sun*. The club was definitely in a deep financial crisis. Each time there had been a problem (e.g. rumours of debt, the embargoes, failing to pay other teams, etc) Jordan had played the rumours down. Claiming that everything was under control seemed to be his favourite pastime. Maybe he should have spent more time actually dealing with the issues rather than telling the fans not to worry.

Unfortunately for him, our patience was running out. Each time he said that everything was fine; his nose seemed to grow a little. He was trying to patch up a sinking ship using nothing but a glue stick. Not even a new one. An old one that a kid has left the lid off so that it dries up and goes hard.

Jordan also had a history of lying. In 2006, he'd very publicly claimed that he'd purchased Selhurst Park from Ron Noades. He even released DVDs, posters and t-shirts for the momentous occasion of reuniting the club and ground. It was pure fantasy. A third party had purchased the ground which gave Jordan the option to buy it at a later date, for a price that he couldn't afford. What was soon to come to light was that in the clever little sausage's plan to rid the club of Ron Noades, he'd managed to quadruple the rent. Yet another reason for our finances spiralling out of all control.

It's amazing that our mood in the pub was so different from the previous weekend. After the Watford game, we'd been flying. We were two points off the playoffs and were unbeaten in six. Losing just once in twelve matches. Despite all of the mayhem going on in the background, the players were performing incredibly well. They were as committed to the cause as the fans in the stands.

On the other hand, our opponents, Doncaster, were just above the relegation zone so we were cautiously optimistic. In some cases, you might fear that the players wouldn't give 100% as they hadn't been paid, but we had complete faith in Warnock and the senior members of the squad, such as Derry and Hill, to ensure that wouldn't happen. At quarter to three, we went about the usual routine: bladders were emptied and we made our way to the ground.

Palace started the match well. Neil Danns missed a golden opportunity to put us 1-0 up when he shot wide from six yards with the goal gaping. After the game, Warnock joked that the midfielder must have bet money on the match. I suppose he needed to pay his mortgage one way or another. Danns had tried to start a music career alongside his football. Having listened to some of it, I think it's safe to say that he was more likely to earn a second income (or only income in our current financial state) from match fixing than he was from rapping.

Midway through the half, after yet another misplaced pass as Palace tried to find the killer ball to unlock the resilient Doncaster defense, Colin applauded the player's effort. He turned to Dan and shook his head.
"I don't know what's happened to me mate! I'd have never applauded that crap twenty years ago. I've gone soft!"
I didn't know what to make of his comments. I was used to shocking passes and

featherweight tackles; clapping them was done out of habit in order to keep warm as much as anything else.

"I'll tell you what's happened. You've got used to rubbish because we've had fifteen years of nothing but average-ness." replied Dan, in his usual cynical manner. Colin frowned and nodded sadly. Dan was right. That was my entire Palace-supporting life, and we had been exactly as he'd described – nothing but average. When I pointed this out to Colin, he duly realised that I'd *'never seen John Solako or Nigal Martyn play'*, before he grumbled, *"No wonder Clinton bloody Morrison is your favourite ever player!"*

We'd dominated the first half but fell behind just before the break. The mood in the bar at half time was of disbelief. Ambrose, Danns and Moses had all been guilty of missing chances and Doncaster had made us pay. While downing our drinks, we all agreed that we'd seen more than enough to believe that we could get back into the match.

Unfortunately, it wasn't to be and just after the hour mark, Doncaster scored a second. Again it was against the run of play but it mattered very little to the few hundred Yorkshire folk who'd travelled down. Despite being two goals behind, Palace continued to press. Even the ever-reliable Darren Ambrose couldn't find the net. Twice he wasted good opportunities to get us back into the game as his goal scoring run came to a disappointing end.

A bit like the club's finances, things went from bad to worse. Doncaster hit us on the break to score a third and after that, understandably, Palace looked a beaten side. In the end, we were saved from further humiliation by some poor finishing and good goalkeeping. Doncaster could have gone on to score four or five. As usual with Palace, the rare sound of pre-match expectations in the pub had been our undoing.

Anyone who saw the score that evening might have assumed that the players were not interested after not being paid. Anyone who was at the game knew this wasn't true. While the result was just as embarrassing as the Scunthorpe one, the performances couldn't have been more different. Despite everything going on behind the scenes, the players had given everything. It was a complete freak of a result that didn't match up to the game.

However, as predicted, having not been there, my Dad didn't see it that way when he called me after the match.

"Results like this are why I can't be bothered to travel all the way up there!" he told me.

I couldn't understand his stance. Surely supporting a crap team meant that you had to live in hope and accept the disappointments? I didn't see how he could be so annoyed about the game without actually being there.

After the phone call, I went back to the Railway Club with Kev. Once again, football wasn't our friend. Who wants to be friends with something that could do that to you? However, there was no escaping the football. Manchester City vs Chelsea was on the television. As I've mentioned before, I really have a dislike of Chelsea. I lived with four (well, three now) of their fans and listening to them bleating on about their club was insufferable. Especially as they didn't seem to like me joining in or having any sort of opinion on their club. Chelsea were currently top of the league and seemed set to be heading for yet another Premier League title – a third in four years. For all of City's spending, they sat in seventh place and weren't pulling up many trees.

Sure enough, Chelsea took the lead from an Adebayor own goal. If I didn't like football before, I positively hated it now. I knew that facing my flatmates after a Palace defeat would be painful but doing so after an impressive Chelsea win didn't bare thinking about. If it meant returning home to banter, I wouldn't mind. I could trash talk with the best of them. However, it was worse than banter. It was a mixture of smugness and ignoring me. They'd make a point of telling me the score without wanting to engage in any sort of conversation. *"Another beer Kev?"* I sighed.

He nodded. We both needed something to take our mind off the football. Beer seemed the logical answer.

As the beers disappeared, so did our memory of the first half performance.

"Ultimately, we've now lost 3-0 and 4-0 at home to Doncaster and Scunthorpe. That's not good enough!" I moaned to Kev. I usually try to avoid whining about a result and look more at the performance but after a few beers, I'm a lot less forgiving. 'Crystal Palace 0 Doncaster Rovers 3' is the score that would go down in the record books.

Luckily for Kev, who probably felt similar to how I did around Brian, the ever controversial Adebayor scored again, in the right net this time. At least my flatmates wouldn't be too self-satisfied that evening. Although, being Chelsea fans, I'm sure that they'd find something to moan about. It's never their fault. Every Chelsea defeat at the time seemed to result in them completely imploding and blaming the referee.

If it sounds like I have a vendetta against Mr Shoebridge, it was nothing compared to their hate of Norwegian referee, Tom Ovrebo. They'd been denied five penalties in a Champions League semi-final by him and when I'd made a joke about the matter during a night out, Matt, who I'd known since I was at primary school, had refused to speak to me for the rest of the evening. Charming.

Anyway, Kev and I continued to drink with the game on in the background. There was a certain quirk of fate about supporting the moneybags from Manchester; bearing in mind the financial crisis that Palace found themselves in. Midway through the second half, City went 2-1 up. Fuelled with Guinness, I jumped out of my seat, arms aloft. I suddenly realised something. Everyone else in the pub was supporting Chelsea. I'd slated Coventry for not caring about their local club a couple of weeks previously. But there I was, in a pub five minutes from Selhurst Park, on a match day, and I was getting angry looks for cheering against Chelsea.

I've said before that a club should embrace the local community and that moment highlighted to me quite how out of touch the club was. In the financial mire that we were in, we needed the South London community to rally around the club more than ever. Long term, something needed to be done to reintegrate the club and the community. One observation that I have long held is that the club's academy is packed full with black players from the local area, but unfortunately, this demographic is not represented in the stands.

I guess the price of attending football and the influx of foreign players who supporters can't identify with has made football seem out of touch with reality for many people. In the past, fans would know the players, see them in the local shops and feel close to them. Nowadays, the players are millionaires and a million miles away from the average man. That's not a dig at them either. Our group were giving absolutely everything they had to the club and as the stars of a multi-million pound industry, they more than deserve their slice of the cake. However, it's easy to see how the hard-up residence of the streets around Selhurst Park could find it hard to care about and identify with them.

Thankfully, in the evening kick off, City held on to put a dent in Chelsea's title charge but I left the pub soon after. I was angry that what should have been a Palace pub, in a Palace area, could be filled with glory hunters. Still, I returned home quite happy that everyone in my flat would be miserable. Only in football could misery bring such joy. Although, despite my intoxicated state, I'd learnt not to mention the football. Which, after our result, suited me just as much as them.

Chapter Twenty-six – **The Second Coming**

Tuesday 8th December 2009, Reading vs Crystal Palace, The Madejski Stadium.

Crystal Palace: Julian Speroni, Nathaniel Clyne, Danny Butterfield, Jose Fonte, Clint Hill, Neil Danns, Shaun Derry, Johnny Ertl, Darren Ambrose (Alassane N'Diaye 81), Victor Moses (Freddy Sears 90), Calvin Andrew (Alan Lee 65).
Subs Not Used: Ryan Smith, Claude Davis, Nicky Carle, Sean Scannell.

Reading Federici, Tabb, Ingimarsson, Pearce, Bertrand (Sigurdsson 68), Cisse, Gunnarsson (Robson-Kanu 46), Matejovsky, Jobi McAnuff, Rasiak, Jimmy Kebe.
Subs Not Used: Hamer, Mills, Cummings, O'Dea, Karacan.

Dan, Colin, Jonathan and I met up early to head to Berkshire and we were again joined by... Jesus!

He had returned. Despite our sins of letting him get ridiculously drunk on his previous visit, he had enjoyed the experience so much that he had come back for some more Crystal Palace action (and beer). So there you have it, Jesus is a Palace fan. Maybe if the players prayed to him, they'd get their money.

Rather than heading straight to Reading, we had decided to make the most of some of the many good pubs in Wokingham. Once upon a time, Wokingham held the record for the most amount of 'Pubs per Square Mile' in any UK town. Unfortunately, a crown that it has now lost to St. Albans in Hertfordshire. However, it is still home to a wide selection of decent drinking spots. We had planned to do a pub crawl originally but we ended up staying in the same pub all evening. The Hope and Anchor.

There, we enjoyed vast amounts of the Cornish ale, Doombar, as we prepared for the game. The players still hadn't been paid and we were still a little bit in shock at the previous weekend's result. Like Doncaster, Reading were at the wrong end of the table and they were still suffering a hangover from Palace and Reading legend, Sir Steve Coppell, leaving the club. We really didn't know what to expect from the match that evening so we did what we usually did. Got drunk and hoped for the best.

Shortly before 7 o'clock, we boarded a train to Reading. We'd sent Jonathan to an off licence to try and get us some beer for the journey but he returned with even less than a bag of magic beans. Sod all to be precise. Luckily, the Hope and Anchor landlady sold us some bottles to take on our way. Well, it probably wasn't luckily. We didn't *really* need any booze for the thirteen minute journey.

Once we were in Reading, Colin suggested that we headed to the Wetherspoons. As the Official Wetherspoons Representative, I led the way. It was a short five minute walk to the pub but Colin still had time to moan.
"We don't have time for this. This isn't the Wetherspoons. I said to take us to Wetherspoons."
It was Wetherspoons. My ability to sniff out a 'spoons was second to none and should never be doubted.
"No, 'spoons is by the station!" he protested. For some reason, he'd decided that

The Three Guineas pub, next to Reading station, was a spoons and there was nothing that anybody could do to persuade him otherwise. He finally ended his grumbles with a parting shot, *"Spoons or not, I meant the one by the station!"* Quite how he'd intended me to read his mind and know this, I don't know.

Once we were in the 'spoons, the real one, we began to drink. Coventry had delivered on meeting its stereotype of a town in depression but Reading seemed keen to outdo it in terms of meeting its own pretentious, royal reputation. There was a group of lads in the spoons, wearing Reading shirts, each supping a pre-match cup of tea. It was very sophisticated. Very Berkshire. They looked over at our drunken mob in disgust.

At the bar, we decided to be as awkward as possible and each order something different. There are two ways of working when buying beer in a large group. Either buy in rounds or have a whip. That evening we had gone in favour of the whip system and we suddenly found that it was empty. A horrific discovery.

"Another £10 each?" inquired Dan, with a daft grin. None of us questioned it and despite the lack of time before kickoff, we had put together a further £40. Jesus had decided against paying into the pot.

Dan had discovered the Polish beer, Lech, that evening and in a drunken state, was close to professing his love for it. At one point, I was worried that he would leave his wife and start a new life with his new love. I, on the other hand, was drinking a pint of 'Rebellion'. An ale from a local Maidenhead brewery. I usually try to drink something local when I go to away games. Lagers tend to offer the same choice all over the country but one of the benefits of drinking ale, is the selection changes depending on where you are.

With kickoff fast approaching, having learnt from the state that he'd ended up in for his previous visit, Jesus decided that he needed some sobering food. Some bread to go with the wine that he'd been drinking no doubt. Anyway, leaving us in the pub, he slipped off to find some food as he didn't want to pay the overpriced rates in the ground. Well, that's where he claimed he was going. He may well have been off to have a word with his father about the game. We could certainly do with any help we could get.

It was a bit of a tradition that we would have a shot or short before heading to the ground on away days and Colin decided that it was time to partake in this particular custom. He saw a sign behind the bar that caught his eye.

"Bells Whiskey, £1.09"

He was sold. He went to order but then another sign caught his eye.

"Double up for £1"

He was doubly sold.

"Four double Bells and coke please?" he ordered.

The bar stewardess looked a little concerned, but poured away.

"Not too much coke!" he added, unnecessarily quickly and loudly while leaning

over the bar with his hand making a stop sign as she started to fill the glass. The bar stewardess looked very concerned, glancing across the bar to her manager. He gave her a nod and she continued to half-fill the glasses.

We downed the drinks, saw that we had money left in the pot and went to order the same again. Thankfully, Dan looked at his watch and brought a bit of much-needed rationality to the situation. It was 7:40 and the game kicked off at eight o'clock. Reading is another out-of-town ground that we would need to get a bus to. Fortunately, unlike Coventry, Reading did lay on direct football buses but it would still take fifteen minutes to get there. And that was simply on the bus. We had a walk at the other end of the short trip and would have to wait for the bus to fill up at the stop before it left.

We ran to the bus stop. I somehow remembered to call up Jesus in the panic to tell him to come and meet us. I did consider saying a prayer and assuming he'd listen, but I thought it was best to call him. Just in case.

On the bus, the driver confirmed that he was under instructions not to leave until the vehicle was full. Just after us, a group of ten or so Palace fans got on. They were coked off their face. They jumped about on the top deck, which felt like it was shaking the entire bus, and gave abuse to anyone and everyone. Wankers. Not even Rob Shoebridge-style wankers. Real wankers. They started to hurl abuse towards us before they realised that we were Palace. Worried about the safety of his vehicle, the driver left early and sped through Reading. He was keen to get them off his bus as quickly as possible and who could blame him? Certainly not us.

The flip side of sharing our short bus trip with the scum was that we were dropped off next to the ground at 7:55. We rushed to the turnstiles and bundled into the away end. As we took our seats, which were in the front row, the game kicked off. Somehow, we'd managed to make it from the pub to the ground in twenty minutes, before the game started.

A game that started well for Palace. Young full back, Nathaniel Clyne, scored his first professional goal. He drilled a low shot past the goalkeeper from outside the area. After that, the game went fairly flat for a brief period. Unlike the atmosphere in the away end. Not even Reading equalising could dampen our spirits (whisky in this case). As half time approached, Jonathan and I were sent in with the money from the whip to get some half time beers.

We got five pints and took them to the side of the concourse. Suddenly, there was an almighty roar from above us. Palace had scored in first half stoppage time and we'd missed it. We weren't alone. The concourse was fairly packed already. I'd never missed a Palace goal before and it was a strange feeling. As happy as I was for Palace to be leading, I was disappointed to have missed it at the same time. I had to be a part of it. I hid my pint under my coat and ran out to the stand to celebrate (and find out that it was Ambrose who had scored. Who else?)

As I went back out to the viewing area, Moses hit a shot from well outside the area. It curled and dipped viciously into the top corner. We'd scored twice in first half stoppage time. The beer that I'd hidden under my jacket went everywhere but who cares? It was 3-1 to Palace.

The mood at half time was understandably electric. The concourse was packed with celebrating Palace fans: singing, dancing and looking around in disbelief. The scenes were more appropriate for a Wembley win than simply leading a league match at half time but everyone was on cloud nine. No one could remember anything like it. Two goals in stoppage time. Our financial woes couldn't have been further from our minds. There could only be one explanation for the miracle.

"Jesus, is a Palace fan!" the four of us burst into song, pointing at a rather embarrassed looking Tom. Instantly, other people joined in. In my drunken state, I imagined that there were dozens of us praising the lord but the reality was that it was just a small handful. I'd assumed they'd felt the need to join in because they agreed that he had such a striking resemblance to the Son of God but I later found out the reason was much less exciting. It was simply that the guys joining in were one of Dan's mates, Pavel, and the friends of his that he was with.

We then did something that I don't think I've ever done before or since at football. We had a second half time pint. I'm not sure why. Partly because of the goal-induced spillage, I'd finished my beer about five minutes before the second half was due to begin and there was still a little bit of money in the whip, so it had seemed like the sensible thing to do. It wasn't, but there was no one there to tell us otherwise at the time.

The second half was edgy. Once again, our expectations had been risen and that was a dangerous thing for any Palace supporter. It got even more nervy when the referee awarded Reading a late penalty. This time, Speroni couldn't do anything to stop the inevitable and Reading were back in the game, having threatened very little.

Throughout the match, Moses had been sensational and both managers would praise him in their post match press conferences. But he really was saving the best until last. From a long clearance, he got the ball out on the left touchline. He showed quick feet, power and acceleration to leave two defenders behind him and fire the ball into the far corner of the net from the edge of the area. It was another sensational goal. A performance like this could only increase his value and help to fund the club in our time of need.

Finally, we could relax and enjoy the evening. Any misguided talk of the players not caring as they hadn't been paid could certainly be put to bed after this result.

Colin and I were still in song as we left the ground. I felt a little tap on the shoulder, *"Excuse me Sir, I'm warning you that you should show some respect."*
The pair of us burst out laughing. This guy was clearly angry at the result but that was the politest threat I'd ever heard.

We carried on and I began to think about who I could text. I explained to

Colin that I'd always had a soft spot for Reading as my local club until I'd got into the sixth form. Suddenly, because Reading got into the Premiership, all of the glory hunters at school decided that they now supported 'Manchester United *and* Reading' or 'Newcastle *and* Reading'. That was fine and I was glad that they would finally see some live football so they could understand what being a football supporter was really about.

What I didn't like, was that they would suddenly get on my back about how much better Reading were than Palace. None of them had shown any interest in Reading when they were crap but as soon as they had any form of success, they were all over it. Now they were back at the bottom of the Championship and getting stuffed at home by Palace, I expect the glory hunters had gone back to their TV cheering of Manchester United. Being an armchair fan must be a bit like looking at Megan Fox on TV and calling her your girlfriend.
"I've seen all her films in the cinema. Even when she was rubbish in Transformers 2, I was still there for her!"

Anyway, the world's most-gracious, angry man took offense to my comment to Colin about 'plastic' Reading fans.
"Excuse me Sir, I've already warned you to stop taking the mick," he told us sternly.
Colin and I looked at each other again and laughed. We shouldn't have laughed really. At any other ground, if I'd wound someone up in that way, I'd have got a smack. He was so cross but he was so unthreatening. Without thinking, we burst into song.
"4-2, to the Londoners!"
Can you imagine the reaction of a Leeds fan in a similar situation outside Elland Road or a Millwall fan at the New Den? As it was, we got a final warning.
"Excuse me, did you not hear me before?"
We carried on walking.

Leaving the ground, we had bumped into Dan's dad, Peter. He'd decided to be a lot more sensible than his son that evening, which isn't always the case, and was driving so he offered Dan a lift back home. He also turned to Colin and Jonathan to offer them a lift to Sunningdale to help them get back to Cheam quicker. In the excitement of the win, the altercation with the home fan and not really knowing where I was going, I'd just carried on walking with Colin. It wasn't until we were near the car park that I realised that there wasn't going to be room for Dan, Colin, Jonathan, Jesus and I in the back of Peter's car. As the two who hadn't been offered a lift, I knew it was Tom and I who wouldn't be able to get in.

I pointed out the numerical problem to Colin who simply turned to me, put his finger to his lips and shhh'd. It wasn't the most helpful action he'd ever done but it persuaded me to carry on walking. We were now about ten minutes from the ground and going back would put us right at the end of the long bus queue. As the three of us had been walking behind the others, it was only when we got to the car that Peter realised the problem. He wasn't impressed but he let us all squeeze in the back. So in we got. Jonathan, Colin, Jesus and I. Both

Jonathan and Colin are well over six foot tall and very well built. It was a miracle that we all fitted in...

Getting out of the Madejski Stadium car park is a nightmare and it's amazing that none of the police who were mulling about decided to question the overloaded car. The drive back to Sunningdale was not a comfortable one. Not for the first time that season, I think I embarrassed Dan - I suspect he was beginning to regret introducing me to binge drinking at football. God knows what Peter had thought. I'd turned up at his car uninvited, forced him to break the law and drunkenly chatted rubbish all the way back. I expect he was very relieved when he was able to kick us out at the station.

From Sunningdale, Colin, Jonathan and I got the train back and headed home towards London. It had been a brilliant night. Palace had won and scored four cracking goals. I don't know the facts but I expect you'd have to go a long way back to find another day when we'd scored four goals from outside the area. Just as importantly, I'd had a great time with my mates. Little did I know it but I had even met one of my future close friends.

Nights like that one are what supporting a team is all about. It wasn't part of a challenge at all, it was a joy. For a football fan, there is no better feeling than winning an away game. The atmosphere. The buzz of scoring. Watching the steams of home supporters empty out with five minutes left. It's a feeling of conquering. You've gone behind enemy lines and given them a beating. It brings out the tribal trait in man. Metaphorically, you've walked into someone else's home, put down your flag and claimed it as yours. For that night, the Madejski belonged to Palace. Berkshire belonged to South London.

Two days after the match, the players were finally paid. Maybe they had got the latest Palace fan to have a word with the man upstairs.

In my opinion, when Victor first came onto the scene the previous year, he was better than the year we fell into administration. This is often the case with young players. The second season can sometimes affect the individual when there are demands thrust upon them. That's not to say that Victor didn't deliver. I remember a game away at Reading when he scored two in a key game for us enabling us to win the game 4-2. There was nobody on the pitch in a Palace Shirt that could have got us out of the trouble aside from Victor on that day. It hasn't surprised me to see him go on to bigger and better things

Shaun Derry

Chapter Twenty-seven – **Jordan's Master Plan**

Saturday 12th December 2009, Sheffield United vs Crystal Palace, Bramell Lane.

Crystal Palace Julian Speroni, Danny Butterfield (Nathaniel Clyne 55), Jose Fonte, Claude Davis, Clint Hill, Darren Ambrose (Sean Scannell 46), Neil Danns, Johnny Ertl (Freddy Sears 66), Shaun Derry, Victor Moses, Alan Lee.
Subs Not Used: Nicky Carle, Calvin Andrew, Ryan Smith, Alassane N'Diaye.

Sheff Utd Bunn, Walker, Morgan, Kilgallon, Taylor, Ward (Camara 87), Harper, Williamson, Quinn, Evans (Stewart 80), Cresswell.
Subs Not Used: Bennett, France, Reid, Little, Kallio.

"Hi James! How's it going?"
"Good thanks, you?"
"Yeah great thanks! We're having a massive party for Christmas and all the lads are coming down for it. We've got about eighty people from uni coming around and it would be great if you could come down to Plymouth for the weekend?"
Rob, my best friend, lived in a huge house with seven other friends. Parties at his place were legendary across the campus.
I was excited. Of course I'd love to go. However, then I began to think. What did he say? A weekend? Unlikely I thought.
"Awesome mate, when is it?" I asked, trying to sound positive – desperately hoping that it would fall on an international weekend.
"11-13th December!"
"Ah... sorry mate... I'll be getting a coach to Sheffield and back that day."
"You're not still going to every game, are you?"

What sort of question was that? Doesn't he know me at all? I wasn't going to let the need to spend ten hours on a coach to go and watch a second rate match deter me. I wasn't going to let *anything* deter me. It wasn't all about enjoyment. It was about completing what I'd started and if that meant getting the coach and missing my best friend's party, that meant getting the coach and missing my best friend's party. So be it.

It was hardly a rare conversation. In fact, it was fairly common. Rob wasn't surprised, just a little disappointed. So was I. It wasn't even as if I was particularly fussed by the Sheffield game and the party would be a much more reliable source of fun. But... if a wedding hadn't tempted me into giving it up, a Christmas party certainly wasn't going to interrupt my challenge.

When I arrived on the coach at Selhurst Park on the morning of the game, I was still on a high from the performance of the Tuesday before. Even if I was a little tired. The coach left at 8am, which meant I'd needed to get up just before six after getting in from work around 2AM the previous evening. I would certainly be getting some sleep on the way there – or trying to, if Brian's relentless moaning would allow. The Reading game had left us just two points off the playoffs. However, while the football morale was high, the money situation was dire.

Any good feeling about our finances after the players had been paid was long gone. The previous day a 'Financing Opportunity Document' had come to light. Jordan had hired the company 'Inner Circle Sports' to create a brochure inviting people to invest in the club. It claimed that *'The Club is seeking to raise £7.50M in senior secured financing to retire existing indebtedness and for general working capital purposes.'* In reality, this meant that we were in a load of s*** with a hedge fund and desperately needed to pay them off. The whole article was badly written and full of spelling, grammatical, mathematical and factual errors. Basically, it was desperate and pathetic.

The prospectus opened:
'CPFC is an English football Club competing in the Coca-Cola Championship, the second tier of English Football, currently ranked 13th out of 24 Championship Clubs (23 points through 17 matches), 4 points off a play-off spot, with the team having lost only once in the last 11 games. The Club is seeking to raise £7.50M in senior secured financing to retire existing indebtedness and for general working capital purposes. CPFC is owned by Simon Jordan, a successful UK entrepreneur, and plays its home matches at Selhurst Park, a 26K-seat stadium where it has been based since 1924.

CPFC is seeking to conclude the above financing in anticipation of a near-term sale of the Club. The sale process will commence subsequent to the end of the January transfer window when the Club is planning on selling certain non-core players. These sales will generate transfer fee revenues while also reducing the Club's wage bill. Inner Circle Sports ("ICS"), a NY-based sports-focused merchant bank with signifcant experience in UK football, will be retained to sell the Club.'

In order to attract investors, it discussed largely irrelevant facts, such as our playoff win, a whole five years previously, or that we had been founder members of the Premiership in 1992. Other than stating out of date facts, it simply made things up. It falsely claimed *'The Club's Academy is only 1 of 5 Academy structures that exist outside of the Premier League.'* Although, perhaps the best line was that *'CPFC is owned by Simon Jordan, a successful UK entrepreneur'.*

The document used this table to prove that we were successful at developing and producing players who we could sell at a profit.

Recent Player Transfers						
Transfer Out		Transfer Received	Transfer Paid	Net Proceeds	Academy?	Purchasing Club
Player	Date					
Ben Watson	Jan. 2009	£1.6	£0.0	£1.6	Y	Wigan Athletic
Tom Soares	Aug. 2008	1.3	0.0	1.3	Y	Stoke City
Johnny Bostock	Jul. 2008	0.7	0.0	0.7	Y	Tottenham
Leon Cort	Jan. 2008	1.2	-1.0	0.2	N	Stoke City
Gary Borrowdale	Sept. 2007	0.5	0.0	0.5	Y	Coventry
Jobi McAnuff	Jun. 2007	1.8	-0.4	1.3	N	Watford
Wayne Routledge	Jane. 2006	1.3	0.0	1.3	Y	Tottenham
Emmerson Boyce	Aug. 2006	1.0	0.0	1.0	N	Wigan Athletic
Fitz Hall	Jun. 2006	3.0	-1.5	1.5	N	Wigan Athletic
Andrew Johnson	Jun. 2006	8.6	-0.8	7.9	N	Everton
Total/ Net Proceeds		£20.9	-3.7	£17.2		

Not only did the table choose to ignore players that we'd made huge losses on, such as Shefki Kuqi, who was purchased for £2.5m and released on a free transfer, but it also had simple mathematical errors that I wouldn't expect from a Year Four child in my class. I'm fairly certain that Andy Johnson could not have been purchased for 0.8m, sold for 8.6m and given us a profit of 7.9m. It simply doesn't add up. Neither did the figures for Jobi McAnuff. I don't suppose such basic errors are likely to provoke much interest in investment.

The brochure went on to claim *'Over the past 18 months, the Club has engaged in a full operational and financial review in an effort to reduce the Club's wage bill and other central costs to improve the financial viability of the Club.'* Which, roughly translated from bullshit, means that the club was making huge losses so they sold a load of players and are now making slightly less losses. Using projected player sales, the document predicted a profit making club for the following financial year. Of course, it didn't take into account any spending on players or extra wages to replace the mass exit. I suppose our academy was ready to produce eleven new superstars every season or in a worst case scenario, Lord Jordan himself would dust off his boots and save the club again. On the pitch this time.

The problem was that Agilo, who were now known as the hedge fund that we owed money to, had secured their debt against player sales. Jordan was desperate to use this requested-investment to pay them off and in his fantasy world, that would allow him to have a profit making club who someone would buy off him for a huge price. This pathetic plea for cash was his way of freeing the club from the self imposed clamp that he'd put Crystal Palace Football Club in.

As documented here, the plan was to flog five *'non-core'* players to raise funds.

Expected Future Player Sales			
Player	Transfer Date	Transfer Amount	Annual Wage
Player A	Jan. 2010	£0.75	£0.50
Player B	Jan. 2010	0.75	0.10
Player C	Jan. 2010	0.50	0.45
Player D	Aug. 2010	4.00	0.16
Player E	Aug. 2010	1.00	0.10
Total Proceeds		£7.00	£1.31

The table provided much debate among Palace fans as to who those five players were. We had expected to lose Moses in January but we hadn't anticipated losing five players. The squad was small enough already. The other cause of amusement was which *'non-core'* player did we have who was worth £4m. This simple answer was that we didn't have one. The article was lying and referring to our star player. Moses.

The begging letter explained that the £7.5m would be used in the following way; £4.4m to repay 1st Lien Debt (Agilo), £1.2m to repay other liabilities (HMRC) and the rest would be kept as working capital for the club, a loss-making organisation. If that wasn't a good investment, I don't know what is.

If people weren't already withdrawing the money to send it to Simon Jordan in cash, then they surely would be after seeing the benefits of investing in the prosperous club.

'New financing benefits from significant asset coverage providing downside protection

— *Championship Clubs have recently been acquired in excess of £30M (Mean of 3.3x revenue) meaning PF for the transaction the financing would be at a conservative LTV*

— *Security benefits from priority repayment from player sales - Playing squad is currently valued in excess of £20M providing salable assets to further reduce debt burden as needed*

— *Simon Jordan has invested over £30M of equity into the Club to date and is committed to providing additional funding, if required*

After securing this financing, the Club will undergo a formal sales process in the near-term, providing significant visibility towards an exit

— *ICS is uniquely positioned to coordinate a sale process and source potential investors given its successful track record of executing team acquisitions (Recently executed transactions for Liverpool FC and Sunderland FC)*

— *London location and strong academy make Club a likely acquisition target for foreign London-based investors as well as other football owners seeking to leverage academy expertise*

Financially oriented management team which has led successful restructuring of the business

— *Mindset of operating the Club on a cash-flow positive/break-even basis, which provides a significant advantage vis a vis the Club's Championship peers*

— *Management is adept at entertaining transfer interest in several of the Club's players which could produce meaningful transfer proceeds while carefully balancing squad performance'*

However, like Moses on the Tuesday before, Jordan had left the best bit until last. The valuation of the club. By now, it was established that we were roughly £30m in the red and this desperate document was hardly going to help player sales. Why would other clubs pay top money to Palace, who were openly so desperate to sell?

Jordan used, at best, bent facts, and at worst, lies, about the values of other Championship team's takeovers to claim that a business that was £30m in debt and making a year-on-year loss was worth forty-six million pounds. He was living in cuckoo land. He was so used to lying to everybody else that it seemed he was lying to himself too. Well, to hypothetical, non-forthcoming investors anyway. And yes, the spelling mistake in the title is Jordan's, not mine.

Precedent Championship League Transactions (£ in MMs)					
Franchise Acquired	Acquiror	Transaction Date	Enterprise Value	Revenue	Ent. Value/ Revenue
Coventry City FC	SISU Capital	12/14/2007	£58.0	£9.7	6.0x
Ipswich Town FC	Marcus Evans	10/31/2007	44.0	15.5	2.8x
Birmingham City FC	Grandtop International	6/29/2007	50.2	25.0	2.0x
Wolverhampton FC	Steve Morgan	5/23/2007	40.0	16.0	2.5x
Queens Park Rangers FC	Flavio Briatore/ Lakshmi Mittal	1/9/2007	28.2	8.2	3.4x
Mean: Overall			£44.1	£14.9	3.4x

Implied CPFC Valuation (FY '10)	£46.2	£13.8	3.4x

Frankly, anyone that was going to invest in the club based on this pile of s***, isn't the kind of person that we wanted anywhere near our beloved Palace.

If Jesus really was a Palace fan, he needed to step up now. No one else was going to invest in our sinking ship. Tom would have to walk on water and hold the club above his head to keep us afloat. The truth was that Jordan had been trying to sell the financial burden of a club for an unrealistic price ever since we'd been promoted in 2004. However, there was no one remotely interested in his inflated valuation.

The majority of the coach to Sheffield was spent discussing the pathetic plea. Brian certainly wasn't the only one in a moaning mood that day and sleep was out of the question. The overriding question was 'What the hell has Jordan managed to do with all of the Premiership money, all of the parachute payments and all of the £17m profit from selling players? On top of that, he claimed he'd invested £30m of his own money. It simply didn't add up.

We got to Sheffield around 1:30 and headed into the away end. It was £4 for a bottle of Carling. I was skint after overspending in Reading – not for the first time that season. It seemed that a trip to Reading ensured that I wouldn't be able to drink at the following game. On top of the high price and low funds, in the previous season at the same ground, I'd had a bottle that tasted flat. I passed on the chance to suffer in the name of alcohol. For the second time in three away games, I was going to watch Palace sober. I guess I'd had enough booze at Reading to cover all three. Brian had a 'VK', which is a teenage vodka-based alcopop. The Sheffield United beer experience really is that bad.

We lost 2-0 and it could easily have been more if it wasn't for Speroni. After the game, Warnock claimed that half the team had come down with a virus in the morning, which certainly explained the performance. It had been as dismal and flat as the beer. The contrast from the midweek match was striking. Unlike our centre forwards.

The coach journey home was long and uneventful. It would have had to be a pretty dull party in Plymouth to have not been an improvement on my day in Sheffield. The game was crap, the journey was crap, the beer was crap and our chairman talked crap. Life as a football fan was summed up in one foul, depressing statement.

Well, it felt like that anyway. Of course, it was simply a case of focusing on the negatives as football fans love to do. Just read an internet message board or listen to a football phone in. Liverpudlian or Birmingham accents are excellent on 6-0-6 for emphasising just how abysmal a side has been.
"Twenty years without a title, it's not good enough Alan, not good enough. Arbeloa, not a Liverpool player. Vladimir Smicer, not good enough. Accrington Stanley, who are they?" was an all too familiar whine from a thick scouse accent on the way back from games. Still, that was better than a London accent moaning about Manchester United.

The truth is, football fans would be a lot happier if they focused on the positives – no matter how hard the clubs make that sometimes. As a fan of most teams, you have to take the dross in your stride, lay back and enjoy the ride. A bit like if referees got every decision correct, what would football fans talk about if they won every game? Ok, Sheffield hadn't been great. However, at Reading, the beer had been great, the journey had been fun, the football had been amazing and the chairman had come up trumps. Four days really had been a very long time. I could accept the odd virus-affected poor performance from the players but coach travel was killing the fun of away games. Unfortunately, it was a necessity. I didn't want to go to games if the only viable method was on the tiring, cramped and sober coach but in order to complete the challenge, I needed to.

Chapter Twenty-eight – **How the Hell did that Happen?**

Saturday 19th December 2009, Crystal Palace vs Barnsley, Selhurst Park.

Crystal Palace: Julian Speroni, Nathaniel Clyne, Clint Hill (Lee Hills, 90), Shaun Derry, Jose Fonte, Darren Ambrose, Neil Danns, Victor Moses, Freddie Sears, Alan Lee (Calvin Andrew, 90) , Claude Davis
Subs: Nick Carle, Sean Scannell, Johannes Ertl, Ryan Smith, Alassane N'Diaye

Barnsley: Luke Steele, Bobby Hassell, Darren Moore, Hugo Colace, Daniel Bogdanovic (Iain Hume, 49), Emil Hallfredsson, Anderson De Silva (Adam Hammill, 66) , Andy Gray, Carl Dickinson, Ryan Shotton, Nathan Doyle
Subs Not Used: Rob Kozluk, Stephen Foster, Jamal Campbell-Ryce, David Preece, Jon Macken,

It was the game before Christmas but the chances of Santa bringing Simon Jordan a seven and a half million pound gift in his stocking were slim. He'd been a very naughty boy and no one was willing to even give him a lump of coal.

As usual, I headed to the pub with my normal group of friends. While we got ourselves ready for the usual Saturday afternoon torture by drinking beers, we reminisced about the glory of the night in Reading. I apologised to and thanked Peter for the lift, Colin still couldn't believe the politeness of the post match threats and Dan was disappointed not to find Lech in the Railway Club. I told them everything that they needed to know about the Sheffield United match. Which wasn't much.

But inevitably, the conversation turned to Jordan. There was still a disbelief between us about the situation that we had found ourselves in. How the hell had we lost so much money? Sure, we'd thrown away a lot of money on crap players. The previous manager, Peter Taylor, had wasted his budget on some horrendous big money signings such as Shefki Kuqi, Paul Ifill and Scott Flinders but we hadn't spent a penny on new players for a long time. We'd also sold players and only just stopped receiving parachute payments. The Premier League's life support machine to the teams it has half killed.

When the '£30 million pound debt' rumours had first surfaced, we had refused to accept them. However, it was now clear that not only were they true but there was a severe cash flow problem and a hedge fund putting pressure on the club. Never mind being up s*** creek without a paddle. We didn't even have a canoe.

I also had my own problem. The Feltham Wetherspoons Christmas Rota had just come out. I was due to be working on Boxing Day, when Palace were playing Ipswich. Everyone had to work two shifts out of Christmas Day, Boxing Day, New Years Eve and New Years Day. I was down to do Boxing Day and New Years Eve. I'd tried to protest but I'd been told by the big boss, Gary, that everyone had to do their bit and make sacrifices. I already dictated that I wouldn't work on Saturdays, which annoyed some people, so they weren't going to change the complicated rota for the busiest time of year.

There was a deputy manager, Rich, who liked trying to express his limited authority. He often tried to get me to have to work on a Saturday so that I'd miss a game. In his words *'to see the reaction.'* He was a typical 'massive' Arsenal fan. He would talk them up whenever they were winning and dismiss defeats as not bothering him when times were hard. Obviously, he had never actually watched a game at The Emirates and had been limited to the occasional Highbury visit as a kid. He was one of those people who just didn't get football.

Someone had offered to take my shift as he needed the money. Gary had agreed to it but then Richard stuck his ore in. Technically, covering my shift would have meant Billy (the guy who wanted it) would have done over the allowed daily hours. When he found out, Rich ran to Gary like the teacher's pet in the classroom. Knowing Rich was right, Gary had to change his decision and insist that I did the shift. Rich gave me a smug grin that was thoroughly deserving of a smack in his stupid gob. Thankfully, I stopped myself.

Admittedly, the correct legal decision had been made based on employment laws but I knew full well that they would break those rules when it suited them. Rich had simply wanted to stop me going to every game. The guy was a little weasel. I later found out from Phill that Rich wasn't actually a manager as he'd failed his exams. It was only because of his friendship with Gary that he wore a smarter uniform than the rest of us and was allowed to be left in charge.

"Just don't show up," suggested Dan *"It's only a crappy bar job!"* He couldn't believe that I was going to let a job, which I was only doing to fund making it to every game, stop me achieving exactly that. He did have a point. However, I had a few concerns.

Firstly, I did have a moral belief that I should respect the company that employed me. Up until now, they had been very accommodating of my studies and football.

Secondly, I felt I owed it to Phill and my colleagues to not let anybody down. While I'd have relished the chance to leave Rich in the s***, my friend Phill had gone out of his way and put his reputation on the line to employ me. As well as that, someone not turning up would leave them short staffed which would make for a crap, break-less shift for the other bartenders. They hadn't done anything wrong to me and didn't deserve that.

Thirdly, it would be bloody obvious what I'd done even if I did phone in sick. I'd risk losing the job and not being able to afford to complete the challenge anyway. Besides that, as university jobs go, I didn't mind it.

Finally, the idea of going all the way to Swansea and Sheffield Wednesday over Christmas wasn't exactly filling me with excitement. For every brilliant away trip, there was a distinctly average one. These were trips that I was simply 'doing' rather than relishing. If I missed the Ipswich game, I'd decided that I'd give up on those two and be more selective about the games that I attended after Christmas.

Anyway, short of deciding that I'd rather stay in the pub, I wouldn't be missing *this* match. Our opponents, Barnsley, were having a surprisingly good season. They were sat just three points behind us in mid table and had won their previous two. Despite that, they were one of the smaller teams in the division and one that we were *expecting* to beat at home. There's that bloody 'e' word again. Expecting.

The Sheffield game had left us three points off the playoffs but more importantly, eleven clear of relegation. With all of the financial troubles, entering administration was now a real possibility. Not only did we have to try and work out what the table actually looked like, we then had to try and visualise it with the ten point deduction that administration would bring. Nowadays, there's probably an app on your smart phone for that.

When we arrived at the ground, we found that the area of our season tickets had been closed. It was proving to be the coldest winter since Narnia froze over and the floor by our seats was covered with ice. In order for the ground to be declared safe, our block, and the one next to it, needed to be shut off. I'm sure that someone could have just got a lighter and melted the ice. Simple solutions are the best. However, the steward simply told us to *"Find another seat."* So we did. Which turned out to be someone else's season ticket. So we found another. Which also turned out to be someone else's season ticket.

Once we eventually found a seat where we could stay, Palace, as seemed to be becoming a regular theme, looked to have got off to the perfect start. Moses beat his man in the penalty area, only to be hacked down. The form that he was in, that was the only way to stop him. Ambrose stepped up to take the penalty and... missed! It was a dreadful effort, sailing high and wide. How the hell had he managed that? It was a rare blip in his outstanding season up to that point. I blamed the fact that Barnsley had forced us to switch ends pre-match.

Palace usually attack towards the White Horse Lane Stand in the first half and the Holmesdale Road end in the second half. They have done this since long before I started to attend matches at Palace. As far as I know, it's been the norm since we moved into our then-state of the art stadium in 1926. The first time I remember the tradition being broken is when Watford won the toss and made us switch ends before kickoff in the 2006 Playoff Semi-final. We lost 3-0. Being superstitious, as football fans tend to be, I've never been comfortable when the away team breaks our routine ever since that fateful day.

Things went from bad to worse for Palace. Barnsley took the lead after nineteen minutes and we went to the Red'n'Blue bar thoroughly depressed at half time. How the hell were we losing at home to bloody Barnsley? Bloody expectations. I tell you, the undoing of any football fan. We finished our beers and returned to our seats with little or no hope for the second half. The Doncaster game had taught us that much.

Ten minutes after the break, Victor Moses scored a goal that no words can do justice. If you haven't seen it, I urge you to look it up online. A free kick was launched forward from the halfway line by a Palace defender and flicked on by Alan Lee to Victor Moses. He chested it down on the edge of the area and then acrobatically flipped himself over, volleying the ball with an overhead kick. It flew into the top corner. Not bad for a *'non-core player'*.

I genuinely have no idea how the hell he did that. Other than Trevor Sinclair's wonder goal for QPR, ironically also against Barnsley, I don't think you'll see a better bicycle kick anywhere. I'd rate the goal even higher than Rooney's effort in the Manchester derby as it was further out. In the many years of Kev's thick, all-weather jumper attending games, which for once was justified in the freezing conditions, it was certainly the most impressive goal to have been witnessed. Maybe, just maybe, Moses' form and goals could save the club from administration.

After the game, Warnock made another come and get him plea to the Premier League's big boys. He spoke as if he was a proud father. He asked *"What can you say that I've not said before? I look at the top of the Premiership and think there must be something wrong if they do not come down!"*

The rest of the game was fairly uneventful. However, there's a phrase *'That goal/moment/piece of skill/etc was worth the entrance fee alone'*. In this case, I think it justified my season ticket. Especially at the rates I was paying. When I was 16, Jordan had offered long term deals to get money into the club. The deals allowed you to carry on paying your current rate for a number of seasons. As a further incentive, he'd also knock money off for each year that you signed up for. Stupidly, he hadn't changed the deal for people who would go from being a child to an adult during the period of their ticket.

Aged 20, I was still legitimately paying around £120 a year for my season ticket in one of the more expensive parts of the ground. Selling so many advanced season tickets had brought in money at a time when he was desperate but was another reason that the club's cash flow was now so low. Thousands of people, who would usually each be paying hundreds of pounds every year, were now redundant as a source of income for the club. Jordan really did come across as a dodgy salesman who'd do anything to make a quick quid.

However, that evening wasn't for reflecting on Jordan. That evening, was for reflecting on Moses and his incredible journey. From a terrified child in his home country, he had become a potential superstar in England. All the papers were talking about him on a daily basis. As Warnock had said after the Reading game, *"You could tell that Victor was on his game and he has been since I bought him back into the team. Everybody is looking at him now. They pay £17m for players like that in the Premier League. You don't get 18-year-old British players like that very often and he will go for sure."*
While it was depressing to know that he'd be leaving soon, it made us even more determined to enjoy watching him play while we could.

That evening, I left the pub deep in thought. I was wondering if I was about to fail in my challenge. If after going to the first twenty-four games and possibly being past the half way stage, I was going to have to find another way of following the Boxing Day match, rather than actually being there to cheer the boys on. It was a strange feeling. I couldn't decide if it was for the best or not.

Chapter Twenty-nine – **Thank You Mike.**

Tuesday 22ⁿᵈ December 2009

"I hear you want to swap shifts on Boxing Day. I'll do 12-6 if you do 6-close?" said
my colleague, Mike.
"Done!" I replied. F*** you Rich. The dream lived on.

Saturday 26ᵗʰ December 2009, Crystal Palace vs Ipswich, Selhurst Park.

Crystal Palace: Julian Speroni, Nathaniel Clyne, Clint Hill, Shaun Derry, Jose Fonte, Darren
Ambrose, Neil Danns, Victor Moses, Freddie Sears (Johannes Ertl, 70), Alan Lee (Calvin Andrew, 90),
Claude Davis
Subs Not Used: Nick Carle, Sean Scannell, Lee Hills, Ryan Smith, Alassane N'Diaye

Ipswich: Arran Lee Barrett, David Wright, Damien Delaney, Gareth McAuley, Owen Garvan (Alan
Quinn, 69), Jaime Peters, Jon Stead, Jack Colback, Colin Healy (Pablo Counago, 69), Liam Rosenior,
Carlos Edwards (Connor Wickham, 45)
Subs Not Used: David Norris, Tamas Priskin, Ian McLoughlin, Tommy Smith,

The day, and indeed Christmas, couldn't have been any worse. I have
three brothers. Mark was having a family Christmas with his wife and two kids,
Simon was ill so he couldn't come and Will was in America. I spent the day with
my mother and her partner, Argie. We'd been to the most horrendous Christmas
service in the morning. I am not a Catholic but I was brought up that way. I used
to attend Christmas and Easter services to please my mother as I believe that it is
a family time of year. However, that miserable Christmas morning, the priest
spent his entire sermon moaning that the church was packed full with non-
regulars. I'm even less of a regular now. I haven't returned to a church service
since.

Christmas evening had brought terrifying news. My beautiful baby niece
had been taken back into hospital. As extended family, we couldn't go to visit her.
We'd barely slept all night and my mother spent most of the evening on the
phone to my brother. Nemie was in the best possible place and she was stable,
but it was scary all the same.

I had passed my driving test a couple of months previously but I couldn't
afford a car. Kindly, and maybe stupidly, my Mum had insured me on her Citroën
Saxo over the Christmas period so that I could get some practise. The plan had
been for me to drive to the game and then go to work. However, understandably,
she was desperate to be with my brother and as close to her granddaughter as
possible so this wasn't an option.

She may not have understood my love of Palace and was certainly
frustrated by it on a regular basis but she always wanted me to be happy. I drove
the three of us to Selhurst, where I left them and headed to the ground. She then
took the car and her partner to Tonbridge to see my brother, look after her

Grandson, Zak, and take Mark, who didn't drive, to the hospital. After the game, she would drive back to South London, pick me up and we would go to Feltham to drop me off for work. When I finished at the pub, I would be able to jump on a No.33 bus to my Twickenham flat, sleep there and finally get on a train back to Egham the next day.

Looking back, it was an amazing sacrifice that my Mum made. It would have been a lot easier for her to simply tell me that I couldn't go but she knew me too well. She knew how much Crystal Palace Football Club meant to me. She knew how much my challenge meant to me. I'd spent twenty years showing her and disappointing her by putting the club before family.

There was one slight hitch. As she was desperate to get to Tonbridge as soon as possible, I was at Palace for 10AM. With the Railway Club not even open, I wondered up to the ground to have a look in the club shop and see if there were any bargains to be had. There weren't. Another Jordan quick-quid master stroke was to sell off the club shop. Not actually owning it or any of the food outlets inside the stadium closed off yet another avenue of revenue. More reasons for our 'minor cash flow problem'. i.e. lots of people were owed money, but no one had a chance in hell of being paid.

I finally bought a coach and match ticket for the Sheffield Wednesday FA Cup game. I was really doing this. If I failed in my challenge now, I would be bloody pissed off. I also bought a match ticket for the Swansea game, which I would travel to on my own, and three tickets for the Plymouth match. Once again, my wallet felt a lot lighter.

I did have to question the challenge. Here I was, while my baby niece was in hospital, spending well over £100 that I didn't really have, on matches that I didn't really want to go to. There's an addiction in football. It might not offer AA style meetings but it should do. There was no logic to my actions yet I was still doing them. I hadn't even had a beer.

I then slowly strolled back to the Railway Club as I tried to kill time. Once there, I sat on my own, drinking alcohol free-Holston Pils. I don't like the booze-filled version of the drink so I'm not sure why I thought the alcohol-free version would be any better. It was a sad, lonely and pathetic moment in the name of football. Sitting there was made even more frustrating because Peter, Dan's dad, had actually offered me a lift to the game. I expect it would have been a lot more comfortable than my previous journey in his car too. However, I wouldn't have been able to make it back to Feltham for work if I'd taken up his kind offer.

Dan wasn't coming because he was attending the local pantomime with his family. Part-timer. Who puts their family ahead of football at Christmas? Boxing Day football in this country has a long tradition of giving men the perfect excuse to escape their wives after being cooped up together as a family for a couple of days.

"Sorry Love, I've paid for the season ticket and don't want to waste it!" they'd apologise to their wives.

"Alright lads, what time are we meeting in the pub?" they enthuse to their mates

in a hushed voice so they aren't heard by their deserted partner.

Colin could take his excuses to the next level.

"But Adam wants to go!"

It was definitely not a case of him simply wanting to go to the pub and cheer on the Palace himself. It was one of the many sacrifices that he made in the name of fatherhood.

Eventually, shortly before I went mad talking to the pub potman who had dyed his hair red and blue for charity for the umpteenth time, I was joined by Kev, Colin, Jonathan and Adam. Which was just as well. Sitting in the pub on my own was only serving to make my depressing Christmas even worse. I had paid into the potman's charity collection. I always do. Everyone does. But there is certainly something dodgy about them. He seemed to collect thousands for the charity 'children's party' each year. I hope the kids get the best party ever for that price.

We all shared our Christmas Day stories and talked about the overhyped TV from the day before. Apparently Jonathan had eaten about fifteen Turkeys at Colin's house. Colin had had about fifteen bottles of wine and Adam had eaten about fifteen tons of chocolate. Kev, on the other hand, had gone for multiple bottles of Jack Daniels. Although, thankfully, not quite fifteen. Everyone has their own Christmas delights.

If football was the perfect excuse to escape the house, Christmas is the perfect excuse to abuse your own body in whichever way you choose. I must admit, hearing about everyone else's day, particularly Colin's family Christmas, made mine seem all the more lonely. Adam, in the way kids are, was still on a high from his new presents the previous day. I was disappointed for Kev that he hadn't been given a new woolly jumper for Christmas – the old Umbro one lived on for another year. Even though I wasn't drinking, it was good to be back in the pub with my mates after the miserable day before. I could almost take my mind off my niece.

We finished our drinks about twenty minutes before kickoff and for once, I didn't need to empty my bladder. The atmosphere was flat in the ground. Boxing Day matches often lack the usual rowdy vibe. It was an early kick off and there were quite a few people missing. Presumably other over-trained husbands who had made the same family sacrifice as Dan. I expect a lot of the people who were there, were still hung over from the festivities of the day before. Those that weren't hung over, had probably come as a family and were unlikely to behave in a noisy and unruly way that helps to create a loud atmosphere.

Palace went 1-0 down midway through the first half and looked poor. The usually faultless Speroni had dropped a cross right at the feet of an Ipswich forward, leaving him with the simple task of putting the ball into an empty net. Like the crowd, the team seemed to have had too much turkey and booze the day before. The passing was poor, the defending was a mess and we didn't look like threatening.

However, the whole game changed in the space of a minute. First, Jose

Fonte volleyed home an equaliser. He was a very good centre back but a highly unlikely goal scorer. Ironically, his previous goals had come against Ipswich's arch rivals, Norwich, on Boxing Day the previous year. The amount of coincidences like that in football are astounding.

Ipswich had been the better team up until that point but as any football fan knows, goals change games. The psychological difference that conceding a goal can have on a team is staggering. It was Brian Clough who said that it only takes a second to score a goal. He was right and that second can change everything.

The away side had been playing well while Palace looked hapless, their players were running after lost causes while ours let them go, and their fans were making some noise while we sat on our hands. One goal sapped the life out of them. They couldn't believe it. They were angry. They let themselves go.

Within a minute, Ipswich striker, Jon Stead, had made a rash tackle on Freddy Sears. It wasn't dirty but it was thoughtless and needless. The referee sent him off. In the space of sixty short seconds, Ipswich had gone from cruising at 1-0 up to being level and down to ten men with over half the game remaining. In the same short period, Palace had gone from seeming lost and clueless to being team on a mission. The mental state works both ways. We just needed to keep our heads and the result would come.

At half time, we headed to the bar and I decided that I'd earned a bottle of real beer (well, the crap lager they served anyway). I'm not sure what I'd done to deserve it, but I felt I did nonetheless. We were fairly optimistic during the break as Ipswich were struggling down the bottom and we knew we had the players to make them panic. Especially against ten men.

Palace dominated the second half as Ipswich and their manager, Roy Keane, felt sorry for themselves. The red card had been harsh as there was no malice in the tackle but it was 'dangerous play' so, by the letter of the law, it probably deserved the card that it received. It was an 'old-fashioned striker's tackle'. That phrase always makes me laugh. It's as if being a centre forward gives a player sanctuary from referee's punishments and an excuse to foul the opposition.

I couldn't help but feel Keane would have had a different attitude if he'd been playing. As a midfielder in the heart of Manchester United's most successful ever team, he'd epitomised their never-say-die attitude. As a manager, he came across as an angry playground bully, who no one really liked or was even that scared of.

Neil Danns gave us the lead half way through the second half. Towards the end of the match, Ipswich finally offered something in the way of a fight and it was from one of their late attacks that Palace finished the game off. We counter attacked at pace and Darren Ambrose unselfishly passed to Moses, who beat his man and fired a left footed shot past the keeper. It went in at the near post, which is often seen as a mistake by the goalie, but Moses hit the ball with such pace and accuracy that the Ipswich stopper had no chance.

Moses celebrated by waving to the crowd. Everyone knew that this could be his final home appearance. There was a lot of mutual love and respect between the crowd and player in that moment. It was a rare flash of closeness between the two. With their obscene wages, players can seem distant and un-relatable to the man in the crowd, but that celebration made us all feel that we were in it together. He didn't want to leave for the big money. He was happy being loved in South London. The other players mobbed him and joined us in our moment of togetherness.

Although he was born in Nigeria, Moses had grown up in Croydon. He was essentially a local boy done bloody good. This was the message that Palace needed to get out into the local community to win back the local support. Hopefully then we wouldn't see any local pubs cheering on 'The Chels'. A repulsive phrase used by middle aged men in pubs wearing Chelsea shirts, who have no affiliation to West London.

After the game, I sat in the Railway Club on my own for an hour until my Mum came back with the car. I wondered how little Nemie was, thought about having to now head to work, and reflected on the game. It was lucky that the football had been good as there had been little else to cheer. My mum returned with the best news of the day. Nemie was going to be ok and would be out of hospital within forty-eight hours.

I took over the driving and headed to work. Rich was the duty manager that evening. I couldn't help but feel a little bit smug. Twenty-six games down, 23+ to go. Depending on how we did in the cup or if we had any playoff games, I might have been over half way through the challenge.

Chapter Thirty – **Excuse me Boyo**

**Monday 28th December 2009, Swansea City vs Crystal Palace,
The Liberty Stadium.**

Crystal Palace: Julian Speroni, Nathaniel Clyne, Clint Hill, Jose Fonte, Lee Hills, Shaun Derry, Neil Danns (Sean Scannell 90), Johnny Ertl, Darren Ambrose, Victor Moses (Freddy Sears 69), Calvin Andrew (Alan Lee 57).
Subs Not Used: Alassane N'Diaye, Nicky Carle, Ryan Smith, James Comley.

Swansea: De Vries, Tate, Serran, Williams, Bessone, Britton, Pratley, Allen (Monk 22), Butler, Van der Gun (Dyer 59), Pintado (Orlandi 79).
Subs Not Used: Cornell, Gower, Stephen Dobbie, Trundle.

As I have already alluded to, this was not a game that I was especially looking forward to. It's a long trip to Swansea and I didn't know anyone else who was going to the game. Also, I was missing a large family party to attend it. I doubt anyone was surprised that I was missing the celebration after my antics for my cousin's wedding, but I was still a bit disappointed not to be there.

The plan was to head to my Dad's place in Salisbury after the match as I hadn't seen him over the festive period. This involved me making a four hour journey, most of which would be completely alone after changing at Cardiff. To make matters worse, due to the train companies needing to use the Christmas period for engineering works, there was also a delightful rail-replacement bus involved.

In my usual wisdom, I also decided to get cheap train tickets by booking an early train there, which arrived in Swansea just before mid-day and a return train that left at 5:10. That would give me about twenty minutes after the match, which would be tight but should be ok.

After a long, but fairly uneventful journey there, I arrived at Swansea station and appeared to be the only Palace fan on the train. Well, certainly the only one wearing colours. In fact, only about 15 people got off the train at all. This was about the same amount of coppers that were waiting in the station.

As I went through the barriers, a police man called me over. *"Are there going to be many of your lot coming today?"* he inquired. I looked around. Nope, there was not one other Palace fan here. I was out numbered by about 15 to 1 by police. I carefully considered my position and decided it was best not to say anything too sarcastic or flippant. *"No, I don't think so officer. Why, have you heard there will be?"*
I was actually quite curious. It would have been great to have a large Palace crowd down there but I certainly wasn't expecting one. Had they heard of high ticket sales? They must speak to the clubs involved in the game and make policing decisions based on these discussions. *"We don't know, that's why we're asking you boyo."*
There again, maybe not. 'Police Intelligence' does seem to be a bit of an oxymoron at football.

I then made a very important inquiry upon arriving in a new town. *"Do*

172

you know where Wetherspoons is?"
There has to be one, right? There is a Wetherspoons in *every* town! I had been to
Swansea twice before, but both times were on the club coach so I didn't know
the town at all. My intention was to get a taxi to the ground as it was a fair way,
but I had hoped to head to a pub and meet other Palace fans to share a beer (and
the cost of a cab) with first.

However, I was told to avoid the town centre and that all away fans
were to make their way to the taxi rank by the station to go straight to the
ground. One kind officer escorted me to the cab office and informed me to be
careful travelling on my own. He then told the driver that I should go straight to
the ground. I half expected him to follow it up by telling me to not pass go or
collect £200. However, he did give me a final word of warning, *"Plenty of English
folk come to Swansea all cocky, and leave with their head kicked in. The locals
don't take too kindly to away folk from London!"*
Welcome to Wales.

My cab driver was very friendly. He was called Stew and took huge pride
in telling me he was a Cardiff City fan and how much he hated everything about
their South Wales neighbours, especially the football team. For once, I think the
cab driver was genuine. It was a lot of fake anger if he was simply trying to earn a
tip. He told me how great it was to grow up in Cardiff and how grubby Swansea
was. He took delight in informing me that 120,000 more people lived in Cardiff
than Swansea because it was so much more exciting and prosperous.

I did have to question – why he wasn't one of those one hundred and
twenty thousand people who were enjoying a more 'exciting and prosperous'
lifestyle but I thought it best not to. I also decided not to tell him of my dislike for
Cardiff's football team. I didn't want to be rude. With such a tight schedule after
the game, it would be best to pre-arrange a taxi to pick me up and in this case,
slagging off the Welsh capital wasn't likely to help my cause.

Swansea's ground is right next to the A4067 so Stew pulled into a slip
road to let me out. He explained that the traffic would be bad if he took me right
to the ground. It did cross my mind that it was three hours until kick off, we could
see the ground and it was more like a ghost town than rush hour on the M25 but
never mind. I just about had time for the five minute walk without missing kick
off.

It also occurred to me that this would be a perfect place to meet him
without getting stuck in traffic after the match. We agreed to meet there at 4:55.
He offered to let me to pay both fees when I returned but I neglected the offer. I
was so taken aback by his trust that I felt I should at least pay his first half up
front. I considered paying return journey too but then my rare streak of financial
generosity and trust ended. I was a student after all.

I headed to the Harvester Pub by the ground, which is advertised as
home fans only but I have learnt from previous trips that it allows away fans too. I
went to the bar and ordered a pint of Brains Bitter to try the local brew. Maybe it
would add to my intelligence by drinking Brains? Even if it did sound a bit

vampire-escque. With my Brains in my hand, I began to talk to a pensioner who was a Swansea fan. He was a real old school football supporter. He told me all about the good old days at the Vetch Field, their previous stadium, and he even talked about fans changing ends at half time during his early days.

He was very interested in Selhurst Park, having not been for 40 years. He talked with envy at us having a 'real ground'. I knew exactly where he was coming from. These new grounds all look the same. Swansea, Cardiff, Reading, Derby, Hull, etc. Apart from the colour of the seats, they really do have very few differences. In his words *"Selhurst Park may be an outdated s***-hole, but at least it has character and it's your shit-hole!"*

While I agreed with his sentiment, two things crossed my mind when he said it. Firstly, I wasn't sure how I felt about Selhurst Park being described as a s***-hole and secondly, technically, it wasn't ours.

I discussed all things Swansea, Palace and football over a few beers with my new surrogate grandad until well after two o'clock. Around one thirty, we were joined by a few other Palace fans that I knew, who had arrived on the club coach.

While in the pub, I got a text from my friend, Karina, saying that she was at the game. I'd met Karina at secondary school and we created an instant friendship upon discovering we were the only Palace fans in the year group. Supporting Palace just isn't the done thing in an Ascot school, so it was enough. Enough to form a friendship that has outlasted many of my other school companionships. My instant thought upon receiving the text was *'Bugger! She always drives to games and could have given me a lift.'*

I finished my drink and headed to the away section. When I got into the ground, I found the bar and got myself another pint before finding Karina. We discussed our hopes for the game and our opinions on Freddy Sears returning to West Ham, which had been announced in the week. Inevitably, conversation turned to the pointless subject of what we had done over the festive season. Everyone has always done exactly the same; either eaten and drank too much or been miserable and alone. Football fans are always glad to be out of the house and have an abundance of football to watch. We wished each other a late Merry Christmas and headed to our seats.

The game started fairly quietly. Both teams seemed to be recovering from their Christmas hangovers and didn't have any real sense of purpose. Then suddenly, Victor Moses brought the game to life. In his current form, no one in the league could handle him. He collected the ball on the left wing and glided past a couple of players before he was ungraciously clattered by a big defender. Presumably, the lump had remembered how Moses had torn them apart the previous year in a 3-1 Palace victory.

Their crowd cheered with pride. The Palace fans took one large gasp en masse. Moses getting injured would not only put the brakes on our good form but could feasibly risk the future of our club. We were relying on the money of his sale to keep the sharks at bay. The defender got a talking to by the referee and an abundance of abuse from the Palace faithful. Moses gingerly got to his feet and received a mountain of disdain from the home fans for diving.

That seemed to change the game. Both sets of players and supporters were fired up. The match became incredibly 'niggly' as both teams scrapped to stop the other team playing and leave a few bruises on their opponents. Just seventeen minutes into the game, Danns poked the ball passed his man, Albert Serran, and was unceremoniously blocked off.

The home crowd went nuts. They believed he dived. The Palace fans went nuts. We believed he was fouled. The referee went nuts. He sent Serran off. It was a brave but ultimately harsh decision from the referee. For the second game in a row, our opponents went down to ten men in the first half. The vocal home crowd were now baying for blood. At Cardiff, I felt that their new ground had killed some of their hostile atmosphere. That certainly wasn't the case here.

Minutes later, Moses was at it again, ghosting past one defender before nut-megging a second. Then a defender crashed into him. *"You dirty sheep-shagging Welsh ****"* I screamed. Although the red card had been harsh, I was getting pretty worked up about the constant fouls from the home side. An elegant lady turned around and looked at me. *"Excuse me boyo, my husband and I are from Wales,"* she said, while pointing at the man next to her as if to prove his identity. *"But we're Crystal Palace fans and would prefer it if you didn't abuse us."*

I felt like letting out a scream akin to Victor Meldrew. What were the bloody chances of sitting behind the entire South Wales Crystal Palace Supporters Club? What on earth made them support Palace if they came from Swansea? Did they make the 400 mile round trip to Selhurst every other week? And only I would manage to sit behind them in their bloody home town. I didn't bee-lieve it! I kept quiet for the rest of the reasonably uneventful half.

During half time, I got myself another pint of Brains Bitter (still hoping it would boost my intelligence) and started to talk to a Palace fan who I have had many discussions with at games but never caught his name and never thought to ask for it. To me, he always has been, and always will be, Santa. The first time I saw him was at a game in Reading about seven years previous and he was dressed as St Nick. It was the game before Christmas and my Dad had taken me to the match to cheer me up after my guinea pig, called Clinton after my Palace hero, had died.

I'm not sure why my father decided this was likely to improve my depressive mood as Palace's form was about as healthy as my pet. We were in the relegation zone, hadn't won for about 407 games and Reading were flying high in the play offs. Despite all this, we strolled to a 3-0 win and went on to gain promotion. Who says Santa's magic isn't real? It's a shame that he wasn't in his plump red attire in Swansea that day. Maybe he couldn't afford a suit after putting £7.5 million pounds in Simon Jordan's stocking? We could but dream.

Anyway, 'Santa' claimed to know the Welsh couple and spoke about them with real warmth. I had no doubts they were lovely people. I mean, Santa knows who's naughty and who's nice, right? But I was still thoroughly pissed off with my bad luck of managing to sit behind and insult the only Palace fans from the region.

While Santa was sipping on his beer and chewing his pie, (no, it wasn't a mince pie) he gave me some advice. *"You know the mistake you made don't you?"*

I looked blankly at him. How dare he suggest it was a mistake on *my* behalf. It's perfectly normal for an English away fan in Wales to insult the Welsh. In fact, it's almost expected.

*"You said they were dirty welsh sheep shagging ****s,"* he continued. I looked around. He was luckier than me. No Welsh Palace fans happened to be passing by at that moment. *"What you should have said is 'You dirty sheep shagging bastards!'"*

"Why?" I replied, puzzled. As far as I could see, all he was doing was repeating the insult as many times as he could without his Welsh friends hearing.

"Because then they couldn't take offence without admitting that they were either dirty, sheep shaggers or bastards!" explained Santa with a huge grin, as if he had just delivered his gifts to Anna Kournikova during his Christmas Eve rounds.

Santa's logic was sound, but I still decided to sit elsewhere for the second half. It was uneventful and boring. Moses didn't dare run at Swansea's defence again and they had an extra defender marking our star player to block any service into him anyway. The kind of tactic that is seen as 'anti-football' when it is done against your side and 'sensible' when your team deploys such an idea. And to be blunt, the other attacking options available to us were hardly inspiring.

Calvin Andrew looked his usual useless self, until he was subbed for the uncompromising Alan Lee, who enjoyed a long tussle with equally uncompromising defenders for long balls that had been lumped forward in his general direction. Freddie Sears was given a late run about for what was going to be his final appearance for the club. Would he finally do something close to scoring? West Ham had recalled him and we were quite happy to save on wages and send him home. His whole time at Palace had rested on 'what ifs?' and none bigger than that goal at Bristol. Bloody Rob Shoebridge. His ten minutes or so in red and blue mirrored the rest of his short Eagles career. He created chances for himself and looked lively but ultimately, didn't score.

In the final minutes, I decided to leave early because I was tight on time for my train. I waved to a couple of friends as I dashed off to the concourse. I only had 15 minutes and didn't fancy spending more money on a replacement train ticket home or spending any more time than I had to in Swansea if I'm being perfectly honest. However, when I got to the concourse, I discovered that the Police had locked the exit and we were trapped in. To make it worse, we were told that we would be kept there until all the home fans had left the area.

This was a typically stupid action of people who haven't moved their views on from the 1980s. I have no idea what they thought 500-odd Palace fans were going to attempt to do. Besides, I had a taxi to get. There had been no signs of crowd trouble before or during the game, yet we were being held behind like caged animals. Apparently it's their policy to do it after every game. A frankly ridiculous and unnecessary procedure that only manages to antagonize football fans, making it more likely that trouble will start.

There was now ten minutes until the train left and I was supposed to have met Stew in his cab five minutes previously. My phone began to ring. 'Swansea Cab' showed up on the screen. I answered and said I was on my way. *"Hurry up boyo or the traffic will get too heavy and you'll miss your train,"* remarked Stew. Really? I hadn't thought of that. Idiot. Pleas to let us go as our train was due to leave in what was now a matter of minutes time fell on deaf ears. Karina and her Dad were nearly falling down the stairs from the seats while laughing at my predicament, which was particularly useful I felt. Bastards.

Finally, they let us out, four minutes before the train was due to leave. My phone rang again. I didn't answer. We charged onto a bus. I had no hope of meeting that taxi now. The fee was £2. I don't think a single Palace fan paid it. The Welsh Police looked likely to have cost me forty odd quid for a second train ticket. I wasn't in any mood to put the little money that I had left into the poxy Swansea Transport System. To be fair to the police, they did hold up the traffic for us.

We went past the small slip road where I was due to meet Stew. He was waiting there. I felt bad for him. His loyalty to someone he had only just met was credible. However, I didn't have time to feel sorry for anyone. My train left in 30 seconds and we were still a few minutes away from the station.

We arrived at the train station around 6 minutes late and the police were waiting at the bus stop to escort us into the station. They really were quite paranoid about us. There was a mere 40 or so fans on this bloody bus. All of which were far more concerned about getting the hell out of Swansea than starting a brawl there. One of the coppers spoke with self importance *"Move quickly please."*

Move quickly? You bastards have made us miss our train and now you want us to move quickly? Move quickly to where exactly? We can't go anywhere now! In fact, if we can't get the train, we'll all go to the pub and get pissed up. *Then* we might start a brawl. No, actually, we'll start a riot, a war, against you. This is entirely your fault, you gits. *"Move quickly, we've held the train for you!"* he announced. Maybe they weren't so bad after all?

The train journey back was a long one. Going from Swansea to Salisbury isn't a particularly easy or natural train journey at the best of times. Needless to say, my friend Mr Carlsberg was on the train to keep me company. Well, not so much my friend, more of an old acquaintance, whom I still sent a Christmas card to once a year.

After parting with my fellow Palace fans, who were heading back to London, at Cardiff, I had to get a replacement bus to Bristol before eventually getting another (delayed) train to Salisbury to meet my Dad.

When I got there, he asked me briefly about the game and that was it.

He was enjoying a rare chance to have his family around him for Christmas and he didn't want to sour the mood by talking about football. For me, it was all I wanted to talk about so I sulked off to read the Palace forum, the BBS, on my laptop, alone. I saw Palace as part of our family. A bond that held us together and it certainly had in the past, when my Dad used to go to games. However, with his interest waning, he sometimes didn't even know the players that I was talking about, having never seen them play.

Chapter Thirty-one – **So what for 2010?**

Saturday 2nd January 2010, Sheffield Wednesday vs Crystal Palace (FA Cup R3), Hillsborough.

Crystal Palace: Julian Speroni, Johnny Ertl, Jose Fonte, Claude Davis, Shaun Derry, Natheniel Clyne, Clint Hill, Sean Scannell (Calvin Andrew, 58), Neil Danns, Alan Lee, Darren Ambrose (Alex Wynter, 90)
Subs Not Used: James Comley, Alassane N'Diaye
Sheffield Wednesday: Grant, Simek, Purse, Beevers (Buxton, 70), Spurr, Potter, O'Connor, Tom Soares (Johnson, 69), Tudgay (Esajas, 81), Jeffers, Clarke
Subs Not Used: Jameson, McAllister, Boden, Palmer

It might have been a new year but for Palace's finances, nothing had changed. For the third month in a row, the players and staff would be paid late...

This was the second of two games that I wasn't particularly looking forward to. I did consider not going. It was, after all, *only* a cup game. I could still go to all the league games and chauvinistically boast about going to every league game of the 2009/10 season, even if I secretly decided to miss this one. However, the challenge drove me on – I would know if I'd cheated the task. I wasn't particularly bothered about the game, or even the result. It was the need to go to *every* game that meant I had to make the journey north. I simply didn't have a choice in the matter.

The Christmas excuse for over-eating and over-drinking had long passed. My second Christmas, one of the benefits of having separated parents, had been slightly less boring and painful than the real date that year. There'd been more family involved in the 'Christmas' with my Dad, which makes the season nearly as jolly as the football does. Although, admittedly both football and family can bring just as much misery as they do joy to millions of people across the country.

Both of the relationships are actually quite similar. You can't change your family. You can't change your football team (and if you do, then it's not a real relationship. It's merely a bit of flirting). You get pissed off with your family. You get pissed off with your football team. However, you know that you'll return to both with optimism and smiles because no matter what, you have an underlying love for them. You go to Sheffield (in this case) when you don't want to because it's Palace. You go to events that you don't want to because it's family (although I did seem to be making an ever increasing habit of missing such family events for football). But if either of them are in trouble, you'll get into their corner and fight for them against all odds (as I was soon to find out with Palace)

And finally, you can't get rid of either of them because as much frustration, pain and inconvenience as they bring, your life is better with them than without them.

The New Year had come and gone in the most uneventful circumstances possible. I'd worked at the pub until around two in the morning before I went to a party which had long since wound down. Although my flatmate Dave was there and it had been really good to have a long chat and catch up with him. Something that I hadn't done for months. Unlike Boxing Day, I had no qualms about having to work. I hate New Year's Eve. It's a night that can only disappoint and provide an opportunity for over-spending. I resent having to pay to get into my local, which is free to enter on the other 364 nights of the year.

What fuels my hatred even further is the one year that I decided to ignore the nonsense and refused to go out. I went to bed early but I was woken up throughout the night as every pissed contact in my phonebook sent me a badly typed message wishing me a Happy New Year. It would have been a much happier New Year if they'd let me sleep. Inconsiderate bastards. As with most things, I can remember the date with a football context as I spent the miserable hangover-free New Year's Day at the New Den, watching Palace lose 3-0 to Millwall. January 1st 2011. Happy New Year indeed.

Before heading to work on New Years Eve, I'd had the usual conversation with my mum.

"What were the highlights of 2009?"

"Well the win at West Brom was brilliant. As was that night at Reading, but it would have to be Moses' goal against Barnsley!" Nothing else entered my mind.

My Mum gave me a familiar disappointed look and a role of her eyes.

"What about passing your driving test? Or meeting your new-born niece? Or your mini-summer road trip with Phill and Rob? Or going to Reading festival? Or going to Prague? Or Edinburgh? Or all the nights out at uni? Or your cousin's wedding? Or your nephew's first steps and words and his face lighting up when he sees you?"

They were all important moments. I'd had a great year. But I'm embarrassed to say, they weren't what came to my mind first. It wasn't a conscious decision. It was the mind of an addict. Are you sure there aren't any help groups? Maybe I should google it. Incidentally, it's amazing how language develops and 'googling' is now an everyday verb. A verb that could just have easily evolved into 'Binging', 'Jeavesing' or 'Duckduckgoing'.

"So what do you hope for the New Year?" she continued.

"Palace to get new owners and avoid financial oblivion. Maybe even get promoted so the Premiership money can save us. Oh, passing my degree and getting a teaching job would be good too."

While Palace's plight had been my first thought, the two did have equal importance to me. They shouldn't have. Clearly, having a career should prioritise over a Saturday kick about but as any football addict will understand, they did. I spent just as much time worrying about football as I did worrying about my degree and getting a job. I spent just as much time reading the BBS (the Palace forum) as I did reading teaching books. I wasn't even being lazy. I was working bloody hard. It was just that everything to do with Palace seemed as – if not more – important than anything else. I was only getting a job so that I could fund my addiction.

Looking back, I was devoting so much time to supporting Palace and studying and working at the pub and failing in chasing girls around nightclubs, I really don't know how I had time for anything else. Even sleep. Students have a reputation for lying about in bed, achieving very little other than a dent in their mattress. Although I hadn't achieved anything yet, I was certainly devoting enough time to my football, women and qualification challenges. Even hangovers were treated with contempt. I didn't have time for them. I would simply head to work or the library or Palace or the pub or a nightclub and carry on through them.

Out of my three challenges, I know which two I was better at. I didn't even think about going to Palace. Yes, I had the odd question mark against it at the end of a long away trip but I was still looking for cheap train tickets on a daily basis and was booked up for every game until March.

The teaching had been my dream since I was a child. Well it was once I'd established that I wasn't going to be the next Palace goalkeeper. Although, I still haven't completely given up on that dream. Goalkeepers do tend to break through into the first team later than outfield players. I'd looked after my younger neighbours when I was 11 or 12 and the teaching idea had begun then. Throughout secondary school, I'd taken every chance that I could to gain experience in primary schools and loved all of them. I'd applied to train to be a teacher with little more thought than that and hadn't found a reason to regret it yet.

I found some of the lectures a little bit tedious and the assignments an irrelevant nuisance at times because being young, naive and arrogant, I couldn't relate them to the classroom in the way that I should have done. I simply saw them as a means to an end. Obviously I couldn't see it at the time but that ignorance during lectures would hold me back when I started teaching. However, in terms of working with children, I was a natural. My first two placements had gone well and I was looking forward to my final upcoming placement. While, at the same time, nervously hoping that Palace wouldn't have any games rearranged to a midweek while I was on the work-based training.

While it didn't stop me trying, having a girlfriend could have easily distracted me from what I was really focused on. Palace and qualifying as a teacher. Both were a huge financial burden and neither of them took preference over the other. Besides, using an opening line of *"Would you go with Alan Lee or Stern John up front?"* never did work with the ladies.

Anyway, the challenge took me to Hillsborough, which was a ground that I had visited three times before and had never seen us win at. The first was a 0-0 draw, which I mainly remember for Brian moaning at Freedman missing our one and only chance late on. The second had one of those surreal moments in football (or indeed life) that over time make you begin to question your memory and make you feel the need to check with others that it really happened.

Palace were losing 2-1 and lacking ideas. With ten minutes left, heavy snow began to fall. Suddenly the players were playing in a blizzard and we could barely see past the halfway line. As Palace were heading for a defeat, we sang for the game to be called off. Right in the last minute, we got a free kick on the half way line. The ball was lumped forward and out of our view. A few seconds later, the Palace players came charging back towards us with their arms aloft. We (rightly) assumed they'd scored.

If there was any doubt that it wouldn't have happened without the snow, it was quashed when we discovered the goal scorer. Matt Lawrence. It was his only goal for the club in 121 games and his first in over 300 matches for any club, spanning back over an eight year period.

"Oh Matty Lawrence, he scores when it snows!"

Terrace 'wit' is never far away.

The third match at Hillsborough had been a forgettable 2-0 loss.

The steel city is a place that interests me a lot. Traditionally, it is an old person's place. It's grey, it's dull and it lacks work opportunities. Redundancies have always been high so anyone with a skilled trade tends to leave the area to look for work. However, my favourite band, The Arctic Monkeys, were proud 'Sheffielders'. Yes I did have to look up that term. Unlike Mancs, Liverpudlians, Geordies, Brummies, etc. there isn't an obvious collective term for the people of Sheffield. Although t'Sheffielders might be more apt because of their Yorkshire accents.

t'Arctic Monkeys represented a new 'cool' wave coming from Sheffield as one of a few popular indie bands that came from Yorkshire at the time. Suddenly, a pair of skinny jeans and a chequered shirt was the look around the city rather than a grey jumper under a dark green jacket. Unfortunately, I didn't have a chance to go to the city that day, let alone head to one of the many clubs that were persuading young people to stick about. Yet again, I was going on the coach.

In fact, forget clubs, I couldn't even go to the pub. All of the pubs around Hillsborough are home fans only. To make matters worse, since the tragic 1989 disaster, they haven't served beer in the away end. Previous coach trips to Sheffield Wednesday have proved to be sober occasions. However, this time, we had a plan. We'd heard a rumour that Hillsborough Leisure Centre served beer and were trying to attract away fans as an extra source of income.

I made the short walk with two of the coach regulars, Helen and Phil. They were absolutely Palace (and drinking, two concepts that go hand in hand in my opinion) mad. I'd tried to convert them to train travel because of the cheaper prices and greater beer drinking opportunities but they'd stayed loyal to the coach.

It was the first time that I'd entered a Sports Centre in years and I couldn't help but feel both guilt and irony as it was only with the intention of getting a beer. We were directed to the 'sports cafe' where they had a few cans of Tetleys Smooth Bitter in a fridge behind the counter. I saw it as a crap version of what I'd usually drink and the other two 'didn't drink bitter'. But that wouldn't stop us. We had three cans each, which drank the bar (or cafe rather) dry. The look on the girl behind the counters face was brilliant. She was used to the odd freshly showered gym-monkey coming in for a *Powerade* but she was now serving three pot-bellied, football piss heads.

It was around quarter past two when they ran out of supplies. I didn't really care about the game. We were going well in the league and our small squad couldn't cope with a cup run. It was a ground that I'd been to a few times before and, such was my indifference, it was one of the rare occasions where I wasn't going to let the football ruin my mood. I expected us to lose and that didn't concern me. Therefore, drinking to gee myself up for the meaningless match was essential.

"Errrm... do you have anymore?" I asked after deciding the need for beer was more important than the embarrassment of looking like an alcoholic in a sports centre cafe.

"We'll have a look..." she replied in a slightly anxious voice. Five minutes later, she returned with two more cans of Tetleys and four bottles of Smirnoff Ice alcopops. *"That's all the alcohol that we have on the site,"* she told us. I don't know where the sports centre rumour had come from but they obviously weren't expecting or wanting a larger crowd of football supporters. Three of us were out-doing their supply and quite enough for them.

"We'll take them all!"

Short of starting on the swimming pool water, we'd drunk the leisure centre dry.

The game was uneventful and once again memorable for only one reason. Being a football geek (*A common trait of your average football addict. Despite the reputation, most of us would be a lot happier quoting statistics than giving someone a whack around the head*) I remembered three things about the game. Neil Danns had given us a first half lead which was cancelled out by a Clint Hill own goal but no, neither of them stayed with me as important.

However, what did stick with me was that Palace got a winner from Calvin Andrew. Despite being a striker, Calvin Andrew goals were about as regular as Matt Lawrence's. Maybe we needed to leave our strikers in Sheffield as it seemed to provide the rarest of goal scorers. It was his first for our club and he'd been with us for a year and a half. Before that, he'd scored four goals in fifty five matches in the lower leagues while playing for Luton. Not a great record.

The second memory of the match that I have kept with me was Alex Wynter being subbed on. He didn't do anything of note (in fact, he played out of position for a mere two minutes) but he was yet another youth player to be given a professional debut at Palace. The feeling of seeing local lads making the grade is special. It gives the club an identity. And as I've said before, it should be used to help the club to re-build links with the local community. The 'Chelsea incident' in the Railway Club still horrified me.

Since Warnock had been appointed two years previously, he'd given professional debuts to Jon Bostock, Victor Moses, Sean Scannell, Lee Hills, Royce Wiggins, Ashley-Paul Robinson, Ben Kudjodji, Nathaniel Clyne, Kieron Cadogan, Kieran Djilali, James Comley and now, Alex Wynter. They would all go on to have very varied careers but each one of their debuts gave me a huge sense of pride and optimism.

It was the club's academy that gave us hope. Moses' impending sale was hoped to save the club this time. Maybe Alex Wynter would be the next young lad to give us a couple of years of entertainment before moving on to bigger things and providing vital money for the club to survive. As it turned out, he didn't play for the first team again for another four years.

The third personal memory of the game, was that it was the first time that I heard the now-standard Palace song 'We Love You'. We'd ripped it off Celtic, who had taken it from the German side, St. Pauli. Within a year, it was being sung by most sets of fans around the country.

I returned to the coach as a happy boy. The football *had* affected my mood. It does. No matter how much you try and kid yourself that it doesn't. It does. There really is no such thing as a meaningless game to a football fan and I had been a disrespectful fool to try and persuade myself that the FA Cup provided that. People (men in particular) hate losing. The context of the defeat doesn't matter. A loss at Wembley holds the same hurt as a defeat in a playground kick about. Both feel like the end of the world.

However, despite the result, I was very relieved when the long coach journey ended as I got out at my usual motorway-side spot. I'd be lying if I didn't admit that I'd wondered if I'd made a mistake in going. I could have missed the game and still completed the challenge. Kind of. It would have still been impressive to go to every league game of the season. Yet I knew, deep down, that my absence would have haunted me forever more. I would have failed. The next day, I watched the draw for the fourth round from the pub while I was working. Palace were away at Premiership Wolves.

Chapter 32 – **A Wasted Day**

Monday 5th January 2010

As everyone was now aware, Palace's finances were dire. Agilo (the hedge fund), Her Majesty's Revenue and Customs, the players and a selection of other clubs all wanted their share of the money. None of them were likely to get it any time soon but Agilo were by far the most aggressive of the creditors. Therefore, the news that broke on Monday 5th January 2010 was probably our biggest result of the season so far.

"I am close to signing a new deal with Agilo so that we are not going into administration tomorrow."
Simon Jordan

The words that every Palace fan wanted to hear. Against all the odds, Jordan had come up trumps. He was in full arrogant swing but for once, he had every right to be. He'd saved us. Again. I half expected Simon's brother, Dominic, our Director of Football, to present him to the crowd at our next home match from above the White Horse Lane end, by triumphantly lifting him up in a manner akin to the way Rafiki raised the new born cub, Simba, to the Lion King pride. The Jordans were the unlikely heroes.

Saturday 9th January 2010, Crystal Palace vs Bristol City, Selhurst Park.

As usual, I was working in the pub on the Friday night while the regular bunch of lonely individuals got drunk in the Feltham Wetherspoons. Geoff was slumped over the bar, 'Roy the ticket' was ranting about the trains running late, Conner was staring at his stale pint, his ninth of the day, and Gillian was picking at her nails as she sat on a lonely table in the corner.

The mood was dead as pubs often are in the long month after Christmas. Not even the Wetherspoons January Sale had tempted the punters to join us. There was a group of friendly armchair football-supporting alcoholics stood by the bar that I could talk to on such depressing evenings to fill the time. Although it was (and still is) quite worrying that half of them work on the buses.

As it was so empty, my shift was ended early. I was tired and all too happy to miss out on the extra couple of hours' pay. I went around to the other side of the bar, sat with the alcoholic bus drivers and bought a pint. I was only going to have one as I'd planned a full day of drinking at Palace the following day. Unfortunately, something caught my eye on the TV screen behind me. Sky Sports News had that little yellow ticker running along the bottom of the picture.

'Breaking news; Crystal Palace v Bristol City called off due to a frozen pitch'

Bugger. Well that ruined my plans for the next day. January 2010 had been the heaviest snow fall that I had witnessed in my short life, with temperatures staying below zero for a prolonged period. 7-10 inches of snow had allowed me the opportunity to have the kind of fun that the small slushy offerings of my previous years had deprived my childhood of.

Throwing (and receiving) a ball of soft snow to the head was much more fun than spending hours trying to scrape together the rare bits of frozen white mud that lay around the unforgiving secondary school playground, as had been my previous snow experiences. However, in January 2010, snow turned to ice and stayed on the pavement for weeks, which wasn't so much fun. It was amazing that no games had been affected up until that point really.

Anyway, it left me with a problem. All of my plans for the next day had revolved around Palace. I now had a day to fill. I had another pint to help me think of something to do. Then I came up with an idea. I decided to go and watch Brentford. I sent Chris a text. I received one back fairly quickly. Damn. They were due to be playing away from home anyway but their match had also fallen foul to the weather. It had been a stupid idea. Of course, if Palace were off, then the odds of a worse ground in the same city allowing a game to go ahead were slim at best. I'd need a better plan. I had another beer to help me think. And another. And another. And a few more after that. Needless to say, I ended up incredibly drunk.

I had sent a few enquiring texts out throughout the evening and received nothing of any interest to me in return but the truth was, I didn't want to do anything else. I'd wanted to go to the football and I was gutted that I wouldn't be. It was a meaningless game in terms of our overall season. Of course it wouldn't be meaningless during or after it as I'd discovered in Sheffield. And yes, like any match, I could big it up to myself. I could, and often do, persuade myself that each match is nearly as vital as life or death.

For example; it was a chance for revenge over Bristol for *that* Freddy Sears goal. If we'd got that goal, we'd currently be in the playoffs with the three extra points. And that's simply taking into account the points from that match. If Mr Shoebridge had done his job properly, Sears would have got his first goal and his confidence would have grown. By now, he'd have twenty goals to his name and god knows how high Palace would be in the table. Yes, revenge was a must. Winning this game was about more than three points. It was about the justice system and integrity of football. See, vital.

But the reality was, no one outside of South London or Bristol cared in the slightest. Well, not many people. Evidently, there was at least one couple in South Wales who it meant a lot to. But to the vast majority, unless it happened to be on their accumulator, the game was meaningless. It was a clash between two, mid-table Championship sides.

However, I did care. And so do thousands of others every Saturday. I wanted my Saturday to be filled with football. I didn't want to go to the cinema or go bowling, or even simply to go the pub to watch the other scores come in. I wanted to see real, live football. I wanted my Palace. It certainly wasn't meaningless to me.

As it was, I did something that I hate doing. I wasted the day. I spent most of it in bed. Doing nothing. With a hangover. Maybe I wasn't so different to most students after all. However, it did show me that without the Saturday fix for my addiction, I was very, very lost. Football is about friendships and emotion and escaping real life and cheering and loving and caring and hurting and releasing anger (and that's all usually just in a first half at Selhurst Park).

But it's also about habit and routine. Something that is essential for children to be given in the classroom and as I found out that day, something that is essential for me to have on a Saturday as a football fan. I couldn't cope with the change in routine and I didn't know what to do with myself. It is a feeling that thousands of people up and down the country have on the first weekend after the season draws to a close. As the summer goes on, you learn to enjoy your Saturdays again. But that first weekend is a real shock to the system and that is how it felt to have a game snatched away from me. It was ok for Colin and Dan, they had families and responsibilities to fill their day with. What did I have? I was stuck without football and stuck on my bed with a hangover.
It was a miserable realisation that without Palace, my Saturdays were dull and empty.

On that Saturday afternoon, when I still wasn't over the emptiness of Palace's cancellation or the discomfort of my hangover, I had the same horrible feeling of something being taken away from me for the second time in a day. Jose Fonte, our centre back and one of our best performers, was sold to Southampton for £1.2m.

Clearly, Simon Jordan's deal with Agilo wasn't enough on its own. Warnock later revealed that Fonte had been reluctant to go and he'd had to personally ask him to leave so that the rest of the players could get paid. It was one of the most depressing transfers that I'd ever known. In football terms, it didn't suit Palace, Warnock or Fonte but financially, it had to happen.

Thursday 14th January 2010

Five days after Fonte left, the players and the rest of the staff were finally paid their wages.

Chapter 33 – **Palace. My Friend's Worst Nightmare.**

Saturday 16th January 2010, Plymouth Argyle vs Crystal Palace, Home Park.

Crystal Palace: Julian Speroni, Nathaniel Clyne, Claude Davis, Clint Hill, Lee Hills, Neil Danns, Shaun Derry, JohnnyErtl, Darren Ambrose (Danny Butterfield, 80), Victor Moses (Calvin Andrew, 67), Alan Lee (AlessaneN'Diaye 72)
Subs Not Used: Matt Lawrence, Kieran Djilali
Plymouth: Larrieu, Duguid, Arnason, Barker, Sawyer, Judge, Summerfield (McNamee 58), Carl Fletcher (Folley 70), Clark, Barnes (Gow 46), Fallon
Subs Not Used: Saxton, Wright-Phillips, Noone, Joe Mason

"I'm not concerned. It's under control and being dealt with."

This had been Simon Jordan's reaction to the club being served with a Winding Up Order by HMRC over unpaid debts of around £1.2 million – the same fee that Fonte had been sold for. The court case was going to be on 27th January 2010. There had been rumours about it for a couple of months but this was the first official confirmation. Maybe the Agilo deal hadn't saved us after all. My brief moment of faith in Simon Jordan had passed.

On the day of the Plymouth game, I woke up at around 6:45 in Putney, at my friend Robin's house. The two of us had decided that the previous day should be spent pub crawling the many excellent free houses up and down Putney High Street. We'd returned home as pissed as a fart, which had left his girlfriend almost as unimpressed as I was with my early alarm call. My friend, Ash, was going to drive the pair of us to Plymouth so that we could go to the football and stay the weekend with our friend, Rob.

As I've said before, the close friends that I have kept from school are not really football fans. My friend Ash certainly wasn't but he was keen to go and visit Rob. When I bring up football to my mates, it's usually met with a communal groan. However, when I bring up Palace, it is usually greeted by the words *"Shut up James. Nobody cares."*
That's the polite version anyway.

Ash's preparation for the journey had been nearly as bad as mine. He'd not slept that night and now planned to drive 235 miles to Plymouth. In his words, *"My girlfriend wanted to do other things."* The sensible thing to do would have been to give him a couple of hours sleep before setting off - but we didn't have time for that. I didn't want to risk missing out on the football or any pre match drinking. Despite being extremely close friends, we spent the journey making small talk. My hangover and his tiredness didn't lead itself to deep or meaningful conversations.

We arrived in Plymouth around eleven-thirty, which gave us plenty of time to drop off our stuff at Rob's before heading to the pub. By the time we arrived, Ash was basically in a coma. Rob and I suggested that he stayed behind and had a sleep but he seemed reluctant. He is someone who doesn't like putting other people out and goes well beyond his duty to say yes. In his twisted logic, staying behind was betraying us. He had no interest in going to the football but didn't want to miss out on time with his friends. In the end, we compromised and it was decided that he would come to the pub before going back to Rob's for a sleep while we went to the match.

Coventry had been a city in depression but Plymouth is a bit of a mixture. During my university years, both Rob and my brother, Simon, lived in the traditional navy town and had very different experiences. Rob loved it. Simon hated it. The university area is filled with cheap, late-night bars and a social student buzz. The rest of the city, despite the odd nice spot such as The Hoe or The Barbican, is basically a s***hole; full of angry navy boys. Students soon learn the places to avoid so they don't get a kicking.

We got a bus to the Wetherspoons by the ground. I'm not proud to admit it but it was the fourth different 'Spoons that I'd visited in Plymouth. I seemed to be fast turning into a connoisseur of the establishments. This one is an old mansion house and like most 'spoons, it was an impressive building from the outside but dim and highly unimpressive inside. We had a couple of pints of badly kept ale and had a catch up. Of course, being so soon after Christmas, we didn't really have any fresh news for each other so we just repeated the same jokes that we'd made over the festive period when we'd all been home from university. However, going for the weekend seemed to give the trip a bit more purpose.

At 2:50 we finished our beers and made the short walk across the road to the ground. As he was half asleep, Ash hadn't taken any notice of our route from Rob's to the ground so he reluctantly followed us to the game. Even with my two friends boosting the away attendance, there was only a small Palace following who had made the long trip. Almost a year to the day previously, six of my school mates and I had headed down to Plymouth for a weekend on the piss and to watch the football. Unfortunately, the Palace game had been frozen off. We'd had a great weekend anyway and only I had been gutted that the football had been cancelled. I guess the combination of bad memories from the year before and 'The Big Freeze' that was hitting the UK had put people off travelling. It was our coldest winter since 1978-79. Luckily, the negative temperatures had begun to rise and, this year, the game went ahead.

Inside the ground, I bumped into my friend, Charlie. I'd met Charlie at a match between Torquay and Port Vale a few years previously. He lived in Torquay and had been to the game with his young cousin, who was wearing a Palace shirt so I'd instantly gravitated towards him. We got chatting and spent the day together in the town. After swapping MSN details (the cornerstone of all social activity for teenagers growing up in the 'noughties'), we stayed in touch and became friends. We have very little else in common but the Palace bond had brought and kept us together. I still see him now. Another friendship made by Palace.

It might not have been played in negative temperatures but other than that, the weather couldn't have been much worse. There was heavy rain, which cut up an already dreadful pitch. Playing anything that resembled decent football on that surface was going to be impossible.

Ash sat there looking miserable. Watching a frankly dreadful game in the cold rain wasn't his idea of fun. It was pushing my understanding of the word too. It wasn't actually his first football match. He'd attended a windy, Friday night game between Wycombe Wanderers and Mansfield for a friend's eighteenth birthday in 2007. Wycombe had won 1-0 and Ash's main comments were *"When is it over?"* and *"Wycombe's forward* (Tommy Mooney) *moans a lot."*
I don't think he could believe that he was going through the whole horrible experience all over again.

He moaned about being cold but he could hardly blame the football for that. He hadn't brought a coat. He moaned about the rain. He moaned about the food. He moaned about the cost. He moaned, starting to sound a bit like his football nemesis, Tommy Mooney, about the crowd. He couldn't understand why people would travel half the length of the country and spend more time geeing up our fans or abusing the home end than actually watching the game.

He didn't get the emotion of the occasion either or why we all cared so much. He simply saw our obsession as an entertainment event, such as going to the theatre or the cinema, and if you approach lower league football expecting the players to provide value for money, you *will* be disappointed. I could see how he wasn't won over by the Crystal Palace Experience that I loved so much. He was cold, tired and watching a s*** game of a sport he didn't like. His face was a picture.

Even the terrace wit couldn't cheer him up. 'Pilgrim Pete', the Argyle mascot, had given us some 'banter' as he walked past. He wore a giant green hat and an oversized bushy ginger tash. The Palace fans amused themselves by singing about 'Paedo Pete'. The poor dressed up character took it well, waggled his finger at the naughty boys in the away end and left.

I couldn't help but feel conscious of how much Ash wasn't enjoying the experience. Ash likes relaxing. Ash daydreams about sitting on a beach in his mother's native country of the Philippines; doing nothing, calm all around and being totally at peace with the world. Ash doesn't like cold, frantic championship football. In one way, I laughed at it. He'd chosen to come and now he had to deal with it. But on the other hand, I felt guilty that after driving me nearly three hundred miles there, he was doing something that I loved so much at his own expense. Literally his own expense –match tickets aren't cheap.

I don't suppose that my expression was much more enthusiastic than Ash's either until yet again, Moses lit up the match. After seventeen minutes, he beat two players with one touch and rifled the ball past the goalkeeper. The entire away end jumped up. Except Ash. He stayed sat down.
Miserable.Shivering.Bored.And grumpy. Not even Victor Moses could cheer him up. And if Moses' piece of skill couldn't win him over, the rest of the game certainly wouldn't. It was abysmal as a spectacle but it finished 1-0 to Palace. A second away win on the trot, which despite Ash's indifference, left me delighted.

In their press conferences, both managers commented that the weather made for an awful match. They also both praised Moses – no one else on the pitch had the ability to win the game. Warnock gave a brilliant summary on our team when he said that *"We had to match them and I went with a team with a spine, and I thought the spine was very strong today."*

I don't think Ash appreciated how strong the spine of our team was in those conditions. I don't think Ash appreciated *anything* that afternoon. Not even Pilgrim Pete.

We always had a strong spine. We could match any team in the league in that way and would continue to do so after Moses left. However, while he was with us, we also had a moment of magic in us that other teams could only dream of. That moment of magic that makes watching dreadful football worthwhile. That moment of enjoyment that Ash just didn't get. Despite our precarious financial position, thanks largely to Ambrose and Moses, we were now just one point off the playoffs.

After the game, we headed back to Rob's before heading for a night out. Once again, not wanting to miss out, Ash didn't go to sleep. Despite being in a sleepwalking state, I think he got more pleasure out of the evening than he'd taken from the afternoon. He's never been to a football game since.

It's amazing that football can enrich my life so much, yet be so torturous for one of my best friends. However, I still manage to link my football experiences to most of our conversations. He's never amused. Ash just doesn't get how Crystal Palace can be relevant to teaching, nights out, the banking crisis, relationship advice, or even trying to pull. I guess that it could be argued that having such a one-track mind is another sign of an addict. I beg to differ.

I just don't get how people can't relate to it. So far in my life, no one has managed to stop my brain from constantly obsessing and regularly drifting to thoughts of all things Crystal Palace. As a child, I would sit in my classroom wondering who we'd play up front on the following Saturday or dreaming of scoring a winning goal at Selhurst Park. As an 'adult', I sit in my classroom wondering who we'll play up front on the following Saturday or dreaming of scoring a winning goal at Selhurst Park. The difference now is that I'm the distracted teacher rather than the distracted pupil. I should have grown up a bit by now but when it comes to football, growing up doesn't come into it. When it comes to football, the little boy lives on forever. He needs to. A child can rationalise and justify most things to his own mind in a way that a (sober) adult can't.

Chapter 34 – **Football Rivalries**

Saturday 23rd January 2010, Wolverhampton Wanderers vs Crystal Palace, Molenuex, FA Cup R4.

Crystal Palace: Julian Speroni, Danny Butterfield, Claude Davis (Matt Lawrence 22), Johnny Ertl, Nathaniel Clyne, Darren Ambrose, Neil Danns, Shaun Derry, Alessane N'diaye, Victor Moses, Alan Lee (Calvin Andrew 78)
Subs Not Used: Kieran Djilali, James Comley, Nicky Carle
Wolves: Wayne Hennessey, Zubar, Berra, Mancienne, Elokobi (Stephen Ward 72), Foley, Henry, David Jones, Surman (Mujangi Bia 63), Ebanks-Blake (Kevin Doyle 63), Vokes
Subs Not Used: Hahnemann, Craddock, Iwelumo, Milijas

Unlike the previous round, I didn't consider avoiding this tie. It might not have been a league game but it was a game against Premier League opposition, and having made the long trek to Sheffield earlier in the month, Wolverhampton was a doddle in comparison. I travelled up on a train full of Brighton supporters as they were away at Aston Villa in their fourth round tie. I met my friend, David, the 'Liverpool fan' from Warwick University, on the train at Coventry (he told me that the city was still depressed) and we spoke in hushed voices until the 'seaweed' fans left the train at Birmingham.

Once we were in Wolverhampton, a place that I have visited for football on numerous occasions, we had to hide our identity once again. A few years previously, West Brom fans had smashed up the Wetherspoons, which resulted in all of the pubs on the high street being strictly 'Home Fans Only'. I'd learnt this the hard way the year before when I'd been unable to get beer anywhere outside the ground, so I hadn't worn any Palace colours this time. Something that I'd been grateful for when I was on the train as Brighton aren't Palace's biggest fans.

Undercover, we went into the Wetherspoons to get some food. The bar tender did question that I was using a London payslip for my staff discount. The fact that I didn't speak in a slow, depressed accent as the locals do didn't help my cause either. In the end, David's student card from a nearby university persuaded the dubious barman that we weren't Palace fans. We had a couple of uncomfortable pints and a bite to eat before heading to the ground.

We didn't have tickets as there hadn't been a home match since the Sheffield game in the previous round so we needed to get there early. We went to the ticket office and asked for two student tickets but our request was declined. They believed our student cards to be fake. For the second time that day, we were forced to argue our cause for letting us into a venue. Going to a football match in Wolverhampton seemed to be a similar experience to being interrogated by the FBI.
"Who do you support?"
"Why are you from London?"
"Where do you go to university?"

"When did you join?"
"What are you doing in Wolverhampton?" (to be fair, this is a question that anyone in Wolverhampton should ask themselves)
"What are you studying?"
"Where is Twickenham?"

Refusing to pay the full price when we were eligible for a student ticket, we went around to the away fans entrance. Luckily, they were selling tickets on the gate and we got in for the rightful discounted amount.

There was a large Palace following of over fifteen hundred who had made the trip to the midlands. Colin saw the size of the away crowd in the next programme and couldn't believe it. He'd regretfully related to his old mate *"Dan, 1500 fans going to an FA Cup match and we didn't even consider going. We're no longer the hardcore."*

It was an upsetting realisation for him that he'd moved on to a different stage of life. Dan frowned but pointed out that they were simply waiting for their sons to be the next generation of Palace hardcore supporters.

Palace fans and players started brilliantly. Alan Lee put us one nil up early on with a powerful header. The away end erupted. Even David. While he wasn't a Palace fan, the contrast between him and Ash couldn't have been more different. He was loving it. Palace could, and maybe should, have got more but after an injury to Claude Davis, which broke the flow of the game, Wolves came back into the match and equalised before half time.

During the break in play for Davis' injury, the Palace fans came up with a song to the tune of 'Que Sara Sara' for our captain, Shaun Derry.

"SHAUN DERRY, DERRY
HE'S BETTER THAN STEVIE G
MORE FAITHFUL THAN JOHN TERRY,
SHAUN DERRY, DERRY"

John Terry had recently been exposed as cheating on his wife with his teammate's girlfriend. It was a silly but clever adaptation of a common football chant which made me chuckle. Something that football crowds can often do.

Early in the second half, Darren Ambrose scored another direct free kick. Maybe it was lucky for Colin that he hadn't come. Offering Adam an amount of money on the condition of a free kick being scored was now a tradition. A football ritual had been born. Colin couldn't stop now or we'd never score a free kick ever again.

Towards the end, Wolves piled on the pressure and scored with just six minutes left. It was depressing as it felt like the Premiership side had got out of jail free. Palace had given them a real game. There was still time for Ambrose to miss a great chance to win it with practically the last kick of the match but it finished 2-2. The teams, and fans, would head back to Selhurst Park for a re-match. Yet more money to spend.

I'd booked a train back at 7 o'clock so that I could spend some time with David after the game. Unfortunately, David and I were turned away from all of the pubs on the high street. As we weren't wearing colours, I'd assumed that we could sneak into somewhere to enjoy a quiet pint or two but everywhere seemed to be checking match tickets. It was impossible. Yates, O'Neills, 'Spoons, none of them would let us in. Eventually, after considering spending two hours in KFC, we asked a bouncer if there were any pubs that would let us in.

"*Go under that subway, and there's a pub called The Wanderer,*" was his unconvincing reply in his deep Black Country accent. David and I looked at each other and went to investigate.

The pub was right next to the ground, run down and from the outside, looked terrifying. It was built from old, chipped red bricks and the name of the pub was written in Wolves' gold and black colours above the two daunting entrances. I must admit, it looked like the most 'home' pub that we'd seen. David wanted to turn around and settle for KFC but I wanted a beer.

Well, the pub had been suggested to us so it couldn't be that bad, right? We walked in and made our way to the bar. A couple of non-regulars walking in to the dimly lit pub turned a few heads. And not pleasant looking ones either. I'll be honest, I did consider trying to use my best Black Country impression to try and make us look inconspicuous. However, I decided that it was likely that I would be found out, which would only make things worse. Despite my beliefs when I'm drunk, my attempted fake accents are terrible.

After getting a couple of pints, we went to a small corner table where we could watch the football on the TV while causing minimal offense. Almost straight away, a large middle-aged man, wearing a gold Wolves shirt came over to us.

"*You aren't regulars. Are you Palace?*" he said in his impossibly slow and stupid sounding accent. David and I looked at each other.

"*I am, he's Liverpool,*" I said, pointing at David. I didn't want him to be implemented in any nastiness. Not that being a Liverpool fan would save him at all if this guy or anyone else wanted to start any needless trouble.

We'd been stupid to go into the pub. Wolves have a reputation for a reason and this was exactly the kind of place where you'd expect trouble to stem from. He paused. I noticed his sleeve of Wolverhampton Wanderers tattoos on his right arm. An arm that looked like it could be every bit as dangerous as Victor Moses on the right wing. He looked us both up and down. I looked at the exits. We were in the far corner from the escape. There was no chance of legging it. I could feel my legs wobbling under the table as they wanted to go. Neither Palace, drinking or the challenge were worth being there; sat in the corner of the dirty and dim Wanderer pub outside Molineux, looking up at the six foot giant in gold who was staring down at us.

"*I thought you boys were unlucky today. What did you think lads?*"

I should have had more faith in football fans. Like 99% of them, this guy had never hit anyone at football in his life and just wanted to talk about the game he loved.

We stayed in the pub, chatting to the surprisingly friendly locals for a couple of hours while League 1 Leeds gave Spurs a scare in the evening cup tie on the tele. Afterwards, we went back to the station to head home. We looked for an off-licence on the way without any luck. You really do need to be committed have any chance of getting any beer in Wolverhampton. David ended up getting a different train to me so that he could go directly back to Leamington Spa. We said our goodbyes and went our separate ways.

As I'd stuck around in Wolverhampton, there weren't many Palace fans on my train so it was a lonely journey until I got to Birmingham when the train filled up.

"Hark now hear, the Brighton sing, The Palace run away!" echoed around Birmingham New Street station as my train pulled in. Brighton had taken six and a half thousand fans to their game, which was more than they got for some of their home matches that season. They'd lost 3-2 but had clearly had a good day out. I hadn't really experienced the Brighton rivalry at the time. I'd been to both games in 2006 when they'd been relegated. However, their stadium, The Withdean, had a running track and a hammer throwing net between the pitch and the away section. I'd been about as close to the moon as I had to a Brighton fan on my one away game there. This train journey was my first experience of dealing with a large group of their supporters and the start of my understanding of the two way hatred.

My carriage was filled with them. Most of their songs were about Steve Coppell or Neil Warnock and not particularly complimentary. To anybody outside of the two clubs, the rivalry is a mystery. The clubs are *fifty* miles apart for a start. It all stems back to the seventies as the clubs rose through the leagues together and the respective managers hated each other. Alan Mullery of Brighton and Terry Venables of Palace. It had reached boiling point in an FA Cup second replay at Stanford Bridge in 1976 when Mullery lost the plot over a last minute, re-taken, missed penalty.

Until that train journey, despite knowing the stories, the rivalry was a bit of a mystery to me too. But on the train, for the second time in the day, I was consciously concerned. The loudest group of Brighton fans looked a couple of years younger than me but they still talked the talk. I knew they were kids who were after a story to brag about rather than hardened hooligans but I was still wary.

In between their songs, they talked about 'doing some Palarse fans'. This was their big day out and they wanted to make it memorable. If they'd realised that I was a Palace fan, I would have been an easy target. I was a sitting duck for some serious verbal abuse at best and a slap around the head at worst. The drunker they got, the more hate filled their songs and chat became. Football does allow for some dubious insults that wouldn't be accepted in most other social environments. However, I thought that singing 'Steve Coppell is a paedophile' was unnecessary and crossed the acceptable lines.

I decided to get up and find a quieter carriage. I found a spare seat on a table of four, which was being used by just one single old guy. I checked the other three seats were free and sat down. Within a couple of minutes, I received a phone call.

"(drum intro)*You say that you love me...*"

The Palace song, Glad All Over, was my ringtone at the time. It was incredibly lucky that I'd moved but I still used a hushed voice on the phone to my Dad. It would probably be fine but I didn't want to give away my identity to anyone.

As soon as I finished my call, the guy opposite spoke to me. *"You're Palace then?"*
I nodded. *"You?"*
"God no! Seagull, born and bred!"
A reference to our rival's nickname, which they changed to mimic us in the seventies after we chanted 'Eagles' in their direction. Quite how they thought that picking a 'flying rat' as an identity could compare to the beauty of our glorious bird of prey, I don't know. Although, seagulls or not, we prefer to call them by the much more apt, in our eyes, name of 'seaweed'.

I started to talk to him. He'd lived through the rivalry building up and had a deep rooted hatred of Palace. He was bitter about the success that Coppell had given us in the nineties, Andy Johnson still gave him nightmares after scoring a hat-trick in a 5-0 win and he had been at *that* FA Cup replay. However, none of that mattered because, ultimately, he was a lovely guy.

He'd got football rivalry sorted in his head. He hated Palace and everything to do with the club. However, when he looked at me, he didn't see Palace, he saw a person. Yes, I was Palace and he hated that part of me and could insult that part of me but there was no edge to it. He wasn't going to lose the plot and give me a smack simply because of the team that I supported. We chatted the whole way home about the all things football.

Since that day, I have learned to hate Brighton. I hate Bobby Zamora, Alan Mullery and Gus Pooyet. I hate their fans and I hate their stadium. I hate hearing about their attendances and I hate their hatred of Steve Coppell. However, I would never throw a punch at any of them because at the end of the day, it's not real hate. It's football 'hate'. It's an escape from reality. Football has rivalries like no other sport. A pack mentality is created by separating fans in the grounds so they can join together to sing abuse at each other as one. Going to an away game is like a tribe invading a rival settlement. It sparks a deep rooted feeling in man of conquering somewhere else. It gives you a sense of pride and something to fight for.

And having a bitter rivalry with another team simply heightens those tribal emotions. The joy of beating your arch rivals in their own back yard is unexplainable to anyone who isn't a football addict. The shame and hurt of losingto them is just as incomprehensible. Rivalry makes everything that is good about football even better. The emotion, the commitment, the atmosphere, the tension, the passion, the dreaming, the love, the desire, the joy, the relief, the friendships inspired by sharing the same feelings as strangers. All of them are sky high after beating your rivals.

Yet at the same time, rivalry makes all of the bad in football even worse and not only the pain and misery side of it when you inevitably lose. Some fans, like the youngsters in the carriage along, find it hard to understand the emotion without wanting to turn it into a violent situation. It's easy to see how it happens. Football is an escape from real life but it means so much to us fans and the emotions that it provokes are so real, that it gets entwined with real life.

Talking to non-Palace fans, such as the Wolves and Brighton fans that I'd met, gives an away day another dimension. They give you another point of view and no shortage of good-humoured teasing. Both of them were lovely guys who I could identify with - even if I didn't agree with their choice of football team. I knew that if I'd been born in a different part of the country with a different father, I could just as easily be writing about my hate of Glenn Murray, Mark Bright and Wilfried Zaha.

The whole experience did make me reflect on how lucky I was. Not because I'd 'escaped' from the kids in the previous carriage or anything like that. I'd simply been able to walk past them and take myself away from a situation I didn't like. I felt lucky because they were *all* I'd had to worry about. Being stuck on a train full of pissed up football fans of your arch rivals wasn't a pleasant experience and meant that I had to be aware of what I was doing. However, doing the same thing twenty-five years previously would have been incredibly dangerous.

I'm very fortunate that I've lived in the safest possible era of going to football. Since the Hillsborough disaster and the Bradford fire, stadiums need to pass extensive safety tests. As well as the actual stadiums being better built, more spacious and better policed, the majority of dangerous fans have been banned or simply priced out of football. On top of that, high quality CCTV at grounds means troublemakers are easily identified and removed.

Inexcusable behaviour isn't tolerated as the norm anymore. Any signs of fighting are highlighted by the press and slated. Clubs don't want and can't financially afford the reputation of football being a dangerous afternoon out. Even Millwall make every effort to distance themselves as a club from the lunatics who they used to embrace as their identity.

I've been to over 600 games at over 100 grounds around the country and my experience of hooliganism is limited to say the least. Why should it be any different? I've got no interest in hitting anyone at football so why should anyone have any interest in hitting me? It's only a game. The most passionate and important game in the world in many people's eyes as it can bring real joy and real pain. It can affect your everyday life like no other sport. But it's still only that. A sport.

I've seen the odd individual act like a pratt, I've seen plenty of kids trying to act hard and I've seen Millwall fans rip up a few seats and throw a few coins. All of which were easy for me to distance myself from. Past those rare incidents, football has been an environment where I'd deem it safe to take a child. In fact, there's even an argument that these days some games are 'over-policed' and simply an easy way of earning overtime for coppers.

Contrast that to going to English football in the 70s and 80s where there was organised fighting around the ground and away fans would routinely go into the home ends with the intention of 'taking it over'. For thousands of people, football was an excuse to get pissed and have a punch up. The vast majority, who simply wanted to follow their team, regularly had to consciously make decisions to maintain their safety. You can't help but be impressed with the work done to improve football. Nowadays, you need to go out of your way to find trouble whereas back then, it could easily find anyone.

That evening, I returned to Twickenham tired, but surprisingly sober. It was typical that the one time I wouldn't have a hangover, I wasn't working until the evening of the following day. That allowed me to watch the draw for the next round of the cup at home. If we won the replay, we'd be at home to Premiership big guns, Aston Villa. If the 'seaweed' had won the previous day, I'd have learnt even more about the rivalry.

Chapter 35 – **A Dark Day**

Tuesday 26ᵗʰ January 2010

Some dates just stick in your mind forever. Saturday 11ᵗʰ September 2004 is one of them for me. It was the day that my best friend, Lee, died, aged just 15. It is the biggest tragedy that I have had in my life so far. Since that horrible day, I have tried to stay close to his family but in January 2010, his father died while both Lee's brothers (Craig and Blake) were still at school. Tuesday 26ᵗʰJanuary 2010 was his father's funeral.

Rob had come up from Plymouth to be there for Judith, Lee's mum, and we, along with a few of Lee's other friends, headed down memory lane as the funeral service was performed at the same crematory as Lee's fairwell. As was the wake, at The Belvedere Hotel, Ascot. And it was there that I got the text.

'Palace are in administration'.

I looked at my phone. I didn't believe it. I rang my Dad, who was at work, so he could check the BBC website. It was true. By now, I'd received a host of texts from a mixture of horrified Palace fans, concerned friends and laughing berks. I turned my phone off and put it in my pocket. I was at a funeral (and not Palace's just yet). Some things are more important than football.

I can't think of a lower feeling. I felt for Judith, Craig and Blake. They had already been through so much pain. However, I couldn't help but feel for me. My actions were the 'right' thing to do. I'd put my phone away and prioritised Judith but you can't control your thoughts. My mind was racing. What would become of Palace now? When I returned to Twickenham, I spent hours reading the BBS, trying to make sense of what had happened and how I felt.

The feeling was empty. I'd felt empty at having one Saturday Selhurst afternoon taken away from me a couple of weeks previously. But this was a new level altogether. This could be every Saturday afternoon taken away from me. Forever.

We arrived in Newcastle airport after our short trip up from London. While we were waiting for our luggage to arrive, all you could hear was phones ringing and beeping with text messages. Right away I thought *'Something ain't right here'*. Had someone been sold without us knowing? Had the gaffa been sacked? - even though he was here with us! No, it was much worse than that. We had been deducted 10 points and placed into administration. We had gone in the space of 90 mins, from being a comfortable mid table team to being in one hell of a relegation dog fight.

And from then on it was one problem to the next, PFA meeting after PFA meeting. They would come in one week and say *"Lads, the club is struggling to pay wages this month, would you mind deffering the money till next month?"* or *"I'm afraid we are gonna have to sell Victor Moses to Wigan, so the club can survive"*

One thing I can't speak highly enough of, was the character and strength of that dressing room. It was unbelievable, not one person moaned or chucked the towel in about the situation we found ourselves in. Instead, it galvanised us as a group and we achieved the unthinkable. We used to have dance offs before every game, adopting songs like The Proclaimers & Black Eyed Peas (Tonight's Gonna be a Good Night). You used to see teams walking past our dressing room and looking in and going "What the hell are they doing?"
Them moments will live with me till I die. Looking back now, it was our way of switching off and taking the mounting pressure off our minds for a little bit at least.

Clint Hill

Chapter 36 – **My Only Palace**

Wednesday 27th January 2010, Newcastle United vs Crystal Palace, St. James' Park.

Crystal Palace: Julian Speroni; Nathaniel Clyne; Clint Hill; Shaun Derry; Darren Ambrose; Neil Danns; Nick Carle (Alan Lee, 83); Lee Hills (Kieran Djilali, 75); Calvin Andrew; Danny Butterfield; Johnny Ertl (Matt Lawrence, 5)
Subs Not Used:
Newcastle United: Steve Harper; Fabricio Coloccini; Jose Enrique (Fabrice Pancrate, 26); Kevin Nolan; Mike Williamson; Danny Guthrie; Peter Lovenkrands (Wayne Routledge, 62); Alan Smith; Jonas Gutierrez (Nile Ranger, 73); Andy Carroll; Tamas Kadar
Subs Not Used: Nicky Butt; Tim Krul; Ben Tozer; Ryan Donaldson
Going into administration was a really strange feeling.

The points deduction had meant we'd gone from being one point off the playoffs to being one place above the relegation zone without a ball being kicked. I'd barely slept the night before as one of our terrace chants was going round and round my head.

"You are my Palace,
My only Palace,
You make me happy,
When skies are grey,
(Skies are grey)
You never notice,
How much I love you,
Please don't take
my Palace away!"

I certainly wasn't ready to have my Palace taken away but I might not get a choice about it now. It was like hearing that a friend is seriously ill. Someone that I loved and cared for and met up with all the time and spent money on and I thought about constantly was metaphorically lying on a hospital bed, unwell and alone. I wanted to help but there was next to nothing I could do.

Agilo had panicked about the HMRC winding up order that was due the next day and also given up on Simon Jordan's bullshit. They didn't believe that they were going to get their money so they forced the club into administration. Something Jordan claimed had shocked him. However, after months of telling everyone that everything was in hand, Jordan had failed. The club were in administration and it was all his fault after years of bad management of the club. The more I thought about it, the more I realised it wasn't a metaphorical illness. Palace actually were in hospital as they'd been metaphorically beaten up. By Jordan.

He'd overspent on wages. He'd alienated and lost lots of supporters which, in turn, lost him vital gate receipts. He'd lost merchandise and food revenue by selling off the outlets around the ground. He'd let his spat with Noades get in the way of dealing for the stadium, which had meant the rent had dramatically increased. He'd not listened to advice or taken on support at any step. In fact, he'd ignorantly ignored all the warning signs. And his final nail in the coffin was selling his soul to Agilo, who'd come to claim it back. Unfortunately, it was Crystal Palace Football Club's soul that he'd dealt with rather than his own.

Exactly as he had done when he claimed to have bought the ground, he'd fed the fans a load of lies. As with the ground, he might actually have believed the bullshit that he'd spread but that didn't matter. It was bullshit. *That* did matter. His claim, less than two weeks previously, was that he'd sorted the Agilo debt. However, Agilo obviously hadn't agreed with him.

I felt scared that I'd lose my club one minute then angry at Jordan the next. Then I'd feel determined. *'We will get through this!'* Then I'd begin to worry again. Then I'd hate Agilo. *'How dare they do this to my club?!'* Then I'd think about relegation. Which was suddenly a real possibility now. Then I'd consider that there was four days left of the transfer window. Who would we sell? There were rumours of the administrator, Brendan Guilfoyle, holding a fire sale in the coming days. The same thoughts went round and round my mind at a million miles an hour as I tried to sleep. I simply couldn't contemplate not having Crystal Palace Football Club in my life. The news was entirely indigestible.

God knows what the players were feeling. Throughout the season, they'd shown an enormous amount of commitment and desire for the club. They'd run through brick walls for us. The timing of administration had been cruel on them. They'd taken a flight up to Newcastle for a top of the table clash. As they got off the plane, Sky Sports News were waiting for them because the news of administration had broken while they were up in the air. Texts from friends and family had informed them of the harsh facts. They'd left London dreaming of the Premiership and arrived in Newcastle in a relegation battle.

The one calming influence was Neil Warnock. He felt like the father at the head of the family, holding everything together in a crisis. *"The supporters can rest assured that me and the players will fight every inch of the way,"* he said. Warnock was an experienced street-fighter and he was up for the biggest battle of his career. He'd often talked about his friendship with Jordan and told the press of his intentions. *"He*(Jordan) *wants me to continue and that's exactly what I'll do until told otherwise."*
His dedication to the club was inspirational.

Someone asked me how the administration would affect my challenge of going to every game. I replied *"It's no longer a challenge, it's my duty."*

After a bad night of sleep, it was surprisingly easy to get up at 4:45 so that I could make my way to King's Cross for the 7am train. I was in Newcastle for 10am and went for a 'Geordie breakfast'. A discounted Wetherspoons fry up (minus the egg) and a bottle of Newcastle Brown Ale. Incidentally, the beer is no longer actually brewed in Newcastle but is now made in Yorkshire. I guess marketing purposes dictated that the name wouldn't be changed to Tadcaster

Brown Ale.

Later in the day, I was meeting a friend, Matt, who was studying at Durham University. Despite being a Newcastle 'fan' and going to university so close by, he'd never been to St. James' Park. Thirteen years previously, Matt joined my primary school and I was the first friend he'd made. We'd been very close during primary school but drifted apart while we were at secondary school. Our primary school friendship had even survived being 'rivals' to play in goal for the same Sunday team, as well as the school football team. In the sixth form, we became close again as we started to drink together. However, I hadn't seen him for a couple of years. Matt was always a hard worker so it came as no surprise to me when he said that he needed to study during the day rather than getting on the beers with me in Newcastle.

I realised that I wouldn't be able to drink all day and make it to the match in any kind of fit state so I went to have a look at the city. I strolled around the city centre, which was much like any other in the UK, and mulled around the shops for a bit. I then went to the River Tyne and had a look at the impressive Tyne Bridge. As I headed back into town, I bumped into another Palace fan. We eyed up the Palace badges that both of us were wearing and gave a nod in each other's directions.

"Fancy a pint?" he asked.

I glanced at my watch. It was just before midday and still eight hours until kick off. Starting to drink now would be very irresponsible.

"Yeah, why not?" I replied with a smile.

We headed to one of the many sports bars around the city. It turned out that my new friend's name was Dave. He'd flown up to Newcastle that morning and, like me, was being joined by a mate later in the day. We tried to talk about things other than the administration but it was impossible. It was always in our mind. Talking to Dave was like meeting a friend of a friend who's in hospital. It doesn't matter what you think of each other or how well you know each other, as you're both just concerned for your mutual friend and desperate for them to get better. We'd both just met at the ward with a bunch of grapes in our hands.

We had a couple of beers in the sports bar, as waiting for the grapes to turn into wine would have taken far too long, before heading to the O'Neills opposite Newcastle train station, where he was meeting his mate. I had a couple more pints with him there and I bumped into some of the regular Palace away followers. Once again, we talked about the administration. The same things were repeated time and time again: anger towards Jordan, concern for Warnock and the players' mentality, and a fear for the future of the club.

There were a few people who weren't concerned. They believed that the club were in a better position now that it was Jordan-less and administration would make it easier to find a new, less-orange, owner. Others talked about how it would affect the performances. We'd been going so well in the league. Would that be ruined now?

The other hot topic was which players would go? While we were in the pub, the news broke that the administrator had decided Moses would not be allowed to play that evening to ensure he avoided getting an injury. Obviously he would be leaving, but how many other players would we need to sell? Did Agilo want to raise their money as quickly as possible, in any way possible? They'd been so aggressive in putting us into administration. Would they simply sell players until they got their share, without caring how it would affect the team's performance or whether they got good value for the players?

By putting us into administration, they'd become secured creditors along with all the football debts e.g. money owed to other clubs or players. However, if a new buyer was found, all the other creditors would get just a fraction of what they were owed from the takeover. Organisations like HMRC and St. John's Ambulance, who were owed money, were now going to lose out.

I could have happily stayed in the pub but, having learnt from my Manchester City experience, I didn't want to get too drunk. I left Dave, his mate and the other Palace regulars in the bar while I went to have a look at Newcastle's ground. I hate out of town grounds like Coventry or Swansea and St. James' Park is the absolute opposite of that. The ground proudly towers over the city as its centre piece. In Coventry, the town seemed to have forgotten that it had a team to support but in Newcastle, the city seemed to be an afterthought to the football. Having such a large stadium right in the centre of town is what makes Newcastle a city like no other. They're football mad and the stadium ensures that no one can ever forget it.

I couldn't help being impressed by the ground. It was my first visit to the stadium and was my sixty-second of the ninety-two, thus taking me over two thirds of the way to completing my other challenge. As you approach the ground, it looks enormous and appears to have been built on raised ground. The Milburn stand and the Sir John Hall stand are incredible. They tower above the rest of the city, including the other two much smaller sides of the stadium. After briefly looking around the four sides, I walked back through the city to meet up with some Palace regulars who I knew would be drinking in the town.

By now, it was nearly five o'clock and had got dark. I had another pint in O'Neills with the Palace fans that I knew and despite it being nearly three hours until kick off, the atmosphere was electric. People had decided that we were going to show the world (well, Newcastle) that despite being in administration and having a points deduction, we were all in this together and we were going to get behind our first love.

In the pub, I started to chat to a couple of guys who were wearing a Palace scarf. As with Dave earlier, our red'n'blue armour meant that there were no barriers in talking to strangers. We all embraced each other, all of us hurting for our mutual friend. We all wanted to be there for Palace. The 'conversation' started with linked arms and jumping around the pub as we sang a song that would soon become associated with that evening and the coming months.

"Going down?
Are we fuck!
Minus ten,
And we're staying up!"

I rang Dan, Colin and my Dad from the pub during renditions of the song. I wanted them to celebrate the moment of unity with me. They probably wanted me to go away. Although, I'm sure the call must have been enough to put a loving smile on their faces at a time of worry. At least the calls weren't in the early hours of the morning as they often were from me at the time – singing of my love for the club. After a few beers, the over-riding emotion from our fans was defiance. We were not going to let our friend down. We were going to fight it.

As one of the chants calmed down, I introduced myself to the two lads that I'd been leaping about with for the previous few minutes.
"Hi, nice to meet you James. I'm John and this is Connor, we flew in from Copenhagen today!"
The pair of them had heard the news the previous day, called in sick and booked a flight. They'd arrived in Newcastle that morning and found a hotel that afternoon. They simply had to be there for Palace. A common feeling that night. A thousand fans made the 297 mile midweek journey from Croydon to Newcastle and at least two made the 737 mile trip from Copenhagen.

Shortly afterwards, I started talking to a bloke who'd flown in from Dublin at the last minute. I think he was a bit disappointed that he'd been outdone to be honest. But there were plenty of other people in the pub who had booked accommodation on the day, and even some who didn't know how they were getting home the next day. Palace needed us and suddenly, real life commitments, such as money worries or jobs, didn't matter. When a friend needs you, you're there for them. No matter what.

I was in the pub for well over an hour but I only had one pint. I'd drunk quite a bit prior to that and I didn't need any more. I was buzzing for the game. There was a real feeling that we were going to get a result that night but in many ways, the result didn't matter. What mattered, was to put on a defiant show to the world. We're Crystal Palace and we are bigger and more important than Simon Jordan, Agilo and administration. We will not go quietly. In a bizarre way, we needed to put on a show for the players too. We needed to show them that we were with them.

By the time Matt arrived, at six o'clock, I was already beginning to lose my voice. We decided to go to the 'spoons so we could get some discounted food and a couple of beers while we had a catch up. I was surprised to find out that despite being in his third year at Durham, Matt had only been to Newcastle once before. I'd assumed that it would be a regular night out.

After our food, we made our way to the ground. It looked even more impressive at night - now that it was busy as nearly 50,000 people arrived for the floodlit match. While Newcastle hadn't been selling out their ground since getting relegated, it was still going to be the largest second tier attendance that I'd been part of. We each had a picture outside the ground before going through the turnstile.

I'd been warned of the Newcastle 'climb' before. There are seven sets of stairs to make it up to the away section and we passed quite a few older fans, (and younger ones who had far less of an excuse) who'd stopped for breath on the way up. Eric, a lovely old boy who went to every away game on the coach, had boycotted the match because he wasn't up to the long ascent. At one point I began to wonder whether I should have brought a helmet, harness and mountain boots with me. By the time that we finally got to the top, we'd definitely earned a pint.

After getting our well-deserved beer, I bumped into Karina, the fellow Palace fan from my secondary school. Like me, she'd also lost her voice but unlike me, it wasn't because she'd been drinking and singing all afternoon. She really wasn't well. Despite being ill, she'd decided to head up to Newcastle after hearing our news from the day before. Her Dad, her brother and herself all looked incredibly unwell and weary but they all felt a duty to be there as a Palace fan. By now, all feelings of concern for the future had been put to one side. We were here for the Palace and that is what was important.

By kickoff, the noise from high up in the gods of the away section was deafening. Even though Matt was a Newcastle 'supporter', he couldn't get over how good the Palace fans were that night. Palace had only named three subs as we didn't have enough players to fill the bench and one of those players was used within four minutes. Ertl went off injured and was replaced by the committed Matt Lawrence, which was hardly ideal after our already disrupted preparation for the match.

Despite the setback, Palace started quite well and caused Newcastle some early problems. As the beers had flowed and our confidence grew, our chant slightly changed.

"Going down?
Are we fuck!
Minus ten,
*And we're **going** up!"*

Unfortunately, Shaun Derry scored an own goal to put us behind but still we pushed on. Warnock was proved right. The players did give absolutely everything. As did the fans. They sang defiantly for 90 minutes, and after the game too. We didn't deserve to lose 2-0. The second goal came in stoppage time as the Palace fans sang of their pride of the team.

Matt and I went for a quick pint in O'Neills after the game, where the locals couldn't believe how loud we'd been. They generally wished us well, both on and off the pitch. I received a text from Karina. She and her family were too ill to drive back so they'd ended up spending yet more money on a hotel for the night.

Matt and I then headed back to Durham and a pub called Varsity, where we had a couple more beers. We discussed going clubbing but I wasn't in the mood. Firstly, I was quite drunk by this point and secondly, although the defeat had filled me with pride, it had also been a reality check. We were in administration and had a huge task ahead of us.

In the Durham pub, I barely had any voice left. However, not for the first time in our lives, I still had enough of a croak to bore Matt with talk about my love of Palace. At least on this occasion it had a context. He'd seen my love firsthand. Despite being in the north of England and it being the coldest January for years, we went to another bar called ' The Boat House', where we sat outside and had a couple of pints by the river. I'd love to say that the sense of pride of supporting Palace that evening kept me warm but I suspect it was the alcohol.

Around two in the morning, we headed back to Matt's halls and had a couple more beers before I settled down on the floor of his room for the night. The next morning, I headed back to Newcastle after getting a fry up (minus the eggs) from a local pub. I then went to the Newcastle 'spoons in the town centre and watched Andy Murray get to the Australian Open Final – his second Grand Slam Final.

The train home was full of very tired Palace fans. The guy opposite me had only booked his train and hotel the day before. It had cost him over £150. However, despite the result, there wasn't a hint of regret in his voice about spending money he didn't have to go and watch the team. That game wasn't about winning or losing. It was about being there for Palace. My only Palace. They'd made me happy in grey skies on many occasions and I wasn't ready to let my Palace be taken away.

Chapter 37 – **A Proud Moment.**

Saturday 30th January 2010, Crystal Palace vs Peterborough United, Selhurst Park.

Crystal Palace: Julian Speroni; Nathaniel Clyne; Clint Hill; Shaun Derry; Darren Ambrose (Sean Scannell, 88); Neil Danns; Nick Carle; Lee Hills (Kieran Djilali, 70); Alan Lee (Calvin Andrew, 70); Danny Butterfield; Claude Davis;
Subs Not Used: Matt Lawrence; Kieron Cadogan; James Comley; Charlie Mann

Peterborough: Joe Lewis; Kerrea Gilbert; Tom Williams; Charlie Lee; Lee Frecklington (Aaron Mclean, 58); George Boyd; Craig Mackail-Smith (Reuben Reid, 72); Chris Whelpdale; Ryan Bennett; Josh Simpson; Jake Livermore
Subs Not Used: Paul Coutts; James McKeown, Tommy Rowe, Ben Wright, Exodus Geohaghon

I'd spent the previous few days glued to the BBS; trying to get every speck of information that I could in a desperate attempt to make sense of it all. Unimportant things, such as my degree, were now very much in the background and to the back of my list of priorities.

The night before the Peterborough game, it had been my friend Natalie's birthday and we'd been out in London. I hadn't got in until about 5:30 so I was incredibly tired and hung over when I got to Selhurst Park. But even so, it was great to be back. It had been five away games on the trot because of the Bristol City game being called off and having two away cup draws. I'd missed Selhurst and I'd missed the Railway Club. Neither are what could be described as picturesque but being back at both was a bit like visiting my friend in hospital. The club wasn't ok but it felt good to be close to it.

The pre-match talk in the pub was all about the administration, as you would expect. Like me, Colin and Dan both felt a lot of anger towards Jordan. He'd bullshitted to us and left us facing oblivion. It was unforgivable. I forced down three pints of Guinness as we vented our anger, before we emptied our bladders and headed to the ground. Although the routine was just the same as usual, everything felt different. Everything felt flatter.

That was until I got into the ground. Glad All Over was played as the teams came out, just as it would before any other game. But it wasn't any other game. It was the home game after Palace had gone into administration. While the attendance was slightly higher than other recent games, 14699 was disappointing in the circumstances. But the passion and emotion that our song was sung with was enough to make the hairs on the back of your neck stand up.

I remember an early cross from Butterfield, which he'd had to stretch to reach, and the ball went straight to the keeper. The entire Holmesdale jumped up to applaud his efforts. Colin observed, *"Last week, he would have been slated for that!"*
He was right. He would have done. It was a rubbish cross but we weren't applauding the cross, we were celebrating his efforts. He'd shown desire to get to

the ball and that was enough for us. That was the attitude of the fans. Like at Newcastle, the players were giving us everything.

Once in each half, the whole ground rose as one to sing *'Stand up, if you love Palace'*.

Even Kev and his jumper, who would usually be reluctant to muster up the effort to move in such occurrences, stood proudly alongside me. It was nothing to do with the action that was happening on the pitch; the first time was at 0-0 and the ball was in the middle of the park. It was a sign of unity. It was something I had never previously seen and am unlikely to ever see again. I have never been as proud to be a Palace fan as I did in that moment. It made me feel entirely at home. I felt like I belonged. Players and fans. We were all as one. It could only have been more perfect and uniting if my father had been stood alongside me.

Soon after the magical moment, Palace took the lead through Neil Danns, which meant we went to the Red'n'Blue bar in a happy mood. Well, we would have done if Jonathan hadn't bought us flat half time pints. We'd long since given up on buying pints in the ground because the draught beer was always crap. Jordan had shown no interest in customer care and didn't give a monkeys that his business was serving an appalling product. As a result, we always got bottles but Jonathan seemed to have forgotten this.

Palace cruised through the second half after Neil Danns scored his, and our, second. Ambrose and Butterfield both missed chances to make the lead more comfortable but it didn't really matter. At the end of the game, Warnock rounded up the players and led them to the centre circle where he gave them a pep-talk, before leading them to applaud the fans. It had been an emotional day for everyone, crowned off with a win.

After the game, I went to The Falcon with Dan for a couple of (not flat) beers. We were both brimming with pride. The club meant everything to us and it clearly meant a lot to the players too. Warnock had created a tight knit team spirit. We just hoped that he could keep enough of them at the club over the next few days as the vultures circulated in the final days of the transfer window. At the previous home game, I'd been considering giving up my challenge but now, I wouldn't dream of missing a game.

Chapter 38 - **Once Upon a Time at Selhurst...**

Tuesday 2nd February 2010, Crystal Palace vs Wolverhampton Wanderers, Selhurst Park, FA Cup 4th Round Replay

Crystal Palace : Julian Speroni, Nathaniel Clyne, Clint Hill, Shaun Derry, Darren Ambrose, Neil Danns, Nicky Carle (James Comley, 84), Matt Lawrence, Alan Lee (Calvin Andrew, 75), Danny Butterfield (Kieran Djilali, 88), Claude Davis.
Subs Not Used: Sean Scannell, Alex Wynter, Charlie Mann.

Wolverhampton Wanderers : Wayne Hennessey, Stearman, Craddock, Henry, Berra, Vokes (Iwelumo, 59), Milijas, Zubar, Muganga Bia (Ebanks-Blake, 59), Mancienne, Foley.
Subs Not Used: Surman, Hahnemann, Jones, Halford, Castillo.

The day before this match, transfer deadline day, Victor Moses was finally sold to Wigan for just £2.5million. In the real world, this is an un-comprehendible amount of money but in the football world, for an exciting young English talent, it was a robbery. We knew at the time that he was worth much more and his career would prove us correct. He went on to sign for Chelsea for nearly ten million pounds, where he scored goals in European Cup semi-finals, before he moved on to Liverpool.

The only saving grace was that the administrator included a clause in the deal so that we would receive money if Wigan sold him on. When he moved to Chelsea, we received a percentage of the fee and the money was used to sign two or three players that starred in a promotion to the Premier League. I still find it strange (although I am very thankful) that an administrator, who was only being paid to look after the interests of the creditors in the here and now, decided to include such a clause.

Deadline day could have been a lot worse. Nathaniel Clyne turned down a move to Wolves, Neil Danns was heavily linked to a move to Swansea and there were rumours of the administrator trying to shift any player to any club.

In the morning of the Wolves game, news broke that Agilo had lent the club a further £1 million pounds to cover the players' wages until the end of the season. It was a bizarre situation that just one week after putting the club into administration to try and get their money back, they were now lending Palace even more money. It certainly showed why Brendon Guilfoyle had been so keen to shift as many players as possible.

I got to the Railway Club early to meet up with Colin and we were later joined by Dan, Jonathan and Kev. Colin was predictably positive. He saw Clyne turning down the move as a sign that the players were up for the fight. As well as that, he believed the weekend's comfortable win had shown that administration shouldn't knock the club too much and that any new owner would be ten times better than the previous one (which surely wouldn't be a difficult task). Dan was more angry than anything else. He still couldn't believe that we were in administration. Again.

Simon Jordan had spent years telling us that he was putting his own money into the club and had asked fans to do the same. However, he had said in the week that he wanted his money back. He hadn't been giving the club that he loved money, it was a loan. It wasn't the fact that he wanted the money back that annoyed us. He was more than entitled to that if he'd given it to the club as a loan. It was, like so many times during his spell as chairman, the way that he'd done it. At best it was a fantasy, at worst a lie.

Kev was happy to simply have a pint and make jokes about Simon Jordan's orange skin. There'd been plenty of photoshopped images of bouncers taking away his sun-beds. Jonathan was intent on getting very drunk. He'd been in the pub since finishing work at mid-day. Overall, the mood was ok. We were defiant that we would get through this and there was a certainly a feeling that at least the club would now be available for a more realistic price to potential new owners. Jordan had valued it at over forty million pounds for God's sake.

Twenty minutes before kickoff, we emptied our bladders and headed to the ground. As the player's names were read out, each one was met with a huge cheer as normal but Nathaniel Clyne's name was met with the loudest cheer of all. It would have been particularly cruel if he'd made his Wolves debut against us that evening. The first half was nothing special, and I was fairly happy heading up to the bar at half time with the score 0-0. In fact, it had been so not-special that the drunken Jonathan had fallen asleep and we'd needed to wake him up to give him our halftime orders. Thankfully, despite his drunken, sleepy state, he managed to remember to get bottles rather than the disgusting flat pints this time.

The second half will live long in the memory of Palace fans' hearts and minds. As previously mentioned, Danny Butterfield was a bit of a fan's favourite but he'd lost form and his place in the team. However, because of our small squad being so stretched, he'd been played completely out of position as a right winger/inside forward. The atmosphere had been very good despite only being a small crowd but it went wild in the space of six minutes just after the hour mark. From a corner, Matt Lawrence had a header saved and Danny Butterfield stooped low to nod in the rebound. It was his first goal in six years and provoked a pile of Palace fans jumping on each other. Admittedly, it was mainly me diving on top of Dan and Colin, who as more experienced fans, could control their elation and beer slightly more, but it was still a special moment. I suspect that I wasn't the only fan in the ground launching himself onto his mates after the unlikely goal.

Minutes later, Butterfield ran onto an Alan Lee flick on and, despite being fouled, poked the ball past the goalkeeper with his right foot. 'Butts' had done it again. Before Dan had a chance to stop me, I'd jumped up on top of him. He had little choice but to hold onto me or let me fall down a few rows of seats. I was punching the air in delight, while he was trying to hold onto his glasses that I'd knocked off his eyes. It was pure jubilation (certainly on my part – maybe not Dan's by now). 2-0, with two goals in four minutes, from the most unlikely of goal scorers.

A couple of minutes later, Butterfield latched onto another Alan Lee flick on. Lee himself was playing like a Trojan (a warrior, not a computer virus or a condom) with an oversized bandage holding his head together. This was Butterfield's evening but it was also the evening that Selhurst fell in love with Alan Lee. Every football crowd loves a hard worker. Anyway, from this flick on, 'Butts' ran onto it and calmly slotted the ball past the keeper with his left foot in a style more suited to Michael Owen than Palace's back up defender. The ground erupted with laughter.

The smile on Butterfield's face was nearly as wide as the whole of South London. We could see it from the other end of the stadium. He couldn't believe it, he was laughing after each goal. How were we supposed to believe that it wasn't a crazy dream? Having a back-up defender, who hasn't scored for six years, score a perfect hat-trick, in six minutes, against a Premier League side. It is about as likely as the Queen giving her Christmas Speech in a bikini.

The Saturday before had been Selhurst at its emotional best but this was Selhurst at its rocking best! Administration, minus ten, players leaving. Sod that. We were 3-0 up against a Premiership side and having a party, hosted by Danny Butterfield.

Everyone in football was absolutely buzzing for him. Paul Merson was watching the game on *Goals Express* for *Sky Sports News* and even he, someone with no connection to Palace or Butterfield, was jumping around the studio. It was a fairytale. It had an unlikely hero (Butterfield), fighting against the odds (the crisis club on the brink, playing against a Premiership side), an unforgiving villain (Agilo) and even a happy ending, sprinkled with a bit of magic (It was the FA Cup after all - a competition famed for its magic). I half expected Butterfield to have to sprint off the pitch at full time before the Fairy God Mother's kind spell had worn off.

My brother, William, was touring around Mexico at the time and he couldn't believe it when he walked into a bar to find Palace on the TV. He claimed he had to stop and review whether he'd taken anything suspicious when not only had he entirely coincidently stumbled across a Crystal Palace match in deepest, darkest Mexico but Danny Butterfield then proceeded to score a hat trick.

Wolves pulled one goal back near the end but that really didn't matter. After the game, the atmosphere outside the ground was brilliant. Palace fans continued to sing in the street, all the way back to Selhurst station. We'd spent a week fretting about the future of our club but that evening was one that we could simply enjoy.

I rang my Dad as soon as I was out of the stadium. The game had been on TV and I wanted to share the moment with him.
"Did you see it? Did you see it?" I squeaked down the phone in excitement, unable to believe what I'd witnessed, while still trying to join in with the '*Oh Danny, Danny*' chants that echoed around the Holmesdale Road as fans piled out of the ground. He had seen it. Well, he'd seen the second half. And having not been at the match, or to the pub, his response made a lot more sense than mine

did. However, it slightly bugged me that he'd *only* watched the second half. What on earth had he been doing that was more important than the first half? I couldn't think of anything.

He'd particularly enjoyed the result because his office at work, despite being based in Southampton, was dominated by Wolves fans. He couldn't wait to be at work the next day. Revelling in a win over a colleague's team is one of the many benefits of being a football fan.

It starts at school as aggressive banter. I remember practically harassing every Liverpool fan on my secondary school site after Palace won 2-0 at Anfield in 2003. As you get older, you learn to be more subtle with your digs. A sly grin or a clever play on words will suffice. Adults might be better than children at hiding it, but the pain is just the same. You don't need to get in people's faces about it. After a big result, you walk around the next day, at work, in the pub, doing your shopping, wherever you are and whatever you're doing, as if you are two foot taller. Knowing someone else, who's feeling the exact opposite for the exact same reason, can only add to your smugness and enjoyment.

After the game, Dan, his dad and I went to be smug and happy together in The Falcon. We had a couple of celebratory beers there before grabbing a can of Leicestershire Bitter to have on the train home. Dan's mum has family in Leicester so Peter took great pride in drinking a beer from the area. Well, that's what he said at the time, but I think he was just drunk and anything alcoholic would have sufficed to toast the magical evening. As we got onto the train, we bumped into Matt, a friend of Dan's who also supports Palace. We jumped on him in excitement to tell him the result. He was sober and looked incredibly concerned by us. We were living a (drunken) fairytale and he wasn't sure if it was purely alcohol induced or not.

Away from the stresses we had to contend with in the league, the game against Wolves in the cup stands out for me. The game when Danny Butterfield scored his hat trick. I've never played in a game when a group of players were so happy for one individual to take the glory before. Danny was an integral part of not only the team on the pitch, but also of the feel good factor that we tried to create in and around the football club. For me to see someone so respected score a hat trick which was so surprising to everybody still makes me smile today.

Shaun Derry

"I have nothing to lose, have fun. If I have a stinker, it won't matter coz I'm no forward anyway!"
All the thoughts that were going through my head as I went into the game. But more importantly, my team mates saw me as the joker and found it amusing I was being given the chance to play as a striker. As usual, the pre match "Dance off to the Proclaimers" followed, with the dressing room rocking and our team spirit tighter than ever considering what we were going through. We were ready for an upset! I remember not playing too well myself in the first half and then WOW! 3 goals??? Me??? No??? Still to this day I'm embarrassed it was me, but proud too as Palace are, and will always be, a part of my life.

A massive thanks goes to big Alan Lee, who battered their back four all night, and I took the goals... (Did I just say that?) The fans got a night to remember and most importantly, some more money to get the club out of the mess that we were in. As a group of players and club, it felt like the world was against us but with the togetherness in the dressing room, backed up by such loyal fans, there was no way that season was going to end in failure. On a personal note, I suspected that the hat-trick might sell a few more shirts in the club shop too – and with my name on the back...

Danny Butterfield

Chapter 39 – **An Unhappy Wife**

Saturday 6th February 2010, Scunthorpe vs Crystal Palace, Glanford Park.

Crystal Palace: Julian Speroni, Nathaniel Clyne, Clint Hill, Matt Lawrence (Lee Hills 90), Claude Davis, Shaun Derry, Darren Ambrose, Nicky Carle, Alan Lee (Calvin Andrew 74), Danny Butterfield (Kieran Djilali 64), Neil Danns.
Subs Not Used: Stern John, Sean Scannell, James Comley, Alassane N'Diaye.

Scunthorpe Murphy, Byrne, Jones, Mirfin, Williams,Thompson (Forte 70), McCann, Sam Togwell (O'Connor 82),McDermott (Moloney 78), Hayes, Hooper.
Subs Not Used: Lillis, Raynes, Josh Wright, Woolford.

Dan had messaged me when I was on my way back from the Plymouth away game. He and his wife, Carol, were going to come to the Scunthorpe match. To get a cheaper train ticket, they were going to travel up much earlier than me but they were on the same train back as I was.

On the tube to King's Cross, I bumped into a Palace fan that I knew called Frank. He is an incredibly nice gentleman in his fifties and goes to every Palace game, home and away. I'd met him on the coach but we'd both since defected to train travel. At King's Cross, we met up with two other Palace regulars, Don and Trevor. Don was another ex-coach user while Trevor was of particular interest to me because he was a secondary school teacher, who I would regularly discuss the teaching/Palace life balance with. Both of them are Palace mad. Fortunately, they were travelling on the same train up to Scunthorpe as I was so I wouldn't be alone.

Other than teaching with Trevor, I have very little in common with any of them. However, thanks to our Palace connection, I was more than happy to travel all the way to Scunthorpe in their company. Conversation certainly wasn't in any way awkward. In fact, it flowed easily for the whole two and a half hours of the journey.

When we got onto the train at Doncaster (a station that I was soon to become very familiar with as I would need to go there to get to Scunthorpe, Barnsley, Doncaster and Sheffield Wednesday in the next couple of months – Crewe Station is known as the hub of the north but Doncaster seemed to be the hub of the 2009/10 Championship), I got a phone call from Dan.
"Allllrigghtt Jamesy Boy!" he bellowed down the phone. It didn't take Sherlock Holmes to realise that he'd been in the pub.
"How's it going?" he continued.
"Not bad, I'll be with you soon mate. Just got on a train from Doncaster."
"Ah cool... well Pavel's on the same train as you, you can meet up with him."
"Who's Pavel?" I replied. It seemed like a nice idea but I didn't know who this guy was so I wasn't sure how I was supposed to find him.
"He's a Palace mate who's coming to the game. He's a bit younger than me so might do some future away games with you!"
That *did* seem like a nice idea but I still had no idea who he was or how to find

him. I'd never even heard of him before.

"Ah cool, just, I mean, who is he? How do I find him?"

"Oh yeah, you don't know him, do you?"

A disappointed Dan was finally catching up with me. *"Just look for the Russian. I'll see you at the station,"* he finished. That was his advice. After considering wondering up and down the train to look for an unknown Russian on the basis that he liked Crystal Palace too, I decided to stay with Frank, Don and Trevor.

I arrived at Scunthorpe station and found Dan, and he found the Russian. Pavel was tall, well over six foot, but that wasn't his most notable feature. Neither was his bizarre accent that, after moving country aged 14, was neither Russian nor South London. It wasn't even his Palace shirt that donned 'Butterfield 20' on the back (something he claimed that he'd done at the start of the season as Butts was his favourite player, rather than because of his midweek heroics). No, his most notable feature was his blonde, over combed, centre parting. If Dan had told me to look along the short train for a David Beckham haircut in a Danny Butterfield Palace shirt, it would have narrowed my options down considerably – without having to ask everyone involved to produce a passport.

Pavel was with an older, bald chap named Rodger. He later explained that it was his girlfriend's uncle who was a Palace fan. Another bizarre friendship made by football. I can't imagine many blokes go for days out with their partner's uncle, especially not to Scunthorpe.

Carol's nephew, whose wife was due to give birth any day, had driven Dan to the station to pick us up. Dan had been in the pub since about eleven and was already well on his way. The four of us were taken to the Harvester Pub next to Scunthorpe's ground. Once there, we met Carol and her nephew's pregnant wife and we all began to drink. Well, those of us who weren't pregnant did.

Chatting to Carol in the pub, I was a bit more nervous than I had been before the home game against Scunthorpe and I certainly wasn't going to be getting into any bets with her after our 4-0 drumming in the previous meeting. Wary of our midweek success, Carol wasn't overconfident either. Scunthorpe were only three points ahead of Palace, despite our points deduction.

I went to the bar with Pavel and we began to discuss the season and suss each other out in the way that football fans do. One of the benefits of going to the ridiculously long distance away games is that the other fans there are going to have a similar level of obsession to you. Scunthorpe away isn't for the part-timers, it's for the people with no life. Or, as I would find out later, it is for people (like Pavel) who would rather do *anything* than spend a Saturday with their girlfriend. At the bar, someone gave Pav a tap on the shoulder,

"Did you get that done in the week mate?" asked the stranger, pointing at the 'Butterfield 20' on the back of his shirt.

"NO!" he replied. He was furious. Butterfield had been his favourite player for years and now that everyone was jumping on the pro-Butterfield bandwagon, he didn't want to be tarred with the same newcomers brush. I must admit, I did look at this angry Russian next to me and not for the first time that day, think 'Who

the hell is he?'

We had four pints before kickoff and I discovered two things about Pavel. Firstly, he was impulsive. Secondly, he earned too much money. He'd booked the extremely expensive train tickets at about two o'clock that morning to come 'oop north. Alcohol may well have played a small part in his decision making too. By two thirty in the afternoon, the pub was pretty packed and in fairly high spirits, although there was no rum, whisky or other such preposterous drink this time. Thankfully.

Just before leaving, we nipped to the loos to empty our bladders. While peeing, a group behind us spotted Pavel's shirt and began to sing,
"Oh Danny, Danny... Danny, Danny, Danny, Danny, BUTTERFIELD!"
Pavel did a strange fist pump with one hand, while he was desperately trying to stop himself from spraying everyone around him with the other. As we left the loo, someone grabbed his arm, *"Be honest mate, did you get that done in the week?"*
"No I bloody didn't!" came his even less tolerant reply.

We crossed the large car park between the pub and the ground and took Carol to the home supporter's entrance where she would be sitting. We then went around to the small, shed-like away end. As we were in the queue to get through the turnstile, we heard a voice from behind us, *"I bet you done that after Tuesday night mate, didn't you?"*
"Oh f*** off!"

Once we were in the ground, we found four seats together. We were in the front row, which would usually be disappointing as it makes it hard to see the action up the other end, but the small stand only went back around six rows so it really didn't matter. The first half was fairly uneventful on the pitch, with Scunthorpe being marginally the better team. As the football offered little in the way of a distraction, Dan had spent most of the first half worrying about his wife being on her own in the home section. He even told me that he'd rather be in the home end with her than with the Palace faithful behind the goal. Maybe there is a greater love to man than his football team? I still find it hard to believe.

However, he soon forgot all about his wife when he saw his other love, Clint Hill. He always described Clint as a 'Man's Man' and, like myself and most other Palace fans, he loved his no-nonsense style of play. There is a belief that football fans love flair players, who can entertain the crowd with outright skill. However, there is an argument that in England, we adore tough-as-nails defenders just as much, if not more. I can't imagine the more flamboyant Spanish or Italian football fans worshiping Clint Hill. In fact, I doubt any other countries would love Stuart Pearce more than they loved Steve McManaman or Chris Waddle or John Barnes.

There are very few English genuine flair players and natural dribblers. Power, strength and pace are skills that are preferred to a delicate technique. There's a good reason for this too. You know exactly what you are going to get from hard players like Clint Hill or Stuart Pearce; commitment, desire and strong tackles. If anyone beats them for skill, they'll kick 'em into Row Z and stop it happening again.

With a flair player, other than the very best, they're likely to blow hot and cold. They will frustrate a crowd by being a world beater one week and doing their best 'Eddie the Eagle' impression the following Saturday. Creative players also tend to rely on confidence. If they've been tackled when trying to beat a man three times in a row, they're hardly likely to risk the wrath of the crowd and try it again. They'll play a simple pass to a teammate which anyone could do; thus making their role in the team pointless. Tough players don't care how well or badly they're playing. They'll still go in for a tackle, just as hard, on anyone and everyone, no matter what's happened beforehand.

People moan that while we have this attitude, young English players will never develop the technique to compete at the top level and the national team will suffer. There may be some truth in this and players like Clint Hill offer nothing to the neutral fan. However, when it's your team, a strong, crunching challenge gives just as much satisfaction as a piece of skill to beat a man or a creative pass to spread the play. In our last promotion season, Palace fans voted a tough-tackling midfielder as our player of the season ahead of a thirty-goal striker and two skilful wingers, who made it into the Championship Team of the Year.

It's just as well that I had this attitude too. Palace's 2009/10 team was full of such players; Shaun Derry, Clint Hill, Matt Lawrence, Paddy McCarthy, Alan Lee and Johnny Ertl were all regular starters who would 'let the opponents know they were there' i.e. kick them. I loved them all. Maybe it's because I was a Palace fan and so used to cloggers that I loved that type of player so much. Perhaps, if I'd been taken to Arsenal as a kid, I'd be a fan of the tip-tappy, skilful players that Arsene Wenger has famed the club for. Which itself is bizarre as Arsenal's more traditional reputation is 'Boring, boring, Arsenal'. An identity that older gooners still identify with and embrace. As it is, I'm happy watching the Clint Hills of this world attempt to stop anyone playing decent football against us before we even *start* to think about playing a bit ourselves.

Anyway, my highlight of the first half was when Palace were defending a corner. The defenders lined up, ready to clear the cross and Dan felt the need to shout out, *"Clint! I love you Clint! Clint, Clint, I love you!"*
Ever the professional, Clint ignored him but he was just a few feet away from us and must have heard Dan's calls.

Soon after, Scunthorpe got another corner and Dan was at it again, *"Clint, I love you! I love you Clint! Open my barbeque Clint! You can cut the ribbon! Open my barbeque!"*
Dan was planning a Summer World Cup Barbeque and had often joked about wanting Clint Hill to be the celebrity that would open it. He'd clearly felt that during the first half of an away game at Scunthorpe was the perfect time to send the invite. I'm sure it was nothing to do with the pre-match beers. Clint didn't respond but, as you do when you're in love, Dan forgave him. Pavel, who had previously known nothing of Dan's one way love affair, looked on perplexed and

slightly fearful, while Rodger was presumably texting his niece and warning her of her boyfriend's associates. It was lucky for Dan that his wife was in the home end or she might have been a little jealous.

Half time came and Dan wanted a beer. I'd been to Scunthorpe a couple of years previously for a terrible 0-0 draw and knew there was no beer available in the away section but he was having none of it. We went to the tea-bar at the end of the stand but, unsurprisingly, they only sold tea. Not beer. Just tea. It was a tea-bar after all (and in view of the pitch, which would have made it illegal to sell beer anyway).

Incidentally, Scunthorpe have been very clever in the years since that game and dug underneath the stand to create a drinking concourse. However, on that day, there was nothing available, which was probably for the best. I'd had four pints before the game and Dan had sunk about four or five more than me.

As we queued up for our tea (not beer), someone tapped Pavel on the shoulder... he sighed and turned around slowly, anticipating the inevitable.
"Mate, did you..."
"No, I didn't get it printed this f***ing week!"
Pavel wasn't going to let this guy even finish his sentence. To be honest, I don't think he was far from re-opening the cold war over it.

In the second half, Palace played much better and Darren Ambrose scored an excellent goal to put us 1-0 up. After the goal, I ran along the front of the stand, celebrating as close to the jubilant players as possible. I can be seen on the TV replays, running alongside my hero, arms aloft. If that's not a claim to fame, then I don't know what is.

Soon after the goal, Scunthorpe had a player sent off for bringing our young winger, Dijlali, down when he was through on goal. This had to be our day, 1-0 up with Scunthorpe down to ten men. The only thing that could have improved it further was Clint Hill turning up to Dan's house in Sunningdale with a pair of scissors and a crate of craft beer for the barbeque. However, in typical Palace style, we blew it. With just six minutes left, Scunthorpe equalised.

Dan, which was unlike him when it comes to Palace, tried to see the positives. *"At least a draw will see both Carol and us happy on the way home,"* he offered.
Maybe there really was more to life than Palace? It seemed unlikely at best. To be fair to Dan, we would have taken a draw as a decent result before the game, but after being 1-0 up against ten men so late on, our attitude had changed.

Palace seem to love teasing us. We're used to mediocrity and failure but we're almost happy with that. Like with Clint Hill, we know exactly what we're getting; you take wins as a bonus and defeats on the chin. However, the club can't just give us that and let us be happy with it. Oh no, they have to tease us with hope and belief and the dreaded 'e' word first; just to make sure that the mediocrity and failure cause as much pain and misery as possible. I'm sure every football fan up and down the country feels the same about their team but to be honest, I'd don't care about their team. I only see and feel it through mine, as it's my beloved Palace who torture me.

Just as we were accepting a draw, Neil Danns scored a super last minute winner. Ok, I guess Palace knew what they were doing. They knew that simply holding onto a 1-0 win at ten men Scunthorpe wouldn't be the most memorable of away victories. They wanted something special. Something to remember. A last minute winner.

Danns got the ball on the edge of the area and turned one way then the other before curling it beautifully into the bottom corner. It was one of those magical moments in football where you are right in line with the shot and can see it's going in as soon as it leaves the player's boot. The away end went mad. This time, Dan, losing any sense of maturity or experience, lost himself and followed me down to mob the players.

Warnock summed it up in his post match press conference *"This business has brought us all closer together, players and fans."*
He was right. The players had gone absolutely mental at the winning goal. It meant the world to them. In my fourteen or so years supporting the club, I'd never had a feeling like it. The manager felt like one of us, the players felt like one of us. We were all in the same mess together and we were all metaphorically giving administration a firm right hook. Clint Hill was good for that too.

After the game, the players came over to the away end so that we could celebrate together. Without the points deduction, we'd have actually been in the top six that evening. I guess that played a large part in driving on their determination. None of this had been their fault. They'd done their jobs and were performing well above all expectations, yet they found themselves in a relegation dog fight regardless. It showed in the heart and desire of their performances that they felt personally robbed of the ten points.

Dan went to the home end to pick up his wife, while Pavel, Rodger and I went to look (unsuccessfully) for a programme, before we all headed back to the Harvester. Carol's nephew and pregnant wife met us in the pub as they hadn't attended the game. When they arrived, I tried my best not to rub the result in too much to Carol. I suspect I failed. I was, and still am, in a transition between the in-your-face-child-like reaction of winning a football match to a more subtle-and-clever, wink-and-nod response when we face a side whom I know a supporter of. Beer can only push me towards (and sometimes beyond) the child-like reaction.

We had a couple of pints in the Harvester before agreeing to head back to the station to catch our train home. There wasn't room in the car for all of us so Dan asked Carol's nephew to take Pavel, Rodger and I first. We arrived at the station a few minutes before the train was due to depart and were disappointed to find that there wasn't a local off-licence. We realised on the way to the station that Dan and Carol wouldn't make it to our train. The journey from Scunthorpe to Doncaster didn't require us to get a specific train but the onward journey did. It would be a very expensive mistake to miss it.

Rodger, Pavel and I arrived at Doncaster in plenty of time, having discovered that Pavel was the previously unknown stranger who'd been singing to Jesus at Reading. We found the Sainsburys opposite the station was closed so we decided to make a run for the large Tesco nearby. In that moment, getting beer was clearly more important than getting our train. It could be argued that this is the sign of being an alcoholic but I didn't worry; alcoholics go to meetings...

We legged it to the Tesco and found the alcohol section. I rang up Dan to see what he wanted. He was hoping to make our Doncaster train by getting the next one from Scunthorpe but it was going to be touch and go whether he made it. When he answered, I asked the most important question of any away trip,

"Hi mate, we're getting beer, what do you want?"

"Any lager," came his reply.

"...and what does Carol want? I guess she needs a drink after her team lost... in the last minute... to her husband's team, 2-1, get in, hehe!" I definitely still needed to work on the subtlety of my taunting.

"Errrrm... they're getting beer love, do you want any? ... eerrmm ok ... errr ... Just get her some lager too. I better go!" Dan hadn't sounded too convinced but it would be most unlike Carol to not want a beer so we got a large crate of Carlsberg for Dan, Carol, Pavel and I, while Rodger picked up some bottles of London Pride.

We ran back to the station and arrived with a couple of minutes to spare. There wasn't any sign of Carol or Dan so I rang Dan. There was no answer. I rang him again. He answered, I heard some arguing, it cut out. I might have been missing a social cue or two but I rang again. No answer.

Their train was due in on the platform next to the one where the London train was set to leave from. Less than a minute before our train was expected, theirs arrived. I saw the pair of them so I ran up to them in drunken excitement and relief. I liked Pavel and Rodger but it was these two who I knew well and were my friends.

"It's all ok now guys. You're here and I've got beer!" I joked. Carol marched past us. She wasn't happy. Dan pulled a face, laughed and followed his wife.

Carol was absolutely furious at Dan for letting her nephew, with a wife who was due to drop any minute, ferry around his mates while leaving the two of them behind. We all got on the train. Dan, Pavel, Rodger and I sat together but Carol stormed off to the next carriage. We opened a beer each as Dan went to speak to his angry partner. While he was away, we discovered a fatal error that Rodger had made. We didn't have a bottle opener for his ale.

After about five minutes, Dan came back. Alone. Carol hadn't taken any of his excuses and was refusing to sit with us. Well, specifically, him. He'd decided that he'd had enough of her being miserable and came back for a beer.

"She's mad James. They're all mad James! Don't ever get married" he announced on his return. It seemed legitimate advice. Dan's life counsel had always been sound up until this point so I took it on board.

Pavel and Rodger had a more pressing concern.

"Dan, does Carol have a bottle opener?" inquired a hopeful Russian.

"No, I don't think so," replied Dan.

"Go on, go and check mate," came a now desperate plea, with a wink and a grin.

"I can't open my beer!" added Rodger. Finally someone was speaking Dan's language and he understood the need. A Palace fan, who he'd just met, needed a drink and it was well worth risking the wrath his wife to get one. Dan went to the next carriage to check with his other half. He returned very shortly afterwards with the answer and an inane grin on his face.

"She doesn't have a bottle opener but she told me where I could put one if I found one!"

Putting Dan's marriage problems to one side, we began to drink. Heavily. After a few beers, Pavel managed to open the bottles of London Pride by slamming them down against the side of his chair. The sophisticated twenty first century at its very best. Soon, the four of us were putting on a performance worthy of the Albert Hall and singing Palace songs at the top of our voice for the rest of the train. It's a wonder that we didn't receive a standing ovation from our fellow passengers.

It wasn't long until our songs about Danny Butterfield changed to Dan's chants about his wife:

"Where's the wife? Where's the wife? Where's the wife? Where's the wife?"

"Wifey, give us a song! Wifey, Wifey, give us a song!"

Before we got a rendition of my personal favourite.

"Go down pub,
Drink ten pints,
Absolutely plastered,
Go back home,
*and beat your **husband**,*
You dirty Northern bastard!"

It's fair to say that she didn't give him a standing ovation.

The rest of the train journey involved a mixture of drinking beer, singing Palace songs and Dan telling me that all women are mad so I should never, ever get married.

"She's mad James! Mad"

When we got back to King's Cross, we got off the train and looked for Carol. We couldn't see her. At the time, we thought we'd had a thorough and strategically planned search around the platform. It later turned out that she was watching us stagger around in circles, as if we were Craig Harrison chasing opposing centre forwards, with a lack of amusement. Believing that the 'mad women' had managed to move down the train and rush off the platform specifically to avoid us (well, Dan mainly), the reality of the situation should have hit home. It didn't. We simply sang a bit more about Danny Butterfield and carried on. Dan's marriage might have been on the line but Palace had won three times in a week. Never forget your first love.

Dan's first love was in hospital (as was his marriage at this point). Palace might have been bravely fighting on and recovering well but they still needed our support and that had to be more important than a marriage, right? Maybe that's a decision best made sober. Anyway, undeterred, the four of us sang loudly all the way through the station and down into the tube.

We left Pavel on the underground at Vauxhall (with a final Butterfield song) and then headed home. Dan did agree to go for a pint by Clapham Junction at The Falcon, but as the beer began to wear off, he realised that going home might be a better option...

Chapter 40 – **Crashing back down to Earth**

Tuesday 9th February 2010, Crystal Palace vs Swansea, Selhurst Park

Crystal Palace: Julian Speroni, Nathaniel Clyne, Clint Hill, Shaun Derry, Darren Ambrose, Neil Danns, Nick Carle (Sean Scannell, 81), Lee Hills, Alan Lee (Calvin Andrew, 57), Danny Butterfield (Kieran Djilali, 57) Johnny Ertl
Subs Not Used: Stern John, James Comley, Alassane N'Diaye, Alex Wynter

Swansea City: Dorus De Vries, Ashley Williams, Adam Tate, Leon Britton (Gorka Pintado,89), Darren Pratley, Andrea Orlandi, Nathan Dyer (Joe Allen, 84), Garry Monk, Fede Bessone, Mark Gower (David Cotterill, 67), Shefki Kuqi
Subs Not Used: David Cornell, Lee Trundle, Tom Butler, Ashley Richards

Since the Scunthorpe match, I'd been on a high. However, I don't think Dan had. In fact, he wasn't allowed to come to this game after the weekend's antics. Football might not actually be real life but it can certainly affect it. He'd messaged Colin and simply said *"I've really messed up mate."*
Carol had been far from amused at his lack of consideration for her. Apparently, when your wife is pissed off at you, getting really drunk with your mates and chanting at her is the wrong thing to do. As is asking her for a bottle opener.

News had broken on the morning of the game that an advert had been placed in the Financial Times for the club. It read:
"The sale of the football club and its associated assets presents an opportunity to acquire a long-established South London club (founded in 1905) currently playing in the Championship division of the Football League and currently enjoying success in the FA Cup"

It was an unprecedented move and it was certainly a strange feeling to hear about the club in the Financial Times. Before the game, Warnock moaned to the press that the administrator had tried to loan Neil Danns to Swansea without telling him. As fans, it felt desperate. Danns had turned down the move which reiterated how much the players were giving to the cause. However, we all felt sorry for the players and Warnock having to work in the current circumstances.

I met up with Colin, Jonathan and Kev in The Railway for a few before heading to the game. Palace never really got into the match and managed to lose to a goal from Shefki Kuqi of all people. At least Jonathan managed to get bottles rather than gone off pints at half time.

Kuqi had epitomized the mis-spending under Jordan. He'd been signed for £2.5m to replace Andy Johnson, our greatest goalscorer in recent times, and had flopped. Not only did he fail to produce on the pitch, he also stuck his fingers up at the home crowd for cheering when he was subbed off during a match against Wolverhampton Wanderers. An action that many fans, myself included, never really forgave him for - despite him finishing as our top scorer in his final season at the club. After three unhappy years, he had been released on a free transfer the previous summer, much to the relief of the Palace faithful and presumably the player himself too. His time at Palace can be found in the dictionary as the definition of 'waste'. However, even I felt sorry for him as he didn't celebrate his goal that beat us but he received heavy abuse from fans in the home end anyway.

However, whatever abuse Kuqi received was pale in comparison to the female Swansea physio. Towards the end, with the home support having long since given up on a Palace goal, she ran, well waddled – such was her rather large size, onto the pitch to support an injured Swansea player. Her entrance was met with possibly the loudest noise of the night from the home ends – a cruel laugh, which was followed up with the chant *"That's why you shag sheep!"*
While it was mean and abusive towards the poor girl, I couldn't help but laugh at the spiteful chant. It was certainly more memorable than the game.

A couple of days after the match, a rumour broke on the BBS. Someone claimed that Neil Warnock was in talks to become the QPR manager. It was met with ridicule on the internet. Warnock was one of us. Why would he leave?

One IT-boffin used the user's IP address to discover who it was and his company. The guy was a chartered accountant for a Sheffield-based company called Finance7. The thread that he started soon deteriorated into people claiming that he was a liar and including his name. Within half an hour, if you typed his name and company into Google, the second result was the thread, which had pages and pages of accusations of him being a liar. The forum moderators had to frantically try and remove the libellous posts. It really highlighted to me the scariness of the internet. Anyone can find anyone. This poor guy was only passing on a rumour that he'd heard and it could have ended up harming his livelihood and reputation at work.

Although it was from the same source that had first broken the administration news on the BBS, the rumour from 'BOBday' wasn't taken too seriously. Warnock had continuously talked about being up for the fight and seemed to be relishing the challenge. It simply wasn't worth considering the idea of him leaving.

Chapter 41 - **Cup Fever**

Sunday 14th February 2010, Crystal Palace vs Aston Villa, Selhurst Park, FA Cup 5th Round

Crystal Palace: Julian Speroni, Nathaniel Clyne, Clint Hill, Shaun Derry, Darren Ambrose, Neil Danns, Nick Carle, Alan Lee (Calvin Andrew, 90+2), Danny Butterfield, Johnny Ertl, Claude Davis
Subs Not Used: Sean Scannell, Matt Lawrence, Kieran Djilali, Alassane N'Diaye, Alex Wynter, Charlie Mann

Aston Villa: Brad Friedel, Luke Young, Richard Dunne, Stuart Downing, Ashley Young, James Milner, Fabian Delph (Nathan Delfouneso, 74), Emile Heskey (John Carew, 45), Stiliyan Petrov, Stephen Warnock, James Collins
Subs Not Used: Steven Sidwell, Curtis Davies, Brad Guzan, Habib Beye, Carlos Cuellar

The 5th round of the FA Cup is as far as I have ever seen Palace get to in the competition. The first time was in 1998 and after beating Scunthorpe in the third round, I witnessed us beat Leicester 3-0 in the fourth round thanks to a Bruce Dyer hat-trick. In that season, we only won two Premiership games at home so we actually matched our tally of home league wins with home FA Cup wins. The 5th round pitted us against Arsenal away, which was the first – and for a long time only – Palace game that I've watched on TV. I was seven years old at the time and staying at my Granny's house. The previous day, she'd taken me around Crystal Palace Park and I counted the amount of Palace and Arsenal shirts that I spotted. Palace won 6-5 and I hoped that would be an omen for the game the next day. Unfortunately, the actual match was less free scoring and finished 0-0. Palace then lost the replay 2-1.

The second 5th round appearance came in 2003 after a win at Blackpool in the third round and a win at Anfield in the following round. We'd drawn 0-0 at home to Liverpool in the fourth round, which was the only time that I'd seen us fail to beat the scouse giants. After the game, I remember my Dad being disappointed because we hadn't really gone for it and had 'no chance' in the replay. However, ten days later, we listened in amazement to the radio as ten-man Palace (Brian has never forgiven Freedman for getting sent off) beat Liverpool 2-0 in their own back yard. The fifth round pitted us at home to then-giants Leeds United. Dermot Gallagher, the referee, managed to not notice that a Leeds player punched the ball away from the goal after it had already crossed the line. Firstly, it should have been a goal but if the referee missed that, then he should have awarded us a penalty and a red card for the Leeds player. He gave neither. It wasn't quite on a par with Rob Shoebridge in terms of refereeing incompetence but it was still a pretty horrific decision and Palace lost 2-1.

And, unfortunately, in my years of supporting the club, that's pretty much our FA Cup record summed up in two paragraphs. I often look at the history books in frustration as two years before I started to follow Palace, we got to a semi-final and five years before that, we were actually at Wembley for the final.

On both occasions, we were unlucky to lose to Manchester United in replays.

So because of my personal experience (I'd even managed to miss the Liverpool win) it would be understandable for me to not believe in the magic and excitement of the cup. The third round tie at Sheffield Wednesday had seemed a bit of an inconvenience at the time but I think this was more down to the fact that it was a long distance away and I'd managed to prepare myself mentally for not going. Thanks to Mike for swapping shifts, once again. However, I do love the competition and do believe in the magic of it – the Wolves game had certainly relit my Cup Fever. I think my love of the cup stems back to when I was a child. We didn't have Sky when I was growing up so the only football that I would watch was the FA Cup. As that's what I could actually see, that's what I prioritised. That's the football I fell in love with.

As a child, the terrible Auto-glass adverts that came at the start and end of each advert break were the hot topic at school on a Monday morning. Sometimes even more than the match. The first domestic game that I remember watching was between Liverpool and Chelsea. My oldest brother still supported Liverpool and jumped around the living room as his side went 2-0 up in the first half. Chelsea came out strongly in the second period and won 4-2. My other brothers and I took great delight in jumping around to annoy our sunken, oldest brother.

It was talked about for weeks in our school. Long after other games came and went but that didn't matter. That was the game that we'd seen so that was the game that mattered in the mind of a seven year old. I remember saying to my best friend at the time *"It could only happen in the FA Cup!"*
Total nonsense of course but I'd heard the commentator say it and liked the sound of it.

On the morning of the Villa game, I certainly felt like a little boy again. The papers were full of reports about the potential fairy tale. The 'crisis' club in administration against high flying Aston Villa. Villa are a huge club who have been in the doldrums for most of my football supporting life. They have never dropped out of the top flight and are unlikely to do so. However, for this cup tie, they were on the crest of a wave in terms of their position in the football world. Martin O'Neil had spent big money at the club and they were doing well. They were pushing for the Champions League and had back to back finishes of fifth in the Premier League. They were also due to play in the League Cup final against Manchester United later that month and were doing well in the UEFA Cup. This was as good as it had got for Villa for twenty years or so. It was going to be a huge ask for us to get a result.

But... It was the FA Cup. If Danny Butterfield could score a six-minute-perfect-hat-trick then anything could happen and our name was pretty much already on the trophy. Although, it was even more unlikely that he would repeat his actions in this match as he was going to play in his more familiar role of a defender. I suspect Pavel would peel off the letters from his shirt if Butts didn't get at least one. The ever on-running joke is that he hated him until the Wolves game.

This cup tie had even more of an incentive than usual. In the past, the magic of the cup was purely on the pitch. It starts with non-league teams, who play on little more than a local park, and ends at Wembley, with the biggest and best teams in the country. And in-between the two extremes, there are numerous shock results (such as, picking one entirely at random, Charlton losing to Northwich Victoria). However, in more recent times, the financial aspect of it is almost as magical as the actual football. When Exeter City drew 0-0 away at Manchester United in 2005, the gate receipts and TV money funded their club for well over a year. As a club in administration, we couldn't overlook the fact that we were playing a game on TV in front of our biggest gate of the season. There was even a small pot of gold to play for in prize money for the winner.

Before the game, the mood was extremely positive. We had nothing to lose and everything to gain. Our excitement was only dampened by the extra clientele in the Railway Club. Our usually empty bar was packed and it took over ten minutes to get served. Another reason to rejoice in crap football is that it cuts the queues. Suddenly, a Premiership side were in town and we were forced into buying double rounds.

Dan had been allowed to come to the game but he still wasn't drinking. He'd brought his son, Max, to the match and they were going to sit in the Family Section of the ground. Family sections are a brilliant initiative from clubs to help create a swearing and aggression-free zone to encourage youngsters to come and see the football. I think it's brilliant that a lot of clubs now also have a family section in the away end to make sure that the kids can see the action as people often stand up and block their view otherwise. I can't help but feel Palace have missed a trick by putting our family section next to the away end, where any avoided aggression from the home fans, is more than made up for by the away supporters.

We emptied our bladders and left the pub, slightly earlier than usual to compensate for the larger crowd. Ten minutes before kickoff, the ground was packed and the atmosphere was buzzing. The teams were read out and I couldn't help but notice that only Matt Lawrence was aged over twenty on our bench. Villa had a range of expensive signings and full internationals. They didn't have a huge squad so I had hoped that they might rotate it a bit and give us a bit more of a chance. But they didn't. They played their strongest side. It wasn't quite as daunting as Manchester City's most expensive ever eleven from earlier in the season but it still contained no fewer than six full England internationals; Luke Young, Steven Warnock, Ashley Young, Stewart Downing, James Milner and Emilie Heskey. They also had one of the top goalkeepers in the country and USA captain, Brad Friedal, the captain of the Bulgarian national side, Stilyan Petrov, and Norway's leading international striker, John Carew. Each of those players were worth more individually than the £2 million that our eleven had cost to put together.

The crowd had been buzzing with excitement before the game but they burst into life during it. Villa started as the stronger side but that wasn't going to stop us. Since going into administration, every game had almost had a party atmosphere. We were bricking ourselves all week, reading reports of our impending doom, but when the football came, we were celebrating the fact that we still had our Palace. With this game being on national TV and having no relegation stresses attached to it, we were going to party more than ever.

Midway through the first half, against the run of play, Palace took an unlikely lead. Ambrose swung in a corner and Jonny Ertl headed in his first goal for the club. Selhurst erupted. Scoring was such a rare feat for Ertl that he didn't look like he knew what to do. Maybe he should have asked Butterfield for some pre-match advice.

Ten minutes later, Selhurst was silenced. Well, it should have been silenced anyway. Villa equalised, the shock victory was off again and that should have been that. It wasn't. It was our party and we weren't going to let a bunch of Brummies gate-crash it. Conceding a goal only seemed to fire the players and fans up even more. By now, the game had developed into a classic cup tie and both sides had further chances before the break - Heskey and Petrov heading over for Villa, while Palace's best effort came when Ambrose's deflected free-kick forced Friedel to punch the ball clear. The crowd were playing their part too, even the Villa fans. This was our celebrating-that-we-still-have-a-team-party but they were in the middle of their best season for years and wanted to enjoy every minute of it too.

Half time came and we went up to the Red'n'Blue bar. The pre-match optimism had turned to belief, maybe even expectation. For once, I didn't fear the 'e' word, I embraced it. From this point, win, lose or draw, I would be proud of the players.

The second half continued in the same vein as the first. It was end to end stuff as both sides looked for a winner. With twenty minutes left, Palace got a free kick.

"How much Dad?" came Adam's plea. Although it had only paid off once, Adam was more than used to being offered money as an attempt to tempt fate.

Before his Dad could reply, I jumped in. *"I tell you what mate, if this goes in, I'll give you a fiver!"*

The free-kick was dead centre of the goal and a long way out. We knew Ambrose would shoot but it was probably too far out to test one of the top keepers in the country.

"...and your Dad will match it..." I continued confidently. *"...and Kev will double it!"*

It was definitely easier to tempt fate with somebody else's money.

The referee settled everyone down and marched the wall back ten yards before he blew his whistle. Ambrose ran up. The ball seemed to fly continuously for what seemed like an age towards the goal. Eventually, the keeper got a hand to it but he couldn't stop it. It was too powerful. He'd hit it too well. Selhurst exploded. I frantically grabbed my wallet with one hand while I excitedly grabbed Adam with the other. I presented him with a five pound note and his already beaming face lit up even further. Colin and Kev were trying to pretend to be pissed off at me as they jumped about in delight. Palace were 2-1 up with twenty minutes left and Selhurst went from having a party to having a rave. Even the usually quiet family stand opposite us were leaping about in delight. I couldn't help but wonder if that was Dan's affect.

For the next five or ten minutes, Villa were shaken. Whether it was the shock of being behind, the outrageousness of Ambrose's strike or the noise of the crowd, I don't know. I guess a combination of all three. But they didn't know what to do. Martin O'Neil, their manager, was jumping around the touchline going mad as they couldn't string two passes together. Palace had chances to extend the lead and Ambrose hit the bar, which would have finished the Premiership side off.

Inevitably, in the final few minutes, Villa composed themselves and had one last desperate throw of the dice. They forced corner after corner as Speroni made save after save. When Speroni was finally beaten, Clyne cleared the ball off the line. The whole of Selhurst was on its feet. This was frantic cup football at its best.

Villa lumped yet another ball into the box, which their striker, John Carew, powerfully headed towards goal. Speroni saved it. Nathan Delfouneso, Villa's young striker, and two Palace defenders all threw themselves at the loose ball. It squirmed away for yet another corner. We'd survived again. England international, Stuart Downing, sprinted over to take it – they had just three minutes left and needed to use every second. Villa had everyone forward. The corner was poor. Too low. However, Stillian Petrov, another international star who was leading the siege on our goal, dived in to get a faint header on the ball. Slowly. Ever so slowly. It sailed across the Palace goal. Past Speroni. Past Clyne. Past everyone. And it nestled into the far corner. Finally Selhurst was silenced. Silenced, except for the distant cry of relief coming from the Villa faithful.

I slowly sunk from my feet, on to the back of my chair and then deep into my seat. I didn't speak. None of us did. Kev put his hand on my shoulder to try and comfort me as I sat there, head in hands. The final few minutes are a bit of a blur but I vaguely remember Villa having chances to win the game. It finished 2-2 and the dejected players received a huge ovation as they left the pitch.

After they had departed, the draw for the quarter finals was shown on the big screen in the ground. The winner of the replay would be away at West Bromwich Albion or Reading. Adam turned to his Dad and asked hopefully, *"If we win the replay, and Reading win theirs, can we go to Reading?"*
Colin looked at his child, *"Son, if we get to an FA Cup quarter final, I'll take you anywhere!"*
Even the 5th round had been new territory for Adam. He beamed with excitement. There was a brief moment where Colin had the same expression. When he was eight years old again. However, straight afterwards, he looked at me and puffed his cheeks in resignation, even Mr Positive knew that winning the replay would be highly unlikely. Our big chance had gone.

I spoke to my Dad straight after the game and he told me the corner that Villa had scored from should have been a goal kick for Palace. This really didn't matter to me at the time. I was heartbroken. I wasn't willing to listen to anyone. I didn't want to speak about the game. I knew I should have felt proud. I knew the players had given everything. I knew that a draw was actually a brilliant achievement. I knew that the replay would give us some more vital money. But none of that mattered. We'd been so close and we'd lost it. Well, technically drawn it but it felt like a loss.

I sat in the Railway Club with Jonathan and Kev, barely speaking during my first pint. I just wanted football to go away. Maybe if the club was wound up, it would be a good thing. Sure, I'd be lost at first but at least I wouldn't feel like this. It was the first time in the season that a match had made me feel so low. At least after the Scunthorpe and Doncaster massacres, I'd been able to laugh about it. You need a good sense of humour to support Palace.

Being a student, it didn't bother me that it was a Sunday, so I continued to sulk into pints of Guinness and with each beer, I felt a little less hurt and a little more pride. By the time we left, I was confident that we'd win the replay. My reasoning at the time was that if we could get that close once, we could do it again. And Villa's League Cup final was going to be on the Sunday after our match so they'd surely be focussed on that. And after all, it was the FA Cup. Anything could happen. The reality of my new found optimism was actually that I was, by that point, rather predictably, pissed.

Although, despite my new-found belief, I was conscious of the personal downside to a replay. It might generate money for the club but it would cost me even more in travel, beer and ticket costs. I was also wary of the affect on the squad. We had a small pool of players and because of the two replays and the Bristol City re-arranged fixture, between January 27th, when we played Newcastle, and April 5th, when we played Preston, we would play in ten of the eleven mid-weeks, as well as every Saturday. To say that the squad would be pushed was an understatement.

After leaving the Railway Club, I went to meet Robin in Putney. He was working in his pub, The Bricklayer's Arms by the river, and I wanted to continue downing beers to forget the pain of the football. I was also fed up with my housemates at the time and didn't want to face going home. There were plenty of issues between me and them during that period but the football, which had previously started our friendship, was now one of the many things driving a wedge between us. They thought it was hilarious that Palace were in administration and wanted the club to go bust 'to see my reaction'. I didn't want to return home to hear jokes about Palace conceding a last minute goal so I simply stayed out drinking.

I began to talk to a West Ham fan in the pub. We were both quite drunk and Robin looked on disapprovingly as we argued about whether you could feel pride in a defeat. I was now over my self-pity (mainly thanks to alcohol) and was declaring my love and pride of the team. This guy was saying that there's no place in football for heroic losers.

He talked about how he felt after losing the Playoff Final to Palace in 2004 (a game that I was more than happy for him to bring up) and he said that no level of performance on the pitch or amount of alcohol off the pitch could have cheered him up after that. However, he was missing the point. West Ham had approached that game with arrogance and had expected to win. They hadn't performed and hadn't given everything. There's no pride in that. However, if you can't feel proud after giving everything you've got and coming within a whisker of achieving something against all odds, then I think your mindset in life is wrong.

Admittedly, on paper, Palace hadn't achieved anything by drawing with Villa that day. It was highly likely that we'd lose the replay and exit the cup despite our best efforts. However, what we had achieved was that we had shown that we were up for the fight, we'd shown we would give everything and we'd given a team of international players a genuine scare that day.

The record books will only remember the result but I will never forget Ambrose's strike or the atmosphere after it. I will never forget the roar after every crunching tackle or heroic block as we tried to hold onto the lead and most importantly, I will never forget the pride I had in watching eleven players in red'n'blue give absolutely everything for the cause. That was a feeling that I got time and time again during the administration period of Palace's history. It didn't feel, as it often does, that we were paying to go and watch the millionaire footballers. It felt like we were there to support our mates. It felt like we were just as involved as the players on the pitch.

Sometimes football feels like the eleven players are just there making up the numbers while you're on the side, where the genuine action and passion is. Often, it feels like you're the ones who are actually involved as it is you who has invested the time, money and energy into the game and hundreds of matches before it. The players seem to be simply going through the motions on the pitch in front of you. However, during those dark days of administration, it felt like we were as one. It felt like they were the front line and we were the masses behind them being led into battle, with Neil Warnock in charge of it all as the leading officer. The players and the fans together were the Red'n'Blue Army and we stuck by them and they stuck by us. No matter what. Although it was one of the lowest points of the Palace rollercoaster, it was also one of the most special times to be a part of the ride.

The goal was one of my finest moments in a Crystal Palace Shirt. Glad All Over!

Johnny Ertl

Chapter 42 – **The FA Cup Hangover**

Wednesday 17ᵗʰ February 2010, Crystal Palace vs Reading, Selhurst Park

Crystal Palace: Julian Speroni, Nathaniel Clyne, Clint Hill, Shaun Derry, Darren Ambrose, Neil Danns (Sean Scannell, 43), Nick Carle (Alassane N'Diaye, 63), Calvin Andrew (Alan Lee, 45), Danny Butterfield, Johnny Ertl, Claude Davis
Subs Not Used: Lee Hills, Matt Lawrence, Kieran Djilali, Charlie Mann

Reading: Adam Federici, Matt Mills, Brynjar Gunnarsson, Jobi McAnuff, Jimmy Kebe, Simon Church, Jem Karacan, Ryan Bertrand, Brian Howard (Gylfi Sigurdsson, 77), Andy Griffin, Zurab Khizanishvili
Subs Not Used: Kalifa Cisse, Hal Robson-Kanu, Ben Hamer, Grzegorz Raziak, Alex Pearce, Gunnar Thorvaldsson

I met up early with my Brentford mate Chris to go for pre-match beers. Jak and him had agreed to come to the game as Jak's cousin, Ross, is a Reading fan and would be joining us. Unfortunately, Jak dropped out at the last minute. Chris and I were in the Railway Club from five o'clock and were soon joined by Ross, along with his friend, Richard, and his cousin, Sam, who turned out to be a Chelsea fan who Ross was trying to convert. I didn't know the three Reading fans before meeting them but they were all really nice guys. They were genuine football fans who I could identify with. Having also grown up in Berkshire, we knew a lot of the same places away from football too. Unlike a lot of the Reading fans who I knew from school, who'd started supporting the club when they got promoted to the Premiership, Ross and Richard really understood what it meant to support a crap team.

Reading had been through their peak of winning the Championship and finishing in the top half of the Premiership table in recent years but they were now back down towards the lower end of the second tier. Before the game, Reading sat in the drop zone and Palace sat just two places above it so it was a real six pointer. A win would put us four points clear of danger, whereas a defeat could leave us languishing in the relegation positions.

Soon, we were joined by Colin, Kev, Jonathan and, eventually, Dan. By the time Dan had arrived, I was sat with my group of visitors and although they were next to us, the others almost had a separate circle. He got himself a pint and went to sit with Colin. He hadn't realised that I was with four others when he gave me a nod and a 'hello' as he sat down. Slowly, he noticed each of the people next to me and gave each one a separate nod and 'hello', believing every one of them to be the last. Each nod became more exaggerated as he realised there was yet another person he didn't know to acknowledge. By the time he'd reached the end of the extended line, he was laughing and grinning at the daftness of the situation.

At about quarter to eight, we finished our pints and emptied our bladders. Ross and his friends went to the away end, while Chris accompanied myself and my usual lot to our season ticket seats. It was a strange feeling to sit with a complete neutral for a match. I'd often bring non-Palace supporting friends, who although they couldn't fully understand the meaning and importance of it all, would become an honorary Palace fan for ninety minutes. Which is fine when you win as they can get some enjoyment out of it but when you lose, rather than a sense of understanding that you get with a fellow fan, you receive pity from a mate which only makes you feel worse.

I've always refused to watch a game with a 'friend' who supports the opposition. I have no interest in banter or gloating during a match, I simply want to be with my own type. People who feel the same as I do. The same joy. The same pain. The same hatred of the referee. The only exception that I've made to my rule was forcing myself to sit in the home end (twice) for pre-season games at Wycombe. Once with my cousin as a child and once with my Wycombe Wanderers supporting friend, Greg.

But watching a game with someone who really didn't care about which team won was a strange feeling. Chris enjoyed the game, supplying wit, tactical observations and the odd laugh at a misplaced pass but he wasn't really concerned about it. I've been in his shoes plenty of times. Often with him at Brentford. Watching a game of football and supporting a team are two entirely different things. Unlike Chris, I can't watch a game unless I'd prefer a team to win. I need the tension that it brings and the emotion. However, you can never get close to the genuine feeling of watching your own team. The feeling of really caring. Of it really mattering.

That is why I would rather see a 0-0 draw against Barnsley at Selhurst Park than watch a 6-5 Champions League Final between Real Madrid and Barcelona. It wouldn't matter to me how tense everybody else is, or how exciting the game is, or how 'big' a match it is, there's no replacement feeling for being absolutely desperate for your team to score or hold out for a result. It doesn't mean that I can't enjoy non-Palace games – I've been to more than my fair share – but it will never, *ever*, be as good. Supporting a football team is how I imagine a solid marriage is for a middle aged man. He knows there are other more attractive women out there but he never questions the need to stay loyal to his wife as he has so much history, commitment and love with his life partner. Even if he never gets much back.

The atmosphere felt flat as there were seven thousand less people in the ground than the previous Sunday. A disappointing stat as it was actually a far more important game for the club, even if it was a little less glamorous. Palace fell behind mid-way through the first half and didn't really look like getting back into the match. We sent Chris up to the Red'n'Blue bar at half time to get our refreshments as, like I said, he wasn't really bothered about the game. During half time we all agreed that the next goal would be crucial. It was. And it came to Reading. They scored two minutes into the second half. Palace briefly got back into the game thanks to a Sean Scannell goal but Reading got a third late on to seal the win. The ground emptied quickly after the third and fatal goal went in. Dan led the exodus of our group and I followed soon after. Only Colin, ever the optimist, stayed until the end.

Disappointed, Chris and I headed back to the Railway Club to meet Ross,

Sam and Richard. Well, I was disappointed, Chris didn't care and the three of them were anything but disappointed. Ross's attempt to convert his cousin into a supporter of a real team was going well. Reading had looked doomed earlier on in the season but had been on a fantastic run and this result took them out of the bottom three. Palace were now only clear of it on goal difference.

I didn't know the Reading fans at the time and I dreaded them coming to meet us in the pub post match. I'd enjoyed drinking with them before the game but I wasn't sure how they would react to beating us so comfortably. I shouldn't have been worried. They were gracious in victory as I'm sure they would have been in defeat. They showed genuine class and I'm sure that I could learn a thing or two from them in that regard. As I've said before, I find it hard not to get carried away after a Palace victory.

We continued to drink together until it was time for the last train back to Clapham Junction that we could all get. The football had been very disappointing as both the crowd and players seemed to suffer from a hangover after the heartbreaking end to the Villa game. However, the rest of the evening had been enjoyable and I have stayed good friends with Ross to this day. We've been to plenty of Palace vs Reading fixtures together and he has proved me right about being just as gracious in defeat as victory.

Chapter 43 - **Send them to Coventry! (but not to QPR)**

Saturday 20th February 2010, Crystal Palace vs Coventry City, 2014

Crystal Palace: Julian Speroni, Nathaniel Clyne, Clint Hill, Shaun Derry, 7. Darren Ambrose, Nick Carle (Calvin Andrew, 87), Sean Scannell (Kieran Djilali, 68), Matt Lawrence, Alan Lee, Johnny Ertl, Claude Davis
Subs Not Used: Lee Hills, Danny Butterfield, James Comley, Alassane N'Diaye, Charlie Mann

Coventry City: Kieran Westwood, Stephen Wright, Sammy Clingan, James McPake, Jonathan Stead, Clinton Morrison, Martin Crainie, Aaron Gunnarsson, Carl Baker, Michael McIndoe (David Bell, 72), Richard Wood
Subs Not Used: Freddy Eastwood, Gary Deegan, Dimi Konstantopoulos, Freddie Sears, Ben Turner, Jermain Grandison

Throughout the week, speculation had continued to grow about the possibility of Warnock leaving the club for QPR and Palace fan's dismissive attitude was beginning to look unjust. That morning, rumours had gone into overdrive and were the main conversation in the Railway Club, where I met Colin and Adam. The pre-match mood was calmed and quietened further thanks to the absence of Jonathan's irrational ranting, Kev's sly humour and Dan's all-knowing summaries and dampening of expectations, destroyed by years of abuse from his beloved club.

"Why would he go to QPR?" groaned Colin. I simply shook my head. It didn't make any sense but the rumours were too strong to ignore by now. *"...after everything that he's said, surely he wouldn't walk out now?!"* I replied, as I took a sip of my pint. Or I would have done if I'd had a pint, but I was on orange juice and lemonade. I was pretty skint and had been drinking a lot around that time so I decided to stick to the soft stuff. For the second time that season, I was going to watch us play Coventry while sober. I just hoped that this match would be a less depressing occasion than my visit to their dejected city and stadium earlier in the season.

Thornton Heath might not be the most exciting place to come and visit for away fans. In fact, it's pretty disgusting. The high street is awash with the smells of mouldy vegetables and stinking fish that are on sale outside the grubby grocery stores. The dining opportunities include a take-away pizza joint, which is badly decorated in peeling red paint, a selection of filthy-looking Indian restaurants and a Jerk Chicken shop with an endless supply of smoke, giving it an appearance and smell more like Didcot Power Station than a small fast food outlet. Other delights include the watering holes of a run-down Wetherspoons and a former National Front Pub.

However, regardless of the areas faults, Palace away has to be a good excuse to escape from the soulless ghost town of Coventry. I'm sure that any away fan without family responsibilities enjoys a night out in Central London on the Friday and would only sample our small, grimy corner of South London between 1 o'clock and 5:30 on a Saturday.

To be fair, that's actually the case for myself and a lot of other Palace fans too. While Brighton seem to believe that most Palace fans are all Croydon chavs living in slums, the truth is actually nearer to Millwall's stereotype and a lot of Palace fans have moved out into 'Leafy Surrey'. After moving away, Thornton Heath High Street is quite a culture shock for a lot of returning South Londoners. You only have to type 'Thornton Heath' into Google to discover a range of horror stories of stabbings and gangs from the area.

I've previously mentioned that the club needed to rediscover its roots and get involved with the local area. Supporting a football team has given me an identity and a sense of belonging to something. The absence of these emotions have been highlighted as a couple of the reasons that teenagers find themselves mixed up in gangs.

Football isn't going to solve all of South London's gang troubles but if just one child decides to go to football and obsess over who Palace are going to sign in the next transfer window rather than obsessing over who is 'top dog' on the estate or how they're going to earn 'respect', then that really is something magical. A club should be for the local community and as far as I could see, the immediate community had very little interest in the club. Something that needed to change. Schools needed to be visited, tickets needed to be promoted and going to games needed to feel more like a treat and less like a chore.

One group who were trying to inspire Selhurst Park into a livelier and louder environment were the Holmesdale Fanatics. They are an 'Ultras' group who formed in 2005. A small set of lads were fed up of sitting through crap matches in flat atmospheres and enduring their football, rather than enjoying it. It wasn't the experience they wanted on a Saturday afternoon and instead of doing what the average football fan does and go to the pub to moan, they began their quest to improve the experience for all.

First, they began to create displays before matches to inspire the players with a wall of red and blue. They then introduced huge, Italian-style flags to wave before games and a drum to beat throughout them. In its early days I hated the drum but over time, I have learned to accept it as part of the match day experience. When everyone is singing, it helps to keep the beat and stops songs from gathering too much pace and inevitably stopping for breath. However, the main attribute that they'd brought to the club is a dedication to non-stop singing.

The section where they set themselves up, Block B of the lower tier in the Holmesdale Road stand, has always been the loudest area of the ground but there is no doubting that the Fanatics have further improved the atmosphere. Their smallish group had sung all game, every game, for five years but now, the movement was beginning to grow in size and since the administration, surrounding supporters were joining in with their range of chants. They'd already introduced the 'We Love You' chant, which I'd first heard at Sheffield Wednesday and was now sung loudly and proudly at every game, and they'd also reinvented the 'Pride of South London' chant. Although Dan hated this creation, refusing to sing 'a Boney M song'.

Anyway, back in the Railway Club, Colin and I continued to go around in circles as we tried to get our heads around the idea of Warnock walking away from us in our hour of need. We were still no closer to an answer by the time I waited at the exit of the pub with Adam as Colin emptied his bladder. Orange Juice and lemonade doesn't seem to travel through your body at the same, almost disturbing, pace as beer.

The first half was poor, Palace slightly edged it and the teams missed one great chance each. Throughout the half, the home crowd sang praise to Neil Warnock, basically a desperate plea for him to stay. The club was already on its knees and surely couldn't cope with yet another kick. At half time, for the first time this season, we didn't bother going up to the Red'n'Blue bar. I wasn't drinking and Colin, sensibly, didn't want to continue drinking alone. Half time was about as dull as it could be. I had no money to get some food, the game hardly inspired conversation and there was still a disbelief in the air that Neil Warnock was going to leave us.

The second half was little better than the first. Ambrose went close with a free kick but neither team seemed to be really going for it. Coventry scored a late winner and even that was more down to a very rare Speroni cock up, rather than them having to earn the reward with any genuine skill. He rushed out of his goal but then he realised that he wasn't going to get to the player so he stopped, leaving him in no-man's land. Coventry's striker simply lifted the ball over him and into the net. The few Coventry escapees had a moment of jubilation in London before heading back to their dead Midlands hometown. As soon as the referee blew his whistle for full time, I received a mocking text from my friend, Jak.

':-1' it unsubtly read.

The result left Palace in the bottom three and staring relegation in the face. In the press conference after the game, Warnock walked out when he was asked about the QPR job – further fuelling the now inevitable rumours. I bumped into my friend, Jim, at Clapham Junction, which was good. His wife was now heavily pregnant and it had been a rare 'treat' for him to get out the house and go to Palace. He wouldn't be rushing back. It was unfortunate that seeing a disheartened Jim on the platform at Clapham Junction was the highlight of my day. I returned home to my lonely flat. It's no wonder that I usually drank after matches to hide the pain.

Coventry City had been true to their stereotype. They bring depression wherever they go. Be it Cambridge or South London, Coventry really can bring a despondent feeling to any location. Send them to bloody Coventry and leave them there.

Chapter 44 – **Be Loud, Be Proud, Be Palace.**

Tuesday 23rd February 2010, Aston Villa vs Crystal Palace, Villa Park, FA Cup R5 Replay

Crystal Palace: Julian Speroni, Nathaniel Clyne, Shaun Derry, Darren Ambrose, Neil Danns (Kieran Djilali, 90), Nick Carle (James Comley, 83), Matt Lawrence, Alan Lee (Calvin Andrew, 90), Danny Butterfield, Johnny Ertl, Claude Davis
Subs Not Used: Clint Hill, Sean Scannell, Alassane N'Diaye, Charlie Mann

Aston Villa: Brad Guzan, Luke Young, Richard Dunne, Stewart Downing, Ashley Young, James Milner, John Carew, Gabriel Agbonlahor, Fabian Delph, Carlos Cuellar, Stephen Warnock
Subs Not Used: Brad Friedel, Steve Sidwell, Nathan Delfouneso, Curtis Davies, Emile Heskey, Habib Beye, James Collins

Although I hadn't seen him since meeting him in Scunthorpe, I'd been in regular communication with the Russian, Pavel, by text and he had offered to drive me to Birmingham for the replay. This made it much cheaper for me and much more convenient. The last train back to London from Birmingham was at ten past eleven so if the game went to extra time and penalties, I would be cutting it very fine to make it. I had tried to work on Colin's pie in the sky expectations and persuade him to jump in the car with us but the days of him going to a midweek away game in the Midlands were long gone. In fact, I didn't even attempt to convince Dan, Jonathan or Kev to join us. I knew the game wasn't for them.

I had to be at Aldegate East tube station, near where Pavel worked, for 1:30 so we could go straight up north from there. I'd never been to that part of London before and I couldn't believe the state of it. It was very similar to Thornton Heath High Street. I arrived early and took in my surroundings in horror as I walked along the grubby street to get some snacks from Tesco. Pavel's new Chrysler Neon was kept behind a locked, gated entrance and I doubt he would have taken it to work if it wasn't.

As well as myself, Pavel was driving his friend, Neil, up to Villa Park. Neil is slightly older than Pav, in his mid forties, and bald. He's divorced and got two kids, who are both Palace fans. The kids – not his ex wife. Presumably. He brings them along to games on the weekends when he's looking after them. The three of us met up on time and set off nice and early to the Midlands. My fifth of seven trips to that part of the country during the season: Wolves, Aston Villa, Nottingham Forest, West Brom, Coventry, Derby and Leicester.

The journey up was fairly easy. We'd left in plenty of time and the traffic was quiet. As Pavel had work the next day, I didn't know where he was going to drive me back to, so I was very relieved when he said he'd take me to Twickenham, which was quite out of his way. Most of the talk on the journey was about Warnock leaving. It was being reported in the press that he was only staying on as he wanted to see the cup run through. If true, this was a disgusting attitude. The cup run was good fun but the league was vital. Results, for whatever reason, had dropped off and we found ourselves in the bottom three. Despite the rumour gathering pace over the previous two weeks, I still wasn't willing to accept that Warnock was going to turn his back on us when we needed him most, let alone that he was using us as an ego trip before buggering off.

On the way up there, I texted one of Plymouth Rob's university friends, who had moved back to Birmingham, to see if he wanted to go for a drink with us in the town centre. Pavel had spent a year at Birmingham University so he wanted to go to the actual city, have a couple of drinks there and then get the train to the ground. Our plan was to head to Broad Street for drinks and food.

Unlike Coventry, Birmingham is a Midlands city that I do like. I know it reasonably well - both from visiting for football and because I have cousins who grew up there. Some of the Victorian architecture is stunning, including the pub that I'd drunk in before the West Brom game. The city has a great shopping centre in the Bull Ring and there are some brilliant markets that are located in the centre of town. There are plenty of good bars and clubs too. I've had two or three really memorable nights out in the city and hope to have a few more. On top of all of that, Birmingham actually has more canals than Venice. It has 35 miles worth of canals compared to Venice's 26 miles. A stat that's definitely worth quoting when discussing holiday locations with a partner. Although, so far, I'm yet to find anyone who thinks that Birmingham holds the same romantic charm as the Italian city. If I do, I guess she's 'The One'.

When we arrived, much to Pavel's horror, I did my usual trick of sniffing out the nearest Wetherspoons. This definitely didn't have the romantic charm of Venice. I promised them discounted food (they could have had a lasagne if the canals weren't enough to give them an Italian feeling) and that was enough to get Neil on my side. We went into the large, empty pub and ordered one ale, for me, one lager, for Neil, and one coca-cola for Pavel. We were soon joined by one of Pavel's friend, Adam. They'd met during Pavel's brief spell at the university and stayed friends ever since.

Adam is a Birmingham City fan so he wanted us to win almost as much as we did, such is the rivalry between the city's two teams. It's amazing the emotion that hating another team can create. On plenty of occasions, I've watched matches desperate for one team to win; not because I care about them, but because of my dislike of their opponents. I guess for Adam, it was a case that he'd love Villa to lose rather than hoping we'd win.

After a few beers, we took the advice of a rather large breasted Birmingham City supporter. She suggested that we got an early train to Whitten, the small station that served Villa Park, as it gets incredibly busy close to kick off. We headed to Birmingham New Street Station, via Tesco to pick up some cans of lager, around six-thirty to go to the match.

Once we were off the small train, we found that not only were there no away fan friendly pubs near the ground, and not only were there no off-licences near the ground, there was also no beer sold in the away end. I can't understand why a club would cut off its own revenue in this manner. Unless they're run by Simon Jordan as he seemed to specialise in cutting off revenue. There were three and a half thousand Palace fans in the away end that night. Some wouldn't drink, some would binge heavily. On average, I would guess that each person would have one pint. The beer would be sold at a minimum of £3 (often, it's far more inside grounds). That's ten thousand pounds worth of cash to be handed over. Even if I've over estimated and half of those people have one pint, that's still a huge amount of money to be made, especially when you consider that the ground will host over twenty games a season.

In the ground, I received a phone call. No, it wasn't the 90's asking for Pavel to return his hair cut. He still proudly wore his David Beckham centre parting as he had done since his school days. The call was from Rob's friend, Chris, who hadn't replied to my earlier invitation.

"Hi mate, how are you doing?" I shouted, trying to rise above the loud pre-match music that was being boomed out around the ground.

"Sorry, I can't here you mate!" was my predictable next response as I dug my finger into my other ear to try and block out the surrounding noise.

"Are you up for the football?" he asked. What sort of question was that? Why else would I be in the Midlands? He knew I was a Palace nut and from his comment, he was aware of the match taking place in his hometown so I don't know why he felt the need to check.

"Yes mate! I was just seeing if you fancied a drink while I was about but I'm at the ground now so don't worry." I was about to hang up as I could barely hear him so it seemed pointless to try and scream a polite end to the conversation down the phone, which, as we'd been mis-hearing each other anyway, would only have led to further misunderstanding. However, he then said something entirely unexpected.

"I'm at the game mate!" Chris had no interest in football what so ever. His reaction to being invited to the Plymouth away game had been similar to my friend Ash's. However, whereas Ash took no initiative and found himself stuck in the middle of his freezing worst nightmare, Chris ran a mile and refused to have anything to do with the football. He'd basically put a finger in each ear, lowered his head and screamed "lalalalala! Not listening!" Yet here he was, in Villa Park, in the away end, about to watch Palace play.

It turned out his Dad was a Palace fan and had persuaded Chris to come along. Unfortunately, due to the large size of the away following, the Palace fans had been split into two parts. Chris and his Dad were in another stand to me so I wondered across to the other side of our stand and gave him a wave.

Just before kickoff, I received a text. It read: Are you staying about for a night out afterwards?

It sounded like good fun. I'd got on well with Chris whenever I'd seen him and I didn't have much planned for the following day. However, we weren't staying about afterwards and I thought asking Pavel to not only drive to Birmingham, stay sober, go to the game and then take me back to Twickenham but to also go to a club, stay sober, wait until 3AM and *then* drive me back to Twickenham was a bit too much to ask. Especially as he had work the next day. I thanked Chris and explained that my friend was driving me back so I couldn't. He replied, *'Why don't you stay up here overnight?'*

I hadn't thought of this idea. I liked it. You can get a cheap train from Birmingham to London on the day if you take the slow one, so it would be affordable. Pavel was quite keen on the idea too as it would knock an hour off his journey. I replied *'That sounds good. Would I crash at yours?'* There was no immediate reply.

Palace once again came up against Villa's strongest side. They had their Wembley final on the following Sunday but that hadn't persuaded their manager to rest any players. He was taking the FA Cup seriously. Our team was our strongest eleven too. We'd have loved to have rested players for our upcoming league games (well, Warnock wouldn't have if rumours were to be believed but that's another debate) but we couldn't. Our strongest eleven was our only eleven. Still, pre-match, the large away crowd had a feeling of optimism about them. It was the FA Cup and anything could happen...

The game kicked off and as expected, the 3500+ Palace fans made an amazing atmosphere. Villa dominated the first half and finally took the lead three minutes before half time, from a corner, which should have been a goal kick, sound familiar? I hadn't realised the referee's error during the original match at the time so I hadn't been as angry as I might. However, this time, I had a clear view and was fuming.

"S*** refs! We always get s*** refs!" came the usual cry from the Palace faithful. We'd started singing the song (almost every game) since Mr Shoebridge's incompetent decision. I'm sure it's a feeling that every team has but we certainly felt we were more entitled to the chant than most. Warnock helped create the feeling too. He loved to moan at and about referees to create an 'everything's against us' mentality. As supporters, we're more than happy to lap up the feeling of being hard done by. Everything and everyone is against us as football fans.

After the injustice of the Villa goal, I could certainly have done with a beer. Another £3 that Villa lost out on that night. Although it was only 1-0, it felt like we'd taken a beating. Speroni, not for the first time, made save, after save, after save. Ashley Young had caused us all sorts of trouble on the wings and each time he failed to deliver the final ball or he had a shot saved, the Palace fans would burst into song, singing *'You're just a s*** Victor Moses'*. It was less than a month since we'd had a player terrorising defences in the way that Young was now terrifying us. The Moses-shaped hole in our side was still very much evident. Despite the despondent feeling as the side were heading out of the cup and our manager was heading out of the club, the crowd continued to give their all. As did the players. They were being overrun by Villa but it was certainly not from a lack of effort, commitment or desire. During the interval, I received a text from Chris. It read, *'No, but stay out anyway.'*

Quite what he wanted to me to do at the end of our proposed night out, I don't know. Student budgets don't stretch to last minute and unnecessary hotels. As I didn't fancy a night under the Birmingham stars (maybe on a canal barge?) or, more realistically and less romantically, on the floor of New Street Station, I had to politely decline his invitation.

In the second half, Palace were much better and pushed Villa back. Whether this was because we managed to up our game or Villa simply sat back, not wanting to be tired or injured for their Wembley appearance, I don't know. I expect it was a bit of both. However, against a strong defence, Palace still struggled to create many clear chances. Until, with 20 minutes left, Alan Lee won a penalty, which was superbly taken by Darren Ambrose.

The fairytale was on once more. We were level at Villa Park. The already loud away crowd turned up the volume even further. Suddenly, this could become our night. Even Ash might have enjoyed that moment. There was so much emotion, so much excitement, so much release of pain. Warnock leaving, or being in administration, or the crap referee, or being in the relegation zone, or any personal financial, love or work problems, couldn't have been further from anyone's mind. For ten minutes or so, there was a pure feeling of love for Crystal Palace Football Club and a belief that we could get another to make three and a half thousand people feel as proud and rejoiceful as anyone, anywhere on the globe could have been at that moment.

Unfortunately, the fairy tale was just that. It was fiction. We weren't going to live happily ever after in the quarter final. Twice in the last ten minutes, Villa striker, John Carew, had the ball in the area but in a harmless position. Twice, Palace's defender, Matt Lawrence, dived into a needless tackle. Twice, Matt Lawrence missed the ball. Twice, John Carew went tumbling. Twice, the referee pointed to the penalty spot. Twice, even the Palace faithful couldn't argue. Twice, John Carew dusted himself down to score from the spot. Twice, the Palace fans tried to sing even louder and prouder to inspire the team to come back but on each occasion, the singing was a little more painful and sung with a little less belief.

At full time, the Palace fans sang of their pride of the team and as Neil Warnock walked past the away end, the three and a half thousand devoted supporters gave him one last plea to stay. They sang *"There's only one Neil Warnock! One Neil Warnock!"* as one. He clapped us for our support but he couldn't even bring himself to look up at the away end. He knew he was letting us down. The heartfelt song continued until he left the pitch and entered the tunnel. I turned to Pavel, we knew that was going to be the final time that the song would be sung by a Palace crowd.

Surprisingly, it wasn't. The morning papers had been wrong. He explained his position to the press after the game. *"This could have been my last game - but it won't be and we'll now get ready for Doncaster. But can I deny speculation about going to QPR? No."*

I really wasn't sure how I felt about this. I was desperate for him to stay but QPR were just four points ahead of us in the league. If he was leaving, why should he stay in charge? Surely it was a conflict of interest. A Palace win would put us just one point behind the West London side and drag them closer to the relegation places. It was a bizarre situation.

Once again, I was met by an immediate text from Jak, revelling in our defeat. However, this time, it was me who could smirk. He'd got it wrong. There was nothing to mock here. Palace players and fans had given their all against a genuinely huge club and briefly, very briefly, it had looked like we might actually pull off another shock. There was no shame in that. Only pride.

The journey there had been quick and simple but the journey home was to be anything but that. First, we were caught up in traffic because of roadwork's going onto the M40. A genius idea to do overnight works when nearly four thousand people need to use that stretch of road. We then got caught behind an accident, which forced all eight lanes of the motorway to be closed. I've never known that to happen before or since. We sat, mainly in silence, for well over an hour as we waited for the debris to be cleared from the road. It had obviously been an even worse car crash than our season was turning into. Finally, the road was opened and we pulled away.

However, just a few miles down the road, we were brought to a standstill again. This time, just our four lanes were closed so we could watch the other side of the road move freely as we, once again, waited. It was obviously a night where people were finding it hard to concentrate, whether that was drivers on the road or Matt Lawrence on the pitch. None of these lapses were good for us.

I eventually got home at about quarter past three. Pavel got in, after dropping off Neil in Bromley, well after four and had to get up soon after for work the next day. Despite the journey home, it had been a good evening and a proud one. Without the stresses of the league, we could enjoy the night. That wasn't going to be the case for the remaining fourteen fixtures of the season. They were going to be tense, highly stressful experiences. Anyone who thinks going to football is a watching form of entertainment is wrong. It's not. It might not build any muscle or get me into shape (although the stress of it might make me lose a few pounds – not always from my wallet) but I was certainly *doing* rather than simply *watching*. I might not have been on the pitch but I most definitely would be kicking every ball and screaming every breath with all that I had from the stands. The fans are as much a part of a live match as the players themselves and we knew that we had an important role to play in the run in to the end of the season.

Chapter 45 – **An Expensive Day**

Saturday 27th February 2010, Doncaster vs Crystal Palace, The Keepmoat Stadium

Crystal Palace: Julian Speroni, Nathaniel Clyne, Claude Davis (Lee Hills 6, (Johnny Ertl 46)), Matt Lawrence, Clint Hill, Nicky Carle, Shaun Derry, Kieran Djilali (Calvin Andrew), Darren Ambrose, Danny Butterfield, Alan Lee
Subs Not Used: Charlie Mann, Sean Scannell, James Comley, Alassane N'Diaye
Doncaster: Neil Sullivan, O'Connor, Ward, Hird, Chambers, Wilson (Shields 90), John Oster (Mutch 83), Coppinger, Roberts, Hayter (Emmanuel-Thomas 76), Sharp
Subs Not Used: Smith, Mustapha Dumbuya, Guy, Spicer

Having worked late the night before and still being tired from the midweek trip, as well as the early morning and late night university work and numerous shifts at the pub (yes, I am getting as many excuses in as possible), I had forgotten to check for engineering works on the tube. It was only when I arrived at Vauxhall station that I discovered there was no Victoria line. As a result, I had to frantically head to Central London, take an alternate route and managed to miss my train at King's Cross by a single minute.

I stood alone at the station, staring in disbelief at my now-worthless ticket. I was skint, I was tired and I had missed my train. My train which was taking me to see a team who'd lost their last three league matches with a manager who wanted to leave. I couldn't believe where I found myself. I went to the ticket office to see if there was anything they could do. I knew the rules but I hoped that one of the ticket operators would show me some mercy and give me some leniency. No chance. It would be £57 for a replacement young-persons single to Doncaster. I thought about it. Could I give up my challenge now?

There was an argument that it wouldn't make the slightest bit of difference whether I went or not and the players certainly wouldn't notice if I didn't go. Why should they? I was only one supporter. There was also an argument that the club didn't deserve my support. Especially at such expense. They continually let me down and left me feeling hurt, feeling skint and feeling beaten.

However, they did deserve my support, and more. Every time that I'd handed over my £25 or so for a match ticket, I hadn't just donated it to them, I'd received a bit of history in return. Each game, each goal, each player, helped to form the rich tapestry that is Crystal Palace Football Club. The players and managers are the huge pictures in the middle that make people sit up and take notice but the supporters are the thread that holds it all together. No one notices it, but without it the artwork wouldn't be art. No one would care. It would just be some very expensive felt on the floor of an artist's studio.

However, the supporters *are* there and they *do* hold the club together. And right now, there was an auctioneer who cared very little for the fate of this art. He wasn't impressed by it and he didn't really get it. He didn't want it to deteriorate as he had been charged with the objective of trying to sell it to the highest bidder but he wasn't interested in the history or the pride or the details of the art. Even at a discounted price, there was very little interest in it. It was out of the price range of its keen admirers and would cost so much to repair that it had little financial interest to the big business men of this world. If we didn't care as fans and gave up on it, the thread would fray and let go, then the art really would be worthless and thrown on a scrapheap. Palace could play with eleven superstars and win 10-0 every week but without a set of supporters to cheer them on and relish in the glory, it would all be rather pointless.

The fans are why players charge to the stands after scoring a goal and the TV cameras show the crowd so many times during a match. Apparently, the Premier League marketing team did a survey through Asia to gauge why their league is such a popular product in that part of the world. Even more so than La Liga and Serie A. The response was that the stadiums are full and the fans are so passionate. Clubs create an identity and supporters enhance it and spread it. I've always had a theory that every time that I go to a football match, it is a unique experience. Yes, as you may have noticed, I have pretty much the same routine for every game that I go to. Bacon then beer then empty my bladder then football then beer then bed. Yes, I go through the same emotions in most matches (usually negative and depressive ones) and shout the same abuse at the referee. But, the game that I miss could be the game where something happens that people talk about all over the world or for years to come.

I can't imagine people would rush to the cinema or the theatre or to a gig in similar circumstances to the ones that made me make the expensive trip to Doncaster – paying over twice the value of the event ticket on replacement travel. All for a so-called 'second rate' event that has minimal demand. Films and shows and gigs are repeated on other nights. People who are not there at the same time as you, will get the same experience as yourself. Whereas this football game will never be repeated. No one will see it live again. Other sports have the uniqueness of football but none of them generate the same collective passion as a football match. Lots of people follow a cricket team or rugby team or a tennis player but how many obsess over them? How many of them travel 400 miles on a regular basis to go and watch them? Not many. Certainly not many do it for 2nd or 3rd or 4th or even 5th tier teams as thousands of football fans do on a weekly basis.

I think one of the main reasons for this is the magical moment of scoring a goal. Not many occasions can recreate the feeling of seeing your team put the damn ball in the opposition's net. The feeling of thousands of people celebrating together; arms being waved about hysterically above heads, grown men hugging strangers, people charging forward. Eventually, the hysteria settles down and thousands of people unite to proudly sing the club's anthem in unison or point to the opposition fans as one and politely enquire *'Ooh are ya?'* The celebration of one successful strike continues for five or so minutes before your heart rate returns to a normal football watching rate, which, I imagine, is still far too high to be considered anything resembling healthy.

Scoring a goal creates an eruption of emotion that simply isn't repeated by hitting a long range putt or hitting a six out of the ground or playing a point-winning cross-court forehand. All of these are admirable moments that I would get enjoyment out of watching but none of them would generate a huge amount more than a large round of applause. Ok, competition winning ones would but I'm talking about your average mid-match moment in your average game. Long putts and winning forehands happen regularly throughout a match. Unlike goals. Palace goals are *certainly* not 'regular'. I didn't want to miss any goal. I still hate the fact that I didn't see the second goal at Reading, even though I got the emotion and celebrations of it. I couldn't risk missing another moment of Palace history. It was strange to think back to Christmas when I was almost looking for an excuse to not go to Sheffield and Swansea.

So in my final justifying conclusions to my dilemma (although it wasn't really a dilemma as a dilemma has two unacceptable choices and I did have an option that was more than acceptable to myself – no matter how insane it might have seemed to the rest of the world), football is a unique sport and every match has its own unique character. Some games may be more unique than others but every game has the potential to be something special. Something different. Something talked about.

The Rob Shoebridge debacle had made headlines in at least three different continents – possibly more but my contacts at the time were restricted to Asia, North America and Europe. It was talked about all over the world and I was there. Live. As it happened. In the stadium. Sure, I'd had a worse view of the events than the people in the States who'd looked it up on Youtube but I can say that I was actually there. Imagine I'd decided not to go to that match. It's a totally bonkers thing to say but I'd be gutted to have missed it.

Obviously, there are happier moments that have the same affect. For example, the Villa home game had been watched by millions of UK TV viewers and been broadcast across the world. People in pubs and living rooms everywhere had talked about how well Palace had played and Darren Ambrose's wonder strike. The papers had given it a two page spread of coverage, discussing every element of the match, and the BBC National News at Ten had given it a two minute report. Sky Sports News had it as their main headline and ran a five minute piece about the game, focussing on the 'cash strapped club's huge effort'. My Club's huge effort.

It felt like it was about me, not about the club. Crystal Palace Football Club takes up so much of my life that the lines get blurred between what is me and what is the club. As a supporter, I am part of the club and as an obsessive addict, the club is part of me. During the two weeks since the original Villa game, I hadn't been able to see many friends or colleagues without being asked about the match. They were on the outside, looking in with great envy of me being a small part of the event.

Due to bringing up my beloved club in most conversations, some people see *me* as Crystal Palace Football Club and I feel like I *am* Crystal Palace Football

Club. If a player makes an error, it's our error, if they score a wonder goal, it's our goal. It's very rare that supporters talk about these things as individuals. It irritates non-football fans immensely. I've often been told *"Don't say 'we', you make it sound like you actually did something. You didn't score. You didn't make a save. You didn't make a tackle or even take a thrown in. You just watched. You did nothing."*

They might technically be correct but they simply don't understand. As a club, we're all under the same identity and we're all in this whole experience together.

I was there. No one can ever take that away from me. No one can ever make me forget my memories. Sure, thousands of others were in the ground with me but so many thousands more, possibly even millions, were talking about it from elsewhere. Hearing about the game and caring about the game, without actually experiencing the game. The atmosphere. The sheer collaborative joy at Palace's goals. The inconsolable misery at Villa's. Anything can happen at a football match and you never know, the eyes of the world, for whatever bizarre reason, might be about to turn to that game and talk about it. Talk about your event, where you actually are and they want to be. And that, is something special.

Sure, I would get other chances to go to Doncaster vs Crystal Palace, but I would never, *ever*, get another chance to go to *that* game. I had to go. What if this happened to be the first ever match to have eight red cards, or it turned out to be the highest scoring professional game ever recorded, or, simply, Palace scored a goal that would make me jump up, wave my arms above my head and hug some strangers, before pointing at the home fans and asking '*Ooh are ya?*'. I couldn't miss a moment like that. I couldn't risk not going.

If nothing else, going to the match meant that I wouldn't have a feeling of regret. One thing that I have never regretted is going to a football match, which really, is the only choice that I make on the day. I've regretted Ade Akinbiyi being signed and regretted Ben Watson missing a penalty in the play offs, but even after the worst defeats that I've been to, I've never regretted being there. It's strange really because I should regret going to Derby, when skint, to see us lose 5-0 and I should feel no regret at someone else missing a penalty but I don't. I get it arse about tit. I regret the player's errors and ignore my own stupidity for handing over a wad of cash to experience the wretched game in the first place.

Deciding to pay an extortionate price to travel to Doncaster, without a second thought, was a typically irrational decision that could only be made by a football addict. It wasn't the first time that I'd spent a small fortune on going to a needless game and it wouldn't be the last. However, could I give up the challenge? No. Absolutely not. The players didn't even have their manager backing them. They needed the fans. They needed me.

I pulled out my debit card and put it in the cash point at the station. There wasn't enough money in the account for the train ticket. Without thinking, I got my other debit card out, the one for my student account (which had a large, interest-free overdraft, designed to help students fund the essentials such as bread, water, soap and last minute train journeys to Doncaster. That kind of thing) and I withdrew sixty quid. It put me to within £100 of my overdraft limit. Strangely, I wasn't thinking 'we better win this' or 'I hope Palace make it worthwhile' or 'I hope something does happen to turn the heads of the world', I was simply thinking, 'I've got to go'. I had no expectation or belief. I had a pure and natural blindness to any consequences of my irrationality and put football and my challenge above all else. I'd come this far. I'd been to this many games. I couldn't drop out now.

As I went to get a ticket, a Palace fan approached me, who had a spare train ticket as his friend couldn't travel. He sold it to me at a slightly cheaper rate than face value. My frustration was only added to when the ticket inspector on the train checked my ticket.

"You should have come and seen me mate, I'd have let you on the train with your original ticket!" he told me. Great. I can't help but feel I'd have rather not known this ultimately useless information.

I sat glumly on the train, alone. I didn't know anyone going and after my unexpected outlay, I certainly couldn't afford to sit in a pub pre-match to try and meet other obsessed individuals. Suddenly, I remembered something. My Dad owed me some money. He'd said that he was going to transfer it but I didn't think he had actually done it. I text him *'Hi Dad, just texting to check you sent me that money that you owe me x'*

Within a minute, I'd received a reply. *'Yes I have'*

Bugger. It was an unusually blunt text from him but I didn't think much of it. It was annoying that I'd already blown the money he'd sent me. I continued to gaze out of the window as thoughts about Warnock's imminent departure went round and round my head, along with concerns about both mine and Palace's finances. Was my challenge worth it? I hadn't questioned it for months but suddenly it seemed a very expensive, tiring and pointless exercise. If Warnock, who I'd admired and trusted so much, didn't care about seeing the season out, why should I?

Beep-beep!

My phone buzzed and took me out of the deep thoughts that I was in. It was from my Dad's step-daughter. My Dad had remarried when I was 18 and she was older than me so although she was technically my step-sister, I didn't really know her and I didn't particularly count her as family.

It read *'It's your Dad's birthday today. It might be nice if you give him a call.'*

I felt humiliated and it was all my fault. I looked at the date. 27th February. S***! She was right. How could I forget that? I was so wrapped up in my life that I hadn't given my own Dad a moment's thought. No present. No card. No nothing. I'd even texted him asking for money that he'd already given me. I rang him straight away but the damage had been done. I'd been so focussed on Palace's troubles that I hadn't even thought about him. He thanked me for the call but I knew I'd hurt him. To let down someone you care about is an awful feeling.

I arrived at the now very familiar Doncaster station around 1 o'clock. The train guard hadn't signed my ticket and had told me to go to the ticket office to see if there was anything that they could do. I wondered up to the only one of the six ticket booths that was open and explained the situation.

"Sure, you can get a refund, as long as you have the unstamped ticket,"

Wow! What a let off! I couldn't believe my luck. My face brimmed with relief.

"...and the card that you booked the ticket with."

My heart sank. The card that it had been booked with belonged to my fellow Palace fan at King's Cross. God knows where he, and his card, were now. What a waste of money. I'd tried to save a fiver and it had cost me fifty quid. It felt like the 27th February was punishing me for forgetting my father.

After sitting down on a stall outside the station, head in hands, I composed myself and got a bus to the ground, where I had a slow and painful single pint with Brian, congratulating him on getting to all 92 grounds. A challenge that one day, I hoped I would emulate. He was his usual moaning self but it didn't bother me. His words went straight through me. I couldn't focus on anything but my own stupidity and selfishness.

The first half was one of the worst Palace performances I have ever seen. This was summed up by Lee Hills, who was subbed on for the injured Claude Davis early on, and dragged off at half time after a shocking display. Palace were very lucky to be only 1-0 down at half time. Ironically, this was the exact opposite of the previous year at Doncaster, where we had dominated the first half and were incredibly *unlucky* to find ourselves 1-0 behind.

People didn't know where to begin with their rage at half time. I just felt empty – and not purely because I'd decided that I was too poor to buy food up there. Two months previously, we'd been just outside the playoffs and flying. Now, we were in the relegation zone and Warnock was jumping off a sinking ship. For the first time, I really thought we were floating towards relegation. The manager couldn't be bothered, so why should I? It was an expensive challenge that I was forcing myself to do.

In the second half, we weren't quite as bad as the first, although I still wouldn't stretch the description of our performance to 'good'. Midway through it, our young winger, Kieran Djilali, scored his first professional goal as we managed to draw one all. It was a great moment for him as he clearly wasn't ready or good enough to be playing first team Championship football yet but because there was no-one else, he'd been thrown in. Still, despite Warnock's admission that he was leaving, Palace fans sang his name and to be fair to him, he had done well to lift our players after their pathetic first half showing. Leaving or not, Warnock was excellent at getting the best out of players and demanded they gave their all.

I walked back to Doncaster station with a couple of Palace fans who went to Leeds University. I'd seen them at a few previous northern games and they were really nice guys. I've no idea what their names are and I have not seen them for a few years now or given them any thought, but conversation with them was never difficult. They were Palace fans and that was enough. We all shared the same mutual emotions. Having got the bus to the ground, I knew it would be useful to have a couple of fellow Palace fans who could show me the way. That's what I'd assumed anyway. However, like most of the day so far, it went wrong. The three of us managed to get lost. Thankfully, I did just about get back for the earlier train, which I managed to blag my way on to. The plan was to stay in Doncaster and drink until seven when my pre-booked train was, but I didn't have the motivation or money to do so. I returned, alone, to the train.

On the train, I got a call from my Dad as I did after every game. I told him about the match and we discussed Warnock's imminent departure. We didn't mention my failure to realise that it was his birthday. I knew he was still hurt about it but that wasn't going to stop him calling me about the football. Being able to talk like normal, about our shared love, began to fix the hurt that I'd caused.

Had the day been worth the money that I'd spent? No, absolutely not. The game had bordered between shocking and poor, I'd had little or no company throughout, and my obsession with going had blinded me to my own father's birthday. I'd felt that he was falling out of love with Palace and my behaviour that day would have made it easy for him to fall out of love with me. The date 'Saturday 27th February 2010' had made me think of 'Doncaster Away' rather than 'Dad's birthday'.

So why had I done it? Why had I gone at such expense? Had my presence made a difference? No. Had I received something back for the money that I'd handed over? No. Had I even enjoyed it? Not really. What had seemed so easy to justify in the morning, now made no sense to me. Sure, I had my little piece of history that I'd been craving for; I'd seen the game and no one could take that away from me but what was the point? Nothing magical had happened. Nothing special. Nothing unique. It was just like any other northern away trip – except it had cost a lot more and I'd drank a lot less thanks to my own stupidity. I didn't feel part of a spectacular tapestry. I felt alone, stupid, regretful, hungry and skint.

I'd been foolish and reckless. Just like I had been to miss the wedding. My love of the club and my determination to complete the challenge was blinding me to what I was doing. I'd insulted family with my absence at the wedding, I'd financially harmed myself in my insistence on going to Doncaster. I couldn't afford it. I'd been so worried about being there that I hadn't even thought about having to pay for rent or food. Thoughts that were now catching up with me and peeking out of my personal blind spot – Crystal Palace Football Club.

The result actually took us out of the drop zone. In his press conference after the game, Warnock admitted that Palace and QPR were trying to agree compensation over him leaving. It was really happening. A month of speculation was going to end with Palace being manager-less. There was only one name on everybody's lips as to who we wanted. Sir Steve Coppell. A real Palace legend. A man who had led us through the previous administration and a man that we were confident could do so again. Warnock clearly didn't have the fight for the battle but we knew from 1998-2000, when the club had lost so many players in our first period of administration, that Coppell had the mental strength, dignity and determination that Warnock was lacking.

Chapter 46 – **Warnock Leaves**

Monday 2nd March 2010

The midweek between the Doncaster game on 27th February and the Sheffield United game on 6th March was the only week-long break that Palace were to have in a three month spell. It had pushed our squad to the limit and it had pushed my emotions, liver and wallet to the brink of devastation.

I'd taken the chance to go to Plymouth with my boss, Phill, to visit Rob. We were on a day trip to Truro when I received the news. Dan sent me a text *'He's gone – it's now official.'*

I knew exactly what he meant. Warnock had joined QPR. I received dozens of texts after that. Some full of empathy. Some sticking the knife in. I'd known it was going to happen for quite a while now but I still felt low. I felt betrayed. He'd cheated us and it could cost us our club. From the outside, I'm sure that it was a reasonable decision. He'd left a club in administration for a club that would back him with huge amounts of money. But I wasn't on the outside. I was part of what he was walking away from. And it hurt. A lot.

"The supporters can rest assured that me and the players will fight every inch of the way"

That's what Warnock had promised us when we went into administration a couple of months previously but he'd lied. Or at best, he'd spoken with empty words. He *would* fight every inch of the way *until* he got a slightly better offer is what he should have said. He was the managerial equivalent of a whore. Not only that, but he'd taken his entire coaching staff with him. Mick Jones and Keith Curle had followed him out of the Selhurst Park door to Loftus Road. It felt personal. It was like my flatmate, Darrell, leaving all over again. Him staying had become impossible but the manner in which he left, without saying goodbye or giving any reasonable reasons, hurt. Although, at least Warnock had the decency to take his cronies with him. I was stuck in the flat with Matt and Adam, as well as a random Irish student whom the landlord had found to replace Darrell.

I couldn't get my head around his decision or accept it. I was fuming. He didn't need the money – he'd planned to retire after finishing his Palace contract, that despite the administration he would be paid in full as he was a football creditor. I'd been furious at Steve Bruce walking away from us nine years previously and still held a grudge, but this was worse. This was when we really needed an experienced man to guide us. This could cost us our club. I'd previously compared Warnock to William Wallace but I was wrong. He may have been on a quest for freedom but it was his own that he was after, not his peoples'.

Supposedly, QPR were one of the world's richest clubs but they'd been less like Manchester City and more like a city circus since their wealthy owners purchased the club. They hadn't spent the huge money on players that had been promised when the takeover happened. Presumably, because they'd spent most of their budget on sacking managers. Warnock was set to be their fifth of the season.

Within twenty minutes, more news had filtered through. Paul Hart (not Steve Coppell) was going to replace him and Dougie Freedman, much to Brian's horror I'm sure, was going to be his new assistant manager. Former Palace player, John Pemberton, was going to be the third member of the coaching team.

I read about our new manager on the club's official website. I remembered him starting well at Nottingham Forest and he got them into the playoffs but then it all went sour. However, I knew little else about him. Since being sacked by Forest, he'd also been sacked by Barnsley, Rushden and Diamonds, Portsmouth and QPR, with little or no success at any of them. The appointment looked desperate. In fairness to the administrator, I doubt there was a huge queue of potential suitors.

Avoiding relegation was beginning to look like mission impossible. It had been less than three months since my previous trip to Plymouth and our season had fallen apart in spectacular style since that 1-0, Moses-inspired victory. We'd been put in administration, been deducted ten points, gone from chasing the playoffs to fighting the drop, had Moses sold, lost numerous games and now, had Neil Warnock walk out on us.

This feeling of betrayal was too much. I would never forgive Warnock. He might have been doing what was best for him and his family but in doing so, he had cheated on me and my Crystal Palace family. A family that I thought he was part of. The middle of. He'd got up from his seat at the head of the table and left, only muttering a few sound bites of patronising excuses in our direction. It wasn't even like he'd walked out on us for a glamorous younger model. Anyone who's ever been to Loftus Road or has watched the 'Four Year Plan' documentary will understand why it felt that he'd left us for a sad, wrinkly, old tart.

As I remember the boys were a little bit down. They had just lost their manager and received a 10 point deduction. So they had gone from being potential play-off candidates to relegation fodder. However, we had a strong core of senior players. I quickly realised they were up for a fight. Speroni, Derry, Hill, Lee, McCarthey and others. These senior players became the rock on which we built.

Paul Hart

The dressing room was full of big characters (Derry, Hill, Ertl, McCarthy, Lee, Lawrence) and was great to be part of. I'll always remember the shock on Paul Hart's face when he took over later in the season as he saw 15-20 players and staff bouncing off the walls to 'The Proclaimers – 500 miles before we went to warm up, which happened before every game!

Danny Butterfield

Chapter 47 – **The Return of a Legend**

Saturday 6th March 2010, Crystal Palace vs Sheffield United, Selhurst Park

Crystal Palce: Julian Speroni, Nathaniel Clyne, Clint Hill, Shaun Derry, Darren Ambrose, Nick Carle (Sean Scannell, 90), Calvin Andrew (Alassane N'Diaye, 86), Alan Lee, Danny Butterfield, Johnny Ertl, Claude Davis
Subs Not Used: Stern John, Lee Hills, Matt Lawrence, Kieran Djilali, Charlie Mann

Sheffield United: Mark Bunn, Nick Montgomery, Chris Morgan, Nyron Nosworthy, Mark Yeates (Ched Evans, 78), Lee Williamson (James Harper, 70), Richard Cresswell, Jamie Ward, Kyle Bartley, Stephen Quinn (Henn Camara, 58), Toni Kallio
Subs Not Used: Ian Bennett, Andy Taylor, Jordan Stewart, Marcel Seip

It had been five days since Warnock's departure and I still felt angry. In the morning, my Dad came over and took me out for a fry up before we headed over to the Railway Club. Over breakfast, I apologised to my father about his birthday, repeatedly. I also gave him a couple of books that I'd bought on the way back from Plymouth as a token present to try and repair some of the damage I'd caused. He thanked me and smiled. Then we moved on to talking about the football – that was much easier conversation.

Despite our anger at Warnock, there was one bit of good news to come out of the sorry mess. A club legend had returned. It wasn't the one that we had wanted, Steve Coppell, but Dougie Freedman. Despite Brian's hatred of him, he was a club legend and would be welcomed back with open arms in his new role.

Freedman had signed for Palace in 1997 from lower league Barnet and had been an instant success. It was around the same time that Kev's famous Umbro jumper had started to appear at Selhurst. He'd stayed for three years (Freedman, not the jumper – that lasted much longer) and left as a fan's favourite thanks to his creativity, intelligent play and most importantly, his ability to score goals, including two stoppage time strikes in a Playoff Semi-Final against Wolves. I'd listened to that season on the radio and Freedman was my favourite player. My first ever live match was the resulting Play-Off Final when Freedman was suspended. Despite being my hero, the closest that I got to seeing Freedman play in his first spell was watching him warm up on the touchline in a game against Blackburn Rovers the following season.

However, four years later, he returned. Again, my love affair with him would begin on the radio. He scored point-winning goals away at Wolves and Bolton as I danced around the living room with my father. Eventually, after five years of loving Dougie Freedman, I got to see him play live. He didn't disappoint. He scored one and made one in a 4-1 win over Sheffield Wednesday. From then on, the love only grew. He stayed for a further seven years, scoring over 100 goals for the club, including the goal that kept us up against Stockport in 2001 (the only time that I've been in the wrong end at a competitive Palace match), his 100th and 101st goals for the club in a 3-2 win at B*ighton and possibly the greatest

Palace goal that I've ever seen in a 3-0 win against Sunderland. Warnock had eased him out of the club a couple of summers previously as age had begun to catch up with him and Freedman had a testimonial for ten years service to the club.

Since leaving Palace, he'd been playing for Southend. He started well. Scoring four goals in his first four games but since then, injuries had cursed him and he'd barely played. The previous weekend, Freedman had been a sub for Southend against Charlton. However, he'd given up his career and retired with immediate effect to become our assistant manager. He told the South London Press:

"What was I supposed to do? I was asked to help out. I couldn't say no."

Having a legend, one of us, with such an amazing attitude, return to the club was the only safety mat stopping us from crashing head first after being dropped by Warnock. When my Dad arrived at my Twickenham flat, we sat and admired a ten minute *Youtube* compilation of all of Freedman's best moments for Palace. We absolutely purred at some of the strikes. There was such a variety in the types of goals and he had exquisite technique in so many of them. And now, to add to all that, he'd given up his playing career for us. For Crystal Palace Football Club. Other than Steve Coppell and maybe Jim Cannon, there really was no one else above him in the list of Palace legends.

After reminiscing over Freedman's greatest moments, my Dad and I had actually started to feel quite positive about the whole situation. If that lying, selfish bastard, Neil Warnock (or if you re-arranged the letters, Colin Wanker), didn't want to be at the club, then it was best for everyone that he left. Lingering around like a bad smell had left us plummeting down the table with three potentially crippling consecutive home defeats.

The mood in the pub was dampened by comparison. Dan and I had been texting each other throughout the week after finding more and more reasons why Paul Hart was not the right man for the job. Colin, ever the optimist, was trying to be slightly more positive about it all but the pair of us were having none of it.

"Have you not seen his record? It's a list of failures!" groaned Dan, *"The statement on the website was hilarious. About four times it read 'he started well before being sacked five months later'. We're doomed!"*

I had to agree with him. The worst thing was that the media seemed to love him. Lots of reports claimed that he was the perfect man for the job because of his recent role as Portsmouth manager.

"If I read that 'he's got the experience for the administration battle' one more time, I'll cry!" I added to Dan's discontent.

Seriously? Experience of what? Getting sacked? Being the first Premiership manager ever to lose their first seven games of the season? So he knew what it was like to be the manager of a club in administration?That was hardly a reason to appoint him. He'd done a terrible job as the manager of a club in administration. At least at Portsmouth he'd had a large squad and quality players to work with. He wouldn't have either with us.

My Dad sat fairly quietly in the pub, reading the programme. It was only his second game of the season; despite being my 40th. He'd re-married two and a half years previously and his life was busy. He'd given up his season ticket after four years when I was 18 as he'd become fed up with the numerous night games. He travels from near Salisbury so it's a long journey each way for, what he says *"Is usually a crap game of football."*

He'd had a hiatus from football before. He'd barely missed a home game between 1969 and 1974 but as he entered his late teens, he lost interest in Crystal Palace and only really began to follow football again in the late eighties when my oldest brother started to get into it. I'm always astonished and slightly disappointed when he tells me that he never even considered *trying* to get a ticket to the FA Cup final in 1990 *or* the replay. As my brother got more into football, so did my Dad. By the time that I was gaining an interest, the idea that he'd ever not followed it was absurd. As my obsession grew, so did his.

When he and my mother split up, he bought us a half year season ticket each so that we could spend every other Saturday together. Still, that wasn't enough for me. I hated missing games. I nagged and nagged and nagged. Eventually, as I chipped in a large contribution towards both season tickets, using saved up birthday, paper round and pocket money, we got one each. And yet still, that wasn't enough for me. Every other week, we played away and I had to be glued to the radio or teletext or Sky Sports News or anything. I had to know what was happening. I remember once charging around my friend's garden aged fifteen in excitement after an Andy Johnson goal at Norwich. My friends looked on in horror as I made a fool of myself and they tried to persuade the girls who were present that they weren't all as strange and sad as their companion.

Worse still, I remember another teenage afternoon when I was shopping in Reading with Plymouth Rob while Palace were away at Newcastle. The Palace game ended 0-0 but the Southampton against Norwich match was just as important to us in our battle for Premiership survival. I made strange noises, pulled bizarre faces and jumped up and down in Reading's Oracle Shopping Centre as I received a text from my Dad each time one of the seven goals went in that changed the match's (and Palace's) fate. It finished 4-3 to Southampton with a last minute goal. I was exhausted just receiving texts about the game because of the importance to Palace. God knows how the poor sods in the stadium felt.

No, not being there wasn't good enough. I started to persuade my Dad to go to the odd local away game at Watford or Reading or Southampton. Soon, we'd got into a tradition of going to the last game of the season each year, wherever it was. Still, this wasn't enough. By now, he had the bug nearly as badly as I did. One year, we planned our yearly summer break around away games at Wolves and Norwich. After those two games, I started to attend away fixtures alone and began to ignore any obstacles in my way – often lying to my mother in the process. By this point, I was totally hooked. I couldn't bear to miss a game. Anywhere or any time.

The peak of sadness came when I went to Sunderland for a meaningless midweek game the day before my university interview. It finished 0-0. I remember that after the game, our manager, Peter Taylor, apologised to their manager, Roy Keane, for the negative manner of our performance. He didn't send a word in the direction of the 150 mugs who had travelled 600 miles for the game. Quite frankly, I don't give a toss what Roy Keane thought. Either it was a necessary performance and up to Keane's side to break us down or, if the negativity wasn't necessary, it's not Roy bloody Keane who deserved an apology.

Anyway, at some point, the graph for my father's Palace obsession had peaked and started to slip down, whereas mine had simply continued to climb and climb and climb. I'd missed just 19 league and cup games over the previous 4 and ¾ seasons. Although I'd made up for them by attending numerous friendlies, reserve and youth team matches.

Before arriving at the pub, Dad and I would talk non-stop and after the game we'd happily chat, but he always seemed reluctant to speak up too much in the dingy Railway Club. From his quiet corner where he was reading the programme, Dad cleared his throat and pointed out the poster in the centre of the book. It had the three new members of coaching staff, each holding up red and blue shirts with their name on the back. He once again commented on the fact that he believed appointing Freedman was the most important of the trio as he would raise morale around the ground, which was vital after Warnock's exit had demoralised supporters.

We were like the dumped boyfriend, who'd despairingly locked himself in his own house as he was unable to cope with the devastating rejection. Freedman's arrival was like an ex-girlfriend, who'd left to fulfil her dreams and go travelling, returning to your door at the perfect moment to bring you out of the doldrums. We still had reservations about it all, but we certainly felt a lot better because of the return. The reservations might have been down to Paul Hart's inability and Freedman's inexperience. Although it's also possible that they were because you would have to seriously question any girl who left you to go travelling in Southend.

At about twenty to three, we followed the regular routine and emptied our bladders before heading to the ground. Within minutes of the game kicking off, a familiar song, sung to the tune of 'Winter Wonderland', echoed around Selhurst Park:

"There's only one Dougie Freedman!
One Dougie Freedman!
Walking Along!
Singing our song!
Walking in a Freedman Wonderland!"

It must be the only time in the history of football that a new assistant manager has been worshipped while the new number one was ignored. When you appoint a new manager, there is always a good atmosphere at the next home game as a new era begins. There's a sense of renewed optimism and a fresh start which gives both the players and supporters a lift. Even Trevor Francis, who despite being our manager for eighteen months, I still think of more favourably for the mention of his tracksuit in the Only Fools and Horses theme tune than I do for his time in charge of the club, received a warm reception when he first came out of the Selhurst Park tunnel.

As Warnock had deserted us rather than being sacked, and Paul Hart was such an underwhelming appointment, we'd been robbed of that new manager feeling. Luckily, having the returning legend as his deputy, gave us the emotion that was lacking. For that reason alone, appointing Freedman was a good move.

Alan Lee gave us a first half lead, which we just about deserved. He'd expertly volleyed home a Danny Butterfield cross. This was more the kind of thing that we expected from the two of them linking up, rather than Lee winning aerial knock-ons for Butterfield to score a hat-trick. Earlier in the season, I'd slated all of our strikers. While Stern John was barely playing, Calvin Andrew still didn't seem to know how to play and Freddy Sears had been sent home, Alan Lee had certainly won me over. He was yet another player who was giving absolutely everything for us.

We headed up to the Red'n'Blue bar for a drink at half time. Well, Colin, Kev, Jonathan and I did. Dad and Dan bonded over their wish for a Bovril to warm them up. Well, I say Bovril, it was actually labelled as 'Beef Drink' at Palace. Apart from inside a football stadium, I don't think I've ever seen Bovril on sale in the South of England. Let alone a cheap alternative. Apparently it's *all* that is available 'oop north.

It was a badly named cheap alternative at that. I'm sure they could have been more creative than 'Beef Drink'. Calf Time Drink? I'd buy that on the pun alone. I'm sure there has got to be other options too. What about 'The Udder Hot Drink'? Or how about simply calling it 'No Bull, Just Beef'? Any of them would be a lot better than the tame and boring 'Beef Drink'.

Palace controlled the second half and we should have doubled our lead through Alan Lee, when he reacted quickest to Ambrose's well struck free kick being saved. Unfortunately, he fired the rebound high above the Sheffield goal. Although, in the end, it didn't matter. We comfortably held on to win 1-0, without Speroni having to make a save. It was a vital victory because when a new manager comes in, they need a result straight away to get the players and fans behind them. Paul Hart would have been desperate to avoid giving the press and supporters a chance to start discussing stats about a lack of wins since his appointment. It would have been worse for Hart than most managers, as his losing streaks at Portsmouth and QPR from earlier in the season had given him a pretty horrific personal record of two wins in eighteen previous matches during the 2009/10 season.

As we left the stadium, we heard that QPR had beaten third placed West

Bromwich Albion. Bugger. The perfect start for Warnock. The results left us just above the relegation zone on goal difference but if QPR had lost, we'd have actually gone above them. The new manager effect had worked for both teams. Although, I couldn't help but suspect that the feel-good factor would last longer in West London than it would for us. The relegation battle was incredibly tight. All thirteen of the teams in the bottom half of the table could have feasibly got relegated at that point.

Position	Team	Played	Goal Diff.	Points
13	Preston North End	34	-8	43
14	Derby County	34	-7	42
15	Bristol City	34	-10	42
16	Queens Park Rangers	33	-6	40
17	Watford	32	-5	39
18	Reading	32	-9	38
19	Ipswich Town	34	-9	38
20	Scunthorpe United	34	-20	38
21	Crystal Palace	33	0	37
22	Sheffield Wednesday	34	-17	37
23	Plymouth Argyle	33	-15	30
24	Peterborough United	34	-21	24

The amount of time that a football fan can spend staring at a league table is worrying. In your head, you consider every permutation. What happens if we lose? If we win? What fixtures do I need to look up? What's the best possible scenario next weekend? Where would a win take us? What's the worst possible scenario? Where could a defeat drop us to? I've killed hours looking at league tables. Of course, it's a completely pointless use of my time. Without knowing the next set of results, it means nothing.

However, it's a comfort. Knowing everything that is possible to happen, makes watching it happen a lot more bearable. As soon as a game finishes, people want to see the table. They want to know the effect of the match that they have just witnessed. So that evening, I spent hours doing the BBC's predictor. I looked at the table as it swayed one way and the other. I tried all sorts of permutations to see which would keep us up and which would send us down. Eventually, the scenario that I had going into the final day (I never predict the final day as everything goes out the window then and anything can happen) was that it would be between us or Sheffield Wednesday to get the final relegation spot. Sheffield Wednesday were due to host us on that final football weekend of the season. My finger nails were going to take one hell of a battering between now and then.

Chapter 48 – **A Chance for Revenge**

Tuesday 9th March 2010, Crystal Palace vs Bristol City, Selhurst Park

Crystal Palace: Julian Speroni, Nathaniel Clyne, Clint Hill, Shaun Derry, Darren Ambrose, (Neil Danns, 68), Nick Carle, (Stern John, 80), Matt Lawrence, Calvin Andrew, Alan Lee, Danny Butterfield, Johnny Ertl
Subs Not Used: Sean Scannell, Lee Hills, Kieran Djilali, Alassane N'Diaye, Charlie Mann

Bristol City: Dean Gerken, Bradley Orr, Liam Fontaine, Louis Carey, Lee Johnson, Nicky Maynard, Paul Hartley, Cole Skuse, Jamal Campbell-Ryce, Lewin Nyatanga, Chris Iwelumo
Subs Not Used: Jamie McAllister, David Clarkson, Gavin Williams, John Akinde, Ivan Sproule, Stephen Henderson, Danny Haynes

This was the rearranged game from January. When the game was originally meant to be played, we had been going for promotion, but two months on we'd lost all form, lost our manager, lost ten points and it was a vital game for different reasons. However, one thing that was the same was that we wanted revenge. Revenge on Bristol and revenge on Rob Shoebridge.

Earlier in the day, I'd had an interview to get into the Richmond Borough NQT Pool. This is basically a selection process, where each borough can pick out the best Newly Qualified Teachers and recommend them to their schools. Richmond has a reputation for being the hardest one to be accepted into.

After the interview, I'd headed to Kingston where I did my ICT skills test. In order to qualify as a teacher, you need to pass a test in Literacy, Numeracy and ICT to prove that you are of suitable intelligence to educate the little minds of the country. Personally, having met some of the people who failed the tests, I think it's a great idea. Seeing as I passed, I'm sure there are people who'd like the standard raised even higher, but the only change that I would make is to add in a fourth test on the history of Crystal Palace Football Club. I think that it is a pivotal subject that should be taught in every school.

The previous evening, I hadn't been frantically revising for my test. I hadn't even been reading up on interview techniques or looking at the possible questions. I wasn't ironing a shirt or dusting off my under-used suit. I was reading the Crystal Palace internet forum. On a daily basis there were new rumours of possible takeovers or impending liquidation. The mood of a Palace fan could swing up and down two or three times a day. And that wasn't even on match days.

I arrived at Palace for 5 o'clock, straight from Kingston and headed to the club shop. I bought some tickets for the upcoming away games at Barnsley, Blackpool and Nottingham Forest. Three games that I would be travelling to alone. However, there wasn't even the slightest question in my mind that I would be going to them. I also bought a pink Crystal Palace fleece for my niece, Nemie.

I'd been chosen to be her Godfather at her upcoming Christening. I felt that it was important that she was not only welcomed into the church, but she was also welcomed into the Crystal Palace family.

On the way to the Railway Club, where I met Colin and we were later joined by Kev, Jonathan and Dan, I received a phone call to tell me that I'd got into the Richmond NQT Pool. The mood in the pub was slightly more upbeat after our victory over Sheffield United – the phone call had helped my mood too. We sunk pints until it was accepted that Palace would definitely win that evening and not only that, they would win with a really dodgy goal to send the away fans back to the West Country with the same sense of being cheated as we had felt seven months previously.

The reality was quite different. The first half was dour, with neither keeper having a save to make. Both teams had set up negatively and both teams lacked any genuine quality. The busy fixture list was taking its toll on our thin squad. Our players looked knackered and were running out of steam.

After a half time beer in the Red'n'Blue bar, Palace had their only real chance of the game but Alan Lee headed it wide. Bristol scored a stunning goal with 17 minutes left and Palace never looked like coming back. Paul Hart was booed by discontented supporters when he substituted Stern John on for Nicky Carle, our one creative player. Bizarrely, in the eyes of the all-knowing supporters, he left the awful Calvin Andrew on the pitch, who unsurprisingly, didn't look like scoring. On the cold March evening, the small crowd had considerably shrunk in size long before the referee finally put us out of our misery and blew his whistle for full time.

I hadn't left the stadium when I received what was now a familiar text from my friend, Jak.

':-1'

It was a terribly hidden jibe, which had very little thought or imagination behind it but it was enough to make him feel slightly more smug about our defeat and enough to irritate me into muttering the words 'F*** off Jak' with a shake of my head and a weary, thin smile on my face. As childish and spiteful as it was, I actually quite liked it. It's how I'd longed for my flatmates to react to football. With a joke and a bit of a laugh. To be able to dish out the abuse and hit me when I'm down, knowing that they'll receive it back when their time comes.

Before meeting me, Jak had absolutely no interest in Crystal Palace. They were simply another team. Now, whether he was at a Brentford match, sitting at home or even in the pub with mates or his girlfriend, he wanted to know the Palace score at all times. To him, it wasn't about how Crystal Palace had got on, it was about how James Howland had faired. Just as I wanted to know Brentford's results because I wanted to know Chris and Jak's results. As far as I'm concerned, the classified results might as well read like this:

Chris and Jak 0 Rotherham United 1

I have lots of friends (and probably some enemies too) who hear the words Crystal Palace and simply think of me. To them, I am Crystal Palace Football Club. I like that. I suspect there are people who I went to school with and haven't seen or thought about for years, but who can't help but think of me when they hear the words Crystal Palace Football Club. It goes back to a football club giving you an identity. And growing up in Ascot, supporting Palace is a rare identity. I doubt supporters of Manchester United or Liverpool are thought of in the same way as they have such a generic and widespread identity. Every Saturday (and Tuesday during this period of Palace's history) there is a reminder to hundreds of people that they once knew me and without speaking to me, they know exactly how I am feeling.

There are people who hate Crystal Palace and are desperate for them to lose because of me and there are people who follow Crystal Palace and are desperate for them to win because of me. They don't actually care about the club but they know what makes me tick. They know that the club can hurt me or fill me with joy more than they ever could. To most people I meet, Crystal Palace Football Club is simply too big a part of my life to ignore. Many people see it as my life. And to a degree (or lack of if my obsession got in the way too much), they have a very good point.

Chapter 49 – **Running Out of Time**

Saturday 13th March 2010, Barnsley vs Crystal Palace, Oakwell.

Crystal Palace: Julian Speroni, Danny Butterfield, Nathaniel Clyne, Clint Hill, Matt Lawrence, Kieran Djilali (Calvin Andrew, 70), Shaun Derry, Neil Danns, Nicky Carle (Johnny Ertl, 46), Darren Ambrose, Alan Lee (Alassane N'Diaye, 87)
Subs Not Used: Charlie Mann, Stern John, Sean Scannell, Lee Hills
Barnsley: Preece, Hassell, Foster, Shotton, Dickenson (Potter, 45), Teixeira (Jacob Butterfield, 79), Colace, Doyle (Hallfredsson, 72), Hammill, Jon Macken, Bogdanovic
Subs Not Used: Lund, Hume, De Silva, Andy Gray

I was tired. Tired from work, tired from life and tired from football. Deadlines for my assignments were upcoming and I was beginning to struggle to keep on top of all eight of them. The last thing I needed was another long away trip. However, the idea of giving myself a free Saturday to rest and catch up didn't even cross my mind. I had a challenge to complete, a pledge to keep and a team that needed me. The challenge drove me on so I set an early alarm call and off I set to Barnsley...

I got the train as far as Doncaster on my own and I was exhausted after working late at the pub the previous evening. I saw Chris and John, the guys who I had travelled back from Cardiff with, at the Hub of the Championship, Doncaster Station, and continued my onward journey with them. As usual, John was worrying about everything from Palace getting relegated to us missing our train. We got a small 'Transpennine Express' train to Meadowhall, a purpose built station for The Meadowhall Shopping Centre just outside of Sheffield. I call it a station but it is literally a stop in the track and a tiny bridge. I then got an even smaller 'Northern Rail' train to Barnsley. Northern Rail trains are a unique experience. They are usually only one or two carriages and rattle louder than a small aeroplane while they bump along the line.

When we arrived in Barnsley, we came across Don, Frank and Trevor, who I'd travelled to the Scunthorpe game with. The six of us went into the town centre to get a fry up. I always think of Barnsley as a small club from a tiny town in the North of England. South Yorkshire to be precise. I consider them to have no right to a second tier football team, which is what they have been for most of my football supporting life. The town centre itself feels small and is instantly forgettable. It has all the same features as many northern towns: the usual banks, the usual fast food chains, the usual clothes retailers and a Wetherspoons, all of which are situated in average and forgettable 1960's architecture. There was probably a Bisto factory somewhere too. Maybe it was in one of the banks. I'm led to believe that gravy is currency 'oop north.

Traditionally, Barnsley was a small industrial coal mining and market town. Since the closing of the mines, the area relied on the glass making industry that it was famed for but that can hardly sustain an economy. Even more so than Coventry, Barnsley should be a town in depression. However, it seemed to have slightly more of an unexplainable buzz to it. There were more young people around and more faces with smiles on them. I was shocked to discover that the Metropolitan Borough of Barnsley has a population of over a quarter of a million people. That is much bigger than Ipswich or Norwich, who got far higher average attendances than Barnsley in the 2009/10 season, by eight and twelve thousand respectively.

I guess it's the combination of the size of their football following, and the fact that the name Barnsley sounds like a tiny place that made me assume that it's smaller than it is. The name of the town comes from the Saxon word 'Barn' and to be honest, the whole place looks about as comfortable and welcoming as a concrete barn. Although there is a certain charm to that. It is what visiting a Championship or League 1 football town is all about. It was big enough to support a football club but not big enough to offer much else. Like so many places in England, football is the only reason that people unconnected to the area would ever choose to visit it.

After some bacon and sausage in a bizarre school-canteen style cafe in the main shopping centre, I left my fellow Palace fans and made the short walk to the football ground. It takes less than ten minutes to walk from the town centre to Oakwell but once you're there, it feels like you are in a small countryside village in the middle of nowhere.

Before going into the ground, I went to the *Metro Dome – All in One Leisure Centre* at the top of the hill for a pint. On my two previous visits to Barnsley, for a 2-0 loss and a 0-0 draw, I'd drunk with Garry and Brian in the sports centre that overlooks the ground. I hoped that the coach regulars, such as Helen and Phil, would join me as quite frankly, drinking alone is pathetic and watching Palace in Barnsley is not an experience that has ever been especially enjoyable. The idea of doing it sober, was unbearable.

I got myself a pint of Guinness. The rest of the bar was empty so I decided to sit down outside as the Spring weather was just about warm enough to make use of the balcony overlooking the ground. After the long and cold winter, I was more than happy to use any excuse to sit outside. My enthusiasm was more than a little optimistic. I lasted about five minutes before I gave up on Barnsley's rare March sunshine and returned inside. I had barely sat down when I felt a tap on my right shoulder.

"Are you a Palace fan?" inquired a middle-aged, grey haired bloke. I looked down at my red and blue striped football top. I don't think it needed Sherlock Holmes to work out that I was indeed following Palace. In fact, I don't think it really required a question at all.

"Errm... yes," I politely replied, with a nod to reassure him even further.

"Me too. Do you mind if I join you?

Mind? Of course I didn't mind. I was sat on my own in a pub in bloody Barnsley. The idea of company was a good one. Especially Palace company.

Bob, as it turned out his name was (and still is), had travelled up from Northampton. He doesn't tend to visit Selhurst regularly but tries to get to as many away games as possible, particularly in the Midlands. He'd decided to make the further than usual drive up to Barnsley at the last minute – simply because he didn't have anything else on for that Saturday. Another rational decision in the name of football.

The more that I spoke to him, the more I liked him. He was very level headed and knew his football well. He'd been born in South London and moved to the East Midlands in his thirties. He played in a classic rock band and loved his music just as much as he loved Palace. As with many fans, since the club had gone into administration, he'd tried to get to more games. The connection between loved ones is always stronger when it is threatened.

We stayed in the bar and chatted happily about all things Palace until around two forty, when we made the short walk down the hill to the ground. As I went through the away turnstile, I remembered something that grumpy Brian had done at Barnsley a couple of years previously. There is a twenty foot or so gap between the turnstile and the concourse behind the stand. Next to the entrance to the concourse, there was a sign saying 'No smoking beyond this point' and by the exit of it, there was a sign saying 'No alcohol beyond this point'. Brian had stood half in and half out of the concourse with a fag in his left hand and a pint in his right. He would simply lean to the necessary side to be permitted to partake in each activity. It was little wonder that he had recently been hospitalised for health reasons.

The game was really poor, Palace were extremely negative. The starting line up was designed to defend rather than attack and Hart's subs only made us crawl further into our shell. Fortunately, Barnsley had some awful strikers and they spurned chance after chance. Although it would be unfair to ignore the role of Speroni, who made a series of outstanding saves to keep Barnsley at bay. Despite having to endure the dreadful football, we got the draw that the team came for.

In three games and more than 270 minutes, I still hadn't seen a Palace goal in Barnsley. That's 1,116 miles worth of travel. I don't know what is an acceptable amount of miles is to see three goalless performances, but it is certainly less than 1,116. To be honest, Bob's 224 mile round trip from Northampton for one such performance would have been enough to make the men in white coats question whether he held the mental stability to be allowed to maintain his freedom. If I'm ever questioned by a psychologist, I think it would be for the best if I neglected to tell them of my repeated Barnsley self harming.

After the game, I said goodbye to Bob and we swapped numbers. We'd got on well so he suggested that we could go to future games together as we both travelled alone. It made sense to me. Once again, the Palace connection had made me the most unlikely of friendships. I still text Bob regularly and we meet up at the occasional away game.

I got the train back to Doncaster, via Middle-of-nowhere-hall, with John, Chris, one of their friends called Warren, and his group of friends. I had an hour in Doncaster so I went to a pub called 'The Plough' and had a couple of pints with

Warren and his mates. Once again, I had little in common with these guys, but they were Palace – that was enough. I liked the pub just as much, if not more, than the company. It was a small and friendly 'locals' pub but as it was situated in between the station and the town centre, they were more than used to visitors. Especially on a Saturday afternoon.

The exterior of the pub was built with large stone bricks and had a Victorian style lantern above the door. Inside, there was a warm log fire and a time-honoured wooden bar. All of the decoration was well kept and traditional. It still had many of the original 1930 features, such as the low, long wooden beams on the ceiling and the impressive brick mantelpiece. It felt like a pub should do. Just like you were walking into someone's living room. I had a pint of Acorn brewery's 'Barnsley Bitter', which summed up my mood quite well. Although, I must admit, the beer went some way to cheering me up as it was far better than the Barnsley football match that I had witnessed that day.

In the pub, there were supporters of Palace, Doncaster, Derby, who'd lost at Doncaster, and QPR, who'd drawn at Sheffield United. All four sets of fans drank happily together, discussing the different matches that we'd gone to. I must admit, I was relieved at the tame nature of the QPR fans. It would have been very easy for them to be in a smug and taunting mode. Warnock had made a good start to life in West London and had lifted them away from the relegation battle that we were still locked in.

The pub was a real ale pub and I must say, I find ale pubs a lot more pleasant to drink in. Of course, preferring to sup on ale rather than lager does help, but I also find the clientele that congregate in ale pubs tend to be less aggressive and more knowledgeable than your average Fosters drinking type of chap. Therefore, it seems to me that you are less likely to get a smack in the gob in a real ale pub. That's not to say that you can't find those qualities in a lager drinker. I know plenty of perfectly pleasant people who regularly indulge in many of the cheap lagers readily available in England. I am also aware of the hypocritical nature of my claims as I have, on many occasions, described myself drinking lager in this book. However, as an overall generalisation, I've found ale pubs to be friendlier and more welcoming.

I would guess the reason is that if people have made an effort to frequent a specialist pub, then they are more likely to appreciate the beer rather than simply get hammered. I will make another huge hypocritical generalisation and state that people who don't care what they are drinking and simply want to get pissed, are more likely to have repressed aggression and give someone an undeserving smack after a few pints.

Thanks to the welcoming atmosphere, traditional feel and excellent beer, it came as no surprise to me that the following autumn, the pub would win Doncaster's Pub of the Year. Although I'm dubious as to how much competition it would have had for the award.

I could have happily stayed chatting to the other football fans in the pub all evening. However, I was the first to leave as I was booked on the earliest train out of all of us. I said my goodbyes and grabbed some cans for the journey home. I'd started drinking so I had no intention of stopping now. I didn't want to get a 'football hangover' and start to feel the adverse affects of the booze during my journey home. I was more than happy to delay that until the next day.

However, I was still in no mood to drink alone. I wondered along the train until I found a group of drinking Palace supporters. I introduced myself and we began to chat along. The irony of their names being Matthew, Mark and Luke was lost on them. I asked them where John was but they simply looked at me blankly. They obviously hadn't had the same Christian upbringing as myself. Their ignorance towards the joke ruined my opportunity of following it up by asking if they wrote for the Palace programme. I didn't have a lot in common with them but they were what I wanted from the journey home. They were Palace fans. As always, that was enough.

The trip home was spent drinking and singing. The songs were the same repertoire as usual but something felt different. Coming home from Scunthorpe a few weeks previously, there'd be a defiant edge to our songs. We'd been beaten and bruised by so much throughout the season but we'd still felt untouchable. However, the flatness and tiredness of our performance in Barnsley had been yet another right hook planted perfectly on our nose. The singing on the train reflected the player's performance. Time was running out both on and off the pitch. The players were tired from their busy schedule and I was tired from mine.

There was little or no substance behind any of the takeover rumours and without the club being bought, whether we stayed up or not would be irrelevant. Without a takeover, the decision of whether I should spend a small fortune and travel 372 miles for *another* 0-0 draw at Barnsley would be taken out of my hands. While I had (and still have) no intention of ever returning to Barnsley, the thought of not being *able* to do so, didn't bear thinking about.

On the way home, I received a text from my cousin, Bernard. He was at university in Manchester but was in Richmond for the weekend as he was visiting friends. When I arrived back in London, I went to join him. He frowned when I arrived. It wasn't that he wasn't pleased to see me. He was. At least, I think and hope he was. It was the fact that I was wearing a Palace shirt. As a kid, he used to come and stay with me in the summer holidays. On one such visit, I'd worn a different Palace shirt on each of the seven days that he was with me. He'd never let me forget it.

In my mind, I'd grown up since those days but here I was, in a student bar, wearing a bright red and blue football shirt. It wasn't a good look. I wasn't going to impress any ladies that evening. I wasn't going to impress *anyone* that evening. Bernard introduced me to his friends, explaining my shirt and addiction by embarrassing me with the story of missing Emily's wedding for the football. His friends looked at me with a slight fear and a complete lack of understanding. Any football addict is used to this pitied and disappointed look.

However, I did have a good night - drinking lager, like the rest of the bar, and not even coming close to receiving a smack in the gob. Maybe those lager drinkers aren't so bad after all. I returned home well after midnight and incredibly drunk. A few hours later, I was rudely awoken by my alarm. Sure enough, I was feeling the adverse affects of the booze; my head was pounding, my throat was dry and the room was spinning. Perhaps I should have opted out after leaving the pub in Doncaster and taken a small headache on the way home.

I picked up a paper to read on the way to work. I say to read but all I really wanted was the Championship table. I had looked at it when I'd got in the night before but I couldn't remember all of the permutations of the previous day's results. There was now just eleven games left and Palace were sitting right on the edge. We were only out of the drop zone on goal difference and the administrator had made it clear that there would be no money to continue to fund the club after the end of the season. We needed points and we needed a buyer. And quick.

However, the club weren't the only ones having a financial crisis. I was too. I'd put off purchasing my train ticket to Middlesbrough for the start of April as each week my pay packet seemed to disappear before I got a chance to buy one. When I got in from work, I decided that I needed to bite the bullet and pay for the long trip north. I couldn't believe it. The cheapest ticket was £54 return, even with a railcard and the match being nearly a whole month away. I'd cocked up and left it too late. I hadn't paid more than £25 for a train journey all season. Well, other than Doncaster, but I'd only actually paid £14 at the time of purchase.

Having learnt absolutely nothing from my experience in Doncaster, I winced as I pressed 'buy now' – the previous day's performance had hardly inspired me to rush out and spend more money on watching further uninspiring and substandard football.

I didn't want to pay it but the challenge forced me. It had taken me over. I'd come this far and made so many sacrifices that it would have seemed almost disrespectful not to go. Disrespectful to Emily and Mitch for missing their wedding, to Mike for switching shifts at Christmas, to all the friends that I'd had to cut short or missed parties of, to myself – I hadn't sat on a train outside Newport Station for hours as the police faffed about over some kids, and spent a fortune to get to Doncaster and travelled all over the country for nothing. No, I had to go. The challenge wouldn't let me miss it.

At the price that I was paying for the Middlesbrough train, I expected it to be the most luxurious and enjoyable train journey of all time, with picturesque scenery throughout. Although, in the precarious position that we found ourselves in, I'd have settled for a scrappy Palace win at the end of it, whatever the journey was like.

Addiction is a state that is characterized by compulsive drug use or compulsive engagement in rewarding behaviour, despite adverse consequences. Classic hallmarks of addiction include impaired control over substances or behaviour, preoccupation with substance or behaviour, continued use despite consequences, and denial.

Behavioural addiction consists of a compulsion to repeatedly engage in an action until it causes negative consequences to the person's physical, mental, social, and/or financial well-being. Behaviour persisting in spite of these consequences can be taken as a sign of addiction.

The definitions were damning. My substance might not be illegal but it was having adverse effects, impairing my control of my behaviour, preoccupying me, stopping my ability to learn from my mistakes and choosing the substance over logic. I had made a pledge to the challenge and a pledge to Palace. I couldn't give either of them up for anyone or anything.

Chapter 50 – **P Diddy's Red and Blue Army**

Tuesday 16th March 2010, Crystal Palace vs Leicester City, Selhurst Park.

Crystal Palace: Julian Speroni, Nathaniel Clyne (Lee Hills, 45), Clint Hill, Shaun Derry, Darren Ambrose (Sean Scannell, 79), Neil Danns, Calvin Andrew, Alan Lee (Matt Lawrence, 45), Danny Butterfield, Johnny Ertl, Claude Davis
Subs Not Used: Stern John, Kieran Djilali, Nick Carle, Alassane N'Diaye

Leicester City: Chris Weale, Michael Morrison, Nolberto Solano, Matt Oakley, 10. Andy King, Lloyd Dyer (Dany N'Guessan, 79), Bruno Berner, Martyn Waghorn (Steve Howard, 64), Richie Wellens, Paul Gallagher (Nicky Adams, 85), Jack Hobbs
Subs Not Used: Robbie Neilson, Ryan McGivern, Conrad Logan, Yann Kermorgant

I met up with Chris in Putney before the game and had a few pints with him, as well as a cheeky bottle of London Pride on the train. I'd only meant to meet him for one pint but I was enjoying his company and lacking motivation to go to the game so much, that I ended up only just making it to the match on time. When I left him and arrived in South London, I had the dubious pleasure of having some jerk chicken from the West Indian takeaway in Thornton Heath that belts out smoke throughout matches. I got into the ground and met the guys just before kickoff, spicy chicken in hand. Soon the fumes wouldn't only be coming from the chimney of the fast food outlet.

Palace were incredibly negative during the first half. Once again, Hart had set the team up to defend. We'd hardly been a 'gung ho' style team under Warnock but the change in playing style was very evident. It wasn't Hart's team and he didn't believe in the players that he had been left with.

In stoppage time of an uninspiring first half, Claude Davis stupidly punched one of their players in an off the ball incident and got sent off. Fortunately, despite being in the area, no penalty was given. However, it was a ridiculous action from our central defender. Throughout his career, he had been notorious for being a hot head and making rash decisions. Fans of his previous club, Derby County, had nicknamed him 'Calamity Claude' as his irrational nature had cost them so many points. Until this point, he hadn't let us down. He'd harshly been given a ban for an alleged elbow against Cardiff in the previous season but other than that, his Palace disciplinary record was very favourable compared to his spells at other clubs. But that night, he let us down badly.

We went up to the Red'n'Blue bar at half time and all of us were in disbelief at what had just happened. We were angry. Why had he done it? Why had he been so unprofessional? Every point was vital to us, not just in our plight to survive the drop but also in terms of simply having a club for the following season. There were still no obvious takeover candidates and surely being in the division below would put off any potential buyers. No matter what provocation he received, there was no excuse for lashing out.

As we took our seats for the second half, our anger grew even further. Hart took off Alan Lee, our only striker, as well as Clyne, our best defender, for

Lee Hills and Matt Lawrence. There was total disbelief in the crowd. The subs had left us with no striker on the pitch. Not even the usually ever-positive Colin could justify the manager's decision. Dan was furious. He continually shook his head in astonishment as he stared into his Beef Drink.

"That might just be the worst double substitution ever made by a Palace manager. Some of the clowns we've had might have made one of them but together, that's just unbelievable."

He wasn't wrong. It wasn't anything personal against the players that were coming on. They were both decent players. It was simply the negative intent behind the substitutions.

For eight long minutes, we watched the most pointless bit of football that I've ever seen. Leicester would attack, Palace would eventually get a tackle in and lump the ball forward to... no one. One of the, rather bored, Leicester defenders would then bring the ball forward and start another attack. It was painful to watch. Inevitably, it didn't work. Leicester scored on 53 minutes. At least that forced Hart to move Calvin Andrew up front. Andrew may have been about as likely to score as I was that night but even he was better than having *no one* up front.

Palace never looked like getting back into the game and Hart hardly helped matters. He took off Darren Ambrose, our main and only goalscorer, much to the continued bafflement of the crowd. We huffed and puffed in the closing stages, as our players always would, but we were unable to get anything out of the match.

We'd now gone 337 minutes since our last goal, having fired blanks in our last three outings. Hart's defensive instincts we're not doing us any favours as the baffled crowd, of barely over twelve thousand, went home disappointed. It was little wonder that it was played in front of such a small crowd. Our home form was appalling – five defeats out of six matches, with only two goals scored in that time. I guess that it was no surprise, if a bit disappointing, that my father forgot all about the game in his busy life – he only remembered when I phoned him up on the way home to moan about Hart's inability. I repeated Dan's sentiments about it being *'the worst double substitution ever made by a Palace manager'*.

Two days after the game, one of the most bizarre rumours to ever grace Selhurst Park was splashed all over the front and back pages of the papers. It started on one newspaper's website and quickly spread from one website to the next and then, one paper to the next. Before long, there were quotes from associates, which gave the sensational rumours a little bit of credit.

P Diddy, the world famous rapper, was set to try and buy the club. Allegedly, he'd looked into buying an English football 'franchise' and he'd decided on Crystal Palace as it reminded him of his favourite drink, Cristal Champagne. The papers claimed that the hip-hop mogul, worth over $700m, wanted to not only clear the club's debt but also fund a return to the Premier League. P Diddy had made a surprise visit to London in the previous week and the papers were claiming that he had been discussing a deal to buy the club then. It wasn't quite on the same scale as when Colonel Gadafi was rumoured to want to purchase the club but it was almost as ridiculous.

Over the previous few weeks, the pressure of supporting my club had become too much. Going to a game on a Saturday was supposed to be a relief from the stresses of real life. However, the constant checking of the internet forums for updates, continuous watching of Sky Sports News for any hint of hope and the forever worrying, both in conscious states and in my sleep, about the future of my Saturday afternoons, about the future of my club, about my friend, was taking its toll. Palace's administration had taken over my life. The stress of university and work and applying for jobs didn't come close to the stress created from the fear of losing my football team. Real life had become an escape from the football.

Whether the P Diddy rumours were true or not, and if we were being honest, we all heavily suspected that they weren't, it provided our pot-less and goalless club with something to laugh about and enjoy. Fun was something that had been missing from my football club for some weeks now. I was so engulfed in the drama and panic of losing my club that I hadn't realised how much its plight was getting me down. I'd always recognised the effect that a victory or a defeat could have on my mood in the hours and days after a game but this was something new. We were constantly fighting a huge battle. Every day, every night, every moment, we were constantly playing the biggest game of our history.

The P Diddy rumours gave us an escape from that game in the same way that a couple of streakers could give the crowd something to cheer about and release the tension during an important fixture. P Diddy was metaphorically streaking across a metaphorical football match. It could only happen at Palace.

People dreamed of 'Cristal' being the official club sponsor and being available to drink in the concourse at half time. It would certainly be an upgrade on 'Beef Drink' or flat pints. People imagined a board room filled with his 'bitches' and a club shop stocked with his fashionable clothes range, Sean John. Yes, I had to Google that. I'm nowhere near fashionable enough to be strutting around in his clobber. There would be sell out gigs every summer at Selhurst Park to raise money for the club. It would even outdo Watford's regular Elton John concerts. Crystal Palace would be world famous and the first club to be tapping into the hip-hop market. We would officially be the coolest club to support.

Unfortunately, as suspected, the rumours turned out to be nonsense. Well, partially. He had actually investigated buying the club but had decided that it wasn't financially feasible. However, there was more fun had by Palace fans in the couple of days around the 'P Diddy Incident' than there had been in the previous few weeks of matches. I highly recommend watching this light-hearted *Youtube* re-creation of the whole event –
https://www.youtube.com/watch?v=ZXMhWO8xBzo

Chapter 51 - **Finally, a roof!**

Saturday 20th March 2010, Blackpool vs Crystal Palace, Bloomfield Road

Crystal Palace: Julian Speroni, Danny Butterfield, Matt Lawrence, Clint Hill, Lee Hills, Darren Ambrose, Neil Danns, Johnny Ertl, Shaun Derry, Nicky Carle (Alassane N'Diaye, 82), Alan Lee
Subs Not Used: Charlie Mann, Stern John, Sean Scannell, Calvin Andrew, Kieran Djilali, James Comley

Blackpool: Gilks, Coleman, Baptiste, Evatt, Crainey, Adam, Southern, Husband (Burgess, 37), Barry Bannan (Taylor-Fletcher, 76), Stephen Dobbie, Clarke (Ormerod, 68)
Subs Not Used: Rachubka, Euell, Edwards, Butler

I'd found an insanely early (and cheap) train from London Euston to Manchester so I left Twickenham, exhausted from working the night before, at five am. As well as saving myself some money, it also allowed me to meet up with my friend Shane, who was at Manchester University, for breakfast and a few games of *FIFA* on the *Playstation*.

I then left Shane and got the train to Blackpool. When it stopped at Bolton, a large bunch of skinheads, draped in St. George's flags and England football shirts, got off the train, aggressively chanting. I thought of Lee Young-Pyo and reminisced of my experience of Bolton Wanderers fans in West Bromwich. I remember thinking that I hoped they would be able to avoid this lot and wondered which team possessed such unruly looking thugs as supporters. I grabbed the cheap newspaper that I had with me and checked who Bolton were playing. Everton – away. That's odd, I thought to myself. Who the hell were these guys? I was certainly glad that they weren't associated with my team.

I eventually arrived in Blackpool around mid day and bumped into a couple of Palace fans at the station. We made small talk about what the line up should be. They were discussing whether or not they would start our Australian International, Nicky Carle. I'll be completely honest. I didn't care.

You may have noticed that I talked a lot about football being a game of opinions in the first half of this book and that I have barely mentioned it in the second half. There is a reason for that. Entering administration changed everything; our ambition, our aims and our outlook. Whether you hated Warnock or could understand his decision, whether you were giving Hart a fair chance or not, whether you would start Nicky Carle or Neil Danns in midfield – none of it mattered. All that mattered is that we all stuck together. Palace had to stay up and Palace had to survive - who, how and why didn't matter.

Players and fans alike both had something precious and life changing to lose. For us, it was our club. The idea of not having a team to go and watch on a Saturday was incomprehensible. For the players, it was a job. Not knowing if they would have a wage to take home to their families after the end of the season must have been terrifying. We could empathise with each other. I guess that's what made us so strong.

The other argument killer was that there simply wasn't much debate about who should play because there weren't many options. If you were fit, you played. The squad was threadbare. Subs weren't debated as the manager simply didn't have any choice in players to bring on (Ok, the ones in the last game were but that was more down to who he took off and that he decided to play without a centre forward. In terms of bringing players on, he had little alternative to the ones that he did bring on). During his first four games, Hart had used just fourteen different players. In the same time, Warnock had used over twenty at QPR.

At the start of the season, I would have happily spent hours discussing who should start, who should be a sub, who didn't deserve to wear the famous red and blue ever again and should be shipped out to the lower leagues at say, Brighton, Millwall or Charlton to inflict their s***ness on them. However, we could no longer be so picky. Things had got so desperate that Dougie Freedman, the assistant manager, had asked the FA to allow him to change his contract to a playing one, but as we were still working under a transfer embargo the request was declined.

Rather than find a pub, I decided to wonder over to the ground as Garry was going to make a rare appearance, so I decided to meet Brian and him there. On the way to the ground, I met a journalist from 'The People' newspaper. He was extremely excited to be reporting on the game. Not that he cared about Blackpool or Crystal Palace. He didn't. In fact, he told me that he'd thrown a big sulk in the office when he'd originally been designated the game. Very rude of him if you ask me. He was clearly clueless about football. He was moaning about being paid to travel fifty odd miles to the game from Manchester but I was paying a small fortune to travel 274 miles each way to watch the same game. He defined the phrase 'ungrateful git'.

He was your typical football journalist. Arrogant and clueless. He spent our entire walk name dropping Manchester United players that he'd met at parties, while he showed absolutely no knowledge or interest in either of the teams that he'd been sent to watch. He clearly believed that he should have been sent to bigger and better things. However, once he was over the initial disappointment of his assignment, he'd found out something about the game that made even the biggest resistor of lower league football excited.

Blackpool were finally going to open the fourth stand at their ground. On my previous visits, they'd had two fairly new stands, one temporary, unroofed stand and nothing behind one of the goals. Naturally, they seated the away fans in the unroofed temporary stand down the side of the pitch. This had resulted in me getting drenched during a two all draw in the previous season. I was wearing a high quality coat but even that couldn't hold out. Over ninety minutes, the heavy rain found a way through. I was still ringing my clothes out back in London. However, while the prospect of a new stand and more importantly, a roof, excited me, it wasn't this that excited my new journalist friend.

The new stand was to be named after and opened by Jimmy Armfield, the former England and Blackpool star. He is a true legend of the game and the opportunity to not only meet him, but interview him too, did excite the journalist.

Certainly more than Blackpool against Crystal Palace did, which wasn't hard as he spoke with such disdain for both clubs and all lower league football.

To be fair to the guy, when we got to the ground, he showed me his press pass and said that he had a spare if I wanted it. He was going to watch the game in a box. It was a brilliant act of kindness from someone that I didn't know but I wasn't interested. When Palace made mistakes and continuously gave the ball away cheaply, I wanted to be with my own type. People who would over-enthusiastically clap encouragement, sing their hearts out and believe that the players were about to suddenly turn into world beaters. I certainly didn't want to be sat next to a host, who I had to mind my p's and q's around, while listening to him tut, sigh and roll his eyes at every mistake before scribbling down some condescending notes for his inevitably ignorant match report.

I politely declined before I went to meet Garry and Brian in an old working man's social club by the ground. I liked it for two reasons. Firstly, its dingy outside and surprisingly friendly inside reminded me of the Railway Club, but the main reason behind my fond memories was the price of beer. Bottles of Carlsberg were just £1 (or 5 for £4). However, I decided to push the boat out and go for a 'pricey' pint of Guinness at £1.30. The north has its faults but I couldn't moan at this.

Garry and Brian were both on good form. Brian was relieved that Freedman hadn't been allowed to come out of retirement for us. I suspect he wouldn't have been in the surprisingly positive mood that he was if he had been. The combination of no Freedman and cheep beer was obviously all that had ever been required to cheer him up. It saddens me that I have just realised that this would be the final beer that I ever had with Brian. In 2011, his health issues caught up with him and he passed away. We had a good catch up and a light hearted reminiscence of the previous year's soaking, while enjoying a few beers, before we made the short walk across the road to the ground.

As the players came out, it began to rain. Not the torrential rain that we'd received the previous year but a shower nonetheless. It was exactly what we wanted. We felt smug. The roof had been justified.
"We're not getting wet,
We're not getting wet,
We're not getting,
We're not getting,
We're not getting wet!"
was the chant from the dry and covered away fans.

Palace came out of the blocks flying. Nicky Carle and Darren Ambrose put us 2-0 up. I could just imagine the pro-Carle supporter from the station jumping on his mates back to further amplify his loyalty to the Aussie. The small Palace following were in great voice and why shouldn't we be? At certain points in the season we had sung louder, prouder and longer than expected. However, in Blackpool, we not only had a two goal cushion but we also had a roof. What more could you ask for in life? We got to half time with our lead still intact. I had a quick beer with Helen and Phil as we listened out for the other scores. It was coming to that dramatic time of the season when the other results seem to matter almost as much as your own.

Minutes after half time, Blackpool pulled one back. As the second period continued, we defended deeper and deeper into our own half. Soon, we had Speroni in goal, nine defenders sat on the edge of the box and Alan Lee left all alone on the halfway line. Blackpool pushed and pressed for an equaliser but lacked the quality to break us down. Despite the Palace faithful's fingernails disappearing, our voices didn't.

Eventually, in the very last minute, they scrambled an equaliser. I sank deep into my chair. Blackpool celebrated. 'Glad All Over' boomed out over their PA system. Some of the Palace fans tried to sing along. Blackpool copied our song over twenty years after we had started to sing it and some of our fans couldn't let them have it, especially not at that moment. However, I couldn't muster up a defiant voice.

I was anything but Glad All Over. I was fuming all over or, I would have been, if I had the energy to be. I was beaten. I hadn't particularly expected anything from the game. Blackpool were going well and we were sinking but having been 2-0 up and cruising at half time, it was gutting.

After the stolen song had ended, I caught one pair of the jubilant, yet threatening eyes of an orange-shirted home fan. He displayed anger and menace, yet sheer joy and relief at the same time, as he pointed his boney finger, at the end of his chubby arm, towards me, while screaming '2-0 and you f***ed it up!' at the top of his over excited voice from one side of the stand to the other. I felt a rush of irrational hatred fire through me. It echoed around the stadium and my head. Thousands of them were singing it at us.
'2-0 and you f***ed it up!'
At Palace. At me. They were doing nothing that I wouldn't do myself but I couldn't take it. They didn't understand. They didn't know what Palace had gone through. What I was going through. Within minutes, both Chris and Jak had texted me to mock. I tried to make up some saving face crap about taking a point beforehand but all three of us knew that wasn't what I was thinking.

On the way back to the station, I grabbed some fish and chips and a stick of rock. I was at the seaside after all so it seemed rude not to. I just needed to go to an arcade and a strip club to complete the Blackpool experience. I have discovered during other trips to the Hen and Stag Capital of the UK just how horrific the Blackpool nightlife is. Every girl (and some blokes), aged between twelve and sixty, seem to wear hot pants, a fluorescent boob-tube and a thick layer of fake tan. I definitely think that I got the better end of the Blackpool experience with my cod, chips and confectionery.

I jumped on the small *Northern Rail* train back to Preston and as I had an hour there, I nipped into the pub opposite the station and got a cheeky pint with Warren and his mates, who I had drunk with after the Barnsley game. Like myself, they were now only interested in drinking to forget the football. The same football that we had travelled so far and spent so much money to see. None of these guys were what I would consider a 'friend' but I knew them all by name and I could quite easily hold a conversation with them throughout the long journey home. Provided, of course, that the topic of conversation didn't veer too far away from all things Palace. That was our only connection but it was a strong one.

On the pub radio, something caught my attention. Unfortunately it wasn't a good tune or even happy news from Bloomfield Road that we'd all missed the linesman's flag and Blackpool's late equaliser had actually been ruled out. No. It was from Bolton. Seventy-four 'people' had been arrested during English Defence League marches. The thugs in England flags and shirts hadn't been football thugs at all. They were racist scumbag thugs and thankfully, a reasonable amount would spend the night in a cell. I say 'thankfully' but that's not really the right word. I would have been more thankful if no arrests had been needed to be made and even more thankful if the march hadn't happened at all.

I can understand, without supporting them, some of the views about the need for tight rulings on immigration and ensuring that people who want to live in this country, have something to offer. However, the people who tend to show up for EDL marches are, on the whole, ignorant, racist thugs who I would much rather left our country than the vast majority of law abiding, hard working, immigrants, who the generally unemployed racists want out.

That said, the opposition who turned up on the day, the UAF (United Against Fascism) were just as provocative and aggressive in their demonstrations and deserve absolutely no sympathy whatsoever in my opinion. That is simply saved for the intelligent locals, such as the friends from Bolton that I'd met in Birmingham, who wanted nothing to do with the criminal activity in the town centre that day. One report read that *'Missiles were thrown across the barricades keeping the two sides apart, with the demo growing uglier as the day went on. Some protesters tried to smash down the barriers.'*
I struggle to see how any of this is anything but the actions of scum.

I texted 'Lee Young-Pyo', my Bolton friend, to check he was alright. He was fine. He was pissed in Liverpool after watching his side lose at Everton, but he later told me that his grandmother had nearly been hit by a missile while out shopping that day. I must admit, having had one short look at them, I was very relieved that my first impression had been wrong and they were nothing to do with football.

English football has had its problems in the past. I have heard stories from older Palace fans about Paul Canoville's horrific debut at Selhurst Park for Chelsea, where his own fans chanted abuse and threw bananas at him. However, thankfully, before I got into the game, football stood up, realised that it had a problem and has pretty much eliminated it. You still hear abusive and homophobic songs and shouts from spectators but I can honestly say that I haven't heard more than a small handful of racist comments at football and certainly nothing on a large scale. It simply isn't accepted. If football was still played in an environment that tolerated that behaviour, I honestly believe that I wouldn't go. I definitely wouldn't be as addicted as I am.

I got the train back with Warren and his friends, drinking all the way home. As we got drunker, there were a few renditions of '*P Diddy's Red'n'Blue Army*' echoing around the carriage. We needed a reminder that this whole pilgrimage was supposed to be in the name of fun. The challenge was supposed to be in the name of fun. There were moments of fun but it was also expensive, stressful and tiring – and it was those emotions that were taking over the challenge, that were taking over me. Going to games had become robotic and entirely out of habit. The whole string of northern away games were blurring into one. Just as the regular home defeats were too.

Back in London we headed to the Wetherspoons outside Victoria station for a quick pint. One of Warren's friends, Simon, was really drunk. He could barely stand up and certainly couldn't string a sentence together. I think he'd achieved his mission of forgetting the football and our two goal slip. Eventually, around eleven o'clock, I said my goodbyes and headed home, exhausted after an extremely long day and filled with dread for my 9AM start to work the following day.

Chapter 52 – **Career vs Football**

Tuesday 23rd March 2010, Nottingham Forest vs Crystal Palace, The City Ground.

Crystal Palace: Julian Speroni, Clint Hill, Lee Hills, Matt Lawrence, Danny Butterfield (Sean Scannell, 5), Johnny Ertl, Shaun Derry, Darren Ambrose, Neil Danns, Stern John (Calvin Andrew, 80), Alan Lee (Kieran Djilali, 85)
Subs Not Used: Charlie Mann, Kieron Cadogan, James Comley, Alassane N'Diaye

Nottingham Forest: Camp, Chambers, Morgan, Wilson, Gunter, Anderson (McGoldrick, 90), Cohen, Moussi, Majewski (McCleary, 74), Earnshaw (Tyson, 80), Blackstock
Subs Not Used: Smith, McGugan, Dele Adebola, Boyd

Since arriving back home from Blackpool, I had barely stopped. That week, I had been scheduled to do twenty four hours of work at the pub, all of my assignment deadlines were upcoming, and I also had a couple of friends' birthday nights out to attend. On top of that, I was applying for teaching jobs for the following year. I would finish work at the pub after midnight, buy some energy drinks and sweets for a sugar boost and then head home to do a couple of hours work to finish off my essays. The last thing that I needed was to have to rush off to the Midlands for yet another Palace game. At least the busy schedule meant that I was far too occupied by my life to notice how lonely I was in the flat.

The previous day, I'd got in from work at one and gone to sleep around 4AM. My alarm had rudely awoken me from my slumber less than five hours later for a nine o'clock lecture. The plan was to finish my lecture at eleven, jump on a bus to Hampton Wick, where I would hand in my CRB check and proof of identity ahead of an interview for a teaching job, and then get the train to Selhurst to catch the official club coach that was leaving Palace at the absurdly early time of 1PM.

Unfortunately, my lecture overran. Considering the extortionate tuition fees that universities charge, leaving you with a lifetime of debt, I shouldn't have moaned about having an extra 'free' twenty minutes of tuition but, at the time, it wasn't particularly helpful in my quest to get to Selhurst Park. Come to think of it, I'm not sure it has been majorly helpful and made any groundbreaking difference to my teaching practice either. I suppose it's just a case of how many sets of 'un-essential' twenty minutes you can afford to miss at university before it does make a difference. Missing lectures is a fatal and slippery slope that is easy to fall into for many students.

I prided myself on the fact that come illness, hangover or tiredness, I refused to miss a lecture. Admittedly, I was there in body and not mind for some, but come rain or shine, I turned up to every single lecture of my university life. I did actually skive off one lecture to go to an away midweek game at West Bromwich Albion in my first year but I later discovered that the lecture had been cancelled. I may not have been the most dedicated or hardworking student but I sussed out, Palace permitting, it was worth going to the lectures and hoping that something would stick in my brain.

Anyway, after twenty minutes of watch-watching and mentally weighing up the professional acceptability of walking out of the lecture for football, it finally ended and I dashed off. If traffic was on my side, I could just about make the short trip to Hampton Wick in time to drop off my paperwork and still make the train. As it was, the traffic was ok. I then power-walked to the school, almost breaking out in a run, while desperately trying to read the map that I had printed out. Upon arrival, I quickly checked that my hair looked as respectable as it ever would and buzzed to gain entry to the main reception of the school.

I was welcomed by a large, middle aged, smiling lady. She wore a dress covered with Mickey Mouse faces and embraced me with an overly zealous handshake. She introduced herself as the head teacher. It was immediately evident that she was the kind of head teacher who was very visible to the students; she knew everyone by name and was liked by all. Some head teachers wear a suit and hide in their office, working budgets and booking meetings, having lost sight of the fact that the school should be all about the children and not simply making decisions based on statistics.

I gave her a nervous smile in response to her enthusiastic greeting and introduced myself. Immediately, she broke out into a long spiel about the school and all of the great things that they were doing to enhance the lives of the children who attended. It sounded amazing but I was finding it hard to focus. I wasn't thinking about the expanding playground or the six school trips a year promised to the children or even the support offered to NQTs (Newly Qualified Teachers) and the extensive training program that the borough of Richmond would give. I was thinking, how could I end this conversation politely so that I could get a train to go and watch a game of football?

As she promoted her school, I couldn't help but be impressed by her gusto and desire for improvement. She was interested in what I had to say and believed that her staff should be free to create an environment that they believed in. Staff morale was obviously as important as the children's morale to her. I could imagine myself working for this lady and in this school. I nodded and agreed at the right moments and tried to drop in a few lines that I'd picked up from university and previous placements about how I believed a school should be run, to make myself seem like an intelligent and suitable potential employee. Rather than the football obsessed lunatic I was/am.

While we were chatting, one of her teachers came over to ask her about a certain child. She knew everything about the kid and their situation, so she immediately broke out with some suggestions of how to support the child's needs. The break in conversation gave me the perfect opportunity to look over her shoulder at the clock hanging above the receptionist's desk. 11.35. I just about had time to run to the station and get the train to Selhurst to get the coach. At least I would have done, had another teacher not come and asked for some advice. She too was met with a patient smile and the requested support from her boss.

The short conversation ruined everything. I was going to miss the train. Therefore, I was going to miss the coach. Therefore, I had no idea how I was going to get to Nottingham that evening. Having previously been in awe of this lady, I was beginning to go off her. It seemed to me that her main problem was that she was far too approachable. If only her staff had no respect for her or she was the kind of person who viewed going to your boss for support as failure. But oh no, she had to be the perfect superior and be there to assist all of her staff with little or no concern for a potential employee getting to a game of football. I was wrong. Not everyone liked her. I didn't like her.

As I mulled over my new found irrational hatred of the woman in front of me, I stared in disbelief as the receptionist's clock seemed to go faster and faster until my train had actually left the station. I really couldn't concentrate on the information being placed on me now. I wanted to leave. I wanted to sulk. This wasn't supposed to happen. How could I get out of this? How could I get to Nottingham? Suddenly, she said something that took me out of my Palace-related daydreaming.

"Would you like a tour of the school?"
I took one last look at the clock to double check that I hadn't misread it. Nope, I certainly hadn't so it seemed harmless enough to have a wonder around the school.

She took me on an impressive tour. The children were certainly lucky to attend the school. No money was spared on resources, every classroom was fitted out with the latest technology and the commitment and happiness of its staff was commendable. I might have been feeling that I wanted to work at this school but I certainly wasn't thinking it. I was thinking, *'What is the cheapest way for me to get to Nottingham tonight?'*

Looking back, it seems hard to justify. I was in the middle of one of the most important meetings of my life and all I could think about was how I was going to get to a fairly meaningless football match. I had to work hard to ensure that I didn't let any comments slip out about football as I tried to discuss the school with it's head teacher. Well, she called herself a head teacher but I viewed her more as a dream destroyer.

Eventually, the tour ended and I left with mixed emotions. I was impressed by the school and definitely wanted the job but that wasn't my immediate concern. Getting to Nottingham was. Being polite and boosting my job prospects had been an expensive mistake. I got the bus back home and assessed my options. On the way, I bumped into Jak and our friend, Marco. After laughing at my situation, they followed me back to mine for a cup of tea. I got out my laptop and looked up trains to Nottingham.

I could get a single ticket to Nottingham, watch the game, get the coach back and jump off in Egham for my usual walk to my mother's house. £61.55. F***ing hell. Considering that was the price with a third off thanks to my young person's railcard, it seemed like daylight robbery. I checked the price again on a different website. Inevitably, it was the same price.

"Why don't you ask Chris to drive you?" asked Jak.

It seemed unlikely. Chris had no interest in the game and he had work the next day. He did, however, have a car so it was worth a try. I rang him up.

"Hello,"

"Hi, Chris, eerrm... how are you?"

"What do you want? I'm at work."

"Ah, yes, errm, work, errrm what time do you finish?" I asked, trying to avoid letting the large, cheeky grin that I was giving Jak come across in my voice on the phone.

"3:30, why?"

"errrrm.... do you fancy driving me to Nottingham tonight? (Pause) *I'll pay you £50?"*

There was a pause. I winced and gritted my teeth as Jak, Marco and I waited for his reaction.

"I'll do it for fifty quid."

"Ah wicked! Nice one!"

"Get yourself to Brentford train station for four o'clock and we'll go from there."

Chris' voice hadn't changed from its monotone expression the whole way through the short exchange of words. It was almost as if it were the kind of request that you got every day. I suppose he wasn't exactly surprised to hear me make a Palace related plea. I did worry that we were cutting it a bit fine but I couldn't be too picky. Not only was it saving me a tenner but it also meant that I would be returning home to my own front door. I certainly couldn't think about the money that I'd wasted on the coach or the £50 that I was handing over.

Behavioural addiction consists of a compulsion to repeatedly engage in an action until it causes negative consequences to the person's physical, mental, social, and/or financial well-being. Behaviour persisting in spite of these consequences can be taken as a sign of addiction.

I was going and that was the end of it. I was in no mood to disrespect the challenge.

Chris and I had a good chat on the way up there about all things football. Brentford's season was already over. They'd been promoted the previous year so to be sat securely in mid-table suited them just fine. Our season was alive for all of the wrong reasons. He'd listened to me ramble on about Palace so regularly that he knew our team and the club's predicament quite well.

This was to be my third visit to The City Ground and Nottingham is a city that I quite like. I'd been apprehensive before my first visit thanks to its then-label as the *'Knife-crime capital of England'*. However, I've never encountered anything but friendly locals and welcoming pubs in my experiences of the city. One of the highlights is *Ye Olde Trip to Jerusalem Pub* that incorporates the caves under Nottingham Castle and claims to be the oldest pub in the UK; with proof of its existence dating it back to 1189 – making it precisely 800 years older than me. The pub brews its own ale and although it's turned into somewhat of a drinking tourist attraction, it is still well worth a visit. I like the size of Nottingham as a city too. It is big enough to have a lot going on but it isn't too large to be intimidating for visitors.

I also love the fact that one small area of Nottingham, on the banks of the River Trent, is host to three sporting stadiums. The City Ground, Nottingham Forest, Meadow Lane, Notts County and Trent Bridge, Nottinghamshire County Cricket Club. The three stadiums are just a few hundred metres away from each other and the two Nottingham football clubs are the closest stadiums in the country. Unfortunately, there would be no time to see any of the city on this visit. We were simply going to The City Ground as opposed to going to Nottingham. We were simply there to complete my challenge.

Chris and I ran into traffic going into Nottingham so we only arrived at the ground as the teams were being announced. Chris missed the kickoff as he needed to go and buy a ticket. As a true friend, I obviously refused to go with him to check that he could get a ticket on the day. He may have been willing to drive me all the way there but I wasn't going to put him ahead of the football.

Bob, the Palace fan from Northampton that I'd met in Barnsley, also arrived late and sat with us. In the first half, Palace did ourselves proud and played well. Unfortunately, Forest scored in stoppage time. Their defender, Wes Morgan, scored with a low drive from well outside the area. As Chris and I had a beer each, the half time mood was quiet and flat. Forest were going well in the league and even the most optimistic Palace fan didn't see a way back into the game.

I started to chat to a Palace fan that I'd seen at plenty of away games. I must have had dozens of conversations with him over the previous five years but I have absolutely no idea what his name is. It's the kind of relationship that could only happen at football. I had no interest in becoming friends with him, just as he had no interest in becoming friends with me but we were both so addicted to Palace that we would see each other regularly, chat happily and not care in the slightest about each other's lives outside of the concourses of remote football grounds in the North of England. He summed the situation up perfectly by groaning *"We've done ok but when Wes Morgan scores from 30 yards, it's not your night."*
We finished our pints and headed out for the rest of the match.

Early in the second half, Matt Lawrence stupidly got sent off for a needless handball and we were never in the match after that. Forest got a second late on and should have scored a third but they missed a sitter in stoppage time. Being 2-0 down and out of the game didn't stop the Palace fans cheering the miss as if we were clinging on to a vital lead. Football fans have a bizarre mentality where no matter how down and hurt they may be feeling, they won't show it. They'll admit to their fellow supporters how they're feeling but they'd never let on to the opposition. There's far too much pride in their own image and male testosterone involved to allow for that.

Once again, as with Blackpool, Barnsley and Doncaster, it had been a long trip with little reward. I enjoyed chatting to Chris in the car but I can't help but feel we'd have enjoyed each other's company even more in a London boozer. The game had been flat, the crowd had been flat and the challenge was falling flat. As much as I loved the club and wanted to be there for them, mad dashes up motorways and arriving just in time for kickoff wasn't what I wanted from away games.

I grabbed a couple of beers for the journey home but I decided against drinking them as Chris banned toilet breaks. He wanted to get home. Quickly. Thankfully, the drive home was a lot faster than my journey back from the Midlands with Pavel a few weeks previously. Although, the relief of a shorter journey didn't stop me noticing that my Dad had once again not realised that we were playing. We got back to Twickenham at around half twelve and I set an alarm for 6am the next day. I had plenty of work to do and an interview to prepare for.

Chapter 53 - **Football Stress**

Saturday 27th March 2010, Crystal Palace vs Cardiff, Selhurst Park.

Crystal Palace: Julian Speroni, Clint Hill, Shaun Derry, Patrick McCarthy, Darren Ambrose, Neil Danns, Stern John (Wilfried Zaha, 80), Sean Scannell, Lee Hills, Calvin Andrew, Johannes Ertl
Subs Not Used: Kieran Djilali, James Comley, Alassane N'Diaye, Alex Wynter, Charlie Mann, Jack Holland

Cardiff City: David Marshall, Gavin Rae, Gabor Gyepes, Peter Whittingham, Michael Chopra (Ross McCormack, 89), Steve McPhail, Chris Burke, Tony Capaldi (Mark Kennedy, 60), Paul Quinn, Kelvin Etuhu (Warren Feeney. 75), Darcy Blake
Subs Not Used: Solomon Taiwo, Peter Enckelman, Adam Matthews, Aaron Wildig

It was amazing that despite being in the relegation zone, our defeat at Forest had only been our fifth away loss of the season and three of the teams that had got the better of us were in the top four. The other two had been to Sheffield United and Bristol City – thanks to Rob Shoebridge, whose unbelievable error was looking more and more costly. Unfortunately, our home form wasn't quite so impressive, which left me less than optimistic ahead of our match against sixth placed Cardiff.

Having stayed at Robin's the night before, I headed off to Palace from Putney early as it was a 12:45 kick off thanks to Sky. Robin and I had been out for a drink after my interview the previous day and I still hadn't heard back from the school. I should have been nervously waiting for the life changing phone call but I was far more focussed on Palace getting a vital three points. The early kick off meant that both Dan and Colin were taking their kids to play football so couldn't make the game. I honestly don't understand the mentality of people sometimes. Choosing their children over Palace? Don't the kids have mothers who could have taken them?

I met Jonathan, Kev and his jumper in the Railway Club pre-match after getting six tickets for Sheffield Wednesday away on the last day of the season. Wednesday were four points and two places above us so the game had potential to be huge. However, none of my Palace friends wanted to commit to getting a ticket with eight games left. As,

a)   We could already be relegated by then.

b)   Sheffield was a long way to go if we got ourselves out of trouble before then and it was a 'meaningless' game.

I, however, didn't want to risk missing out on the game and completing my challenge so I bought tickets as soon as they were on sale. I also didn't want to have an anti-climax of finishing my challenge alone. I'd worked bloody hard and spent a lot of money to get to this stage so I wasn't willing to complete the task without friends to celebrate my achievement with. Sure, there would be the regulars who went every week, but they did this every year; going to every game wasn't a challenge for them but an expected yearly achievement. There was also no guarantee that I'd book the same travel as any regulars that I knew so I organised a night in Leeds on the Saturday - before going to Sheffield for the match on the Sunday. I invited Chris and Jak, as real football fans who understood what the challenge had meant to me. I also invited Phill, my mate and boss from the pub, and two plastic Liverpool supporting friends, Martin and Steve. If nothing else, it promised to be a lively weekend away.

Trying to persuade Jonathan and Kev to join me in Sheffield was predictably fruitless. It had been a minor miracle to get Kev to leave the M25 and travel to Bristol earlier in the season. Whereas Jonathan's venture to Clapham Junction and the Falcon had proved to be too far for him. Dan and Colin, using their older and, slightly, wiser heads, had decided to wait and see what the game meant before making any decisions about going.

It was only after getting the important business of the Sheffield game out of the way that I began to tell my companions in the pub about my Teaching interview from the previous day at the Hampton Wick school. An interview that I'd taken a lot more seriously than my Wetherspoons one in the previous July – although the same 'magic' suit had come out and no-one had said that I looked like a 'twat' for wearing it this time. Boosted by the confidence gained from nobody insulting my suit, I felt that the interview had gone reasonably well.

With the early start, we only had one pint before heading to the ground. As always with lunchtime kickoffs, the atmosphere felt flat. Fans haven't had enough time to recover from the previous night's hangover, let alone lubricate their throats sufficiently to allow for constant vocal support.

Palace dominated the first half, despite falling behind after just four minutes. Ambrose had two great efforts saved and Clint Hill had a header that cannoned off the bar but we still managed to go into the break with a one-nil deficit. At half time the three of us headed upstairs to the Red'n'Blue bar for a quick beer and we were all frustrated beyond belief. It just felt like the game and our season were slipping away from us. The players were giving everything and it was all to no avail.

After the restart, Palace continued to dominate. Stern John had what looked like a stone wall penalty turned down.
"S*** Refs! We always get s*** refs!" echoed around Selhurst Park and was sung with a mixture of anger, frustration, hatred and desperation. Of course we didn't always get s*** refs. Well, no more than any other football team in the history of the game, but, at that moment, it certainly felt like it.

We needed someone to blame. The players were as dedicated as the fans with their relentless efforts so they were untouchable. Jordan or Warnock would have been obvious candidates for the blame and hatred but they weren't there thanks to varying degrees of incompetence and selfishness. Blaming Cardiff, who, as we'd learnt at their ground, were quick enough to blame other people, would have been acceptable but the Welsh side simply happened to be the opponents who were benefiting from our lack of fire-power and distressed situation. They couldn't be blamed, yet. Although, it would have only taken the slightest bit of time wasting or play acting or a provocative chant to redirect the wrath of the home crowd. But no, the only person suitable for vile threats and abusive obscenities, which would be seen as entirely unacceptable in any other walk of life, was the referee.

Eventually, just as we were beginning to give up hope, we scored. Clint Hill, presumably because Dan wasn't there to distract him with calls to open his barbecue, managed to send a bullet header past the goalkeeper from a Darren Ambrose corner. I leapt up and punched the air in front of me. Weeks of pent up anger came out in one moment. I jumped and stamped and screamed and swore and punched and kicked.

The players dived on our latest hero and clenched their fists to the crowd as they too released the frustration and disappointment of the last few weeks and months. The celebrations lasted for what seemed like an age. I turned to Kev, grabbed him with both hands and screamed "Come on!" in his face. He grabbed me and did the same back. In our minds, it was a hug that showed mutual affection and relief for the team. If we did the same action in a pub or in the street, away from the context of scoring a goal, people would have waded in to pull as apart, assuming we were fighting. However, we were as far from fighting as you could be. We were celebrating. Aggressively celebrating, but celebrating nonetheless. And harmless with it. No one was in danger; we were simply physically releasing the emotion of the goal.

I don't think any other sport could provoke an action like that. Certainly not for an equalising moment in a second tier match, which wouldn't even decide the outcome of the game, let alone the season or the tournament. It was purely the frustration of going over 190 minutes without a goal. Imagine a tennis player going 190 minutes without winning a point or a cricketer going 190 minutes without hitting a run. It wouldn't happen. Their scores are too regular. If it did, then maybe then the crowd and players of those sports might grab each other and punch the air and lose the plot a whole lot more. The rarity of a goal is what makes it all so special. There really is nothing else like it.

Selhurst was now in full voice. Hangovers had been forgotten and there was a belief about the place. However, ten minutes later, we conceded. It came indirectly from a free kick, which should never have been awarded in the first bloody place. I checked the programme to make sure that it wasn't Mr Shoebridge who was officiating, but I couldn't even blame him. I couldn't blame Paul Hart either. He'd selected a team to try and attack and they'd done that for most of the game, yet we still found ourselves behind.

It was then that I decided to look at the subs to try and plan our great escape. Charlie Mann, a goalkeeper, aged 19, Alex Wynter, a defender, aged 18, Jack Holland, a defender, aged 18, Kieran Djilali, a winger, aged 18, James Comley, a midfielder, aged 19, Wilfried Zaha, a striker, aged 17 and Alassane N'Diaye, the 21-year old midfielder who'd played so well at the start of the season. Other than N'Diaye, who'd played less than twenty professional games himself, they had a mere nine professional appearances between them. If anyone doubted the task in hand, they only needed to look at that bench. For the first time, I felt huge sympathy for Paul Hart and the task that he'd taken on. What I would have done to have Dougie Freedman named amongst the substitutes.

The only one who was thrown on was Wilfried Zaha, for his first professional appearance. I knew a little about him as he had scored quite a few goals in the FA Youth Cup that season. Being a football addict, I tried to follow and watch Palace at every level. Seeing the under 18s and trying to get a glimpse of the future seemed like a perfectly legitimate use of my limited spare time. Zaha went on one exciting run where he beat a couple of players but then he ran out of space as the ball went for a goal kick.

Alex Wynter's debut at Sheffield Wednesday had given me a huge sense of pride but this was different. This didn't seem like the latest local lad to be given his big chance. This stank of desperation and reminded me of all of the local youngsters that Coppell had used during our first administration, who frankly, were out of their depth. No one who saw his debut could have possibly predicted that three years later, he would sign for Manchester United for £15million and become Sir Alex Ferguson's final signing.

Despite being the better side for most of the match, once we fell 2-1 behind, the game slowly eased away from us. At the end of the game, we stayed to applaud every Palace player off the pitch. Once they'd disappeared down the tunnel, I turned to Kev, we both shook our heads and I gave a huge puff of my cheeks. We now had no wins in six (or one in thirteen if you went back further) and we couldn't see where the next result was going to come from.

Jonathan, Kev and I slowly sauntered our way to the Railway Club. It wasn't even that we needed beer for once. Admittedly, drinking until we forgot about Palace's whole sorry situation would have been a good way to cheer us up. However, going to the pub on this occasion wasn't about getting pissed or trying to make the most out of a bad day. It was about following the other results. The benefit of playing at midday on the Saturday is that you can put pressure on the teams around you by winning. Managers of the title chasing clubs often moan about when their games are played as they don't want their rivals to have any kind of psychological advantage. However, we'd been given the perfect chance to up the heat on the teams above us and we'd blown it. In fact, we'd given everyone a lift, just before they kicked off at three o'clock. Their results would be just as important as our own.

Our latest loss had left the table looking like this:

Position	Team	Played	Goal Difference	Points
19	Scunthorpe United	38	-19	44
20	Sheffield Wednesday	39	-16	43
21	Watford	37	-9	42
22	Crystal Palace	39	-5	39
23	Plymouth Argyle	38	-15	37
24	Peterborough United	39	-25	30

Watford were home to mid-table Middlesbrough, Wednesday had to travel to mid table Coventry and Plymouth, who had gone on an amazing run to give themselves a chance, were home to playoff chasing Blackpool. All three were winnable games for our rivals. Scunthorpe weren't playing until the next day.

Late on in the second half, tension was high in our South London pub. We'd had a few beers, which left our nerves like jelly but it was the results that made us feel sick. Watford and Sheffield Wednesday were both winning and Plymouth were holding out for a draw. Sky Sports News was doing the maths for us and it wasn't looking good. We were set to be five points adrift of safety, having played more games than both of the two teams directly above us.

Thankfully, it all changed. First, Middlesbrough equalised against Watford. Like ourselves, it sounded like Watford had raised their game so being pegged back was heart breaking for them. Next, Plymouth fell behind. It was the least important of the three games but it was still worthy of a cheer.

"Another pint boys?" I asked with a smile.

"Why not?" came the grinning response.

As I turned to head to the bar, there was a loud cheer. Jeff Stelling had sent the attention of Soccer Saturday to The Ricoh Arena. Coventry had equalised. Suddenly, I didn't care how bloody depressive the place was, I loved it. For the second time in a couple of hours, I was jumping and screaming and punching the air. We'd been let off big time. I dare say the goal was celebrated with more passion and emotion in South London than it was in the dead Midlands town where it happened. The idea of being sent there had been torturous a few weeks previously, but I now wanted to run there by foot and kiss anyone and everyone connected to the place.

Suddenly, my pocket buzzed.

"Hello!" I screamed down the phone, still excited at the goal.

The lady on the other end of the line spoke with a lot more calmness, professionalism and authority than my over-excited squeaking "Oh hello, Is that James Howland speaking? It is Mrs Wilson here, you had an interview with us yesterday."

S***! I'm glad to say that although this was my first thought, I refrained from saying it out loud. In all the excitement of the football, I hadn't even thought about the fate of my career. I ran outside the pub so that I could hear her properly.

It turned out that I didn't get the job. They'd interviewed six of us for two positions. One was a full time role and one was an eight month maternity cover. I was offered the maternity cover but I'd already decided that I didn't want that as it wouldn't see me through my NQT year. It was still early in the job hunting process and I didn't want to limit myself to a short term role.

I returned into the pub and told Kev and Jonathan. They agreed that it sounded like a reasonable decision and then we turned our attention back to the football. After the games had ended and we were finishing our pints, I turned to Kev. *"Why do you insist on wearing that jumper?"*
It was the first and only time that I'd questioned my friend on his match day attire.
"I wore this jumper when we won 4-1 away at Southampton," he replied.
I looked at him. That wasn't even the first time that he'd worn it. Far from it. It was nearly ten years old by the time that it had made the short trip down to the south coast. But to Kev, the jumper was lucky. No amount of losses or jokes from his friends could deter him. The jumper, and its so-called luck, was here to stay. However illogical, uncomfortable or unlucky it became.

Later that evening, I went to meet Chris in Twickenham to continue my drinking. The other results had gone our way and I now intended to drink heavily until I forgot all about Palace's sorry situation.

Brentford's season might have been over for a long time but that would never stop a football fan from going. Chris had seen his side beat Leyton Orient 1-0 that day. During the previous season, I'd moaned about going to so many meaningless games as Palace languished in mid-table but I was actually quite jealous of Chris – I'd have loved to have a stress-free match to attend. Non-football fans wouldn't be able to understand his logic of going.

My friend Ash, who'd hated the Plymouth game, joined us and out of politeness, he tried to take an interest and build up a football based conversation with Chris.
"What was the score at your game?"
"We won 1-0!" Chris replied, flatly.
"That's good. So what does that do for you?" asked Ash, desperately trying to sound enthusiastic.
"Not much!" Chris replied, flatly.
"Ah, well at least you didn't lose. That would have been a disaster?" continued Ash, trying to gain some understanding of the purpose of Chris' expensive day out.
"Meh" Chris replied, flatly.

Ash didn't get football. He doesn't like football but even he could see why I was investing my time and money into Palace's season. He could see on my face what it meant. He could understand that if we kept losing, we'd get relegated. If we got relegated, the club would lose money and players and I'd have to watch worse teams and there'd be smaller crowds. He could see why I went. I was watching a team trying to achieve something.

However, he had no idea why Chris was still bothering to watch a team that had nothing to play for in matches that he didn't seem to care about. To him, it was like continuing to play Cluedo once someone had worked out the murderer and they'd been locked away. As far as he could see, Chris was a detective, wondering around an empty crime scene – I guess the price of football tickets does leave fans feeling like they've been robbed sometimes. All the mystery and excitement of the crime scene had gone and as far as police work went, being there was pointless.

What Ash didn't get was that although Brentford's season was petering out, going to the football was about a lot more than the ninety minutes on the pitch. Despite his apathetic feelings towards the end-of-season matches, Chris wasn't able to give up his Saturday routine. He still wanted an excuse to go to the pub with his mates (although, I suppose you can do that without football but afternoon drinking is more socially accepted if there's a game involved). Chris still wanted something to cheer and even if he cared less for the outcome, he still cared. He still wanted a referee to scream abuse at and blame for all that's wrong with the world, even if he did it with slightly less venom than he would if the result really mattered. He still needed an escape from real life and he still needed to feed his addiction.

Chris still got all of the ingredients that make football so important to so many, but he got it without the tension. The binding agent. Without anxiety and stress, football loses its edge. It becomes simply something to do, like going to the theatre or cinema. Losing becomes an irritation rather than a devastation and winning becomes pleasant rather than euphoric, and when that becomes the case, you know that it is time for the season to end. You need a chance to re-charge over the summer and the new season to arrive for a fresh chance to feel invincible or distraught each Saturday. Because when you stop caring so much about the result, football becomes an expensive pass time as opposed to a brainwashing way of life. However, the routine and escapism of football stays and fans continue to attend matches without questioning the use of their time.

In a way, football fans can never be happy. If you're stuck in mid table, football is boring and simply a hobby that you attend out of routine. If you're in a promotion or a relegation scrap, it's all too intense and takes up far more thinking and worrying time than could possibly be considered healthy. Chris was longing for a meaningful match and I was longing for a meaningless match. I'd not only had the stress, and false dawn, and ultimate disappointment of our game, but I'd then had to sit through another ninety minutes of frustration, panic and relief, listening to the scores of three more matches. The next day, I would need to desperately follow the result of the Scunthorpe game while I was at work. At least Chris could happily watch Brentford without giving a toss about any other team in the division.

The fact that I was having to up my hours ahead of giving up my pub job when I started my teaching placement and the fact that my assignment deadlines were now only days away and the fact that I was frantically writing job applications and preparing for interviews, while at the same time I was looking to buy my first car (and not only so I could drive myself to Nottingham in the future), didn't seem to matter. All I could think about was my addiction. All I could focus on was my beloved Palace and their battle to not only stay up, but to stay alive.

Wilfried was brought to my notice by Dougie. I listened to his opinion of Wilfried's abilities and as I have never been afraid of putting talented young players in the 1st team so we gave it a go. He did really well and a star was born.

He is still a very good player and, in my opinion, he is currently at the right club.

Paul Hart

Chapter 54 - **Do or Die**

Tuesday 30th March 2010, Watford vs Crystal Palace, Vicarage Road

Crystal Palace: Julian Speroni, Johnny Ertl, Patrick McCarthy, Claude Davis, Lee Hills, Shaun Derry (Matt Lawrence 20), Darren Ambrose, Neil Danns, Sean Scannell (Nicky Carle 80), Stern John (Alassane N'Diaye 90), Calvin Andrew.
Subs Not Used: Manns, Lee, Comley, Zaha.

Watford Loach, Adrian Mariappa, DeMerit, Taylor (Hoskins 84), Doyley, Lansbury, Cowie (Graham 68), Cleverley, Eustace, Helguson, Buckley.
Subs Not Used: Lee, McGinn, Harley, Noble, Hodson.

Position	Team	Played	Goal Difference	Points
18	Queens Park Rangers	39	-5	47
19	Scunthorpe United	39	-18	47
20	Sheffield Wednesday	40	-17	44
21	Watford	38	-9	43
22	Crystal Palace	39	-5	39
23	Plymouth Argyle	39	-17	37
24	Peterborough United	40	-26	30

Scunthorpehad beaten Sheffield United on the Sunday and left the table looking somewhat bleaker than it had at five o'clock on Saturday evening. The maths was easy. A Year Three class could work it out. Lose, and we would be seven points behind Watford, five behind Sheffield Wednesday and eight away from QPR and Scunthorpe. Win, and we were right back into the mix.

Kev, John, Colin, Jonathan, Dan, Steve and I met up at 4:30 at The Falcon for a couple of pints. We all knew the stakes. Anything but a win would see us all but down.

"In some ways, a draw would be worse!" claimed Dan *"Because we'd convince ourselves that we had a chance but deep down, we'd know."*

As football fans, we knew that it wasn't failure that would kill us. It was hope and expectancy. We didn't dare to believe that we could win.

We nervously drank our pints and tried to build up to the game. It was nearly impossible. This meant too much. I wasn't looking forward to the match. I was looking forward to seeing my mates. It had been a long time since all seven of us had been to a game, let alone an away game. I was desperate to know the result. I needed to know it. Could we survive? Who would step up? Who would make the difference? However, the actual ninety minutes of football was something I dreaded. It would be tense, it would be nervous and it could quite possibly give me a heart attack.

One attitude that had softened was our feelings towards Paul Hart. Dan summed it up well by saying *"I can't help but begin to like him. I still think he's useless as a manager but he's such a nice guy that I have to pander to the press's*

image of him and quite like him,"
And he was right. Hart hadn't been our first choice to replace Warnock and he had done very little to prove that he should have been since being appointed. However, he clearly had a nearly impossible job and, like the players that he'd inherited, he was giving it everything. He was now one of us and in on the fight. For the majority of football fans, that's enough to win them over.

We left the pub at about half five and headed to catch our train, stopping off at the Sainsburys in the station to pick up some beer for the journey. For reasons unknown to myself or any other football fan, Colin and John decided to relive previous away days and got themselves a bottle of wine to share. The queue in the shop was long and, waiting outside, Dan, Kev, Jonathan and I began to panic. Steve had made his way to the front of the line but seemed to be stalling. We called over to him to hurry up but he seemed to be stuck. He had our whip round so he couldn't be short of money. We'd each put £20 in.

Eventually, he got served. By this time, we only had one minute to catch our train. We ran. Sprinting through a station is always difficult but charging through the UK's busiest train station during rush hour was nigh on impossible. True to football fans stereotype, we pushed our way through the crowds and dived onto the packed train, unfortunately losing Steve in the process. I've been to Watford more than I've attended any other football ground as an away supporter and not once, despite written complaints from myself and other fans, have Southern Rail decided to run an extra train or at least put more carriages on the inadequate half-hourly service that they do bother to run.

The result is a highly uncomfortable and almost dangerous journey. For the football fans, this is certainly not a pleasant experience. However, if I was a commuter with a season ticket for this ride, I would be fuming. The rail company are effectively selling them something that isn't fit for purpose. By the time the train reaches Imperial Wharf, where no one gets off as they're all going to the football, nobody else can get onto the train.

If animals were transported in this overcrowded manner, there would be campaigns from animal rights protestors to make it illegal. However, football fans often seem to be treated as equal to or lower than animals. It is bad enough on the tube but it is difficult to see how the underground could create a more regular service and visible efforts have been made to reduce the demand on the capital's overworked system. However, having eight carriage trains rather than four would make a huge difference to the safety and comfort of the journey between Clapham Junction and Watford on match days. Unfortunately, Southern Rail know that they will get their money regardless and no changes to their timetable for Watford games are forthcoming.

Not only would I be travelling for the next forty minutes with my nostrils shoved into somebody else's armpit, but we would also be without the beer that meant we'd nearly missed the train in the first place. Steve was nowhere to be seen. Had he missed it? Colin gave him a call.
"Alright mate, where's our beer?" Not where are you? Or did you make the train?

No, we had important issues to discuss. We wanted our beer, which was certainly more important than Steve.

"I'm on the next carriage," he explained. Brilliant. He may have been only twenty foot away from us but there was little or no chance of getting our booze now.

"What took you so long?" enquired a frustrated Colin, beginning to show his disapproval at Steve's carelessness to be separated from us while in possession of two of the most vital elements of an away day. The whip and the booze.

"Nectar points. Dee (his wife) *would kill me if I didn't get them. We're saving up for a holiday. Their machine wouldn't work"*

Colin shook his head and put the phone down. We'd nearly been the first people, anywhere in the world, to miss a football match so their mate could get some bloody supermarket points. I hope the £15 worth of points would have been worth it for his wife had we not made the train. Come to think of it, I refuse to believe the points made enough of a contribution towards their holiday to make it worth us being separated from the booze at all.

Soon, the train was rocking with song. I genuinely felt sorry for any commuters who'd had three thousand football fans added to their journey home from work. However, we were heading to the biggest game that we'd had in years and we needed to warm up our vocal chords. Mid-song, Colin started to scramble around next to me to try and free his arm so that he could get his phone from his pocket.

"Steve, what's up?" he shouted, pushing his phone against his ear to try and hear his mate. He burst out laughing before ending the call and struggling to get his phone back into his pocket.

"He wanted to know which carriage we're in. He reckons he's going to come and join us," explained Colin. There we were, so packed in on the train that we could barely free our arms to get to our pockets and Steve reckoned he was going to push his way through two carriages. There are plenty of words that I can use to describe Steve and I think the only polite one at that moment was 'optimistic'.

After forty long minutes, we arrived in Watford, stinking from the train and ready for a drink. Steve came and met us on the platform. Unsurprisingly, he hadn't managed to fight his way through the crowd but we were relieved that he'd restrained himself from drinking all of the beer on the journey. Between the station and the pub, we downed our beers, while John and Colin downed their wine. I've previously explained why I don't think I'm an alcoholic but I'm unsure that those two could have made a convincing argument if they'd been observed during our short walk.

We headed to the Wetherspoons in the town centre and relived memories of a playoff game from a few years previously. We'd lost the first leg 3-0 and approached the second match with a carefree atmosphere of having an end of season party. By the time kickoff arrived and plenty of beer had been sunk, we'd convinced ourselves that we were going to turn the match around and make our way to Wembley. A conga of Palace fans marched out of the pub and towards the ground in celebration to the bemusement of the on-looking Watford supporters. The match was flat and our players gave very little fight. It was 0-0 on the night and Watford went on to win at Wembley.

It could be argued that was the evening that our slippery slope towards administration began. What we didn't know at the time was that Jordan had gambled on promotion and failure to achieve our goal would result in the immediate selling of players as debt built, year on year.

This fixture was as far removed from that evening as possible. For the play-off game, we had an underachieving and overpaid side, who lacked the bottle and the commitment needed to succeed at any level of football. At least we arrived at Vicarage Road for this game with a team who would fight for every tackle and challenge for every header and give sweat and blood for the cause.

Both evenings had a sense of hopelessness about them. We were never likely to come from 3-0 down to get a result and we were unlikely to suddenly turn our form around and win the biggest game of the season so far. However, whereas hopelessness had allowed us to relax four years previously and try and enjoy the game for what it was, it was that same emotion that meant this game was not for enjoying but for the important business of getting a vital result. A loss could effectively relegate us and the prospect weighed heavily on our shoulders.

However, relegation happens to twelve football league teams every year in England. That hurts football fans but they can deal with that. They have to or there'd be thousands of football fans hurling themselves off the top of their respective town halls all over the country each May. However, this was more than relegation. This was about saving the club. Each week, the administrator was reminding us that if no buyer was found at the end of the season, the club would be forced to fold. A chilling thought.

The atmosphere in the 'spoons was good but not as lively as previous years. We were all too nervous for that. Although it felt positively spacious compared to the train journey, the pub was packed so we bought a double round with the whip. We also decided to have our traditional chaser just before leaving the pub. John and I went to the bar and asked for seven different shots. We returned with a tray of pink, yellow, green, brown, red, blue and black coloured liquids. 25ml of each. The guys shook their heads. We downed them and headed to the ground.

We all let out loud 'EAGLESSSSSS' shouts as we made the short walk to the ground. By the time the game kicked off, the away end was in full voice. We'd been restricted to just over two thousand tickets but we could have easily taken double or triple that. On my first visit to Watford, we'd been given the whole Vicarage Road stand, which holds 5000 people, but since then, the police had restricted us to just one half of the stand. It was a ridiculous situation where the ground had five thousand empty seats, the demand was there to buy them and the police weren't willing to let them be sold. The result was that there were some away fans in the home end and people turning up without tickets, which has to be a more dangerous situation than simply allowing more away fans into the ground. There has never been any kind of history of trouble with Palace fans at Watford but the Hertfordshire Police force seem to target our games as 'high risk'. I guess I shouldn't complain, at least the police noticed the fans, unlike the train companies.

However, the benefit of the limited tickets was that we were all packed into a smaller area and the noise we created was more concentrated and coordinated. In a larger crowd, it can be difficult to organise everyone to be singing the same song, at the same time, at the same pace. However, being restricted to 2000 loyal fans meant that we could make one hell of a racket. The Palace fans started before kickoff and continued throughout. If we were going down, nobody could accuse us of not playing our part. There were long renditions of 'We're the Red and Blue Army' (to the tune of The White Stripes' Seven Nation Army) and the 'We Love You' chant.

Eventually, the dreaded ninety minutes were upon us. Watford came flying out the blocks. However, we weren't going to let Watford's supremacy on the pitch stop us singing. There was a famous game in our previous administration away at Norwich, which was rumoured at the time to be our final ever match due to the financial crisis that we found ourselves in. Coppell took a team of kids to Norfolk and we won 1-0 in front of a devoted crowd. Many Palace fans speak of it as being the greatest Palace atmosphere of all time thanks to the togetherness of the occasion. This was the equivalent for our second administration. No matter what happened on the pitch, we were there and we wanted everyone to know it.

The Hornets buzzed around our box as they made wave after wave of attack. We barely left our own half. It wasn't as if we were trying to be defensive. We simply couldn't get the ball off our opponents. If I wasn't so focussed on singing, I'm sure that my fingernails would have disappeared within the first twenty minutes and my frustration would have built. I was sweating with fear and singing and clapping and shouting. It was all I could do to focus my nervous energy. If I stopped encouraging the team, I would physically need to replace the action or I would simply stand there shaking, feeling sick, just like a drug addict when he hasn't had his fix.

Our cause became an even harder task when our captain, Shaun Derry, was forced off the pitch after twenty minutes with an injury. Thankfully, a couple of injuries had eased up since the weekend and we had the experienced Matt Lawrence to come on. I take more pride than most in youngsters getting their chance at Palace but this was no stage for a kid.

All of the action was at the far end of the pitch and it was hard to tell what was going on. Watford players and fans rose as one to claim for a penalty early on as the ball struck Paddy McCarthy. My heart froze, the whole ground seem to freeze, but the chant of 'We're the Red and Blue Army!' continued. And so did the play. Suddenly, the referee was my favourite person in the ground. Occasionally, very occasionally, referees can have that effect. Of course, he could easily change himself into a wanker of Rob Shoebridge proportions at any moment.

Watford continued to attack but Speroni stood tall in goal. It was hard to tell from the far end how impressive or routine each save that he made was, but every time he gathered the ball, I breathed a huge sigh of relief, although the Palace crowd were relentless. They didn't even stop singing to applaud individual moments. We were there for the badge and no one is bigger than that.

"We're the Red and Blue Army,
We're the Red and Blue Army,
We're the Red and Blue Army,
We're the Red and Blue Army,
We're the Red and Blue Army,
We're the Red and Blue Army,"

It was almost robotic. It was as if the Palace fans believed that any pause for breath would give Watford a chance to score. We couldn't risk a break in song.

My predicted heart attack can't have been far away midway through the half. Watford's centre back sent a header towards our net. It seemed a certain goal. My heart flew up into my mouth. Somehow, Speroni managed to turn it onto the bar. Minutes later, Watford's Manchester United loanee, Tom Cleverley, hit a fierce effort at goal from outside the area. It sailed past Speroni and once again, my heart did somersaults and visited parts of my body that it had no right to visit. The ball crashed against the crossbar. We'd been let off again. As a child playing in goal, I always used to give the woodwork a 'lucky touch' before games in the hope that it would be on my side. Speroni had obviously given the bar a tap and earned his fortune that day.

"We're the Red and Blue Army!" The chanting was relentless.

The near misses only served to crank the away fans up another couple of notches. It hadn't mattered whether either of their attempts had gone in or not, we were not going to stop singing. I knew this atmosphere was something special. I'd never felt anything like it before. If this was to be one of our last ever games, we were making sure that we were noticed on the way out. The players certainly seemed to be lifted by it.

Just before half time, in a rare Palace attack, Johnny Ertl hit a cross into the Watford penalty area. The Watford keeper started to come for it and then retreated. His hesitance was the chance we needed. He was in no man's land as the ball fell to Stern John. The cross was slightly behind him but he managed to lean back and nod it into the unguarded net. Finally, the away end stopped singing. It erupted. The seven of us found ourselves in a big group hug. Strangers jumped on top of us. Steve picked me up from the hips and threw me in the air. You often hear the phrase in football of there being 'pandemonium in the stands' and this moment was exactly that.

We felt every emotion imaginable. We shouted every word possible and even made up a few. Our voices were croaking from the previous singing but we found new chords to scream. I would love to give you some words to describe the joy and relief and excitement and nervousness of that moment, but I genuinely don't think there are any words to explain it. I guess that is why so many usually eloquent and educated football fans can be seen shouting 'F***ing YESS!' in such moments. When there is no way of being precise in your release of emotion, you might as well stick to the simplest of words. F***ing YESSSS

It is fair to say that Stern John's move to Palace hadn't worked out. He had gone eight months without a goal, his attitude and appetite had been questioned and he was taking a huge wage. There'd been rumours of us trying to get him to walk away from his contract but we couldn't afford to pay it up. John had a clause in his contract that meant he would get a pay rise after playing a certain amount of games. When he was one match away from this landmark, the administrator decided, understandably, to ban him from playing. Eventually, thanks to us being so short of players, Hart, the administrator and John came to an agreement where he would sacrifice the extra money and he had been allowed to play again. The change of attitude in John summed up the ethic of the players at the time and his actions were justified for that moment. Suddenly, from being hated all season, John was the hero. He deservedly milked the new-found love from the crowd.

The party continued into half time. Sometimes, once a team takes the lead, the nerves of having something to lose can dampen the atmosphere. Not on that night. Not a chance. The words to our song were simple but they summed up our thoughts perfectly.

"We love you, We love you, We love you,
and where you play...
We follow, We follow, We follow,
cos we support...
The Palace, The Palace, The Palace,
and that's the way...
We like it, We like it, We like it!"

Followed by the screaming of a *'wooah wooah wooah'* and as much scarf waving, hand clapping, fist clenching and leg jumping as our bodies would physically allow.

The words spoke of our emotion and the second part showed it. We did love Palace and following them around the country was how we liked to spend our time. The celebration afterwards was to show that we had no intention of letting Jordan or Agilo or anyone else ruin our club. We would continue to sing that song for years afterwards but I will forever associate it with that evening in Watford.

The second half started in the same way as the first. Watford hit the woodwork again. This time it was the post. From a breakaway, just after our latest let off, the ball was crossed into the Watford area and our young winger,

Sean Scannell rose to win a rare header. However, this time, it was our turn to watch in horror as the ball came back off the post. He'd fallen over after winning the original header but fortunately, our luck was better than Watford's. It bounced back perfectly to him and, despite being on the floor, he managed to hook the ball into the empty net. We went mad. I jumped onto the back of the seat in front of me and punched the air. Jonathan grabbed me and held me tight. With my head trapped between his large arms, I continued to jump. Again, it would look ridiculous in any other setting. People would be evicted from Wimbledon if they reacted to an Andy Murray forehand smash in a similar style. Yet there was two thousand fans reacting in a 'F***ing YESSSS' manner.

Suddenly, we were in dangerous territory. Suddenly, we were in a position that we hadn't even considered when we were at The Falcon three hours previously. Suddenly, against all odds and against the run of play, we were 2-0 up and had something to lose. If we'd been 2-0 down, it would have hurt, but we'd still be singing and the feeling of pride would have seen me through the night. However, at 2-0 up, I would be a wreck right up until full time. I was still shaking five minutes after the goal.

"We love you, We love you, We love you...."

Looking back, I'm not sure that the continued singing was a sign of defiance to administration as it had been in Newcastle. I'm not sure it was a sign of pride as it had been against Villa or even desperate encouragement as it had been against Cardiff. I think it was simply a case of not being able to stop. If I wasn't singing and thinking of that, I don't think I could have dared to watch the remaining half hour.

A shell shocked Watford tried to get back into the game. They'd already thrown the kitchen sink at us but they now started to rip up the plumbing and throw the pipes too. They had one attack down our right hand side, where their winger beat Ertl and drove into the area towards the unmarked Watford striker. Both Matt Lawrence and Paddy McCarthy threw themselves in front of the ball. It cannoned off the pair of them and bounced out for a corner. They both jumped to their feet, grabbed each other by the neck, slammed their bodies together, thumped each other's back and then punched the air towards the away crowd. That is what staying up and fighting for the club meant to the players. I have never seen such an act of raw passion between two professional footballers on the pitch before or since. Every time I ever doubt the attitude of footballers, I think back to that moment and beam with pride.

With twenty minutes left, Neil Danns put us 3-0 up, sparking wild celebrations. The away end had been rocking throughout but we were now in full festival mood.

"WE LOVE YOU! WE LOVE YOU! WE LOVE YOU!"

The pressure was off. We could have the party that we'd desired in that playoff game. It was our turn to cruise to a victory in the most vital of matches.

Watford did pull one back and Lee Hills was sent off late on but nothing could stop our party. The players came right over to the away end at full time to celebrate like we'd won the cup. Johnny Ertl and Neil Danns stayed out the longest, taking the applause of the crowd with their arms aloft in victory. They knew what the game had meant and they'd raised their performance for the moment. With the tiny squad and the run of fixtures we had, they must have been exhausted. It wasn't that they put in any extra effort that night; they simply found something inside themselves. Indisputable guts. Players often speak about the crowd giving them a lift and how important they are but there seemed to be a genuine sincerity in their voices as they praised us after the game. Paul Hart almost looked in shock during his post-match press conference as he spoke of the crowd.

After the game, we went to Beavers for a celebratory beer. Dan had more than a drink as we all chipped in for a birthday present for our mate, as if the Palace victory wasn't enough. I still hadn't calmed down when we returned to Clapham Junction. It will always be the greatest atmosphere of my Palace supporting life. We simply had to win. And we did.

Dan and I got a can of Leicestershire bitter and then headed home. I couldn't sleep that night. It wasn't the alcohol. Compared to some games, I'd drunk a lot less. The game had been about far more than getting drunk. I just had the tune of 'We're the Red and Blue Army' echoing round and round in my head. I watched Sky Sports News on loop, waiting for the brief highlights to come up each hour. I was searching the BBS for anything I could find about the game. Videos, quotes, discussion, anything would do. Whatever happened at the end of the season, it had been a special night. Older fans were discussing if it was the greatest atmosphere ever at a Palace game. Younger ones, such as myself, had nothing to compare it to. Videos popped up on Youtube but no amounts of microphones or technology could do it justice. I'm sure it wasn't the loudest crowd ever recorded but it wasn't volume that made it so special. It was the heart behind it.

Nothing could catch the emotion and consistency and genuine feeling in which the Palace crowd sung that night. If you could bottle up football emotion and sell it, you would be a very rich man. It is not a feeling that you can get anywhere else. To be honest, the genuine 'F***ing YESSSS' moments are hard to find. They are unique. Winning a trophy or a promotion *could* happen every year. The blind faith in that is what keeps you going each season. However, with success, you have a chance to prepare for it. The actual clinching game is the result of a whole year's worth of build up, natural highs and anticipation. There's no major swing in emotion or element of surprise to it.

Also, clubs that win trophies have either had the feeling plenty of times before or are so shocked by the whole experience that they don't know how to enjoy it until it is too late and the moment has gone. I've been guilty of feeling underwhelmed by promotions as a Palace fan. I expect something to change. I expect to feel different but I don't. I feel proud and happy and satisfied, of course I do. But I don't have the feeling that I got in Watford that night. That pure emotion. Pure elation.

When we win, I think football fans look for a meaning to it all and there isn't one. It simply means that your team was less crap than all the other teams that year. It is not life changing. Not usually anyway. However, that night in Watford, losing the match could have lost us the club. Losing the match could have genuinely changed the life of every Palace fan around the globe.

Unlike the Watford game, cup finals and title deciders aren't desperate occasions. Win or lose, they're to be enjoyed and remembered. The worst that you can achieve is second. A frustrating closeness to victory but a commendable effort nonetheless. It hurts at the time but it softens and you are left with a memorable occasion and a feeling of pride. The only clubs who don't feel that are the big clubs, who more often than not, will be able to erase the losing memory the following year when they inevitably get the trophy that they were so tantalisingly close to the year before. It is not a pain that they have to hold onto for years of growing bitterness. Losing a match at the bottom offers no pride, no memorable occasion and leaves a scar that runs deep into the following season.

Winning also brings arrogance and smugness. Traits which are not to be admired and as a supporter of a crap club, displaying them would turn yourself into everything that you despise about the big clubs. Fear of turning into the monster is sometimes overcompensated for with an attempt to not over celebrate and lack class. Winning gives you a responsibility to enjoy the result without acting like a tosser. Whereas, when you're down the bottom, you don't care what anyone else thinks. It's pure, uncontained joy that can be displayed however you wish. Digs from armchair supporters that you haven't actually achieved anything can be rejected with self righteous rants such as this one that they 'simply wouldn't understand' and are missing out.

No, moments of pure 'F***ing YESSSS' can only be found when there is something to lose. You haven't lost a cup in a cup final because you never 'had it'. Whereas when you're at the bottom of the league, you have a league status and then it is taken away from you. Winning at the bottom is an entirely different feeling to winning at the top. It is unexpected and something that offers relief, which has all been underlined with a feeling of injustice and anger. We certainly had that. It had been aimed at Rob Shoebridge up until Christmas but it was now firmly at the feet of Simon Jordan, Neil Warnock and Agilo.

The element of surprise is also vital. You expect to win when you're good. However, you learn to expect nothing from your side when you support a crap team. You can plan how you will feel after a cup final as there are only two possible outcomes. You can prepare strategies of how to cope with success and failure and plan actions accordingly. However, I genuinely don't know how I'd have felt if we'd have lost that night. Would I have been truly convinced that we were down or would I have let that annoying naive voice in the back of my head persuade me that we still had a chance? I can honestly say that I don't know. However, after weeks of depression, I suddenly believed in my club again.

It takes every element of anger, surprise, relief, happiness, pride, desperation, not-caring about life outside your club's bubble, commitment from your own players, and love from a packed set of fans in the crowd to make a truly perfect football night.

Those 90 minutes in Watford were as close as I have ever come to the perfect match. Football and life had been stressful in the weeks leading up to the game. Long and fruitless trips to Doncaster, Barnsley, Blackpool and Nottingham had given me more questions than answers about why I was doing my challenge. They'd been lonely trips, entwined with home defeats to Swansea, Coventry, Reading, Leicester and Cardiff. Alongside all of the misery on the pitch, Warnock had left and his replacement was yet to inspire us. However, all that pain, all that money and misery, all the damage to the club and worries about the future had built up and combined. Combined to give a truly magical night. A vital win, a special atmosphere and a euphoric memory forever.

F***ing YESSSSSSSS

What a game! I remember before the game keeping things pretty low key. I didn't want to heap anymore pressure on them than there already was. But we were definitely up for it.

The game itself was a little bit too much end to end for my liking but we had great resolve that night and although they had a few chances, we took our chances and finished brilliantly.

After the game, although delighted with the result, I reminded the players that we still had quite a bit of work to do.

Paul Hart

Chapter 55 – **Train Clientele**

Saturday 3rd April 2010, Middlesborough vs Crystal Palace, The Riverside Stadium.

Crystal Palace: Julian Speroni, Johnny Ertl, Patrick McCarthy, Claude Davis, Matt Lawrence, Nicky Carle (Sean Scannell 72), Alassane N'Diaye, Neil Danns, Shaun Derry, Darren Ambrose, Alan Lee (Calvin Andrew 77)
Subs Not Used: Charlie Mann, Stern John, James Comley, Wilfried Zaha, Jack Holland
Middlesbrough: Jones, Hoyte, Wheater, McManus, Taylor (Naughton 42), O'Neil, Rhys Williams (O'Shea 78), Robson, Franks, Killen (Lita 57), McDonald
Subs Not Used: Coyne, Miller, Arca, Grounds

I had barely calmed down from our midweek result when the next game was upon us. I'd been to a party at Robin's house the night before and woke up at 6am on his sofa when my alarm began to ring. With my head thumping, I threw some clothes on and made my way to King's Cross station in a zombiefied state. I certainly wasn't in a condition to 'enjoy' the extremely long train journey that I'd paid such a high price for.

I had a quick look around the station for some fellow red and blue shirts but there were none. I waited until my train was listed as 'boarding' on the electronic time table and then found an empty set of four seats to slump on. I was asleep before the train left the station.

Unfortunately, my much needed snooze didn't last long. I was rudely awoken by a middle aged bloke opposite me.

"AALLLLLRIIIGGGHH Young man!" he yelled in my direction, giving no courtesy to the fact that I was asleep and he had no idea who I was. *"You goin' all the way up to 'boro, are ya?"*

He was thin in the face and lacking most of his front teeth. He had tough, wrinkled skin and was badly shaven. He'd cut himself in more than one place on his aged face and, worst of all, there was a terrible stench coming from his general direction. Embarrassingly, he wore an old Crystal Palace cap on top of his greasy, grey hair. To anyone who had passed us while I'd been napping, it would have appeared that we were travelling together. My personal state wasn't great but even with a horrendous hangover and a lack of a shower, I allowed myself to look on in horror at the mess that had presented itself in front of me.

I squinted at him as my eyes adjusted to the light, having previously been laying face down on the table. I looked at my Palace shirt, realising what had given me away, groaned and then looked at my watch. It was only ten past seven. We'd only just pulled out of the station.

"Errm yeah," I mumbled, *"You?"*

As I regained some sort of conscious thinking, I realised that I was likely to be stuck with this guy the entire way to Middlesbrough. That is a very long way. Especially with a hangover. This was not the travel experience that I was expecting for the extortionate price that I'd paid.

"Nah mate," he replied. I tried extremely hard to not let out a visible sigh of relief

although I don't think I succeeded in this.

The rough old man then leaned over to the seat next to him. I hadn't noticed it before but he had a four pack of Stella Artois. He cracked one open and took a long swig, followed by a release of gas and a grin.

"Want one?" he asked. I winced. Hangover or not, I wasn't about to start drinking at quarter past seven in the morning for any occasion. Not even supporting Palace excuses or explains that behaviour. He insisted that I took one as I'd want it later.

"So where are you going?" I asked, unsure which occasion allowed for drinking at that time. Football has pretty questionable morals in terms of drinking acceptance but this was too early - even for football.

"I'm off to Peterborough," he started, as if that explained everything. I remembered a university friend from Peterborough had once told me that the town had a small celebration when it had got a Nandos as there was so little else to do in the area. However, I didn't think a *second* chicken food outlet party was on the cards. I lowered my eyes and raised my eyebrows, while gesturing with my hand for him to expand his explanation as I was still a little lost. What came next didn't give me any explanations to the reason that he was drinking but it did give me an insight into the poor bloke's life.

"...to see the grandkids."

Whatever happens in my life, I hope that I never end up needing early morning beers before visiting my grandkids. With this guy, being Palace wasn't enough.

I managed to get back to sleep soon after and when I woke up, I hoped that the whole experience had been a weird, alcohol-induced nightmare. Unfortunately, the three empty cans left across the table from me suggested otherwise.

The loopy seat was soon to be filled again. At Doncaster, another middle aged bloke got on. He had an aged, bald head and his neck had a strange stars tattoo on it. He saw my football shirt and launched into conversation. Wearing a Palace shirt has given me an identity and helped me make friends in the past. However, on that Easter Saturday morning, my shirt seemed to be attracting every nutter on the train.

"Palace!" he shouted. He then went off on a ramble about us being the 'Team of the Eighties' and how he'd loved watching us back in the day. He seemed to have a brilliant knowledge of our club for someone who had no connection to the South London area, let alone Crystal Palace Football Club. However, I didn't appreciate the loud volume that he seemed to insist on sharing his knowledge in. He loved our sash kit from the era and Terry Venables was his all-time hero. I was too hungover, and slightly too scared of him, to point out that most Palace fans hate the money grabbing bastard.

"Where are you lot then?" he asked, well shouted – everything that he said was in a loud enough voice to be heard by the entire carriage.

"Middlesbrough," I replied, trying to lower the volume of the conversation.

I didn't recognise his shirt. His jacket had been partly covering it up and

I'd assumed that it was an away top. When I got a glimpse if the badge, I didn't recognise that either.

"So where are you off to then?" I enquired, nodding at his top.

"Leeds!" he replied. Nothing in his voice suggested that he thought his reply was strange. Not for the first time on that journey, I was confused. It certainly wasn't a Leeds shirt but surely if he was following the away side, he would have at least mentioned them.

"So... who are you supporting?" I quizzed, almost suspiciously, such was my lack of understanding. I assumed that my hangover was making me dim.

"Leeds," he replied, slightly louder this time, which I'd previously thought to be impossible. He looked at me as if I was stupid and deaf – one sense short of being being a Pinball Wizard. Maybe the alcohol was still having a negative impact on my levels of intellectuality. However, the smugness on his face made me suspect that he was enjoying my confusion. It was him who'd originally launched into conversation with me yet suddenly, he had restricted himself to one word answers.

I thought I'd try a different approach. *"So who are Leeds playing?"*

"Swindon," he grinned. Another smug, one-worded response. It was almost like we were playing a game that I hadn't wanted and hadn't asked to join in with. He knew that he wasn't giving away any unnecessary clues and was enjoying my confusion. It was a bit like a strange football shirt equivalent of the game 'Guess Who?'

I didn't think he was wearing a Swindon shirt and as he seemed to be being deliberately awkward, I decided to break the rules and change tact.

"Ohh, that's a Swindon shirt then! Go on the Robins!"

He looked suitably irritated and disgusted.

"No, no, no. It's Gainsborough Trinity," he exclaimed, trying to sound shocked that I hadn't instantly recognised the shirt. Maybe his South London knowledge wasn't so good after all if he believed that Gainsborough Trinity shirts were common in the area. However, it was now me who was smug. Whether he knew it or not, (and I suspect that he did) we'd been playing a game and I'd won. He'd let me in on his secret.

He was a die-hard Gainsborough Trinity fan. Before that trip, all I knew about the small Conference North side was that they had been Neil Warnock's first club as a manager. For that reason alone, I didn't like them. Three months previously, I'd have loved to have met a Gainsborough Trinity supporter. Three months previously, I'd loved everything about Warnock. In the same way that you fall in love with everything that a girl likes when you first get together and you start to take an interest in things that you'd never previously known or cared about, I'd wanted to know everything about Neil Warnock and his career. Now he'd run off for another club and left me behind like a single parent to look after Palace, I hated him. I hated everything about him. I irrationally hated Gainsborough Trinity by association and the smugness of my fellow train customer only added to my dislike.

Once we were over the needless confusion, we began to discuss all things football. Gainsborough's game had been called off that day. I have no idea how non-league schedules ever get finished as there seems to be more cancellations than matches actually played. He'd felt exactly as I had on that horrible day in January when our game against Bristol had been frozen off. However, instead of sitting around miserably as I had done, this seasoned pro knew exactly how to feed his addiction. Many supporters of clubs in the top two divisions go and watch non-league matches when they have football-free Saturdays thanks to international breaks. This guy was doing the opposite, he had no non-league football to attend so had decided to take in a professional game.

He left the train soon after and we wished each other luck. I was beginning to wonder if the high price of ticket that I'd paid was for a 'companionship' travel package. If I had paid a premium on it, I certainly wasn't getting good value for money. However, I'd decided to forgive Gainsborough Trinity for their association with Warnock so I gave him the Palace alcoholic's can of Stella that he'd so kindly left me. It was a parting gift to symbolise my forgiveness and off he went.

The final part of my long journey was spent alone. I changed trains at Darlington and took the small train on to Middlesbrough. My hangover was clearing up and I stared out of the window. It must be one of the most depressing train journeys in the country. There were no signs of life. However, there was plenty of empty quarries and coal mines, reminding everyone who went past of the history of the area. That and the faded 'Thatcher Out' graffiti on the walls were the only signs that there had ever been life in that part of the country at all. The wasteland, like its previous employees, had been made redundant.

It was hardly befitting of my most expensive journey of the season – just like some of my company on the long trek north. I briefly considered writing to the train company to complain but I decided that it was likely to fall on deaf ears. Instead, it would simply have to go down as my least favourite stretch of rail of the season. An indignity that any self-respecting track would be horrified to have put upon it. Unfortunately, this stretch didn't seem to have any self-respect left.

During the journey, I received a text from Pavel saying he and his girlfriend, Abby, were coming to the game. I thought it was strange. I'd tried to persuade him to come to the match but the last I'd heard, he was planning to take his girlfriend away for the Easter weekend. When he'd said that, Middlesbrough wasn't where I, or I suspect she, had imagined.

I was in the Middlesbrough Wetherspoons for 10:30 in the morning and bought myself a large fry up. After travelling 255 miles from Putney to the North East, it was the final part of my hangover cure. The pub was large and empty. The manager came over and quizzed me about the Feltham payslip that I'd used to get a discount on my breakfast. He was a Middlesbrough fan and we bonded over the football. Boro had come down from the Premiership the previous May and were having a disappointing first season in the Championship.

The other two newly relegated sides were battling for automatic promotion but Middlesbrough were two places and six points outside the playoffs. Like the area, the club was having a depressing time. They'd just spent twelve years in the top flight, getting to European and domestic cup finals. The club had given the area some hope. Unfortunately, inevitably, the area eventually dragged the club down and it was now as depressed as the rest of the place. The pub manager said that attendances were rapidly dropping as fans became disillusioned. What had previously been an escape from recession hit life, was now an expensive way to waste money.

Conversation moved on to the price of beer. I couldn't help but notice how cheap it was, even for Wetherspoons. £1.09 for a pint of Carlsberg or Tuborg. £1.19 for a pint of Fosters. Or, if you really wanted to push the boat out, you could spend £1.25 on a Kronenbourg. These were all nearly two quid cheaper than in the Feltham 'spoons that I worked in.

"How do you keep the prices so low?"

"We had to!" he explained, *"I needed to get special permission from Wetherspoon's headquarters to go below the lowest price bracket."*

"Why?" I inquired, Wetherspoons have such cheap prices anyway and I was unsure of the benefit of reducing the prices and minimising the profit margins even further.

He looked at me and sighed, *"All the other pubs undercut us."*

It did make me think. I'd paid £54 for my train ticket. Each pint of Kronenbourg that I drank would 'save' me around £3 compared to the same pint in a Central London Wetherspoons. Therefore, if I was able to drink eighteen pints over the day, my travel would be effectively free. At normal train prices, I might have had a do-able target. However, the inflated price meant that eighteen was quite unrealistic. Even for me. Although, I was keen to make a dent in the hefty price that I had paid for my journey. Unfortunately, the ale was no cheaper than back home. Apparently, the locals didn't drink it anyway so there was no point in reducing the price.

After breakfast, still not ready to begin drinking, despite the encouraging prices, I went back to the station and briefly met up with John and Chris, the guys from the Barnsley and Cardiff trips earlier in the season. We found a small cafe and had a cup of tea, while we relived the atmosphere of the previous Tuesday in Watford. Even as fans who were nearing the age of retirement, they struggled to think of many better Palace atmospheres. Not even John could find something to worry about. We were all still on a high from the performance, result and crowd but there was no doubting anyone's favourite moment. It wasn't the goals. It was Lawrence and McCarthy's show of man love and commitment as it summed up how we all felt.

Soon after, Pavel arrived and we headed to a pub called Dr Browns that was near the ground. Pavel had taken Abby for a night out in Newcastle the night before and they were going to spend the second evening of their weekend away in the famously romantic town of Middlesbrough. He had promised, being the modern day Romeo that he is, to use the long weekend to take her away and try to save their relationship. Unfortunately, he'd lacked motivation and the weekend had arrived quicker than he'd expected without him booking Paris or Venice or New York so the obvious replacement was... Middlesbrough. I think it's fair to say that she was somewhat underwhelmed.

Abby is a Chelsea supporter so we had a few pints while we watched Manchester United play Chelsea. Like myself, Pavel is no fan of the West London club but in order for the weekend to avoid being a total disaster, he needed a Chelsea win. Even I cheered Chelsea for him/her. By now, I was so disillusioned by my flatmates that I was beyond caring about Chelsea. When we'd been friends, I'd been desperate for Chelsea to lose but despite living in the same flat, we were so separate that I really wasn't interested anymore. In the right spirit, abusing each other's football teams is great harmless fun. However, without any underlining friendship or respect, it simply becomes abuse, which is no fun to give or receive. Man U and Chelsea held the top two positions in the Premiership and the winner would be in pole position to take the title with five games left. Luckily for Pav, Chelsea won with a late, controversial winner (not that Chelsea ever got any luck according to my flatmates) and his girlfriend's frosty mood slightly softened towards him.

After the game, we headed to the ground to get a cheeky pint inside the stadium before our match. On route, a kid ran up behind us and shouted *"There's only two Simon Jordans!"*
The chant was directed at Pav as his blonde centre parting gave him more than a passing resemblance to our former owner. Just as they had done at Scunthorpe, Palace fans' reaction towards Pavel had pissed him off. This helped Abby's ever improving mood.

The Riverside Stadium was the fourth and final new ground of the season for me. Like most stadiums built since the mid-nineties, it was round and soulless, designed to be filled and maximise revenue in the Premiership. Unfortunately, second tier football was less attractive and there were blocks and blocks of empty seats. Once inside, other than the colour of the seats, there was no way of telling that we weren't at Reading or Southampton or Derby or Coventry or Leicester. The only differentiating feature was the army of swans that surrounded the ground thanks to its riverside location.

During the first half, Palace started well and Alan Lee hit the post after a good run. The Palace crowd was much smaller and more spread out than it had been at Watford but the passion from the 500 travelling fans was as evident as ever. However, fifteen minutes into the game, 'boro took the lead with a goal that looked at least a couple of yards offside. My love of officials from the previous Tuesday had proved to be as short lived as predicted. The useless w***ers.

The goal knocked the wind out of our sails and the half seemed to be petering out but Alassane N'Diaye, back in the side for the first time in months, scored a stunning header in first half stoppage time. We got a quick pint at half time and checked the other scores.

Palace started brightly in the second half but really sat back in the last half hour, which made for a very nervous finale. Thanks to two top saves by Speroni and some great defending, especially considering we had no available full backs, we held on for a vital point.

After the game, Pavel used his Smart Phone to check the other results from around the country. I was relieved to be with a more technically advanced friend so we wouldn't have to rely on taking in the other scores based on one small reading in the ground. Watford and Sheffield had drawn too so, looking above us, the situation had stayed the same. However, our mood was slightly dampened when news of a last minute Plymouth winner filtered through. The result gave them half a chance of surviving.

The end of the season is when football fans reap the benefits of smart phones. By now, the other results were just as important as our own, especially when we failed to win. Thankfully, the days of malicious rumours, dodgy radio signals and incorrect information are gone and fans can follow all of the latest results from their seat in the stadium. The only sight more bizarre than seeing thousands of people celebrate a goal that's happened in another part of the country is seeing a group of fans celebrate a goal that *hasn't* happened in another part of the country as often happened in the days before smart phones.

As I left the ground, Dad rang to find out the score as he hadn't followed it, again. At least he'd remembered that we were playing this time. He had a smart phone so I really thought he had no excuse. He didn't seem to share the same concern as me that relegation was looming, let alone that the end of our club was coming.

Pavel, Abby and I went to Wetherspoons for a couple more pints towards our money saving target of eighteen. I only had about an hour before my train back, meaning that I was going to get nowhere near the target number of pints. However, those two had the whole evening to take in their surroundings – or simply try and drink eighteen pints. I know which one I would rather do in Middlesbrough. Although, the last minute nature of their journey, coupled with hotel costs, meant that they would be required to consume considerably more than the eighteen that I would. Pavel, trying to save some face on his misguided weekend away decided to look up the top rated restaurants in Middlesbrough. If he was going to take his girlfriend away to watch Palace play in a s*** town, he might as well treat her to a nice meal afterwards.

The third top rated place was a small Italian. From what we could gather, it was basically a posh pizzeria. I say posh, but only in the way that Pizza Express would be considered posh compared to Pizza Hut. The second top rated was a kebab house. Now, I love a good kebab and I'm led to believe that in Turkey, some of them are incredible. In fact, even in Kingston-upon-Thames, I have frequented a kebab house at the end of a night that tried its best to be a bit up market. However, we refused to believe that the second top restaurant in any town, anywhere, could or should be a kebab house. Unsurprisingly, they opted for the top rated option, which Pavel later described as an 'average kind of place'.

I know you might find this difficult to believe but Pavel and Abby broke up soon after. His relationship-saving weekend hadn't been exactly as he or she had imagined it.

I grabbed a couple of cans at Darlington station and geared myself up for the long journey home. On the train, I started chatting to a Scottish girl called Lauren. She was returning back to London, where she lived with her boyfriend and worked in a cinema in Leicester Square. The conversation started off quite well. We had good laugh and time began to fly. She even used the train's wifi to add me on *Facebook*.

Soon, I ran out of beer and went to the buffet carriage to get us another one each. She didn't need much persuasion to join me on the booze. She was Scottish after all. As we cracked open our cans, she began to quiz me. She was intrigued at my motive for travelling so far for a football match. She'd been back to Scotland to see her parents over the Easter weekend and hated the journey. It was a necessary evil as her attendance was expected at home for the religious festival. If she'd been allowed the slightest bit of choice in the matter, there was no way that she would have made the long trip.

"So was it a good match then?" she asked.

"It was ok I guess,"

"You must have been a bit disappointed not to win?"

"Nah, not really. I'm used to it. It happens a lot as a Palace fan,"

"Why do you go then? If it's not usually a good match, it's pointless. Why bother?"

"I've got to!"

"Why?"

"Well," I paused to take a long swig of my beer and buy myself some time. As a football addict, you don't question why you go. You simply go because you enjoy it. The whys or how's are best not thought about. However, under such sceptical interrogation, justification was required. *"Well...erm... it's my club and I've got to cheer them and also, we're battling relegation so.."*

"...so they've been rubbish all season..." she *'helpfully'* chipped in with an irritating Scottish twang and an equally irritating oversized grin.

"No," I stated firmly, waggling my finger at her to express my disappointment at her flippancy, *"...so they need my support more than ever and also I'm going to every game this season so there's no point stopping now. I dunno. It's not about the football. It's the social side too."*

She over exaggerated as she looked up and down the carriage before she turned to the empty seat next to me, *"Oh hello there, you must be James' friend. Nice to meet you. I'm Lauren."*

She seemed to find that hilarious. I tried to explain that I wasn't a loner at all and I had loads of friends, including the romantically-challenged Russian that I'd watched the game with but she was having none of it.

"Oh, so you must be the Pavel that he talks about. He mentions you a lot," she enthused to the empty seat next to me.

I'd had enough. I grabbed her bag and brought it up to my eye level. I briefly examined it and gave it a sniff. *"That's strange,"* I quizzed.

"What?" she replied with a thin smile and a pair of suspicious eyes.

"Well... it doesn't smell of left over haggis and it's not big enough to contain a set of bagpipes..." I started. She gave me a look that could only have come from the eyes of an angry Scottish lady. I grinned. 1-1, just like the 'pointless' Palace game I'd attended that day.

I was happy to return to London with two score draws. I suspect that the second one had made time pass quicker for me than the first had made time pass for Abby. I am still learning about women but Dan and Pavel had taught me that when I did meet a special lady, taking them to Scunthorpe or Middlesbrough was not a particularly good idea. Although I'd enjoyed the trip, mainly for the extrovert characters that I'd met throughout the day, it was definitely the kind of journey that I hoped I would be able to wean myself off over time.

Chapter 56 – **Palace Rise from the Dead**

Monday 5th April 2010, Crystal Palace vs Preston North End, Selhurst Park

Crystal Palace: Julian Speroni, Clint Hill, Shaun Derry, Patrick McCarthy, Darren Ambrose, Neil Danns, Stern John, Sean Scannell (Nick Carle, 85), Matt Lawrence, Calvin Andrew, Johannes Ertl
Subs Not Used: Kieron Cadogan, James Comley, Alassane N'Diaye, Charlie Mann, Wilfred Zaha, Jack Holland

Preston Noth End : Andy Lonergan, Darren Carter (Callum Davidson, 66), Shaun St. Ledger, Paul Coutts, Keith Treacy, Billy Jones, Tom Williams (Chris Brown, 80), Matthew James, Elliott Ward, Jon Parkin, Neil Mellor
Subs Not Used: Michael Hart, Richard Chaplow, Liam Chilvers, Wayne Henderson, Adam Barton

I was travelling from Egham as I had been to my Mum's house for Easter Sunday the day before. I met Dan and his Dad, Peter, on the train at Staines and we headed to the Railway Club. Upon arrival, Peter's friend, Chris, got us a round of drinks in, before I got us a second.

The two away games had given us some vital points but they hadn't got us out of trouble. We were still in the relegation zone. Sheffield Wednesday and Watford had home games but QPR and Scunthorpe both had tricky looking away games. Failure to follow up our away performances with a result against Preston, could leave us in a position just as precarious as the one that we'd been in before the Watford game. Palace needed a win to help us rise again on the Easter weekend.

We nervously emptied our bladders and headed to the game. Glad All Over was sung loudly but it lacked the conviction and meaning that it had in some of our previous games. Supporters were far too anxious about the result to worry about that. For away games, there has been a whole part of the day before the actual match. You've usually been for a fry up and to the pub with your mates, travelled as a group and pitched up in someone else's town. By the time kick off arrives, there's been so much build up (and drinking) that you're ready to release your feeling and emotion out in passionate song. Whereas for home games, I'd simply pitched up in the same places that I had for hundreds of other games; the same pub, the same ground, the same seat. I'd spent a mere 45 minutes with my mates and arrived at the ground, still working myself up for the match.

Although, I suspect the slightly calmer mood was also partly because, being a bank holiday Monday, lots of people had spent the weekend drinking; meaning they were now hung-over and not looking forward to returning to work the following day. It was a huge game – they all were now – but it didn't have the same edge to it as the Watford one. However, it should have done.

The wrong results could potentially leave the table looking as bleak as this:

Position	Team	Played	Points
20	Sheffield Wednesday	42	48
21	Watford	41	47
22	Plymouth Argyle	42	44
23	Crystal Palace	42	43
24	Peterborough United	42	30

With four games left, it would have looked an unlikely escape. However, despite the potential disaster, it didn't feel like it was as 'do or die' as Watford. I suppose partly because a defeat wouldn't immediately result in our rivals winning. For the above scenario to happen, not only would we have to lose, four other teams would have to win.

Palace dominated the early stages but Shaun Derry gifted them an opener. Suddenly, this did seem like a big game. After a couple of good results, we'd had a natural positivity about us. Preston were stuck in mid table and mid table teams are traditionally the ones who you want to play at this stage of the season. They have nothing to fight for and are supposed to just roll over and lose. They certainly weren't supposed to take the lead. The atmosphere in the ground changed as we stared disaster in the face.

At Watford, nothing would stop the intense singing but on that Easter Monday, the mood was flat. Palace continued to press on the pitch but we needed something to lift us. Just before I headed off to get the half time beers, it came. Neil Danns equalised, ensuring we went up for a relieved half time beer. For some reason, and I can only assume that it had been carried over from the Watford game, we all had a positive feeling. We weren't scared of the 'e' word. We expected the players to come out in the second half and win.

Palace started the second half just as well as they had ended the first. Darren Ambrose hit a volley against the crossbar; it bounced down, just over the goal line, and then flew back out of the goal again. It had clearly crossed the line but Calvin Andrew tried, and failed, to force the ball back into the goal to remove any doubt. It was definitely a goal, but it wasn't as clear as Freddy Sears' effort in Bristol, which the referee had missed. The entire ground stopped. Ambrose charged towards the referee, arms aloft, claiming the goal. After what could only have been a few split-seconds, but felt like a lifetime, the linesman waved his flag and pointed back to the centre circle. Rob Shoebridge was nowhere to be seen and the referee, rightly, gave the goal, sparking wild celebrations. Any hangover or nerves or holding back of emotions were left behind. Palace were winning again.

After that, we began to sit back. Unlike some of the other defensive moves by Hart, this one was more understandable. It wasn't that he was calling the team into their shell, it was simply that the players, like the crowd, were getting nervous. True to stereotype, Preston, as a mid table team with little to fight for, never looked like getting back into the game. Nothing was happening in the match and that suited us just fine. However, every football fan has seen this script so many times. Your team is one goal ahead and cruising to victory against a deflated opposition when BAM. They score a wonder-strike or your defender slips to gift them a chance or even worse, scores a needless and calamitous own goal to seal your own fate. And those are the worries before Rob Shoebridge or any other *'bastard in black'* shows up. Everyone was far too experienced to feel in any way comfortable with our lead.

As the clock ticked down, the lively crowd quietened down again. At Watford there had been nothing to lose but here, we had a vital lead, were heading out of the drop zone and had everything to lose. Players started to make mistakes. Cheers turned to groans. Joy turned to nerves and time seemed to go slower and slower. Three or four times a minute, I would glance up at the big screen above the Whitehorse Lane stand opposite me and wonder how the countdown hadn't changed.

Our game was on such tenterhooks that I dared not listen to any of the other scores. Smart phones stayed firmly in pockets. With a few minutes left, Darren Ambrose crossed the ball into the penalty area for Stern John. He leapt up with the Preston goalkeeper and punched it past him. Doing his best 'Shoebridge impression', the referee completely missed the infringement. Finally, luck was evening itself out. The ball fell to Calvin Andrew with the goal gaping. He faffed about. He couldn't adjust his body. He was being chased down by the defender and goalkeeper and eventually, he managed to scoop the ball into the empty net for his first, and only, league goal for the club.

It provoked mayhem in the ground. The fans went wild. The tension had been broken and he dived into the welcoming crowd. Well, he tried to. He didn't even get that quite right. Like the goal, he threw himself at it and it kind of worked. He ended up half in the crowd and half smashing himself against the advertising boarding below. However, in that moment, it didn't matter. He was our hero.

After the game, most of the crowd stood and waited for all of the other results to be read out. As a kid, I dreamed of being the stadium announcer at Palace. Having thousands of fans listen to your voice as you introduce the team or inform them of other results must be an amazing experience. In the classroom, I love reading stories which capture every child as they hang on your every word. It is a special feeling to hold the script and have the attention of everyone in earshot clenched in your hand. I once read a story to over five hundred children in an assembly and watching that many eyes focussed on your words is incredible. The idea of having 20,000 Palace fans listening to me had seemed like paradise as a kid although nowadays, I'd be far too scared about making a mistake to want the responsibility. As a kid, I hadn't understood just how important a job it is to read the other scores. The Palace stadium announcer, realising the power that he had, was on the case straight away.

Sheffield Wednesday... 0 Bristol City... 1 *(there was a cheer from the crowd)*

Newcastle United...2 Sheffield United... 1 Newcastle are promoted. *(There was silence. No one cared for their promotion, no matter how deserved or impressive it was)*

Plymouth Argyle...0 Middlesbrough... 2 *(another cheer)*

Swansea City...3 Scunthorpe United...0 *(a slightly louder cheer)*

Leicester City... 4 Queens Park Rangers... 0 *(this one got an especially big cheer)*

Watford...1 West Bromwich Albion...0*(Silence. But we certainly did care)*

What the hell were West Brom playing at? They were second in the league and they were bottling it against Watford. We couldn't afford slips like that. Suddenly, the big screen cut away from showing the results and showed Sky Sports News. They were live at Vicarage Road and there were celebrating fans in the background. Celebrating West Bromwich Albion fans. Watford had conceded. With most Palace fans still in the ground, we too celebrated like we'd scored again. We were not only out of the drop zone but we now had a team between us and the bottom three. Unfortunately, I couldn't stay and celebrate in the pub as I had to rush off to Feltham for work that evening but I did so with a huge grin on my face.

Position	Team	Played	Goal Difference	Points
18	Queens Park Rangers	41	-9	48
19	Scunthorpe United	41	-23	47
20	Crystal Palace	42	-1	46
21	Watford	41	-11	45
22	Sheffield Wednesday	42	-18	45
23	Plymouth Argyle	42	-18	41
24	Peterborough United	42	-27	31

Three points separated 22nd and 18th with four games left. Peterborough had been officially relegated that day thanks to their draw at Barnsley, while Plymouth's defeat against Middlesbrough looked costly for them. I now suspected that they were going to follow Peterborough down to League 1. After that, it looked like one from five but the most exciting prospect was that QPR, and more importantly, Neil Warnock, were in free fall. Staying up would be a fairytale of Danny Butterfield proportions, but to stay up and watch Neil Warnock's side go down would be far too good to be true. Next up for us... QPR, home. A win would put us above him.

Chapter 57 – **Judas and Jesus Return**

Saturday 10th April 2010, Crystal Palace vs QPR, Selhurst Park

Crystal Palace: Julian Speroni; Clint Hill; Shaun Derry; Patrick McCarthy; Darren Ambrose; Neil Danns; Stern John; Sean Scannell; Matt Lawrence; Calvin Andrew (Nathaniel Clyne, 23); Danny Butterfield (Alan Lee, 58 (Johnny Ertl,70))
Subs Not Used: Nick Carle; Lee Hills; Claude Davis; Charlie Mann

QPR: Radek Cerny; Peter Ramage; Damion Stewart (Jay Simpson, 8); Mikele Leigertwood; Akos Buzsaky; Kaspars Gorkss; Alejandro Faurlin; Hogan Ephraim; Dusko Tosic; Tamas Priskin; Adel Taarabt (Josh Parker, 90)
Subs Not Used: Lee Cook; Lee Brown; Joe Oastler; Elvijs Putnins; Antonio German

I was still in Egham after Easter and I went for a fry up with Jesus. Like Palace, he had risen from the dead the previous Easter weekend and was using his new found life to attend a Palace game for the first time in months. Although, in his new life, Tom had cut his hair and no longer had any sort of resemblance to the Son of God – not that he especially had done before.

I went early so that Jesus and I could get him a ticket without missing out on any drinking time. While we were at the ground, I kept up my usual tradition of buying the home shirt at the end of the season. I have bought every Palace home shirt in the last 17 years but I have generally refused to pay full price. I wait until the end of the season and buy them on the cheap. I don't care about having the most recent shirt as they all have the same (well, similar) badge and it is that which I cheer. The badge represents the past, the present and the future of the club. I support and value all three. The eleven players who walk out in the current shirt each Saturday are merely a tiny part of that.

We met Dan, Kev, John, Jonathan, Colin and Adam in the Railway Club, which was quite busy. Middlesbrough, Villa and QPR seemed to be the only clubs who knew about our little drinking bunker. Those three packed it out but I don't think I saw an away fan of any other club that season.

We had a couple of drinks and the mood in the pub was positive once more. Why shouldn't it be? We'd taken seven points from three games, we'd climbed out of the relegation zone and QPR were in our sights. We were no longer discussing whether we could stay up or not, we were discussing whether we would finish above QPR and send them down.

Around twenty to three, for our last home, Saturday 3 o'clock game of the season, we emptied our bladders and made the short walk to the ground. It had been a gruelling stretch of matches and I'd only been watching them. Since I'd been to our cup game at Wolves in January, before the administration had been put upon us, Palace had played twenty one matches in seventy six days. I was exhausted so I couldn't begin to imagine how the players must have been feeling. We'd only used eighteen players in that time and had named just three out of the seven allowed subs on more than one occasion. My liver, my wallet and my heart were glad that the busy fixture period was coming to an end.

There was a large crowd of over 20,000. It was our second biggest of the season, behind the Newcastle game way back in August. Glad All Over was sung with a lot more intensity and meaning than it had been before the Preston game. The crowd were up for this. A win would surely send us a huge way towards safety. Before the previous game, we'd worked out the worst case scenario but now, we had visions of a table with *at least* three teams separating us and the drop zone.

While the QPR team was being read out, it happened. Warnock appeared from the tunnel. Immediately, our group began to boo and shout obscenities and cries of 'Judas'. It was a strange twist of fate that a week after Easter, Jesus was condemning Judas. We certainly wouldn't have been against crucifying Warnock at the time. Especially Jesus, after the stressful week that he'd had, he couldn't stand Judas.

However, much to our surprise and disappointment, we were more than drowned out by the warm round of applause that he received from the majority. There were a few other boos around the ground but the attitude of the bulk of supporters was that he was a returning hero, who'd had to leave to look after his family. In my opinion, they'd fed on his bullshit. I couldn't believe it. Although, the reaction of the Palace fans certainly made me question my hatred and wonder if I was an incredibly bitter individual. My conclusion was that I wasn't and that anyone who'd watched Warnock walk out on us when we needed him the most and then welcomed him back with his new club, who he'd cheated on us with, was a fool. I had no doubts that if Warnock had been able to show us a bit of commitment and bottle, then we'd already be clear of the relegation battle.

It may have left our group feeling bewildered and annoyed but the warm reaction that Warnock received didn't knock the loud atmosphere for our only home London derby of the season. Whatever the motives, the crowd were up for this. The 'We Love You' chant echoed around Selhurst Park as we tried to lift our players ahead of the massive game. Palace kicked off and the referee's whistle was met with a huge roar from the crowd. Within seconds, the game was stopped. Calvin Andrew had clashed heads with a Rangers player. The crowd cheered ironically as the physios of both teams raced onto the pitch, trying to reach their patient first as if it was the Olympic 100m sprint final. However, once they got there, the crowd waited. And waited. It lasted seven minutes until QPR were eventually forced into a substitution.

By then, the crowd were bored. The atmosphere had lost its edge. The Holmesdale Fanatics, the group of Palace ultras, were still singing but the rest of the ground had lost its intensity. The Palace players had too. Johnny Ertl, our limited but combative midfielder, had been dropped for the game and we seemed to lack some bite in the team. Soon, everything fell even flatter. QPR scored with a stunning strike. The Rangers fans went mad and then began to taunt us with songs about Warnock leaving.

It wasn't the first time that a Palace manager had walked out on us, while we were financially crippled, to go to QPR. Terry Venables had done the same in the early eighties and had taken lots of the playing staff with him. There were already rumours of Derry, Hill, Danns, Speroni and Ambrose following Warnock to West London on the cheap and the QPR fans sang about taking Ambrose, our star man. They showed no mercy in the way football fans don't. Palace never really threatened to get back into the game and we conceded a second goal on the hour mark. Finishing above QPR suddenly seemed like a long lost pipe dream.

The stadium announcer had been the hero at the end of the Preston game. He'd added to the delirium of the victory. It had been our day. We'd won and the other results had gone our way. Another reason I'd realised that in the highly unlikely event of being offered the job, I wouldn't want it anyway, was that on some occasions, I'd have to be the bearer of bad news. I can still hear the voice of Rob Fox, the previous stadium announcer, telling the ground that Norwich had beaten Birmingham 1-0 when we were in the Premiership, which hammered another nail into our survival hopes coffin. I'd hate my voice to be associated with such circumstances. Although I guess my voice might echo around the heads of some of my pupils as a voice of doom after I give them a detention. However, I try to only resort to that level of sanction in extreme and deserving cases, such as them claiming to support Brighton or cheering against Palace.

While they weren't quite as damning as sealing our fate, the words from the PA machine were not what we wanted to hear. Most of the results were fine. Obviously, we already knew QPR had won but Sheffield Wednesday and Scunthorpe had lost. But then the killer words came, *"Watford...1 Plymouth...0"*. It had been a bad day. We had been third out of the five teams battling to avoid one spot. We were now third out of the four teams in the battle; with QPR looking safe.

Position	Team	Played	Goal Difference	Points
19	Watford	42	-10	48
20	Scunthorpe United	42	-24	47
21	Crystal Palace	43	-3	46
22	Sheffield Wednesday	43	-19	45
23	Plymouth Argyle	43	-19	41
24	Peterborough United	43	-28	31

After the game, we went to the Balham Wetherspoons to continue drinking. John was going to a school reunion and had invited us all along. At least the others were of a similar age to John and could mix in. Being nearly twenty years younger, there was no way that I would be able to blag a story of being a long forgotten school friend. Throughout the night, John, who had only been to five or six games that season, kept repeating a phrase that really irritated me. *"It's gone now. The football doesn't matter now. We've just got to enjoy the evening."*

Enjoy the evening? Enjoy the bloody evening? And how did he suggest that I did that? Palace had just blown the chance to move ourselves out of the relegation picture, while throwing our former manager right into the middle of it. Not only that, but we were risking losing our club. It was alright for him. He didn't have a season ticket any more. He'd found other things to do on a Saturday afternoon but what would I do? How would I cope?

John is one of those people who there is very little point in arguing with, so I did the only thing that I knew would be able to cheer me up on a Saturday evening after a Palace loss. I got drunk. Really drunk. By the time we were in the O'Neils on Clapham High Street, the pain had eased. An alcohol-fused mind only allows your brain to think about one thing at a time so as long as that one thing wasn't Palace, everything would be ok.

By the time we were downing shots of sambuca in Infernos, where despite being in a night club, Kev was still wearing his black Umbro jumper, for John's school disco, I could barely stand up. It was a party with a load of forty year olds, who hadn't seen each other for years, having a good old dance to some eighties classics and I was the drunkest there. Even if I had worked out a back story to explain my attendance, I wouldn't have been able to spit it out. I was hammered; stumbling around the dance floor, swaying from side to side, eyes glazed over and clinging onto a plastic bag containing my new Palace shirt.

By the time that I was back at Clapham Junction, I was paralytic – lying on the hard station floor like a homeless drunk. Without Dan there to help me, I don't think I'd have made it home that night. However, no matter how pissed off I was at the club, no matter where I stuttered or stumbled or tumbled, I continued to cling to my bag. To my new Palace shirt. I wasn't going to give it up without a fight. The club meant too much to me for that. I might not be an alcoholic and buying cans of Stella at seven in the morning to take to see my grandkids just yet, but I could now see how supporting Palace might have that effect.

Chapter 58 – **A Great Day out in Derby**

Saturday 17th April 2010, Derby County vs Crystal Palace, Pride Park.

Crystal Palace: Julian Speroni, Danny Butterfield, Clint Hill, Patrick McCarthy, Lee Hills (Nathaniel Clyne, 33), Neil Danns, Johnny Ertl (Alassane N'Diaye, 77), Shaun Derry, Nicky Carle (Stern John, 46), Darren Ambrose, Sean Scannell
Subs Not Used: Charlie Mann, Matt Lawrence, James Comley, Wilfried Zaha
Derby County: Bywater, Hunt, Barker, Anderson, McEveley, Tonge, Green, Savage, Martin, Cywka (Davies, 71), Porter
Subs Not Used: Deeney, Croft, Teale, Pringle, Dean Moxey, Sunu

This was to be my last 'normal' away trip of the season. The West Brom game the following week would be at home and the Sheffield Wednesday one was set to be an enormous showdown as the pair of us battled against the drop. Even if it turned out to not be such a dramatic occasion, I was going for the weekend so it wouldn't be a 'normal' fixture. So in many ways, I saw this as the end of my challenge. I couldn't not be at the last two: there simply wasn't a choice in going to them.

Although I'd booked the travel to Derby and match ticket alone, I knew plenty of people going. Pavel was getting the train before mine on the way up with some friends and I was going to meet him in the pub. Some of Colin's friends, who I knew from the Railway Club, were also on my train and going up in a large group. As well as that, I spotted quite a few of the regulars making the relatively short trip. It is an easy enough journey to Derby, which is one of the reasons that it is my favourite away day. Despite all the potential company, I sat on my own for the journey up there and reflected on the season.

I looked back at the start of the year and it was almost as if I was thinking of a happier and carefree time. Sure, we'd known about the money troubles and embargoes but they were simply in the background, rather than dictating everything that happened at the club. The games had been less stressful and held less importance too. The early season trips to Bristol, Ipswich, QPR – twice, and West Brom had been fun occasions. The football hadn't mattered, the company had been good and the beer had flowed. Even the 4-0 Scunthorpe disaster had been fun in its own strange way. I was enjoying the challenge then. I was embracing it and looking forward to each and every game.

In a way, Palace had mirrored my own life. I'd known about my assignments and the upcoming responsibility but it had been very much in the back of my mind. None of it had bothered me and I was free to go out whenever I wanted. Even working in the grotty Feltham Wetherspoons had a charm in the way that a new job does. I was still learning things and meeting new people, which gave it a freshness and excitement in the same way that the new season had. Any worries about my future were put to one side as Palace and I both had unfulfilled potential so we lived for the moment and hoped for the best.

Leading up to Christmas had been a bit of a drag. University work had begun to take over, just as Palace's financial crisis began to shape our season. Uni life became tamer, repetitive and less exciting as Palace drew five consecutive games one all. Nights out were still fun but the voice in the back of my head was telling me that it couldn't last and responsibility would soon be upon me. Palace were having some great moments too. Unfortunately, most of them were Moses-inspired and each goal he scored seemed to add to the inevitability of him leaving. Just like Darrell had done around that time. At least Moses waved goodbye on the way out.

As the fear of having to actually do some work to get a degree took control of me, fear of administration was clouding over Selhurst Park. Both problems were descending into a frantic panic of falling behind. I struggled to stay on top of work as Simon Jordan struggled to control Palace's finances.

Christmas Day had been lonely and depressing for me and the festive trips were more of the same. I had nearly let the challenge slip to do a shift in the pub on Boxing Day and it was only my apathy towards making the long journeys to Sheffield and Swansea on my own that allowed me to come so close to giving it up. Work had become as depressive as working in the Feltham Wetherspoons inevitably would; the customers were racists and the managers were idiots (except Phill of course). Life, and Palace, seemed boring. November and December was a long slog and the only time that I imagined I might possibly give it all up.

January had brought administration to the club. It became a matter of life and death. From trying to persuade ourselves that we had a real chance of getting into the playoffs one minute, our entire season was turned upside down the next and we were in a battle to survive. Just as I realised that university work would have to be done, I found that going to Palace had to happen. Which, in turn, meant working for idiots at the pub had to happen. Palace needed me to work hard, just as the administrator would have to work hard to find a buyer and the players would need to work hard to stay up.

Life became busier and busier. Palace, and I, were both stretched to our limit in terms of resources. I never questioned my challenge during this period but I couldn't say I was enjoying it. I wasn't not enjoying it either. I was simply doing it. I didn't have time to reflect on or question or explain my life. I was frantically doing. Frantically researching or writing, rushing from lectures to the pub to the library. Rushing off here, there and everywhere for exams and interviews, football and work. I'd been to Wolverhampton, Birmingham (for Aston Villa), Barnsley, Newcastle, Doncaster, Middlesbrough, Watford, Scunthorpe, Blackpool and Nottingham in the space of seventy three days. That's three thousand, six hundred and sixty nine miles. All of that for two wins in ten games. Jesus, the addiction was bad. However, I hadn't stopped to think about it. I was just doing it. Rushing through life as Palace rushed through defeats. I thought I was going to fall off the edge a few times and it felt like Palace might tumble with me but we hadn't. We'd just about stayed there. Clinging on.

And where were we now? Well, other than approaching Leicester on a train to Derby. Palace were sat above the relegation zone, still hanging on in there. We'd passed so many challenges. We'd recently had a couple of huge wins and were in a reasonable position to survive. Of course, there was still a lot of uncertainty about the future. We were still in administration but there was now a glimmer of hope. A business man called Steve Parish was trying to get a consortium together to purchase the club and give it a brighter future. He described himself as a 'reluctant' buyer, who didn't want to purchase the club but, provided that we stayed up, he would step in as a lifelong Palace fan. We now had three final games to deal with. Three final challenges at the end of a long season of challenges.

I had also hung on in there in my busy schedule. Lots of people had dropped out of the course, finding the demands too high and they didn't have the dedication to see through what they'd started. They were all Neil Warnocks. They'd had a chilled few months and an easy life but they didn't have much to show for it. It would have been much easier to let the stress hit me and not bother with university. Like Palace, I was tired and I wasn't enjoying it; I was simply 'doing' it. However, like with Palace, I simply carried on with it.

I, like Palace, also had some final challenges at the end of a year of challenges. I had my upcoming teaching placement, which started on the following Monday and would last for ten weeks. However, I wasn't particularly worried about it. I'd always found the placements more beneficial and enjoyable than studying. I didn't want to know the theory behind teaching. No, I'm an impatient and arrogant kind of person and I was itching to get out there and actually do it. None of the lectures made much sense to me. I needed the context of the placements and more 'on the job' style learning to understand what the hell I was trying to do in the classroom. I also needed to find a job. I hadn't had any further interviews since turning down the Hampton Wick job after the Cardiff game and was beginning to worry about getting employment.

At the end of those challenges, as with Palace, there was a reward. The club could get a new owner and I could get a career. Palace and I just needed to get past the final few hurdles. Maybe the similarities suggest that Palace and I aren't so different and that is why we get along so well. Maybe, as I stared out of the window, I was just looking for some meaning that wasn't there. Either way, it made me think about the rollercoaster that Palace and I had been on that year. It was a rare pause for breath in a frantic period before it set off for one last terrifying loop around.

We arrived in Derby and the sun was shining brightly. I always have the same reaction when the sun shines during an end of season match. First, I feel happy as everything seems better in the sunshine. Bad things never happen on a bright day in stories or movies and the sunshine makes me feel safer. If only this was reality. The lowest points in my football supporting life both happened on sunny afternoons in May. One at Selhurst Park in a playoff semi-final against Watford in 2006 and one at Charlton, when we were relegated from the

Premiership in 2005. I guess most heartbreaking football moments happen in the May sunshine as that is when the season ends. It would make a much better setting for the story if it was on a freezing cold, rainy evening, with a swirling wind in February. However, football isn't like a story or a movie. It's much stranger than that. I guess that is why movies about the sport are usually so naff. You couldn't write the script of reality in football.

Unfortunately, as soon as I've felt the sun beaming down on my body at such games, I feel a sense of sadness. Not because of those unhappy memories. The season ending in May means that I've had as many, if not more, promotion and survival sunshine memories as depressing ones so it would be naive to connect the weather with the football. No, I feel a sense of sadness that the season is ending. I feel sad that I'm going to have to try and fill my Saturday afternoons with something else. I don't want the season to end. Sod the player's well-being; I'd keep the season going all year if I could. As I've always been in education, my year runs from September to September. Well, it should. As far as I'm concerned, the year runs from August to May and the rest is just filler. The last day of the season is a far more appropriate time for reflection and celebration than December 31st.

When I talked about the benefit of getting the train over the coach, I touched on the fact that Derby is one of my favourite places to visit but I didn't elaborate on why. The first reason that I love the trip is actually nothing to do with Derby, it could apply to anywhere. I love travelling to places and matches and Derby is the most convenient of places to travel to.

Don't get me wrong, I love London derbies and other local games such as Watford or Reading for the atmosphere and the large followings that we take, but they don't feel like 'away' trips as I haven't had to travel anywhere. In some cases, local away games are actually easier for me to get to than Selhurst Park, which always makes me question whether I should have supported them and if by supporting Palace, I am in fact... a glory hunter. Then I watch us lose heavily and realise that I'm certainly not a glory hunter, I'm a fool. Anyway, the purpose of this local matches ramble is that I'm discounting them from my 'convenient *away* games'.

Some of the longer trips are great fun. I tend to meet more people on them and I like the fact that the people who go to them are the loyalist and sadist Palace fans. They tend to be either very old or very young. People who don't have much else on in their lives. The only people in their late twenties and thirties who can give up their Saturdays to go to Scunthorpe or Preston, either have very understanding partners, fellow-Palace supporting partners or are single. Even the ones with understanding partners tend to have children or other responsibilities, which are more important to them than going to matches. Long trips need to be booked up well in advance and planned well. They require you to set an alarm for an obscene time on a Saturday morning and give up a whole day. Basically, long trips can be fun but they're a bit of a ball-ache and certainly not convenient.

However, Derby is just right. It is under two hours from London and there are plenty of trains, which means there are more cheap deals. Or, if it's your preferred method of travel, you can decide to drive up there on the day and do it with relative ease. It's a distance that allows me to feel that I've 'travelled' somewhere, without spending the entire day on a train. It is close enough to ensure a big away following, without being too popular and making it difficult to get tickets. The ground is close enough to the station so that you can walk rather than get a cab and the station is big enough to avoid queues. Derby fans are passionate and can create an atmosphere, but I've never feared for my safety there either. Everything about it is easy.

The station is also surrounded by a whole host of good pubs – perhaps the biggest contribution to my enjoyment of the day. The further that I've ventured into Derby, the more good pubs that I've found. Thornbridge and Buxton breweries, which are based in Derbyshire, are two of the leading breweries in the 'Craft Beer Revolution' that has spread across the country over the last few years. Their wide range of excellent beers can be found in many of the pubs in the town. It has always been a pioneering place. It was seen as the birthplace of the industrial revolution and now it's leading the way in the beer revolution.

People in Derby seem happy and why shouldn't they be? Their town is reasonably clean and well kept. As well as that, it is lively, yet the countryside is nearby. There's more than enough to do in the town without getting bored but they've also got plenty of peaceful escapes on their doorstep. Like Nottingham, the architecture is mixed and welcoming, a far cry from the concrete midlands cities of Coventry and Birmingham. The gothic style cathedral is lit up at night and stands slightly higher than the buildings surrounding it. Admittedly, it's not as spectacular as Prague's gothic offering, but it's impressive and pretty nonetheless.

On this occasion, I didn't venture far. I went to the Merry Widows pub opposite the station to meet Pavel and his friends. John, the friend of Colin, also led his group of around ten Palace fans into the same pub. Pavel was with Neil, who I'd travelled to Villa with, and his friend Dan – a small and smiling chap with scruffy hair. If I'm being totally honest, I didn't take too much notice of him that day and I would have completely forgotten him. However, in the way football does, I continued to meet him through Palace and within two years, I had a season ticket with him in the lower tier and was helping him to move house. If I'd met him in any other environment, he'd have simply been a friend of a friend (who in turn was still little more than a friend of a friend at the time, making Dan a friend of a friend of a friend. In fact, if I was being truthful, he was a friend of a friend of a friend of a friend. I knew Dan O, who knew a Palace fan called Tom, who I'd never met, who knew Pavel, who knew Dan S. Got it?) Anyway, the point is, he would have simply stayed as the unremarkable guy who was at the end of a chain of people who vaguely knew each other, that started with me and ended with him. He would have stayed as 'that guy' if it wasn't for Palace. We continued to see each other at games and soon we began to meet up away from the football too. Without knowing it, I made a very close friend in the Merry Widows pub in Derby that day.

I spent most of the time chatting to Pavel in anticipation for the game. The pub had a reasonable sized beer garden and we were making the most of the end of season sunshine. As beers began to flow, the Palace singing got louder and louder. A win in Derby would be a huge result and could put us half way towards safety. However, with the QPR result still in our minds, we needed to distract ourselves from thinking the worst. Beer and singing and talking to Palace fans seemed the best way possible. Although, it wasn't just Palace fans. There was a fair amount of Derby fans in the pub too, who were incredibly friendly and well-wishing.

And again, why shouldn't they be? Derby were on the up. Two years previously, they'd become the 'Worst Ever Premiership Team', registering just 11 points and one win. I usually hate the term 'Premiership record' as it suggests that football started in 1992, when Sky TV started investing money into the game but to be honest, I can't be bothered to look up if there has ever been a top flight team, before 1992, who managed to get even less than eleven points. I'm merely grateful to the knowledge that if there have been any teams who were somehow worse than Derby, Palace aren't one of them.

Since their pitiful relegation, Derby had sat in mid table for a couple of years and were finally beginning to recover from the horror of it. Having such a lovely place to live and a pressure-less end to the season resulted in the town's folk having a completely carefree attitude to the day and being more than pleasant hosts.

Around twenty to three, we emptied our bladders and made our way to the ground, singing all the way. On reflection, it could have been considered rude to mark our arrival and invasion of their town in such a way but thankfully, the ever-smiling residents of Derby didn't seem to mind. Once we were in the ground, we began to build ourselves up for the match. Both sets of fans began to sing songs to each other to try and get the upper hand in the terraces, and the teams were met with a huge roar as they walked out onto the pitch.

Derby fans had been applauded for their continued attendance and atmosphere during their Premiership campaign that had seen 29 defeats. They'd even sold out of season tickets for the following season and needed a waiting list. If you were one of the people who had to go onto a waiting list to get a season ticket to watch the 'Worst Premiership Team of all time', you must have stopped yourself at some point, looked in the mirror and questioned your existence. Being there would have been bad enough but wanting to be there and not being able to go and watch the whole miserable experience must have been even worse.

Missing out on the humiliation takes away from it. You need to be there, embrace it and be able to tell any laughing armchair supporters that it doesn't matter because at least you get to cheer your team and see them live. Sometimes, like our loss against Scunthorpe, you just need to laugh at yourself and your team in the same way that a parent may laugh at their teenage son, when he wears some unnecessarily outlandish clothes or has a ridiculous hair cut. It's embarrassing for everyone but you get on with life. You still love them – which was lucky for Pavel as he still wore his own teenage rebellion – a ludicrous centre parting haircut – into his late twenties.

The season of misery on the pitch hadn't stopped Derby supporters from having a party in the Premiership as it seemed that having a pleasant place to live could help you to keep up appearances in the face of football adversity. Middlesbrough fans had gone through much less and given up much easier. I can only conclude that the surrounding area of a football team helps to shape the outlook and attitude of their supporters. A quick wander around the North London streets of Tottenham will explain why Spurs fans are so depressive to listen to, and a stroll down Islington High-street explains why Arsenal fans are so up themselves. While a daring venture into some of the pubs near the South Bermondsey docks explains a lot about Millwall.

However, a couple of mediocre championship seasons had taken the edge off the volume of even the most positive Derby supporter. Although the large home following had the perfect chance to make some noise early on as they took the lead after just four minutes.

Derby controlled the rest of the half. The Palace crowd were loud but nervous. All was not going to plan and we knew it. News of Scunthorpe leading filtered through to the away end on people's smart phones. People groaned and swore as they heard the news, which tainted but didn't kill the atmosphere from the Palace faithful. Not even the news that Watford were losing could raise our spirits and voices to their highest level. Maybe it was the absence of whisky or rum or other such substances. It wasn't that Palace weren't singing, it was that we didn't believe in the songs. As loud as we were, there was a voice in the back of our head telling us that we were doomed, which was reflected in our voices.

Mid way through the half, our left back, Lee Hills, went down with what looked like a serious injury. It turned out that he'd broken his leg. Hills had been very highly rated as a youngster and played for England at youth levels, but it was fair to say that he hadn't really kicked on as a player. Although, bar his nightmare at Doncaster, he was starting to show his potential again as our thin squad had allowed him a sustained run of games for the first time. He was at the make or break stage of his career and, having been around the first team squad for over two years, it was to be that moment that effectively finished him off.

Football can be a cruel sport. He'd burst onto the scene as a seventeen year old kid and seemed destined to make it at the top of the game. By the age of twenty-two, he was playing part time in the Conference South, the sixth tier of English football, for Whitehawk. Who are they? Even Accrington Stanley are more famous than them. Who knows what could have happened to him without the injury that he suffered that day.

Half time arrived and I went for a drink with Pavel and his friends. Something happened during the break. Not between Pavel and I, or anything visible. Something unexplainable. People began to sing. Loudly. Very loudly.

"WE LOVE YOU, WE LOVE YOU, WE LOVE YOU..."

During the first half, the game had felt like it was just happening. It was happening to us and there was nothing that we could do to stop it. However, half time gave us a chance to stop and think. It was almost like everyone said a collective *'F*** this. I'm not sitting here and letting this game pass me by. Crystal Palace Football Club means far too much to me to allow this'.*

Up until then, Derby had been so nice, so welcoming, that we were almost on egg shells, not wanting to offend our hosts. It might have been a nothing game for them but it certainly wasn't for us.

The crowd should have come out for the second half to the applause of the players. It was almost like *we'd* had a half time team talk and we were ready for war. As much as the crowd helped, it was the half time introduction of the divisive Stern John that really changed the game. A first tactical masterstroke by Paul Hart as he changed the shape of the team to accommodate a second striker. Despite his vital goal at Watford, there were still plenty of fans who still held a grudge against John for the way that he had acted all season. His introduction would have usually been greeted with more sighs than applause. However, whether it was our new found 'us against them' mentality with him being more part of 'us' than 'them' or whether it was because Hart was *finally* making an attacking substitution or whether it was simply out of desperation, I don't know; but he was roared onto the pitch by the away crowd.

Palace were infinitely better in the second half. We started slowly but as the crowd continued to sing loudly and proudly, the players began to take the new-found belief from the crowd and show it on the pitch. Ambrose nearly got us back into the game with a fine effort that was well saved by the Derby keeper and after that, John took centre stage.

First, he beat his man and fired a shot away to the far corner, which the keeper expertly tipped wide. Minutes later, he showed outstanding composure and skill to control the ball in the air, chip it over a defender and smash it goalwards. The away end erupted. The ball cannoned off the underside of the bar and away. We couldn't believe it. It had seemed like a certain, magical, goal. Maybe it wasn't to be our day. Time was running out and we were still behind. The other games were all but over, Scunthorpe led 3-0 and Watford were being smashed 4-1 at Leicester. However, neither of those games mattered if we couldn't get the goal that we needed to get back into the game.

Still the crowd kept going. It was like we'd taken a vow at half time to suck the ball into the net and we were not going to be accused of not trying. Palace have always been a club with an average atmosphere. Nothing special but not a club who'd get picked out as being famously quiet like Fulham or Arsenal or Charlton. However, our spell in administration had changed all that. Being so close to the edge meant that just going to Palace was no longer enough, we needed to be heard and we needed to celebrate the club. If we weren't heard, the club would die and there would be nothing to celebrate. Not singing wasn't an option.

With five minutes left, John once again used his experience to expertly control the ball in a packed penalty area. He managed to wriggle himself free of his marker and fire the ball across the goal. This time the net rippled and nothing could contain the explosion of delight and love from the away end. Strangers hugged each other. John dived into the crowd, followed by various other Palace players. I went through the entire happy/relieved routine of punching, shouting, kicking, screaming, stamping, kissing and hugging anyone and anything.

Palace pushed for a winner in the final stages but it didn't come. The players came over to take the applause at full time and return the compliment to us. A draw wasn't a great result but players and fans alike had given it everything. Often, players seem to come over to clap the away fans out of duty but, as it did at Watford, the player's gratitude seemed incredibly genuine. They came close enough that we could see in their eyes what it meant to them.

The difficult thing about the end of the game was that we weren't sure if it had been a decent result or a poor one. Sheffield Wednesday weren't due to play their game until the following day, when they played their city rivals, United. A Wednesday win would put us back into the drop zone. Thanks to their comfortable win against Bristol, Scunthorpe looked pretty safe and it now appeared to be one team from three to go down with Plymouth and Peterborough.

Position	Team	Played	Goal Difference	Points
20	Watford	43	-13	48
21	Crystal Palace	44	-3	47
22	Sheffield Wednesday	43	-19	45
23	Plymouth Argyle	43	-19	41
24	Peterborough United	44	-34	31

After a long standoff, where neither players nor fans wanted to turn their back on each other, the players eventually traipsed off the pitch to the tune of 'We Love You'. Back in the pub, after conceding such a late goal, the Derby fans could have been forgiven for being a bit pissed off with singing Palace fans but they weren't. They'd admired our atmosphere and claimed that it was by far the best that they'd had at Pride Park that season. We were unsure what we could take from the result of the game but the overriding emotion that I would take away was pride, which was especially fitting considering the name of the ground.

In the pub, Pavel, Dan and I (Neil had passed out and was asleep in the corner by this point) spoke of the only topic that was on everyone's lips: Sheffield Wednesday away. Pavel was going to buy a ticket and was trying to persuade his mates to do the same. Well, those of them who were awake.

Sat out in the evening sun, we started to chat to a large Palace fan named Nick. We would continue to bump into him around the country over the following years and happily discuss Palace. Eventually, he would change from a recognisable face, to a face that we sought out and then from someone we chatted to, to a mate, and finally, from a mate to a friend, who we meet up with away from football. I'd spent all season alone and wishing I had more Palace supporting companions and then, in one trip to Derby, I seemed to be creating a small army of football friends.

My train left Derby around six o'clock so I was back in London around eight. I got the train with Colin's friends, led by John, and we sang and drank the whole way home. We had no idea if the point was to be of any use to us or not but we were going to celebrate it anyway. We'd worked hard for it after all.

Back in London, I headed to the O'Neils by King's Cross Station with John, his son Sam, and his friends, Alan and Vance. We continued to sing until we were asked to quieten down by the manager. This annoyed me as I'd gone in there after arriving early at the station in the morning and the pub had been full of loud, singing Manchester United fans, who'd been allowed to do as they pleased. Regardless, we did as we'd been asked and stopped the singing. Five of us chanting in the corner of an uninterested pub didn't have the same effect as two and a half thousand passionate fans in a packed ground anyway. Although in our drunken states, it seemed just as good.

Alan was supposed to be going to a 'fancy' ball with his wife that evening and he'd been given instructions that if he wasn't able to speak, don't bother coming. He was certainly able to speak as he rushed off around the bar, chatting to anyone and everyone who went near him. He was determined to make friends that night. I did wonder if that was because he wasn't likely to have any at home after getting into the drunken state that he found himself in.

The other four of us stood at the end of the busy bar, next to where food was left for the waiters to take from the kitchen, as we supped pints and relived the day. It had been fantastic but it was horrible to have to spend 24 hours agonising over whether the result was a good one or not. I'd known John and Alan all season because of Colin, but I'd barely spoken to them until that night. Like Colin, they all lived in Cheam and as a group, they went to about ten away games each season.

I was really enjoying getting to know them. Sam is my age but the others were in their fifties. In any non-football environment, drinking with guys thirty years older than yourself, who you have no family connection to, would seem strange but as usual, our bond of Palace made the age barrier invisible. They've seen it all with the club and to them, the whole administration thing was a lot more relaxed. They were confident that Parish's consortium would take us over and we'd be ok.

I must admit, while I stood and drank with them, there were two things that should have been on my mind but weren't. Firstly, I was starting my teaching placement on the following Monday and I'd made a half-hearted promise to myself that I wouldn't get too drunk. Secondly, I hadn't eaten since getting a bacon and sausage baguette from the butchers across from my house at ten o'clock in the morning. I was starving. As the food was left on the side, waiting to be taken to tables, I couldn't resist, I was pinching a chip off each plate that came past. This continued for seven or eight poor people's meals until I was caught.

The manager went ballistic but John thought it was hilarious. They threatened to kick us *all* out but realising a) I was in the wrong, b) I should probably go home anyway because of my placement and c) I barely knew the guys that I was with and didn't want to irritate them, I said it was only me and offered to leave. However, the pub manager was having none of it. He wanted all five of us out. I'd started to go but as John finished his pint and discussed going to another pub with his mates, I waited on the side. Mr Pub Manager still wasn't satisfied. He didn't want them to finish their pints. He wanted them out of his pub. Now. Within a couple of minutes, the police had arrived. To say that the situation had escalated quickly was somewhat of an understatement. From me stealing the odd chip, I'd managed to get four guys a police escort out of a pub and a ban for life. Ironically, I was left in the pub, watching the whole bizarre situation unfold. I finished my pint and followed them out.

We continued to Victoria, where we went to the Wetherspoons to have another drink. I regularly drink with John and his group at Palace these days and I occasionally see him away from football too. Although it tends to be for a different sport or an event of some sort, rather than simply meeting up for a pint. That day at Derby will always be remembered as the start of many friendships by me.

Although it wasn't just the friendships that made the day special, it was everything. The determination and togetherness of the crowd and the players. The singing, the passion, the nerves. In some ways, the day was too good. Everything about it felt like an early season fun day out, where everyone went home happy with a point. The seriousness of the whole situation seemed to get lost in the fun. In a way, it was a strange and vicious cycle. Having fun is what football should be all about but I couldn't have fun at football without a club to support. The draw could have been a disastrous result that would leave us in the drop zone with two games left. Therefore, would it have been better to have traded all the enjoyment that I'd had for a s*** day of heavy rain, cancelled trains, aggressive home fans, lonely travel, gone off beer and a scrappy 1-0 win? There was more to this being a football fan lark than was evident on the surface. Did I want a mixture of the two? Was it that I was simply having some good days out and the football was neither here or there? Could I have such days without the football? Could I still go to a good pub with good friends and drink good beer and fill my Saturdays that way?

I certainly wouldn't have met the people that I had met without the football. However, my main conclusion was that yes, I could fill Saturdays in good pubs with good beer and good friends. It wouldn't be unpleasant in the slightest and it would certainly be less stressful than going to football but it was that stress that I craved. That passion is what is important in a person and it was a passion that at the time, could only be lit in me by Crystal Palace Football Club. Not even football in general. Just Palace.

Over time, I have realised that having one passion is far too risky – just as my Dad had done. Palace were showing me that having only one passion left me open to losing everything in one foul sweep and I've learnt to have more. I now have a passion for teaching and I've had a passion for certain women in my life and I've had a passion for writing this story. I've discovered a passion for travel, seeing new places and trying new foods. I've found the rewards in keeping yourself fit and playing a variety of sports, something that I would shy away from in the past. Even football. As much as I loved watching it, playing the game terrified me. At the time, as a twenty year old guy, there wasn't anything in the world that I cared about enough to rival my passion for Palace.

Anyway, what was clear was that I had two more games to endure of my challenge. I say endure because I knew that the last two games wouldn't be like the Derby one. For those two, there would be no escaping the seriousness of the matches and simply having fun. My passion was under threat and we needed to stay up to survive. The Sheffield Wednesday match had loomed as an inevitable showdown for months and it was getting bigger and bigger by the minute.

Chapter 59 – **Other Games**

Sunday 18th April – Saturday 24th April 2014, Watford/Sheffield Wednesday vs Various Teams at Various Grounds.

The potential league table didn't bare thinking about:

Position	Team	Played	Points
20	Watford	45	54
21	Sheffield Wednesday	45	51
22	Crystal Palace	44	47

The one thing worse than watching your own team is watching another team and needing to cheer them on as your own. Over the space of six days I would become a Sheffield United, QPR, Reading and Cardiff supporter.

The dreaded table above was an entirely possible situation. Sheffield Wednesday and Watford had two matches each before we played against West Brom on the Monday night, live on Sky. Playing after our rivals was certainly of no benefit to us. It was terrifying. If our two rivals somehow both won their matches, we would be all but down, without even kicking a ball in anger. Although, I suspect I would have kicked, hit and screamed at most things in anger if that had happened. Football fans will always tell you that this is their worst nightmare. At least when it is your own team, you feel a small amount of control on the situation. Explaining that to non-football fans, who'll point out that it is the players and not the supporters that affect the game, is impossible (although, by contrast, you'll have a tough time justifying that to anyone who was in Derby). However, there is certainly more comfort in needing your team to get a result than relying on others.

First up was Sheffield Wednesday against their bitter steel-city rivals, United. I listened to the game on the radio, which is quite possibly the worst way to follow a match. Between over excited commentators and dodgy signals, you can barely work out what is going on. You shut your eyes and try to paint a picture of what is happening in your mind but irritatingly, I seem to be imagining the ball with the team that I am cheering in an attacking position one moment and with no explanation, the confused voice coming from your radio is shouting that the other team are through on goal the next. You only seem to find out ten minutes later that it was offside anyway or in the worst case scenarios, it was an 'audio replay' of an earlier moment. The whole experience only adds to your nerves and leaves you feeling physically sick. Eventually, I gave up on the radio and turned on Sky Sports News.

Wednesday took the lead in the first half but were pegged back for a draw. They'd only matched our result, which left them in the drop zone and one point behind us. No matter what happened now, we knew a win on the last day would keep us up. Watford did their bit too. They lost 1-0 to Neil Warnock's QPR to leave their survival hopes hanging in the balance. I'd followed the midweek game while trying not to fall asleep as the six o'clock alarm calls for placement and days of actual work were shocking my body.

Position	Team	Played	Points
20	Watford	44	48
21	Crystal Palace	44	47
22	Sheffield Wednesday	44	46

The first week of placement came and went reasonably uneventfully, but I had a few nagging worries about the school. However, nothing serious enough to distract me too much from the football. I set an early Saturday alarm so that I could do some planning in the morning because I knew, come three o'clock, I would not be able to concentrate on anything other than the games affecting the bottom of the Championship table. I'd learnt from the time when I was shopping in Reading with my mate Rob during dramatic non-Palace end of season matches that I needed to be as close to the action as possible. Short of travelling to Watford or Wales, this meant being glued to *Soccer Saturday*. However, by 3:15, I wished that I was doing anything but lying on my bed, watching the football scores.

Cardiff...0 Sheffield Wednesday... 1
Watford... 1 Reading...0

Thankfully, Sheffield Wednesday's lead was short lived. It would have been typical of bloody Cardiff to screw us over, but they had playoff aspirations of their own and needed the points. Two minutes later, they were level. *"...and the Sheffield Wednesday crowd have been silenced!"* we're the only words that I needed from Chris Kamara before I jumped up, heavily stretching the springs of my cheap university bed.

Just after half time, I had one of those moments where you can't possibly decide how you feel. Jeff Stelling announced *"There's been some big goals in the Championship involving Watford and Sheffield Wednesday!"*

They went to Vicarage Road first.

Watford...2 Reading... 0

Bloody Reading.
Then they went to Wales.

Cardiff...2 Sheffield Wednesday... 1
Get in!

Watford got a third soon after. As it stood, they were mathematically safe. It was now down to one from two. Us or Sheffield Wednesday. All eyes were on Cardiff. I was reading the BBS, while listening to Sky Sports News, desperately trying to get any information about the events in South Wales. From what I could gather, Wednesday were on top.
"The Wednesday fans are very quiet Jeff, they can feel this slipping away from them..." Karama told the studio. I really didn't understand how people could watch this all season. As I'd been at every game, I'd never really cared about 'Jeff and the Boys' before. It didn't affect me. However, listening to those guys having a laugh and a joke while I sat on my bed, sweating with fear, only served to piss me off. It certainly wasn't entertainment. Although, with hindsight, I can see why that might reflect worse on me than it does on the show.
Suddenly, I froze. Silent.

"There's been a goal at the Cardiff City Stadium"

Cardiff... 2 Sheffield Wednesday... 2

"It's been coming..." started Karama. I stopped listening after that. ****!

Back in the studio, two minutes later, I froze again *"This goal might have huuuuge ramifications at the bottom of the Championship table. There's been ANOTHER goal at the Cardiff City Stadium!"*

****!

Stelling tantalizingly waited as he tried to build the tension. I frantically refreshed the webpage in front of me as I had done all afternoon. The results of the new page could be disastrous.

There was a whole page full of 'YEEEESSSSSSSSSSS'es on the BBS!

Cardiff City... 3 Sheffield Wednesday... 2

Despite a nervous finale, it stayed that way, which meant avoiding defeat on the last day would keep us up. However, even better than that, a win against West Brom on the Monday night would result in a stress-free party in Sheffield as we'd have already secured our Championship status.

Position	Team	Played	Points
21	Crystal Palace	44	47
22	Sheffield Wednesday	45	46

Chapter 60 – **A Chance of Salvation**

Monday 26th April 2010, Crystal Palace vs West Brom, Selhurst Park

Crystal Palace: Julian Speroni, Clint Hill, Shaun Derry, Patrick McCarthy, Darren Ambrose, Neil Danns, Sean Scannell (Alan Lee, 68), Matt Lawrence (Alassane N'Diaye), Calvin Andrew, Danny Butterfield, Johnny Ertl (Stern John, 77)
Subs Not Used: Nathaniel Clyne, Nicky Carle, Claude Davis, Charlie Mann
West Brom: Scott Carson, Jonas Olsson (Abdoulaye Meite, 78), Marek Cech, Robert Koren (Giles Barnes, 71), Roman Bednar, Chris Brunt, Graham Dorrans (James Morrison, 85), Yousouff Mulumbu, Gabriel Tamas, Simon Cox, Steven Reid
Subs Not Used: Dean Kiely, Joe Mattock, Chris Wood, Sam Mantom

The dilemma that had spun round and round my head after the Derby game was no longer relevant. I didn't give a s*** about anything surrounding the game or the quality of the performance. I wanted the three points that we needed to survive and nothing else would matter.

In the lead up to the game, one of the most important issues of the administration came to light. When HMRC had issued Palace with our winding up order, they'd also issued them to three or four other clubs. Basically, the taxman was understandably fed up of being ripped off by football clubs and they were trying to take action. Clubs were building up huge bills and effectively using the unpaid debt as a loan because if they went into administration, HMRC were not a secured creditor. Therefore, clubs felt limited urgency to pay the money back.

However, the tax man was not the only business being screwed over. St. John's Ambulance, the first aid charity, had been owed £16,000 that they wouldn't see because of the mismanagement of Crystal Palace Football Club. Football supporters, led by Palace fans, raised the money so that they weren't left out of pocket. Unfortunately, a football club going into administration would mean lots of other hard working creditors losing out. I had only really considered the threat to my social life that Jordan's errors were posing. For many people, their working livelihood had been affected and they'd been left short changed by the club. The full list of creditors was published online and was a sick and hallowing thought. I suspect there were plenty of people who thought that we deserved to go down – and worse.

I was now six days into my teaching placement and it was already becoming a nightmare. The school was not a happy environment to be in. Ten of the twelve teachers had handed in their notice and two were signed off with stress. The head teacher's dedication to do her best for the school had somewhere been mixed up with psychotic bullying and an abuse of power. Teachers were made to feel worthless and effectively blackmailed by their controlling boss. On top of that, it was clear that the teacher I was working with neither wanted a student teacher or liked me. Teaching placements are stressful and pressurised but this was too much. Having loved all of my previous school experiences, I was already counting down the days for this one to end and questioning if I was going into the right profession.

The teacher that I was working with suggested that I was being unprofessional by going to the West Brom game. Naively, I tried to explain to her my challenge and the position that Palace were in, but understandably, for a lady in a highly stressed job and a single parent of two, she made no attempt to appreciate the situation. The one saving grace was that I had a huge amount of respect for her as a teacher and I knew that I would learn a lot from her. In order to have any kind of working relationship with someone who you don't get on with, it is vital that you know that they are good at their job. She was outstanding. Unfortunately, this meant that she rightly had very high standards, which it was clear that she didn't think I met, and she wasn't going to invest the time to support me in achieving them.

I have since had a student teacher who I didn't rate and didn't like. However, I used my experience of that horrific placement to try and always appear constructive and supportive as I know what a highly stressful time it is for students. At the time, I was looking at the university standards and feeling that I was meeting them, which I was, but once you're qualified, which I would be in a few short months, those standards are incredibly low by comparison. I will also admit that I haven't had to support a student while Miss Trunchbull was breathing down my neck, as she was having to do.

Despite the game meaning everything, I arrived at the pub just before seven and ordered myself an orange juice. I was going to be interrogated if I appeared tired at work the following day so I didn't want to have even the smallest amount of alcohol. The maths was so easy that it didn't even need discussing in the pub. Win and we were safe. Anything else and it went down to a final showdown the following weekend.

Dan, Colin, Jonathan and Kev filled me in on a few embarrassing missing gaps from the night after the QPR game. I told them about the day in Derby and they told me how well the Palace crowd had come across on the radio. Usually, the final home game of the season would be a time for reflection on the highs and the lows of the campaign (as well as an excuse for a boozy post-match session) but this was different. This season was a long way from being over.

Much of the discussion was about the West Brom striker, Roman Bednar, who had said that he wanted Palace down because one of our players had made a comment about his former drug problem during our win at the Hawthorns earlier in the year. I must admit, I had a lot more empathy with the creditors who would happily see us down than this over-sensitive opponent. West Brom had already secured their promotion and it was hard to tell if they would all be as fired up as their Czech centre forward, or if they would have their flip-flops out and be looking forward to their summer of celebration on the beach.

We headed over to the ground a bit earlier than usual and the atmosphere was outstanding. The Holmesdale Fanatics had given the whole lower tier red and blue flags to wave before kickoff and there was a real eagle flying on the pitch. CPFC 2010, the consortium lead by Steve Parish who were trying to save the club, were having trouble buying the ground, but they were still very dedicated in their attempts to do so. Ron Noades, who'd split up the club and the ground in the eighties, was still haunting the club. The previous day there had been a rumour that the game was to be our last ever at Selhurst Park but a statement had been released earlier in the day, playing down the possibility of this being the case.

When I heard the rumours about it being our last match at Selhurst, I'd instantly rung my Dad to tell him that he needed to come. He said that work was busy and he didn't fancy the drive. I was furious. It had been the least games that he'd been to in a season since we'd started going together and he couldn't even make the effort in the club's hour of need. He'd lost his closeness to Palace and I took it personally. I couldn't expect the teacher on my placement to understand the trauma that my club and I were going through but I expected my own father to. I expected him to be going through the same but he wasn't. He had other things in his life that were just as, if not more, important to him. Unlike me it seemed. Palace were everything. I was wrong to take it personally as it was his Palace bond that had worn thin; not his parental bond but I saw the two as entwined.

Palace started the match brightly in front of a buzzing Selhurst Park. We took the lead through an own goal and the place erupted. As he had done on so many occasions throughout the season, Ambrose made the goal, putting in the perfect cross. For four beautiful minutes, we were safe but then, West Brom equalised. Their fans went into full gloating mode and sung about their already secured promotion and our imminent relegation, which only upped the tempo of the Palace crowd.

Unfortunately, while the crowd were coming out on top, the players were struggling against an impressive side, who wanted to finish their season in style. Speroni pulled off a string of superb saves late in the half and we headed towards the break at one all. The Palace fans really got on Roman Bednar's back, singing *"Does your dealer know your here?"* and *"Takes it up the nose"*. I'd usually find those kinds of responses funny but the situation was far too delicate for terrace banter. I wanted to sing for Palace, I didn't care about Roman Bednar.

At half time, I gave up on the not drinking and went for a beer in the Red'n'Blue bar. One couldn't hurt right? Anyway, never mind somersaults, my stomach was in an Olympic Gymnastics Final, flipping and twisting and jumping with nerves and, while a beer might not calm it, doing nothing was unlikely to either. I downed the bottle of lager as quick as I could and made my way back to the seat; long before the half was due to kick-off. As the referee blew his whistle to start what could possibly be the last ever half of football at Selhurst Park, there was an enormous roar from the disappointing crowd of 17,798. Considering what was at stake, I'd expected more to show up.

The second half had the same electrifying atmosphere; West Brom continued to have chances and Speroni continued to save them. The players were giving everything but they had no answer to the quick passing and movement of our opponents. The best chance of the night fell to the feet of Bednar. He was through on goal and tried to round Speroni. He seemed to be past our Argentine hero but Speroni dived backwards and managed to get a hand on the ball and scoop it away to safety.

However, we had our chances too, especially when Paul Hart threw on Alan Lee and Stern John with twenty minutes left. The double sub against Leicester had killed the crowd but this one cranked it up to top volume. When you need a goal, there's nothing more exciting than seeing two strikers coming off the bench. Looking back, it shows just how desperate we were that Alan Lee and Stern John could provoke such a reaction from the crowd. They'd scored seven goals in fifty eight league games between them. Neither of them were prolific but they had both managed to win over the Palace crowd. Lee with his wholehearted displays and John with his two vital goals.

John bundled a chance wide in the closing stages and Sean Scannell skied a decent chance. Late on, Neil Danns stupidly got himself sent off for a head-butt which left us completely open, especially after the subs. Not only would we have to see out the remainder of this game with ten men, but we would also be without our star midfielder for the final day showdown; unless we could find a goal from somewhere. West Brom looked to seize their chance and make the extra man count but it was the Palace crowd who cheered loudest when the fourth official did his bit and added on 6 minutes of injury time. The difference between a loss and a draw meant nothing. However, a win would see us safe.

In the final minute of the six added on, the moment came. With the West Brom goalkeeper out of his goal, Ambrose received the ball just outside their penalty area. He managed to turn and slotted the ball towards the unguarded net. The entire stadium rose as they took a deep breath in anticipation. A defender slid across the goal and cleared the ball off the line. It wasn't to be our night.

I left as soon as the whistle went, taking a final, heartfelt look at my beloved home, and unfortunately missed a very emotional lap of appreciation for the players. I wanted to show them what their performances and effort had meant to me over the season as I couldn't have been prouder, but I simply had to get home and get to bed as I had work the next day. Unfortunately, Dan and I still managed to miss our train at Clapham Junction so we headed to The Falcon for the final time of the season.

"What do you want James?" he asked.
"Just a coke please mate,"

I was tired and panicked. I was certainly in no mood for drinking. I was worried about my placement and I was worried about my Palace.

Last game of the season away to Sheffield Wednesday we need a point to stay up. For a few of us lads, it would be the biggest game we have ever played in. We boarded the train up to Sheffield to find that the train company had only gone and double booked our seats. So on the eve of our biggest battle, the lads are sitting in walkways; on bags, toilet seats, you name it. We couldn't help but laugh it off.
Clint Hill

In that group of players there was certain individuals who I classed as real leaders. On the morning of the game, we all got together to have a chat and a walk near our hotel near Sheffield. As the captain of the side I encouraged everybody to have their say on the afternoon that awaited us. To each man we all knew the importance of one 90 minutes for our football club. Having left that walk and returning to our rooms, Danny Butterfield and I (who I was sharing with at the time) both turned to each other and gave each other a hug as we knew that possibly that would be the last time we would play together which at the time brought tears to my eyes. We both knew that there was only going to be one outcome that afternoon and that was that we were going to stay in the Championship.
Shaun Derry

Chapter 61 - **The Final Showdown**

Sunday 2ⁿᵈ May 2010, Sheffield Wednesday vs Crystal Palace, Hillsborough.

Crystal Palace: Julian Speroni, Danny Butterfield, Patrick McCarthy, Matt Lawrence, Clint Hill, Darren Ambrose, Shaun Derry, Johnny Ertl, Sean Scannell (Claude Davis 90), Calvin Andrew (Alassane N'Diaye 61), Alan Lee (Stern John, 84)
Subs Not Used: Charlie Mann, Nathaniel Clyne, Nicky Carle, Kieran Djilali
Sheffield Wednesday: Grant, Nolan (Francis Jeffers, 75), Purse, Beevers, Spurr, Verney, Potter, O'Connor (Esajas, 67), Johnson, Tudgay, Clarke (Tom Soares, 45)
Subs Not Used: O'Donnell, Buxton, Hinds, Gray

      I woke up around five am on the floor of our Travelodge room in Leeds. Trying to save money, I'd booked a three person room for Martin, Phill, Steve and myself to share. I'd gone out the previous night and tried to enjoy the evening but it was no use. My heart and mind weren't on the night. I'd left the nightclub early and had a couple of hours sleeping on the bed before the others got in and woke me up, reminding me of my agreement that I'd sleep on the floor.

      With my head pounding, my throat dry and the others still fast asleep – giving little or no thought to the importance of the day ahead – I got up and headed out into the town. I bought myself a soft drink and just wondered around Leeds in my Palace shirt. It was already light but other than the odd wondering drunk, the city was empty. Today was the decider on every front. The decider of our relegation, the decider of the club's future and the decider of my challenge. I'd thought about how I would feel after going to every game in the season plenty of times but I'd never imagined it like this. To be perfectly honest, I didn't give a toss about the challenge anymore.

      The good thing was that there were no ifs, buts or maybes. It was easy. Win or draw and the day was ours. Lose and it was theirs. It was us or them. That phrase kept on echoing over and over through my brain. Us or them. Us or them. Us or them. That week, the stress of placement had kept me occupied. I was thankful for the distraction or I might have gone mad. I'd used every spare moment to watch youtube videos of famous Palace wins and montages of inspiring moments. However, whatever I looked at, there was nothing to compare this to.

      Playoff finals are exciting days out and there is a buzz and anticipation ahead of them, which makes the build up at lot more enjoyable. Ultimately, the worst that can happen is that you stay where you are. You can't go backwards and you get a big day out at a top stadium. Even previous last day showdowns hadn't been all riding on our game. To get in the playoffs in 2004, we'd relied on another game elsewhere. Our last day relegation at the end of the following season had four teams involved in four different matches. Even Dougie Freedman's heroics at Stockport had been dependant on other results around the country in Grimsby, Huddersfield and Portsmouth. No, I'd never known anything like it. Outside the four walls of Hillsborough, nothing else in the world mattered.

In fact, it really felt like the rest of the world were watching us. We were certainly the game of the weekend in the country – from any division. The match was live on the BBC and millions without a ticket would tune in to see what I was watching - live.

Other football fans seemed to have two trains of thought. Some, seeing the hardship that we had gone through, wanted a Palace victory. Others, feeling that entering administration was a way of cheating, felt that we should have been already relegated as the Sheffield Wednesday chairman, Lee Strafford, had suggested. To be perfectly honest, I didn't give a toss about what supporters of other clubs felt.

Dan had texted me on the Tuesday, while I was enduring another day of my unfulfilling and stressful placement. He and John had bought match and train tickets for the game as the last of the six thousand away seats sold out. He'd been debating whether it was worth it as the price of train tickets had rocketed and it was going to be an expensive day out but his wife, Carol, had given him the final nudge to go.

"You'll regret it if you're not there!"

She was right. No Palace fan wanted to go through the torture of the match from anywhere else but in the ground. I felt a little bit guilty for bringing five non-Palace fans along to the sell-out fixture but at the same time, they'd wanted to commit months before most Palace fans had taken an interest in the game.

I couldn't help but think back to the return fixture in September at Selhurst Park. I'd been right at the start of my final university year, with freshers' events still going on. I wouldn't even have bothered going if it wasn't for the challenge; my final fresher's ball was both more exciting and remarkable than the early season league game, played in front of just twelve thousand fans. The game had been as meaningless and forgettable as could be. The teams were twelfth and thirteenth in the league and barely managed a shot on goal between them. What I would have done to guarantee a repeat of such a boring and uneventful 0-0 draw. It's amazing that after travelling around five thousand miles and spending around two and a half thousand pounds, I was desperate for it all to end with a terrible 0-0 draw.

As I wondered around the empty streets, I also thought all about the Freddy Sears goal at Bristol that had cost us at least one point. A point that would have seen us already safe. Of course there had been hundreds of refereeing decisions throughout the season that had both benefited and hindered us and I am a firm believer in decisions evening themselves out over the course of the season. However, throughout the season, there hadn't been any other decisions like that in any other games. And I don't just mean in our own games. It had been by far the most blatant and shocking decision out of the two-thousand and thirty six Premiership, Championship, League 1 and League 2 games that were played in the 2009/10 season. Other than matches down the local park, where there are no nets on the goalposts, I don't think such a terrible decision would be possible to be made, ever again.

Thinking about Rob Shoebridge made me angry so I tried to change the subject. Changing the subject in your own head is difficult. If your brain wants to think of the same thing on cycle then it is quite hard to make it stop. I tried being positive and thinking of my favourite moments of the season and imagining a last minute Palace equaliser from Speroni to keep us up. I thought about the season and tried to go through each game, remembering my highlights. I thought of the Plymouth game and the wedding and I smiled to myself. Then I thought of the Torquay game, where Ambrose had introduced himself to us with a couple of goals. Little did we know back then that he would get a further seventeen that season. I was beginning to cheer up. Who did we play next? Bristol. Ah yes. F***ing Bristol. This clearly wasn't going to work as a distraction.

The good thing about football is that there is always a silver lining or consolation prize. Under usual circumstances, getting relegated would be heartbreaking but there would be some positives. For example, we'd get to play Brighton, Millwall and Charlton. I'd also get to see us play Brentford, where I could visit the four pubs on each corner and enjoy the banter with Chris and Jak. As well as all the local games, relegation would open up a whole host of possible new grounds to help me on my way to the ninety two. In a way, I'd always kind of wanted to get relegated. I was bored with the Championship and playing Preston and Ipswich and Coventry, year in, year out. However, this was different. This wasn't usual circumstances. There was not an intrigue of League 1. There was a fear. Not only a fear of relegation. A fear of losing the club that I love.

After a couple of hours wondering alone, I made my way back to the hotel and lay there for what seemed like an age before the others woke up. The four of us met Chris and Jak at the Wetherspoons in Leeds station for a fry up to prepare us for the day. Chris pulled me aside and spoke to me, *"Jak and I have agreed. If you get relegated, we know how painful it is. We won't say anything until we're back in London. Once we're back, its fair game."*
I understood what he was saying and it was reasonable enough. They had no loyalty to Palace and no reason to want us down or up other than for 'banter'. However, it reiterated to me that I'd made a huge mistake in inviting non-Palace fans to such a game. It didn't matter that they were some of my closest friends. They certainly weren't what I needed on that day. While Chris and Jak understood what I was going through, they didn't care as it wasn't their club. In the same way, I wouldn't be bothered about Brentford slipping out of League 1. The other three were armchair supporters who didn't have a clue what it meant to me.

We made our way from Leeds to Sheffield and were in the Wetherspoons by 11 o'clock. There were a reasonable amount of Palace fans in there and a fair few faces I knew, but I stayed to the side, drinking slowly with my five friends. There was plenty of singing but I didn't join in. I couldn't, I was too worried. I hated the fact that I wasn't with Palace fans. I needed to be around people who understood how I was feeling but I wasn't going to just go and speak to anyone in the way that I would if I was on my own. I felt trapped by being with friends. I'd agreed to meet Pavel, Dan and John in the pub but when their train arrived, they were ushered straight onto a bus that took them to the ground.

Just under an hour before kickoff, we emptied our bladders before leaving the pub, but it wasn't that end that I felt like releasing.

Usually there are trams to take you from the town centre to Hillsborough but amazingly, they weren't running. It was the biggest Wednesday crowd for years, including six thousand away fans and they weren't running the bloody trams. You could either get a tram part of the way and then a replacement bus or simply jump in a cab. We jumped in a cab.

During the journey, Steve, who at the age of 22, had recently decided that he now supported Brentford as well as Liverpool, encouraged me to give a recording of the arrogant put down that I'd given Chris and Jak all season. *"League 1 is a small league, full of small teams."*

I refused. I'd been pushing my luck by saying that all season as it ensured that I won any inane banter and trash talk between the three of us as I always had the trump card. However, it was going to make me look very silly if we went down.

We arrived at the ground with plenty of time before kickoff, but not quite enough to head to the Sports Centre that I'd gone to for a beer before the January FA Cup tie. For that game, there'd been a crowd of around eight and a half thousand, including under a thousand Palace fans. Today, there would be a crowd of nearly forty thousand, including six thousand Palace. As we approached the huge stadium, Jak stopped me and shook my hand.

"Well Done," he said solemnly, *"Every game is quite an achievement."*

He knew the money and time that I had invested in my challenge and was quite aware of the size of it. His kind words were a rare moment of respect and graciousness between two overly competitive friends.

"Just be a shame if it's a relegation season really!" he winked. That was the taunting Jak that I knew and loved. For once, I had no response. I simply carried on walking.

We got to the ground and I got a programme, which I put safely in my backpack. I was only missing one from my collection for the season as I'd lost it on a journey home and didn't want to have to replace any more.

"Typical tourist supporter. He's barely been all season and now he rocks up for the big game and buys a programme so he knows who the players are," sarcastically commented Chris, with a knowing grin, just about loud enough so that everyone around us could hear as he tried to embarrass me. I refused to take the bait and simply grinned back at him.

We went into the ground and enjoyed a pie with a dollop of mushy peas shoved on top. I finished the pie and went to the seats. Sometimes, when you buy tickets early, you get put at the very front and have a crap view. Fortunately, that wasn't the case here. We had the best seats in the stand. We were about three quarters of the way up, right behind the goal and, snow storms permitting, we would be able to see the action at both ends clearly. The two large pillars holding the roof up were evenly spaced away from us and our angle was perfect so that neither of them blocked any part of the pitch.

The atmosphere built and the stands filled far quicker than usual as supporters decided that getting behind their team, even during the warm up, was far more important than squeezing in an extra beer. The fans of both sides were singing ardently, knowing that they had to put more into this game than they ever had done before. Wednesday had only won once in their previous eleven and we had only registered two wins in the same period but none of that mattered. Form would go out of the window in a match like this.

Five minutes before kickoff, I looked around the stadium. It was packed. Crammed full with 40,000 passionate fans. That is what football is all about. Well, it should have been. But I wasn't enjoying this. It meant *too* much. I'd enjoyed the nothing games at Preston and Plymouth a lot more than this, where there had been about 300 of us, who'd be there win, lose or draw. The games where no one wanted to go gave me a relaxation. I could trick myself into believing that winning or losing at Preston was going to affect my life but ultimately, the worst that could happen was that I'd be a bit pissed off until the alcohol kicked in later that night. Even the Rob Shoebridge debacle had turned into a joke by the time that we were back in London. However, this was different. This could affect my life. This is what I lived for and this is what was killing me from the inside.

At that moment, 12:55 on Sunday 2nd May 2010, I wanted to be anywhere but Hillsborough. But there I was, stood up. Game face on. About to watch the most chilling 90 minutes of football that I will ever witness. I didn't want to watch this game but I had to. All around me there was singing but I didn't join in. I had 5 close friends alongside me and 6000 Palace fans in the stand but I felt alone. I stood there, staring at the pitch, teeth clenched, eyes focussed, and every muscle in my body tense. Everything seemed to be happening around me and I didn't feel part of it. I was there but it felt like everything else was miles away; the crowd, my friends, the pitch. It was all a blur. A stark contrast from the minutes before the Plymouth game on the opening day of the season when I had been casually joking and enjoying the pre-match build up.

Once the game began, I could relax a bit. Suddenly, it had a more 'normal' feel to it. It was just another game. I could shout at the referee, I could sing the songs, jump up at half chances and wince at every Sheffield attack. When it was happening, it was the game that I could focus on and not the occasion. The Palace fans were in loud voice, as usual, and didn't let the nerves quieten them down. The Wednesday fans played their part too. The ground was rocking.

Ten minutes in, disaster struck. The ball was looped forward by Palace and Calvin Andrew chased it. The Wednesday keeper came out to claim the ball and Andrew threw a boot at it as he tried to poke it into the goal. The keeper caught the ball and Andrew's boot crashed into his head. Immediately, both players dropped to the ground and the others charged in to confront each other. The Wednesday crowd chanted "OFF! OFF! OFF! OFF! OFF! OFF!" as the referee tried to regain order. The players of both sides pushed and restrained each other, as others argued and surrounded the referee. Eventually, the man in the middle produced a yellow card for our centre forward. It had been a huge let off.

The game continued and was fairly uneventful. Both teams were nervous and no player wanted to make a mistake. The crowd were getting louder and louder and Martin, who I was next to, was loving it. He'd never seen anything like it and was jumping around with me so I felt that I had an ally at last.

Midway through the first half, Palace got a corner. Ambrose went out to take it on the far right hand side. He crossed it in perfectly for Alan Lee, who rose unmarked with the goal gaping ahead of him. Time seemed to go into slow motion as he hung in the air, waiting to connect with the ball. Eventually, he headed it. The net bulged. The away end erupted. Martin and I hugged. Palace were leading. Palace fans raised the noise to an entirely new level and the atmosphere in the home end changed. They went quiet. They knew they needed two goals or they were down.

Half time approached and Sheffield hadn't looked like getting back into the game. Danny Butterfield had the ball in our right back position but as he went to clear the ball, he was fouled by the Wednesday striker, Leon Clarke. All eyes turned to the referee, he did nothing. Clarke didn't care. He ran through on goal and curled the ball past Speroni. The ground exploded with joy.

"YOU F***ing ****!" I, along with six thousand other Palace fans, screamed. "Cheating w*****!"

The foul had been blatant and left Butterfield on his arse, kicking thin air. "You could have just killed our club you cheating ****!"

I looked at Martin. He'd invested in our goal and celebrated it as his own but he was grinning at theirs, looking at me in bemusement as I vented my aggression. He'd cheated me on our goal. I felt alone again.

We weren't the only ones releasing our anger. Their goal scorer, Clarke, was obviously worked up too. He punched the air and shoved away his teammates as he took the applause of the jubilant home crowd. As the other players began to head back to the centre circle, knowing they still needed a second goal, he kicked the advertising board in front of him. It broke. Minutes later, he needed to be subbed off with a self-inflicted injured foot. The idiot had hurt himself while celebrating the most important goal of his career. He was replaced by former Palace man, Tom Soares. The entire away end had the same horrible thought. Surely football couldn't be so cruel? Surely a former youth product isn't going to send us down. It would be typical of football's spiteful nature.

Compared to the build up, the match had been easy. It was nowhere near as nerve racking as I'd imagined on my morning stroll. Palace had felt in control for most of the half and Sheffield hadn't really troubled us. It was only the referee who had allowed them back into the game. I shuffled along the line of my friends to speak to Chris during the break and ranted about the referee. He just looked at me with a knowing smile, saying nothing. No disagreement, no agreement, nothing.

I sent some texts out to Dan, John and Pavel to ask where they were and

I text all the Palace fans that I knew who'd been watching at home. I texted my Dad. I'd spoken to him in the morning and out of everyone, I wanted him there. It was he who had inflicted Palace on me and I wanted to share this moment with him. I sent two messages to most people. A proud one of the team and an angry one about the referee. I didn't get a response from anyone.

Soon, the second half was upon us. Once again, I felt more comfortable after it had kicked off. I could focus on our defending and keeping Wednesday out rather than my hatred of the referee. Although, I didn't neglect to express my opinion of him with every decision he gave to the home side. I can't explain why, but I felt 100% confident throughout. I'd built myself up to be a bag of nerves but I didn't feel it. While it was 1-1, we were still set to survive and that was fine by me. The Wednesday crowd were getting quieter by the minute and the Palace fans continued to sing to see our team over that final line.

Around the hour mark, Scannell won the ball near the touchline to our left and cut it back to the edge of the penalty area. It seemed to take an age to reach its target but when it did, Ambrose connected perfectly. I was right in line with the shot. He'd slotted it calmly past the keeper. Pandemonium. Again. Martin grabbed me to celebrate but I ignored him this time. There were a group of Palace fans dressed as lifeguards behind me, God knows why, but I was in no mood to stop and question them. I leaped into their group hug. Palace fans, young and old, male and female, black and white, all embraced each other in the moment. Ambrose slid on his knees in front of the huge away following before he was bundled by teammates. We now had half an hour to avoid conceding two goals.

I prepared for the time to drag and drag but surprisingly, it felt like time moved fairly quickly. The home side and crowd seemed beaten, while the Palace fans continued to make noise. I'd been so used to clock-watching and time slowing down as Palace held onto a result that I think I'd tricked myself into believing that it was going to be even worse than it actually was so that in comparison, the reality wasn't too bad. That and the fact that Sheffield rarely threatened.

Surprisingly, my heart beat at a reasonable pace, my face wasn't dripping with sweat and I didn't feel sick. That was, until the eighty-seventh minute. In the eighty-seventh minute, Sheffield Wednesday equalised. Darren Purse, their centre back, was completely unmarked as he stabbed the ball home at the far post. It was our first defensive mistake of the game and it was punished. Then, I felt sick, and dripped with sweat, and bit my nails, and wanted to turn it off as if it was a scary movie. I couldn't watch any more. If Wednesday scored again, we were down.

For the final few minutes, our goal was under siege. Wednesday put everyone forward and lumped long ball after long ball towards our penalty area. Their crowd had started to leave but they'd returned and were now trying to drag the ball into the goal for the players. The forth official raised his board and added on five more tortuous minutes. I looked along our line. Jak grabbed me; he put his hands on his stomach, pulled a distressed face and said that even he felt nervous. If the tension was doing that to him, how was I supposed to cope? These next five minutes were to be the first major insight into what real football supporting meant for Phill, Martin and Steve. I felt alone, watching on in despair.

Every blocked shot, well defended cross and long clearance was greeted with huge cheers from the Palace faithful. Wednesday refused to give up. Every ball was contested and every tackle was full blooded and meant. Palace tried to slow the game down but Wednesday wouldn't let it stop for breath. Each time we got the ball, we'd kick it as far away from our goal as possible. From once such clearance, with Wednesday over committed, Palace had two attackers with only one covering defender. Ambrose played in John perfectly. He had Ambrose alongside him as he bore down on goal. He carried it from the half way line to the Wednesday penalty area and, with Ambrose screaming for the ball, released his shot. The Wednesday keeper got a hand to it and it trickled goalwards. The ground fell silent. Time froze. The ball hit the inside of the post and rolled along the line before a Wednesday defender got back to hack it away. That should have finished it. Why hadn't he returned the ball to Ambrose? The game should have ended but now, thanks to the selfishness of our Trinidadian centre forward, we still had two more minutes of hell to hold out for.

Wednesday continued to push as they launched ball after ball into our box but the Palace backline stood firm, as they had done for so much of the season. 93 minutes were up. What seemed like hours later, 94 minutes were up. Years passed by and 95 minutes were up. Wednesday sent one final long ball forward, a striker flicked it on and Matt Lawrence threw himself towards the ball. It went out for a corner. Everyone would go forward. This was it. They were sure to score. But then, we were saved. The referee blew his whistle. It was over. We had survived. With five close friends stood to the left of me, I turned to my right and, in one of the happiest moments of my life, I hugged the stranger next to me. I had more in common with him than any of my friends at that moment. We shared the feeling together.

By the time that I had regained consciousness, Chris and Jak had slipped off, leaving me to enjoy the party. The Palace players charged towards us as the Wednesday ones lay flat on the floor. Beaten. Speroni and Claude Davis tried to console them before joining in with the celebrations. A handful of Palace fans charged onto the pitch to grab the Palace players at the front: Ambrose, Derry, Hill and McCarthy.

A group of Wednesday fans then menacingly marched onto the pitch, towards the Palace fans, angered by them celebrating on their pitch after their relegation. I can understand their frustration and why they felt it was disrespectful but in all the emotion that we felt, I don't think there were any provocative intentions behind the Palace fans' actions. The players were ushered from the pitch and the celebrations were cut short as there was a standoff between Wednesday fans and the Stewards.

Clint Hill, after throwing his shirt into the crowd, was still in with the

Palace fans when he was asked to leave the pitch. He began to make his way to the tunnel when he came under attack from some Wednesday thugs. He threw a couple of punches to set himself free of the yobs and charged towards the exit of the pitch, lunatics chasing after him. He was helped off by Nicky Carle and Claude Davis, who looked like a nightclub bouncer with his muscular 6"4 frame at the entrance to the player's tunnel, showing no concern for the situation.

We waited in the stands for the pitch to clear so that we could celebrate with the players but it didn't clear. Pavel had spotted me from a few rows behind and we greeted each other with a long, tired hug. We waited in the ground for about half an hour, while it slowly emptied, before I took one final look at the heroic setting and left.

Outside, the atmosphere was still hostile from the pitch confrontations and Steve, Martin and Phill were edgy. We lost Pavel as he tried to ring Dan and I tried to ring him. Eventually, I let the other three persuade me to leave with them as they thought we were in danger. Having got a cab there, we didn't have a clue where to get the bus from so we asked a steward. We got confused directions, which involved walking through the crowds of Wednesday fans so Steve lent me his hoody to cover up my Palace shirt.

We saw a bus stop but the queue was full of Wednesday fans so the others didn't want to stop at it. They were all naive to the ways of a football crowd and I should have put a stop to their nonsense but I was zoned out, exhausted from the game. The Wednesday fans that were patiently waiting at the bus stop were families, who, like us, just wanted to go home after the emotional trauma of the match. However, I didn't speak up and we continued to walk. We went past the Sports Centre, where I suggested that we got a drink and ordered a cab to but once again, I wasn't strong enough and let the overly worried fools lead the way. After a while, we realised that we must have missed the bus stop that we required and they decided that we should walk all the way back to the station in the town centre.

Once we were away from the ground, I began to receive text messages. My phone had showed up as having reception in the ground but no texts had made it through to me. I had about twelve from my Dad from before, during and after the game. I had texts from Jak congratulating me and warning me to be careful outside the ground. I had texts from every Palace fan I knew, most of which read as a swear word, followed by the word 'YESSSS'. I had texts from my brothers, my cousins, football fans and non football fans. Anyone who'd seen the result, who I knew, had thought of me. I even had a text from Natalie, the girl that I'd taken to QPR. I was pleased that she'd followed the result. Maybe I had made a Palace fan of her after all.

I rang my Dad as I walked alone, slightly behind the other three. We chatted for about half an hour about the game. About the season. About administration. About the performance. About all things Palace. Like me, he wished he'd been there. It was something that we should have done together. He told me that Butterfield wasn't fouled for their first goal (I guess I should retract some of the obscenities that I'd sent in the referee's direction as a formal apology). He told me that the game had been dramatic enough to keep his wife, who had never watched a whole game before, on the edge of the sofa and that she'd jumped up when we scored. We went through every player and the part they'd played. We marvelled over Ambrose's goal and discussed how we hoped that the game would be the catalyst for the takeover to happen or the whole escape would have all been a bit pointless. As we got to end the call, he chipped in,

"Oh and James,"

"Yes," I replied.

"Well done!" there was a pause. *"On going to every game."*

I smiled. *"Thank you,"*

To be honest, I'd totally forgotten about that.

After the phone call, I caught up with the others. We'd been walking for nearly an hour by that point and were entirely lost. I'd been stupid to let them lead the way but I'd been so exhausted that I couldn't think. Part of me wanted to celebrate but a bigger part of me wanted to sleep. I certainly didn't want to be wondering through the outskirts of Sheffield, lost, with two armchair Liverpool fans and one armchair Chelsea fan. With just over half an hour before our train left, we hailed a cab and got back to the station.

Dan and Pavel had texted me to say that they were in a pub by Sheffield station with John. By the time we arrived, they'd left. Maybe if I'd been with the other Palace fans I'd have felt differently but I didn't feel high. After Derby and Watford, I'd felt a massive natural high that had seen me through the next few days but for the Wednesday game, I just felt tired and relieved. At the station, I saw one of the Palace fans from Doncaster, who went to Leeds University; he and I both let out a huge breath of air as we puffed our cheeks and widened our eyes. We had a big hug and wished each other well for the summer.

In a way, we'd been lucky. We'd won just two of our last twelve games and Wednesday had won just one in that time. Both of us had been poor and couldn't have argued with going down. For us, it was the mental and physical exhaustion that had nearly caught the team out. An exhaustion that I was now feeling as a supporter. I don't think it was the same for Wednesday. I couldn't help but feel if they had put the same level of commitment into their previous eleven games as they had against us, we wouldn't have had the chance to send them down. The division had been weak. Watford had looked in big trouble with two games left but after winning both, they finished sixteenth, five places clear of the drop. QPR and Neil Warnock had travelled to Selhurst Park, just two points clear of us but three wins in their final four games lifted them to thirteenth.

It was interesting to listen to Paul Hart after the game. I'd harshly critised him during the season but he'd won me over. Originally, as a person, and after inspiring results and tactics at Watford and Sheffield, as a manager. His post match press conference was heartfelt and humble. His contract was now up but he'd clearly enjoyed his time at Palace and wanted to stay. However, he didn't use his success and newly found high stock to pressurise any new owners; he simply showed that he wanted what was best for the club. Although it was decided that it wouldn't be him to take us into the following season, he left as a Hillsborough Hero and will always be welcomed back at Selhurst Park with a huge amount of respect.

"I often listen to people saying that they've been emotionally drained and I know what they mean now. It's been a very emotional day. Great relief on our part but there's sadness on their part because Alan Irvine's a friend, I played here as well and I've been relegated. It's not very nice. We're hoping the new ownership gets completed and now Palace can build from a sounder base of Championship football, which I think is important
It's such a great club that I would fully expect, with the correct business practices put in place, that the right visionary people, if handled properly, could make great progress. I've said all along, let's get the takeover done then the new owners can make a decision on the next manager. It would be absolutely no hardship whatsoever to work at this football club, it's been a fantastic experience, but they should be allowed to make their own appointments."

From a personal point of view, the train journey home was long and sobering. I had some cans of M&S bitter to try and perk me up and celebrate, but I wasn't feeling like it. I just wanted to get home, read the Palace forum and go to sleep. The season had been full of amazing days out, tainted by disappointing results but on the final day, the match had been too perfect. It had captured every emotion so well that I was drained. I couldn't possibly think about or enjoy anything else that day. I was certainly relieved to have a Bank Holiday following the game so that I could try and recover before another four long days of placement.

Palace had survived on the pitch but it was relief, not joy, that I felt, which made no sense really because if you can't enjoy winning one of the biggest games in the club's history, what is the point in going? Football really does make very little sense at times.

I'm pretty sure our pre-match dance off is what shocked Sheffield Wednesday on the last day as they must of heard us before the game; we'd left the dressing room door open on purpose!!! There was no way that we were going to leave Hillsborough with the dreaded (r) next to our name!!! What a great way to end the season and end my time at Palace too!!!

Danny Butterfield

We had done it, survival against all the odds! What a massive achievement for that group of lads and everyone connected with the club. And to cap the day off for myself, a few hundred Wednesday fans wanted to fill my head in! In all honesty, no one could have touched me after that final whistle cause I was so full of emotion and high on elation from what we had just achieved. A great ending to my Palace career.

Clint Hill

We all know how the game developed but being sat in the dressing room afterwards I looked around our team and knew that if we were asked to play one more game in that season we couldn't have done it. Collectively we had given everything to the cause since administration struck us and the sense of pride caused many players to cry.

Shaun Derry

Hillsborough on the last day of the season still plays out in my mind as if it was yesterday... who will ever forget Clint Hill bulldozing his way across the hallowed turf in socks, boots and just a pair of under crackers?

Matt Lawrence

Maybe we were all a bit crazy, but those two songs were definitely one of the main reasons that we stayed up. Without a shadow of a doubt.

There was a lot at stake at the Hillsborough game. Palace were in dire straights; most of the players were free agents and were looking into an uncertain future. We didnt know what was going on behind the scenes so it was up to us to play for our football club that we love. We shouldn't have been in this position really, but the ten points deduction made this game a 'special one'. The support from the fans was amazing. I remember the red and blue balloons and the packed Palace stand behind the goal.

I knew we would stay up, because of our team spirit and the work ethic we created within the group. The game was nothing for weak nerves, but as soon as the referee blew the final whistle, the emotions were running high.
"We are Staying up!" was a constant tune that I woke up to over the following weeks and I loved it. We knew it was a bit of history in the making and I hope the Palace squad from that day laid the foundations to the bright future that the club has expirienced over the last couple of years.

That season will always be a special one for me because I will never forget what we achieved together as a group of players and fans.

I'm glad I don't live five-hundred miles away from Selhurst Park – only 80 because I would walk there for Palace!

Johnny Ertl

I have never been more confident that we would get the result we needed. I remember in the week prior to the game Dougie Freedman asked me 'How were we going to play?' and I said some thing like 'We are going to play 4-4-2 and go for the throats!' I thought we did just that and I knew after 10 minutes that everything was going to be alright. The whole team was on the front foot and our centre backs were heading everything.

Our support that day was nothing short of magnificent. To be noisier than the home support at Hillsborough was astonishing and the only disappointment on the day was that because of the pitch invasion, I couldn't go to the supporters and thank them.

I can't remember any low points from my time at Palace. The players were magnificent, as were the supporters. A great club. Given the situation when I arrived at the club, I can't believe how much I enjoyed the experience. Crystal Palace is a 'proper' football club. We had great character in the team and great character in our support. Absolutely brilliant!!!

Paul Hart

Chapter 62 – **Doomsday: The Final Battle**

Monday 31st May - Tuesday 1st June 2014, Crystal Palace vs Lloyds Bank, Agilo & PWC, 25 Gresham Street

There was to be one final battle of the season. Once more, I would need to clear my throat and sing my heart out for Palace. However, this wouldn't determine my mood for the evening or what division we played in. This wasn't just another game. This was the end game. This would determine whether I would be able to have a Saturday evening mood, good or bad, ever again...

Placement was still a nightmare but I was in the half term week and enjoying a trip down to Brighton with some friends. Life was good; the takeover was going to happen, the sun was shining, Palace had survived relegation, Speroni had been named Fans' Player of the Year for the third time in a row, I had two interviews coming up, my placement was nearly over, I'd bought my first car and I was on a day out to the seaside with eight of my best friends.

I'd actually made a decision not to go to the supporters rally at Selhurst Park that day. Twenty nine people had been made redundant at the end of April and a Palace fan on the BBS had decided that enough was enough. He wanted our club and our plight to be noticed so he arranged a gathering of Palace fans at the ground for the Bank Holiday Monday. As I'd already agreed to drive to Brighton, after wrestling with my conscience, I decided that I shouldn't back out. I must admit, looking back, I can't believe that I opted to go to Brighton over Selhurst Park under any circumstances, but I had missed out on so many occasions for Palace that I thought I should put my friends ahead of my team for once.

We got to Brighton and did all the usual things; bought a stick of rock, had an ice cream, skimmed some stones, went for a beer and went on the pier, where I bought a car sticker of a Palace fan pissing on a Brighton shirt. Your average day out at the British seaside. We were walking back to the car when I first suspected something was wrong. I got a text from my brother that read *"What's happening with Palace?"*
I then got one from Pavel, who was at the protests, saying *"Things just got real"*
It was somewhat ironic that I was in Brighton as the news of the potential death of Crystal Palace Football Club broke.

I knew something was up but I thought it was just about the Selhurst protests. I rang my Dad to find out what had happened but he didn't immediately answer. I sent a few texts but I was soon driving home. It was on the radio that I heard the first crackling report. There was something about Palace and liquidation on the five o'clock news bulletin but I couldn't quite hear it. I was driving a thirteen year old Ford Fiesta on the motorway and thirteen year old Ford Fiestas tend to make a lot of noise when driving on the motorway – far more than a cheap, old car radio does anyway. By now, my phone was buzzing continuously in my pocket but as a new motorway driver, I didn't dare get it out.

I dropped off my friends in Ascot and looked at my phone.

*"S***!"*

If a deal wasn't done the next day, things were going to get serious. I drove to my mum's house in Egham, as it was closer than Twickenham, and began to read the BBS, look at the news reports from around the internet and watch Sky Sports News on loop.

CPFC 2010 and the administrator had both released statements.

"We are trying to acquire both Crystal Palace Football Club and Selhurst Park. Everyone would agree Selhurst Park is pivotal to the long-term future of the club and CPFC 2010 have always made it clear they will not proceed without securing it. We reached what we thought was an agreement with Bank of Scotland, who are the major creditor of Selhurst Park Ltd. Subsequent to this agreement we have been sent a contract that does not reflect this agreement and is unworkable. There is an anti-embarrassment clause that allows the bank to see a further return if we realise greater value from the ground in the future. It seems that the bank want to make an unlimited return in the future even if that value is created on the back of the success of the football club or money we have invested in a new infrastructure. We believe that the maximum they should make is the difference between what we will pay for the land as a football ground and what a property developer will pay now as a development opportunity plus interest. Bank of Scotland is currently government owned. As such we would urge the new Prime Minister to intervene personally to resolve the situation or see a club supported by many thousands, and with a 100-year history, consigned to the scrapheap."

CPFC 2010

Even now, I shiver reading that final sentence. Guilfoyle, the administrator, responded.

"I've already made the calls [to other clubs]. What I'll actually do after the deadline is start selling players. The enquiries are out, offers have been received. There are a number of players who have value but once they're sold and if no-one else comes in then I'll have to resign, walk away and then the liquidation process will re-start. I am now genuinely concerned because I can't let the thing drift on into June. The staff at Palace have not been paid since the end of April. I can deal with that by selling the club's star players but what CPFC 2010 have said is if you start selling players we'll no longer be interested. If I start selling players - and I will because I have to - I'm not confident CPFC 2010 will still be around. In those circumstances I haven't got anyone to buy the club because they have, for a long time, been the only show in town."

I felt sick. I couldn't eat, I couldn't sleep, I couldn't function. I read on the BBS that people were going to meet at London Bridge station at 11 o'clock for the final protest. I knew I had to be there. I called up BBC Radio London, as they were discussing the club so that I could raise awareness of the march. I texted every football fan I knew, no matter what club they supported, asking them to come to the protest with me. I got a few apologies and well wishes before a text from

Martin, which read 'hahahahahaha'. He'd obviously learnt nothing in Sheffield about being a real football supporter.

Once I was put on air to voice my views on Radio London, I pleaded with people to show up and support our cause. However, the presenter simply wanted me to blame people. The reasons of who and why we had found ourselves in this mess were of no current concern to me. The inquest would wait. All that mattered now was that Lloyds Bank and CPFC 2010 could come to an agreement before 3PM the next day.

I spoke to my Dad. Again, he wanted to come and said he felt guilty that he couldn't but he said that he needed to work. I spoke to Dan, he couldn't make it either. However, this wasn't about having company, this was about my club surviving. I'd thought a lot about the prospect of losing my club but I had never truly believed it would happen. Well, now it was happening. I barely slept that night. This was it. This could be the end.

I got out of bed around five am and drove to Twickenham. I then got the train into Waterloo and the tube to London Bridge. I arrived at about 10 o'clock. I certainly wasn't going to risk missing this so I'd given myself a ridiculous amount of contingency time. There were about five people stood around in Palace shirts, waiting for the march to start. It looked pathetic. Slowly, people started to arrive. A young fan turned up with a couple of hundred printed red and blue 'Save Our Club' posters for us to carry and the station was soon awash with Palace colours.

We began our march just after eleven and the Palace chants echoed around the old station and out into the streets of Central London. Groups of tourists looked on in horror as a few hundred of us marched, making our point loud and clear. Save our club. A young bloke with a *Talksport Radio* microphone started to interview me about it all. He started off by letting me have a voice but he too wanted me to start pointing fingers and naming names. It wasn't about that so I gave him a 'Save Our Club' chant and let him move on to interrogate the next person.

Sky Sports, who were running late, asked us to delay the protests so that they could film us leaving the station. However, after we refused (I can't imagine they'd be late to a Manchester United protest), they soon caught up with us. Cameras were shoved in my face as I sang passionately in the rainy streets of Central London. My phone went mad as a clip of me singing was used for the Sky Sports Headline News Bulletin. For weeks, people were taking frozen images of me, mid-song, looking thuggish and dripping wet in the rain to post on *Facebook*. I didn't care how stupid I looked. I just wanted the club to be ok.

A couple of years later, I would again be marching through the streets of London as part of the teacher strikes over pensions. One of my fellow teachers commented that I seemed to be quite good at this chanting lark; almost as if I'd had a lot of practise. I had to explain that I had done the whole protest thing before over a cause that I cared a lot more for than a quibble about pay.

We arrived at Lloyds' headquarters on Gresham Street at around 11:30 and began to sing. Bemused bankers came to their windows to take photos. I don't think they were used to having an angry mob of football supporters turn up at their place of work. There was a bright yellow Lamborghini parked outside that was draped in red and blue as we made our point. We then moved around to the main entrance and crowded under the cover as we sang loud and clear to the building. The poor receptionist inside didn't know whether to laugh or run in terror. After about half hour of singing, it began to calm down.

People began to play football and mull around chatting. One lady had brought her dog along, who was now wearing a Palace shirt and getting a lot of attention. People began to discuss the prospect of a phoenix club, such as AFC Wimbledon, if the worst case happened at three o'clock. Soon, the ferocious Palace chants turned into more light-hearted ones such as *'What a bunch of bankers!'*

The intensity eased up and the nerves grew.

While we'd been chanting, it felt like any other match. As I had during the Sheffield Wednesday showdown, I forgot about the game and started to simply enjoy and focus on the singing. It was like nothing could touch me then. My brain was occupied and I didn't feel the pressure. Now, we were simply waiting as the worries were growing.

News of our plight was spreading around the world. I received a text from a friend of a friend in Afghanistan with the army, who had spotted me on the BBC's world news service. Colin had been sitting by the pool in the Dominican Republic when Adam called him into the bar area, shouting *"James is on the tele!"*

Unable to read or understand the Mexican Setanta, he texted me to enquire as to why I was on tele in his hotel on the other side of the world.

I, once again, found myself reflecting on my love of the club. Deep down I knew, however unlikely, that it was possible that I could divorce the club. I'd seen it happen before. People have been devoted supporters one minute and then bam! Completely unexpectedly, they find a new love. Usually a woman but it could be anything. Suddenly, they're cutting back games and continue to go less and less until they stop. Often they come back but sometimes, they never do. As unlikely as I thought it was to happen to me, I knew it was possible. However, the idea of the club divorcing *me* had never occurred. The idea of the club leaving me was terrifying. How could I possibly cope with that?

I spoke to my Dad, one of the fans who'd been through a divorce with Palace, on the phone for the umpteenth time over the two days. It was his love of Palace that had started it all off for me. Since first being bitten by the Palace bug, Dad had finished school, had two marriages and become a father of four. The youngest of those four was now a teacher himself. In that time, my Dad had fallen in and out of love with woman but his love of Palace was still there.

I had fallen in love with Palace as a seven year old primary school child and I was now teaching children of that age. Many things had changed over my life but there was one consistency. Palace. The love of your football team burns brighter and duller throughout different parts of your life but it is always there.

Your football club dying would be just like a close friend dying. You get so used to having them in your life that you can't imagine them not being there. When they're gone, it leaves a burning, painful hole in your life. Your club offers you happiness, sadness, love, comfort, frustration, humour and surprise. You won't find any emotion that you can feel with friends that you can't feel towards your football club. It can pick you up when you're feeling down. It has been around you for longer than most of your friends and introduced you to many of them. I've got more friends from Palace than I do from school, university or work. It can look after you through the rough times in life and celebrate with you in the good times. No matter what, your football club is always there for you, just like a friend. A best friend.

Around 1 o'clock, people were leaving to get some lunch ahead of the final push for the 3 o'clock deadline. There was still no news from inside the building and the atmosphere was beginning to get more edgy. Pavel nipped down during his lunch break with a Palace supporting friend. It was calm when he arrived and I did have to explain that it had been livelier earlier. News reporters continued to try and get quotes and feed on our fear.

The only benefit of the day was that by its very nature, it meant that there was a meeting of many dedicated Palace fans. I had long chats with various people about our fond memories of the club. We were all simply praying that there would be many more to come too. The closer to three o'clock that it got, the nervier it became. I was food and sleep deprived but I wasn't going anywhere. 1:30, no news, 2 o'clock, no news. 2:30, no news. Dad and I were speaking every half hour or so. He might have been at work but he wasn't doing much work that day. An accusation that could probably be levelled at most Palace fans on Tuesday 1st June 2010.

Eventually, the singing started up again. It was more aggressive this time. Partly because we were closer to the deadline and partly because some people had been to the pub for the early afternoon. Loud chants of 'We love you' and 'You are my Palace' were sung outside the foyer of the bank's headquarters. At three o'clock, someone came out and told us that they were close to an agreement. Some Palace fans began to chant 'Let's go f***ing mental' and start to crash about outside the building but they were told to calm it down by older supporters. We were there to raise awareness and public sympathy, not live up to football stereotypes of aggressive, boisterous drunks. Texts started to filter through with rumours that a deal had been done. Eventually, around half past three, a message was got to us that it was official. A deal had been reached to purchase the ground; therefore the club. We'd been saved.

We jumped and hugged and sang and charged to the pub. Champagne and beers flowed for a couple of hours and we victoriously watched Sky Sports News. People pointed at me and shouted of my fame as I popped up on the TV every fifteen minutes.

I went with some Palace fans, who I'd met that day, to Norwood Junction and we continued to drink in Cherries to celebrate our biggest and most important victory, not just of the season, but of all time. I don't remember leaving the pub, such was the volume of alcohol that I had drunk on an empty stomach but I do remember where I came round. Reading Station. The short, fifteen minute journey from Clapham Junction to Twickenham had proved to be too far for me to stay awake on and there were no trains back.

I had no other choice. I rang up my mate Ash, who not for the first time was going to be driving me through the night because of Palace. He drove from Ascot and picked me up. I needed to pick my Mum up from the airport at 7AM the next morning, which I'd entirely forgotten about after the dramatic nature of our battle, so he took me all the way to Twickenham where my car was. I paid him for the petrol and bought us both some food on the journey but I knew he was going far beyond his call of duty. I apologised on many occasions and he just looked at me and said, *"Typical Palace!"*

I guess even Ash was beginning to understand my love of Crystal Palace Football Club.

The next morning, I met my Mum at Heathrow and she showed me her early edition of the Telegraph that she'd bought at New York Airport. She'd happened to look in the sports section and found a picture of me.

"You survived then?" she smiled, happy for me.

"Oh yes, we survived!" I smiled back. *"On and off the pitch!"*

Chapter 63 –*... and so it begins....*

Saturday 7th August 2010, Crystal Palace vs Leicester City, Selhurst Park

After emptying our bladders, Colin, Adam, Dan, Kev, Jonathan, Steve, John, Dad and I strolled out of the bunker that is the Selhurst Railway Club and back into the alley.

It was a hot, August summer's day. Everyone had showed up. Despite the scorching heat, Kev was still in his thick, Umbro jumper as a reasonable, if unspectacular, well-spirited crowd was gathering and heading up the Holmesdale Road towards the ground. As we approached the stadium, with a sense of returning home after a summer holiday, I bought a programme. The excitement of seeing the new programme design, with a new player on the front, in the brand new kit is magical.

The wait was nearly over.

Then it was the chance to use my new Season Ticket for the first time. *"Enjoy the game!"* came the trained, almost robotic, comment from the entrance operator.

"I'll try'" I replied with a smile, in the cynical manner that football fans tend to, refusing to give any hint of optimism that the team might actually win or we might enjoy this whole over-priced experience.

I trudged up the two flights of stairs to the upper tier of the Holmesdale Road Stand where my season ticket was, taking in all the sounds that had been missing from my Saturdays over the previous couple of months.

'Selhurst Half-time super-draw!'

'Daddy, can I have some chips?'

'Programmes, get your match day programmes!'

'Wa'cha reckon today then?' 'Gawd knows!'

There's nothing quite like ear-wigging conversations at football. No one ever agrees on anything other than that the referee is, inevitably, a wanker.

After re-emptying our bladders (once you've opened that seal...) we headed to our seats. In our old season tickets, we lined up in our usual formation: Jonathan and his outbursts (kept as far away as possible), Ron (Colin's Dad, who had joined us in the ground), Adam, Colin, Dan, me, Kev. Dad, next to me, Steve and John slipped effortlessly into the line of addicts – everyone needed to be close to the club we loved and nearly lost. It was fantastic to be back. The group of us were casually joking and enjoying the atmosphere in the minutes leading up to kick-off. Music was blaring out, anticipation was building and the reality of the new season was finally here.

It was the opening day of the 2010/11 season and it felt like nothing had changed from the Plymouth game a year earlier – we were still there and we were still in a light-hearted and relaxed early season mood. Only it had changed.

And I don't just mean on the pitch. The atmosphere at Selhurst Park changed that season. It had previously been tense and critical, with disillusioned supporters, but after going so close to the brink, it became a carefree and party environment. The much lauded outstanding atmosphere at Selhurst Park is down to our relief at simply having a club, as much as the success that we are currently enjoying on the pitch.

As well as that, for the first time in my lifetime, Palace were owned by genuine supporters, who listened to the fans and knew how to treat the club. Also for the first time since my birth, the club and the ground were united as one. CPFC 2010 had learnt from Jordan's errors (something that he had refused to do) and would only purchase the club with the ground. The new owners had been more than impressive in their communication with the fans too, which had been one of my biggest complaints about Jordan. They signed up to the BBS and openly answered questions from the fans. Something Steve Browett, one of the co-owners, is still doing five years on.

In some ways, it appeared that the administration had done us good off the pitch. We had richer and more successful owners. We also had four owners instead of one. Well four heroes, which meant that if anything went wrong for one of them like it had for Jordan, the others would still be there to support the club. Steve Parish, Steve Browett, Martin Long and Jeremy Hoskins will forever be legends at Selhurst Park. They talked of running the club in a financially viable manner and of a healthy future. There were no pipe dreams based on bull shit as there had been under Jordan.

However, on the pitch, although we had survived relegation, administration had weighed heavily on the players, and contracts couldn't be sorted out over the hectic summer. Clint Hill and Shaun Derry had moved across London to join Warnock at QPR, Butterfield had joined Fonte at Southampton, Ertl had left for Sheffield United, Nicky Carle and Stern John left the club to go abroad, and Alan Lee went up north to Huddersfield. The squad had been desolated but they had all left as Hillsborough Heroes, etched into the tapestry of the clubs history and not just round the edges. They were all in prime viewing position and to be admired. They'd all done their bit for the club. Although, in a way, none of it mattered. It seemed shallow to be worrying about individual players or managers as long as I had a team to support.

I have tried to hold that with me throughout my onward journey as a Palace fan. I now support the badge. The players and managers come and go, which is fine, as long as the club lives on. June 1st 2010 taught me that I would be far happier holding my head in my hands as Palace sink to a defeat than I would be if I was sat at home, watching other team's results on Soccer Saturday, while wishing that I could get that unique feeling of being in the ground and supporting my team – win, lose or draw.

Dad had resolved to go to more matches again and he's kept that up ever since. He'd been scared of losing the club before he was ready and felt guilty for not being there in its hour of need. His friend, Palace, had been through a near death experience and he was determined to be around for the club in the future. Our shared love of Palace is one of the biggest reasons that we're so close and why I'd found it so hard to watch his dedication to the club drop. To have him standing next to me at games makes me feel closer to him than ever. A closeness and togetherness that isn't dissimilar to how I feel about my club. Every time I approach the ground with him, I return to feeling like the seven year old boy who walked up Wembley way with his father. We're a mini-family in the huge Crystal Palace Football Club family.

I will never forget the feeling that I'd had on 1st June 2010. Even when we lost 5-0 at Derby a few months later. Presumably our defenders were giving them a thank you on behalf of our fans for the great day that we'd had in the previous April. Although, ironically, that match in Derby would see me make two more close Palace friends, who I see away from football almost as much as I see at the games these days. The friendly nature of the locals obviously infests itself onto visitors of the town.

But despite the score, I was just happy to simply have a football club. To have my Palace. I'd kept my promise to myself and I was going to start missing some games. I could love the club without having to go to *every* game. Although I would be at the first one. Oh, and the league cup tie, away at Yeovil on the following Tuesday as it was a new ground. However, after that, I would miss the next *four* as I went to drive around the South of France with my friend Barlow – an opportunity that I'd passed up for football the year before. I didn't even miss the football and regret it like I thought I would. I'd learnt the need to have other passions in my life. Not attending a game at Barnsley wouldn't be the end of the world. In fact, it would probably lead to an improved Saturday afternoon – particularly as we lost 1-0 and I would still be searching for my first Palace goal at Oakwell.

I'd taken the chance to travel before starting my dream job of being a Primary School Teacher in an excellent school in Surbiton. I'd hobbled through the final placement and then reported the school to the University so that no one else would have to go through what I went through. During that placement, there was a record number of student drop outs (Warnocks) on the course and I felt a huge sense of pride in my ability to stick at the challenge. I'd certainly drawn inspiration from Derry and Hill and Lawrence and Ertl and Lee and Speroni and McCarthy and co, who'd all battled on against the odds with an enormous amount of commitment and desire in their job – unpaid at times, just as I'd had to in mine. Those players should never be forgotten – they are written into Palace folk law. Any future success achieved by the club could not have been possible without them giving absolutely everything for our club. There have been more able sets of players to represent us but few could match them for commitment and effort.

At the end of the placement, I was relieved to be moving out of my flat. I stayed in touch with Dave but I have not seen or heard from the others since. I tried a bit with Matt, out of duty more than anything else as I'd known him for nearly twenty years but I received nothing back. Although I wasn't really fussed. I was excited to be moving to Wimbledon to share a flat with Chris, my close

Brentford supporting friend. I was getting closer to my dream South London home. Maybe, like Dan, once I'd experienced life in South London, I'd long for the sleepy Berkshire surroundings that I'd grown up in.

The Leicester game was a typical Palace rollercoaster with us being 3-0 up and briefly top of the league before having to hold on to a 3-2 win. Soon, I was in France and Palace had a magical day where we made no fewer than seven new signings, including one of the world's best ever central midfielders, Edgar Davids.

We were back to 'worrying' about which players we should sign, rather than researching various financial terminology as we quivered in fear at the latest statement from the administrator. It was nice to feel like a normal club again. The press still described us as 'cash-strapped Crystal Palace' but I knew that I could enjoy games without fearing that it would all come to an end. Win, lose or draw, I'd see my friends, I'd cheer my team and I vowed to always enjoy my football.

I was proud of my 'achievement'. It wasn't ground breaking or life changing but I never set out with the intention that it would be. However, it was still a challenge. A challenge that pushed my energy, wallet and dedication to the limit. A challenge that I had to persist with and motivate myself for. A challenge that I could now chauvinistically and proudly tell people that I'd completed. You could never 'complete' going to matches in the way that I'd satisfied my mind by completing sets of stickers or videos, but this was as close as I could get. It allowed me to ease my football desires and miss some games, especially Coventry away. Who knows, one year, I might actually make it to the Annual Family Christmas Party, rather than go to Palace.

The qualities of supporting a club are ones that should be taken through life: passion, analysis, organisation, budgeting, commitment, reflection, communication, humour and confidence with strangers. The challenge had made me work on all of these qualities. I'd struggled at times to balance football with study and friendships. I'd even struggled over Christmas to *want* to go to games. Forcing myself to go to Sheffield and Swansea had been irrational madness.

Those days were ok but there are cheaper and more enjoyable ways to spend a Saturday. However, that's what made it a challenge – doing things that I didn't really want to do and that's certainly not what being a football supporter is all about. Being a football fan is about wanting to do something irrational, like going to Newcastle for a Wednesday night in January. But is it still irrational and extreme when you religiously do irrational things every other weekend? I sussed that I didn't need to always be irrational and always be there. Only sometimes.

Yet at every point of the year, the club had been there. When I struggled on placement, when I was scrapping to complete my assignments, when I fell out with my flatmates, the club was there. While you could never rely on a club like Palace to give you the result that you wanted to pick you up, you can trust the club to be a Saturday afternoon escape and help you to channel your stresses into an environment that matters less.

It's ironic really. On paper, it was the worst season that Palace have had in my lifetime. It was the lowest league position and some of the darkest days in

368

the club's history. However, I'm delighted I chose that season to go to every game. I don't think we will experience the players and fans being as close as they were in the final five months of the season for a very long time, if ever again. The players clearly had an incredible spirit, which showed on the pitch and infested itself into the crowd. Both supporters and players can look back on that season with genuine pride at what we achieved.

Despite going into administration, goals being ignored, Warnock walking out, the tension of Hillsborough, losing ten points and players being sold to balance the books, we all stuck together and we all survived together. I think the best description of what we learnt about supporting Palace was in the change of motto. CPFC 2010 changed Simon Jordan's image of the club from 'Winning is Everything' to 'South London and Proud'. Winning wasn't and isn't everything. Having a club to be part of is everything.

Who knows? Later in life, I may decide to try and commit to going to every game in the season again. Hopefully in a season when Coventry aren't in our league, Agilo have been bankrupted and Rob Shoebridge has retired. Maybe, if I have a son or daughter, I'll try and do it with them. I certainly don't feel like doing it again now but maybe one day. It's not that I care any less about the club or that I worry about results, signings or even their finances any less than I did in 2009-10 but I have learnt to channel that love. I've learnt to miss some games without moping about at home, just because I'm not going to football that weekend. I've even been known to be pleased about a game being called off at late notice so that I could make the most of my weekend, without being restrained by Palace. However, whether I attempt the challenge again or not, I never, ever, want to come so close to losing my beloved Palace again.

While I hope that you have identified with certain parts of my book, I don't think I'll ever be able to sum up the entire meaning of being a football addict as it means so many different things to me at different times so I'm sure there are people out there who have a completely different relationship with their club. However, what The Year of Going to Every Game did teach me, was that simply having a club and experiencing the emotion of the relationship, with your friends, is what's important. The results. Good ones. Bad ones. They don't really matter. Following the club, being a part of something unifying, cheering the team, despairing at its faults and having a good old moan at a (sometimes) innocent referee, brings me an enormous amount of enjoyment and it is a huge part of what shapes me as the person that I am. I simply couldn't imagine a world without Crystal Palace Football Club.